Designing Secure IoT Devices With the Arm Platform Security Architecture and Cortex-M33

Designing Secure IoT Devices With the Arm Platform Security Architecture and Cortex-M33

Trevor Martin, B.Sc. (Hons), CEng., MIET
Arm Technical Specialist, Hitex (UK) Ltd, Coventry,
West Midlands, United Kingdom

Newnes is an imprint of Elsevier
The Boulevard, Langford Lane, Kidlington, Oxford OX5 1GB, United Kingdom
50 Hampshire Street, 5th Floor, Cambridge, MA 02139, United States

ISBN: 978-0-12-821469-5

For information on all Newnes publications
visit our website at https://www.elsevier.com/books-and-journals

Publisher: Mara Conner
Acquisitions Editor: Tim Pitts
Editorial Project Manager: Franchezca Cabural
Production Project Manager: Sojan P. Pazhayattil
Cover Designer: Victoria Pearson Esser

Typeset by STRAIVE, India

Working together
to grow libraries in
developing countries

www.elsevier.com • www.bookaid.org

Contents

Foreword

The world is undergoing an unprecedented technological transformation, evolving from isolated systems to ubiquitous Internet-enabled "things." This novel paradigm, commonly referred to as the Internet of Things (IoT), is a new reality that is enriching our everyday life, increasing business productivity, and improving government efficiency.

IoT devices are being deployed in massive numbers. Arm estimates that a trillion IoT devices will be produced until 2035. IoT devices are powering industries and market sectors around the globe, generating and sharing large amounts of security- and privacy-sensitive data. The success of this new wave of the Internet is heavily dependent upon the trust built into these billions of connected devices. Notwithstanding, recent attacks on IoT devices have shown that poorly designed connected devices have the ability to bring down critical parts of our infrastructures or even affect our safety. The problem is that designing secure IoT devices can be a quandary, with numerous technologies, requirements, and constraints pushing different design directions.

This book is a remarkable effort in such a direction. Completely in line with the Platform Security Architecture (PSA) vision and principles, the book definitely strives for building "security from the ground up." It starts by covering the Arm Platform Security Architecture and overviews the development tools and platforms. The book then focuses on the basics of cryptography and why it is paramount for securing communication and networking from the edge to the cloud. The subsequent chapters provide insights on software attacks and threat models and highlight the fundamentals to build defenses with the PSA security model. With Arm TrustZone providing the perfect foundation for establishing a device root of trust based on PSA guidelines, the latest chapters take as a reference a TrustZone microcontroller—NXP LPC55S59—and break down the different software components of an open-source secure IoT stack, including bootloader, Trusted Firmware, and Trusted Services. All these topics are explained and accompanied by application examples and hands-on exercises, helping readers to easily understand theory with practice.

I strongly recommend this book to a large spectrum of profiles and broad audience: from students and hobbyists with very little knowledge and experience to well-established system designers and architects with proven expertise. The book is a must-read for those looking for theory and practice. Security is a shared responsibility, where all of us shall play a significant role. Johann Wolfgang von Goethe once said: "Knowing is not enough; we must apply. Willing is not enough; we must do."

Enjoy reading this book!

Sandro Pinto

Introduction

As embedded systems designers, we are all aware that many everyday devices contain microcontrollers and that much of the critical infrastructure that is relied on by modern society rests on functioning computer networks. The growing adoption of IoT networks offers the potential for new services and business models, which will also increase our dependency on these networks. When everything is a computer, the world becomes a computer. For the purposes of this book, we have to consider the potential negative consequences of badly designed IoT networks. The horror stories are not hard to find. Of particular interest was a Nation State-sponsored attack against a Ukrainian power station and substation network in 2015. This was well planned and expertly executed. The attackers not only disrupted the power station IT system but used the power station SCADA system to switch off substations and reprogrammed the station PLCs with malware to damage the generators. Not a good day at the office. It took months to recover the system. Even as I am writing this Introduction, a major attack against the colonial pipeline in the United States is unfolding. Although this seems to involve the IT system rather than the pipeline itself, it is still causing widespread disruption, panic buying, and fuel shortages. At the other end of the scale while researching this book, I also came across the acronym SIMAD, "Single Individual MAssively Destructive." The concern is that the increasing availability of advanced technology would enable individuals and small groups to develop weapons of mass destruction. It would only be a matter of time before a Lone Wolf attack would result in a huge loss of life. The growth of insecure IoT networks will ensure that even if we are not quite doing their job for them, we are certainly enabling them to mount and attack easily and quickly.

To create secure IoT systems, we have a couple of problems. First, since their inception, microcontrollers have been designed as functional devices: a CPU, memory, and peripherals that can be programmed to accomplish a huge range of tasks such as run a washing machine, manage a car engine, or control a medical device. The list is endless. With the growth of internet-connected devices and the Internet of Things, such a "plain old microcontroller" is no longer a suitable device. It lacks many features necessary to create a secure and functional device. Fortunately, we have a new generation of microcontrollers that are based on the Cortex-M33 and contain a sophisticated security infrastructure. Second, many of todays embedded systems developers have never been formally trained in security engineering, and it shows. Over the last few years in my professional work, I have seen many companies start projects where devices have some form of internet connectivity or are to be part of a fully fledged IoT system. Just about all of them have been awful. In most cases, the TCP/IP communication is unencrypted ("nobody would be interested in my data"), and no thought is given to general device security. This is leaving yourself wide open to malicious attacks that will cause at minimum reputational damage and, more likely, financial and real-world physical damage. Currently, the threat may be limited, but the incentive to hack IoT devices will increase in line with the number of deployed IoT networks. It will also get easier for attackers as the techniques and tools propagate from Nation-State hackers to criminal gangs to script kiddies. You will no longer be able to get away with obscurity. Every internet-facing device has to be made secure, with no ifs or buts.

Arm Platform Security Architecture

The purpose of this book is to introduce you to the Arm Platform Security Architecture (PSA) and how to implement it at each stage of your project to create secure and robust IoT devices. The PSA project provides a range of open-source software components and is free to use under a noncontributory BSD-3-Clause license for both commercial and noncommercial projects. The PSA resources use a "security by design" approach that uses the best industry practice to create an inherently secure foundation for all IoT devices. This book will focus on the Armv8-m architecture. However, the Arm Platform Security Architecture is designed to work with any processor, not just Arm devices. It is important to note, however, that a new generation of Cortex-M33 based microcontrollers provide a significant level of hardware security compared to our traditional "plain old microcontrollers," which are solely designed for functionality.

PSA certification

In response to a number of high profile IoT hacking incidents, the regulators in most major geographies have introduced legal requirements for IoT devices which you will need to meet for a commercial product. Devices that have been developed to the PSA standards can be certified through a straightforward self-certification process which guarantees a security baseline that meets and exceeds all the current IoT legal requirements. This gives us a route to the creation of a well regulated IoT device market for all future systems.

How much development effort is required?

Lots! You really cannot do it all on your own. Developing a secure device requires a range of software components, many of which would be a project in their own right. Coding everything from scratch would be beyond the capabilities of most projects, both in terms of time and also the necessary design knowledge. Fig. 1.1 gives you an idea of the security requirements for an IoT device.

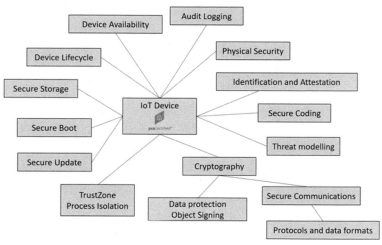

FIG. 1.1

IoT device security requirements. IoT devices have a wide range of security requirements.

This creates a big barrier for many IoT device development projects. Fortunately, the PSA project provides a range of supporting software components that create a full reference platform which provides the security foundations for an IoT device. Once you are familiar with the Platform Security Architecture and Security Model, you will be able to focus on the application code for your particular device.

Assumptions

In writing this book, I have assumed that you have previous experience in developing code in the "C" language and using an RTOS on a small microcontroller. You will also need to be familiar with the Cortex-M processor and the Cortex Microcontroller Software Interface Standards (CMSIS). Where necessary, we will look at the extensions provided by the Armv8-M architecture and also revise some of the more low-level Cortex-M architectural features. I have also assumed that you have no or little previous experience in security engineering and no knowledge of digital cryptography.

Structure of the book

The structure of this book can be split into two halves. The first half deals with cryptography and secure communications, while the second half is concerned with securing a device against a software attack.

Getting started

Introduction to the platform security architecture

We will begin with an overview of the Platform Security Architecture, its aims, and the methodology used to create a secure device.

Development tools

In Chapter 3, we will install a leading tool chain for Cortex-M and build a project that connects a Cortex-M33 development board to a local WiFi network and also adds a file system. This will give us a base platform to use through the rest of the book.

Part 1: Cryptography and secure communications for IoT devices

Cryptography and secure communications

The following two chapters provide an introduction to Cryptography for small embedded devices. Here, I have assumed that you have no previous experience of using cryptographic algorithms. Although there is a fair bit of math involved, you should be able to gain an understanding of how each algorithm works and, more importantly, how to use them in an embedded device without creating security vulnerabilities. The first cryptography chapter covers the most important symmetrical algorithms, ciphers, hashes, and message authentication, as well as random number generation. In the second cryptography chapter, we look at asymmetric algorithms for encryption and signing of data as well as key agreement algorithms. This chapter also covers the TLS protocol and wider public key infrastructure that will allow us to establish a secure connection with an IoT cloud service.

IoT protocols and data formats

Once we have a secure connection to a cloud server, we can start to use the Message Queued Telemetry Transport (MQTT) protocol to transfer data from our device endpoints into a message broker. This chapter will also look at how to format the message data using the JavaScript Object Notation (JSON) and its binary twin, Concise Binary Object representation (CBOR).

IoT cloud service

In the last chapter of this section, we will make a start using a typical cloud server that can be scaled to consume masses of data produced by a fleet of IoT devices. While building a full cloud service is outside the scope of this book, we will look at how to connect our devices and how to store the data they produce in a database and the use of analytics services.

Part 2: Device security

The second half of this book is concerned with making a device secure against network software attacks.

Software attacks and threat modelling

The first chapter in this section introduces common software hacking techniques that exploit software vulnerabilities (aka bugs) and how to take control of a device remotely. We will also look at how to defend against this using secure coding techniques. This chapter also introduces threat modeling, a series of design analysis techniques that, as their name implies, helps you consider your project from a pure security perspective.

Security model

While secure coding gives you the first line of defense, we need to provide "defense in depth" using a partition model that is inherently resistant to software attacks. In this chapter, we will look at the PSA security model, which provides an abstract architecture for an attack-resistant device. Then, we will see how to implement it in the remainder of the book.

TrustZone

The first step in improving device security is to separate the security code from the main application code. This can be achieved by creating separate execution partitions that are isolated from each other. This type of isolation is possible on any device and can be implemented as a pure software solution. However, the Cortex-M33 is designed to create execution partitions at the hardware level using a security peripheral called TrustZone.

Microcontroller

While TrustZone is an important step forward for secure microcontrollers, it is far from the whole story. In this chapter, we will see how a new generation of microcontrollers based on the Cortex-M33 are designed for use as IoT devices. Such a device will extend the TrustZone partitions to create a Trusted Execution Environment. They must also provide a secure boot process that validates the execution images before a device can begin to operate. A Cortex-M33 based microcontroller will also provide a range of hardware security accelerators and other assistive peripherals to enhance the overall device performance and security.

Trusted firmware

The PSA project provides a reference platform for the security software called Trusted Firmware for Cortex-M (TF-M). This creates an execution environment to run in the secure TrustZone partition. The TF-M provides an extensible set of security services to the application code. In this chapter, we will look at the design and communication models of the TF-M software.

Security services

This chapter introduces the mandatory TF-M security services for cryptography, storage, attestation, and audit. We will see how they are configured and how to access them from the application code. We will also look at the lifecycle of our device from assembly and testing through provisioning of device secrets to place it in an operational mode and finally end of life decommissioning.

Secure bootloader

It is highly likely that however well designed your device is, a security vulnerability will be discovered over time. Consequently, a key requirement of the PSA security model is the ability to provide secure updates to active devices either "over the air" or through a local interface.

In the last chapter, we will add a secure bootloader that is able to update and validate the device images. We will also add a firmware update client which co-operates with the bootloader to allow updates to be managed from the application code.

Tutorial exercises

Throughout the book, I have used a tutorial approach, and each chapter contains a set of prebuilt examples that demonstrate key principles. Ideally, you should try out the examples and then try coding from scratch. The examples are also intended to provide a reference for future project work.

Important

At the time of writing, the PSA trusted firmware was still in development, and some function names may change, and new features may be added. If there are significant changes, I will add an updated pdf in the examples to explain any differences to the main text. Also, please check www.hitex.co.uk/blog for new material and webinar recordings. Finally, if you have any questions, please contact me at psa@hitex.co.uk.

Arm platform security architecture

2

Introduction

The Arm Platform Security Architecture defines a software architecture and design methodology along with firmware resources and tools. These resources will enable you to design secure IoT devices that meet and exceed all the current regulatory requirements, laws, and major standards. Devices that conform to the PSA standard can also be certified by independent security labs to demonstrate that good security principles and industry best practice have been applied to your design. The Platform Security Architecture methodology consists of four stages: analyze, architect, implement, and certify (Fig. 2.1). Here, we will take an initial look at each PSA stage while later chapters will cover them in more detail.

FIG. 2.1

PSA methodology. PSA provides a methodology, tools, and firmware for IoT device security.

Analyze

The Platform Security Architecture provides an analysis of key threats to IoT devices and how to mitigate them. The threats against our devices can be divided into four key areas: communications, software attack, lifecycle attack, and device tampering (Fig. 2.2).

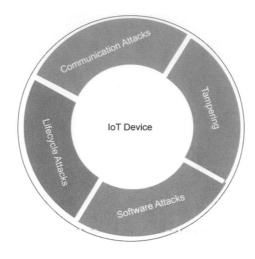

FIG. 2.2

Threats. IoT security threats.

Communications

In our IoT model, a remote device will need to communicate with a server using TCP/IP based protocols. With today's microcontrollers, which feature sophisticated communications peripherals and widely available cloud servers, this has become fairly easy to achieve. However, in order to deploy a large-scale IoT system, we have to consider the confidentiality, integrity, and authenticity of the data as it is transferred to and from each device. This requires a firm knowledge of modern cryptographic algorithms and protocols. Outside of communication protocols, the same cryptographic techniques are used to protect our firmware image and stored data. For clarity, you will not need to code the actual cryptographic algorithms, and indeed, you should not, as this is a job for specialists. You will need to understand their proper application and configuration in order to create a secure communication channel and a secure device.

Software attack

Unlike most other microcontroller-based devices, each IoT device will contain sensitive data such as encryption keys, which must be protected against software hacking attempts. Such hacking attacks have long been a concern of personal computers (PC) using feature-rich operating systems such as Linux and Windows. Today, it would be considered asking for trouble to use an internet-connected PC without a firewall or virus checker. The world of small microcontrollers has not needed to consider such problems until now. In order to understand these threats and take them seriously, we will look at some key software attack techniques and how to mitigate them using the PSA security model. We will also look at adopting secure coding practices to avoid creating software vulnerabilities.

Tampering

Depending on your IoT system's location and physical accessibility, it may be exposed to direct attack from an adversary. This can take many forms, such as attempting to connect a debugger to read the FLASH, glitching clocks and power supplies, and reading and decoding external nonvolatile storage.

Lifecycle attack

When creating an IoT system, we must consider the lifecycle of our IoT devices from their initial manufacture through to eventual decommissioning. It is quite possible that our devices will be manufactured by a third party and delivered directly to a retail chain without ever coming into our possession. Yet, our devices must be provisioned with confidential data and onboarded onto our network. During their lifetime, we must have a way to update the firmware within our devices securely. We will also need to allow technicians access to the device for repair. Here, we may need to provide different debug access levels so that device secrets are protected. At the end of their lifetime, devices must be decommissioned so that any sensitive data are erased or "put beyond use." Any of these lifecycle stages are prone to an attack by an adversary, such as stealing confidential data, suborning a device, or cloning counterfeit devices.

Application-specific threat modeling

While the Platform Security Architecture (PSA) is based on an analysis of the major threats facing IoT devices, it is a generic security platform and as such does not innately provide mitigation for every threat. At the start of a new project, in addition to defining the software requirements for our device, we need to consider the potential security threats against it. Working out these risks is part of the process called "threat modeling." We can discover, document, rate, and provide mitigations against all the security threats to our actual system through threat modelling. It is highly likely that this process will be new to most embedded designers, so we will have a look at several threat modeling methods and tools in Chapter 8.

Architect

While there are many technologies and network configurations that can be used to create an IoT system, in this book, we will concentrate on developing a scalable fleet of IoT devices that connect to a cloud server using the TCP/IP protocols over a WiFi interface. A common temptation is to design an initial proof of concept, which does not consider any security issues. These are seen as an overhead that can be addressed later if the full design goes ahead. Such a system will meet the projects functional requirements, but a poorly designed IoT device will have multiple points of insecurity, which will be difficult or near impossible to fix later in the project. This will result in lots of extra work trying to "design in" security. Then, as we try to scale up such a system, the number of issues that need to be addressed will seem to increase exponentially. By understanding and adopting the PSA, it will be possible to develop a fully secure system from the very start of the project without becoming bogged down in lots of extra "unproductive" work. This will allow us to rapidly move from prototype to production code.

Security model

At the heart of the PSA is the security model. This defines a set of security goals, firmware specifications, and interface API's that you must meet in order to have a compliant device that is resistant to a software attack. The main elements of the security model are as follows:

Secure boot and root of trust

In a "normal" microcontroller project, we are accustomed to thinking of our application code running from the reset vector. With an IoT device, we must establish confidence that the device has not been tampered with before we let it execute the application code. To establish this trust, we must have some secure boot code that is resident in an immutable ROM. The secure boot code executes on startup to validate the application code and establish a root of trust (RoT), which all future operations will be based on. Fortunately, most, if not all, Cortex-M33 microcontrollers have a secure boot process as part of their system ROM code. While each family of devices has a different secure boot implementation, they all achieve similar results. We will have a look at a secure boot implantation and its supporting hardware in Chapter 11.

Secure update with antirollback

The provision of a secure update mechanism for the device firmware is a strict requirement of the PSA security model. In addition, all updates must be verifiable to ensure no unauthorized software is able to run on our device. An adjunct to this is the provision of an antirollback mechanism to ensure that an adversary cannot downgrade the device software to an earlier version with known vulnerabilities.

Isolation of secure code

Once a device has successfully booted, the application code will contain security functions and sensitive data such as encryption keys. As we will see, an adversary can conduct a software attack that can extract data from a poorly designed device. To make our device resistant to such software attacks, the security model defines two software partitions that isolate the application code from the security functions and any sensitive data. For now, you can think of this as an internal firewall where the secure partition provides security services to the application code. We will see how this can be implemented at the hardware level in Chapter 10 and at the software level in Chapter 12.

Security service

The secure partition is used to host the security functions as a set of security services. Each security service must conform to an API defined by the PSA security model. The security model must provide a mandatory set of security services with the following functions: attestation, cryptographic, storage, audit logging, and lifecycle. The secure partition structure is extensible so that other user or third-party services may be added.

True Random Number Generator (TRNG): Strictly speaking, a True Random Number Generator (TRNG) is not a security service in itself. However, a source of random numbers is critical for many of the cryptographic functions we will use. We will look at a typical microcontroller TRNG and how to establish a high-quality entropy source in Chapter 4.

Attestation: The attestation service is used to create security tokens that can be exchanged with an attestation server. The attestation tokens are used to identify and authenticate a device by providing a set of claims about a device and its capabilities. This allows a server to decide whether or not a device can be enrolled onto a network and what services can be granted. Attestation tokens may be generated on the fly, allowing them to contain some process data. For example, a metering system could generate an attestation token that identifies a meter along with its current readings. Ideally, a microcontroller should provide an immutable unique ID that can form the basis of the device attestation ID.

Cryptography: At the heart of the device, security is the cryptographic security service. The cryptographic service provides algorithms for confidentiality, integrity, and authentication. The cryptographic service is used to protect data being sent over a communication channel, "data in flight," and data in device storage, "data at rest." Additionally, the cryptographic service is used to validate firmware images before starting execution or device updates. As cryptography is such an important aspect of device security, it will be introduced over two chapters, which you should read before going to the PSA implementation sections. While there is no getting away from the fact that each cryptographic algorithm is complicated, the good news is that Arm has published a free-to-use open-source library called mbedTLS. Consequently, we only need to understand the purpose and best practice use of each cryptographic algorithm.

Secure Storage: The secure storage service provides two storage volumes: protected storage and internal trusted storage. The protected storage volume provides a storage space that may be located in either external memory or the microcontroller's internal FLASH memory. Protected storage provides a managed storage volume for application and process data. An item is stored with a cryptographic hash to provide integrity. Additionally, the data may be encrypted to provide confidentiality. A nonce (number once) may also be added as an antireplay measure. As its name implies, the internal trusted storage is located in the microcontroller's internal FLASH. The internal trusted storage is used to hold high-value device secrets such as encryption keys and other device intimate data. Consequently, the internal trusted storage always provides confidentiality, integrity, and authentication, so that stored data are held in a secure state and is bound to a specific device.

Audit: The audit service provides a means for the secure partition software to write log messages to the protected storage. The audit messages are timestamped using the microcontroller real-time clock and stored in the protected storage volume with confidentiality and replay protection. The nonsecure software can read and delete records in the audit log but cannot add a record.

Lifecycle: While there is not a specific lifecycle service, the concept of managing the device through its lifetime is built into the security model. Each IoT device can exist in one of six distinct lifecycle stages: assembly and test, provisioning, secured, nonroot of trust debug (service debug), root of trust debug (full debug), and decommissioned. When a device is manufactured, it will go through an assembly and test process and be programmed with an initial firmware image. It must next be provisioned with its device ID and device-specific secrets. At this point, the device will be locked down by enabling the secure boot. Once provisioned, it can then be onboarded or enrolled onto the IoT network to become a secure operational device. During its operational lifetime, it may become faulty, so our lifecycle must be able to place the device into a repair state to allow a service technician to connect a diagnostic tool and view data mediated by the application software while the secure software and data remains hidden. In order to resolve software bugs, our repair state must also have an additional state that allows an authorized design engineer to connect a debug tool to view the execution of the whole system, which is the application code and the partitioned security services. Finally, at the end of its life, a device must be fully decommissioned with any privileged data erased from the device.

Firmware update

The firmware update client is designed to co-operate with the second-stage bootloader so that firmware updates to the system images can be managed from within the application code. This includes multipart download and storage of firmware images, starting the installation process and confirming a successful update.

Implement

The PSA specifications define a wide range of requirements, many of which are a development project in their own right. In order to make PSA easy to adopt, Arm provides a reference platform that consists of both existing open-source projects and Arm-provided software components. The PSA platform components are in Table 2.1.

Table 2.1 PSA implementation resources.

Resource	Type	Description
mbedTLS	Firmware	Reference cryptography library
Trusted Firmware for Cortex-M (TF-M)	Firmware	Reference secure partition and security services
CMSIS-Zone Utility	Utility	Configuration tool for TrustZone Security peripheral
MCU Boot	Firmware	An Arm fork of the MCU boot second-stage bootloader

Secure boot and assistive security features

Part of the implementation phase is selecting a suitable microcontroller. This is no mean feat as there are well over 8000 Cortex-M based devices from over thirteen different vendors. However, the introduction of the Cortex-M33 and the PSA has shaped the development of microcontrollers intended for use as IoT devices. These devices now provide a range of hardware features that "assist" the development of secure IoT nodes. While each implementation is unique to a given manufacturer, we will examine a real-world microcontroller in Chapter 11. In this book, we will use the NXP LPC55S69. This is one of the first Cortex-M33 based devices to be released and was designed with many advanced security features that provide direct hardware support for the PSA security model.

Second stage bootloader

The PSA software resources provide a version of the open-source MCUboot bootloader, which acts as the mandated secure update client. The MCUboot firmware is a sophisticated second-stage bootloader capable of managing multiple update images and validating the existing installed firmware. A set of Python scripts and tools are also included to version, sign, and encrypt update images for downloading into the device. A modified version of MCUboot is included as part of the Trusted Firmware pack (see below). This version uses the CMSIS-FLASH drivers to access the microcontroller memory, making the bootloader much easier to port between devices.

Partition

An essential part of the PSA security model is the ability to separate the device firmware into a nonsecure partition for the application code and a secure partition for the critical security code. While this can be achieved on any Cortex-M device, the Cortex-M33 security extension, TrustZone, is able to do this at the hardware level. This has many benefits such as reliability, lower power consumption, and better performance than a pure software "microVisor" implementation. In addition to the TrustZone peripheral, the Cortex-M33 Memory Protection Unit can also be used to further enforce access rights between the two security partitions. This creates a more complex memory map that must be accurately reflected in both the compiler/linker and software configuration functions across several different firmware subprojects.

Trusted firmware

Once we have partitioned our device, the security services will run in the "secure world" partition to be accessed by the application code in the "nonsecure world" partition. Setting up these services is one of those "projects in its own right" and would consume months of design time if you had to do it from scratch. Fortunately,

Arm also provides an open-source reference implementation of the secure partition software—Trusted Firmware (TF-M). This firmware is designed to manage and provide the default security services required as part of the PSA specification. The TF-M firmware provides a standard API to the application code from its core library. The Trusted Firmware must be customized for a specific microcontroller by modifying a set of platform functions. Ideally, the platform code will be available from the device manufacturer, but you may need to do this yourself and you will certainly need to verify the platform functions. We will look at how to install, configure, and use the TF-M in Chapter 12.

mbedTLS and mbedCrypto

In addition to the trusted firmware, Arm also provides an open-source cryptographic library called mbedTLS, which can be used with Armv7-M and Armv8-M processors. The mbedTLS library was originally developed as a commercial product by PolarSSL before it was acquired by Arm and is now available for commercial and noncommercial use under a permissive Apache software license. A second version of mbedTLS called mbedCrypto is also available. mbedCrypto is a version of mbedTLS that has been rewritten to run as a security service within the PSA secure partition. Typically, this means an Armv8-M processor. Both the mbedTLS and mbedCrypto libraries can be used to provide cryptographic primitives within our application software, as well as creating and managing a secure network channel using the Transport Layer Security (TLS) protocol. We will look at both the cryptographic functions and the TLS protocol in Chapter 5.

Software components

In addition to the cryptography libraries, the PSA support software includes several open-source software components that are used to format and transport data between the device and server (Table 2.2).

Table 2.2 Data transport protocols.

Component	Data format	Description
Paho MQTT	Message Queued Telemetry Transport Protocol (MQTT)	An IoT communications protocol between device and server
cJSON	Java Script Object Notation (JSON)	A lightweight standard for storing and transporting data in ASCII format
QCBOR	Concise Binary Object Representation (CBOR)	A lightweight standard for storing and transporting data in binary format

We will have a look at each of these components and their matching specifications in Chapter 6 and also use them to connect to a commercial cloud server in Chapter 7.

PSA certification

The PSA methodology's final stage is your favorite and mine: certification. Before the IoT became an emerging technology, the IT industry had already considered the security certification requirements for computer systems. Today, there is an established path called the "Common Criteria for Information Technology Security Evaluation," which is used to certify computer IT devices. The common criteria is part of the ISO/IEC 15408 standard and provides a formal methodology that is used by nation-states to provide security certification that is valid for multiple countries.

The Common Criteria provides a set of well-defined protection profiles against which devices can be tested. Once you have your device certified to the common criteria, it reduces or removes the need to test your device in each different country. This sounds ideal, but the common criteria is not well suited for certifying many IoT devices. First, the common criteria documentation is very abstract and typically requires a specialist to understand and implement its requirements against your particular device. This means it is quite expensive and also very time-consuming. This is less of a problem if you are making a consumer product such as a mobile telephone or creating a device for smart card technology. These devices will be made in large numbers and will be in use for a long time, making an expensive certification process less of a barrier. For our IoT systems, this whole process is both a prohibitively complex and expensive process designed to certify devices against requirements than are not really relevant.

We need a different system where we can test a large range of IoT devices and certify them to an appropriate level of security capability. This is the role of the Platform Security Architecture certification process. The PSA certification process is derived from the PSA design and specification documents. This makes the certification process accessible and easy for developers to understand. The PSA certification website provides a full overview of the scheme, a download of the certification questionnaire, plus a database of certified devices and software components: https://www.psacertified.org/.

PSACertified has been set up as an independent scheme that uses a number of security labs, with final certification being given through an international body called Trust CB who already specialize in certifying IT security products. This process allows PSACertified certification to meet multiregional IoT security requirements with a level of security appropriate for each use case and is backed by an internationally recognized authority. At the time of writing, there are five security labs that provide global coverage (Table 2.3).

Table 2.3 Certification labs.

Certification lab	URL
Brightsight	https://www.brightsight.com/
CAICT	http://www.caict.ac.cn/english/
Riscure	https://www.riscure.com/
UL	https://ims.ul.com/
Prove and run	https://www.provenrun.com/

The PSA certification process has three levels. Assurance Level 1 is a baseline security assurance that all Cortex-M based IoT devices and software components should adhere to. Level 2 is mainly focused on proving that hardware devices and software components fully conform to the Level 1 requirements through analysis by a third-party security laboratory, and Level 3 provides substantial assurance against both software and hardware attacks (Fig. 2.3).

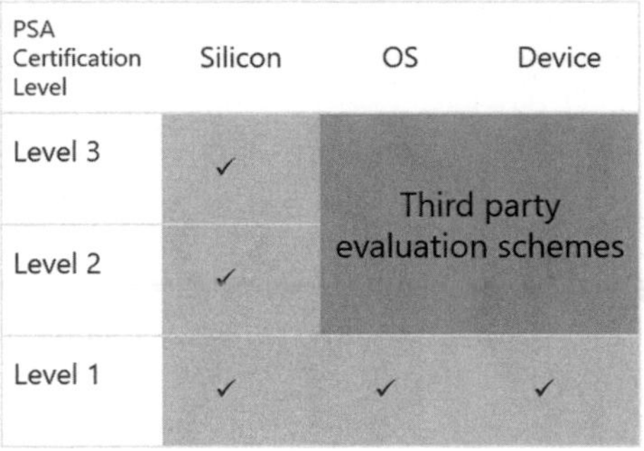

FIG. 2.3

Certification levels. PSACertified certification levels.

PSACertified level 1

Ideally, all IoT products will be certified to a minimum of Level 1 and it is intended to be an easy to follow process relying on a high degree of self-certification. The Level 1 certification is a methodically developed assessment with four key inputs: the PSA threat models and security analysis, security best practice, top 10 security goals, and finally, government regulations and regional requirements. An analysis of all four inputs is used to create a level of certification that exceeds all current government regulations. At the time of writing, there are three major standards that IoT devices need to comply with. These are NISTIR 8259 in the United States, ETSI 303 645 in Europe, and SB-327 in California. These map to the PSACertified Level 1 standard as shown in Table 2.4.

Table 2.4 IoT regulations.

PSA certification requirements	Required by ETSI 303 645	Required by NISTIR 8259v2	Required by SB-327
Authentication/password	Yes	Yes	Yes
Configuration	No	Yes	No
Cryptography	Yes	Yes	No
Hardening	Yes	Yes	No
Logging	No	Yes	No
Privacy	Yes	Yes	No
Secure storage	Yes	Yes	No
Update	Yes	Yes	No

PSACertified Level 1 certification is also used to certify microcontrollers and third-party real-time operating systems. This allows a device developer to base a system on precertified components, thus reducing the overall certification effort.

PSACertified Level 1 certification is based on a questionnaire that can be downloaded from the PSACertified website. The Level 1 questionnaire has under 50 questions covering the microcontroller, software components, and the full device application. Once you have filled in the questionnaire, it can be submitted to an authorized security laboratory who will then vet the questionnaire and provide any feedback where your device may need improvement. Once the security laboratory is happy that your device meets all the Level 1 requirements, it will notify the governing body, Trust CB, who will issue you a certificate that allows you to claim PSACertified Level 1 certification.

PSACertified Level 2

PSACertified Level 2 is currently aimed at silicon vendors. It is an extensive laboratory-based evaluation of the devices' PSA root of trust (RoT) and secure boot code. Level 2 testing is predominantly a white box evaluation against the PSA RoT protection profile. The testing laboratory will conduct scalable software and remote attacks against the PSA RoT to actively prove its conformance to the security model requirements. When the device passes, a certificate will be issued by Trust CB and the device will be listed on the PSACertified website.

PSACertified Level 3

At the time of writing, the Level 3 certification is still in development. This final certification level will provide substantial protection from hardware and sophisticated software attacks.

Conclusion

While you may initially view PSA certification as an endpoint of your project, the PSACertified website is also a good starting point since it carries a listing of all certified microcontrollers and software components. This should be your first port of call for device selection at the start of a project. It is also possible to download the certification questionnaire, which can be added to your project requirements. Again to be absolutely clear, you must include security requirements in your project from the start to have a fighting chance of creating a reliable IoT device.

Development tools and device platform

Introduction

In this chapter, we will set up a software development toolchain and install the platform libraries that we will use to create our device. To test out the board, we will try a simple Hello World program that uses a real-time operating system (RTOS) and go through the compile, download, and debug cycle. Once we have the basics working, we will set up a base project that adds a WiFi connection to your local network and add a file system to read and store data on an SD card. This will give us a basic platform that we can expand through the course of this book.

Hardware

The examples in this book are designed to run on an NXP LPC55S69 XPRESSO evaluation board, which has been fitted with an ESP-Wroom-2 Mikro Click WiFi module and an SD memory card, as shown in Fig. 3.1.

Full details of the hardware are available from the URL's below:

https://www.nxp.com/design/development-boards/lpcxpresso-boards/
lpcxpresso55s69-development-board:LPC55S69-EVK
https://www.mikroe.com/wifi-esp-click

The NXP LPC55S69 microcontroller was one of the first Cortex-M33 based microcontrollers available. As we will see in the second half of this book, it contains many security features that complement the Arm Platform Security Model.

Software

To build the examples, we will use the Keil MDK-ARM, which is a reference toolchain for both the CMSIS standards and the Arm Platform Security Architecture.

- Download the evaluation version of the Keil MDK-ARM using the URL below:
  - https://www2.keil.com/mdk5
- Once downloaded run the executable to install the toolchain.

This installs the core toolchain, which includes the Microvision IDE, ArmM Compiler, RTX RTOS, and the Microvision debugger.

FIG. 3.1

NXP LPC55S69 Xpresso board and WiFi module. The exercises in this book use the LPC55S69 Xpresso board fitted with a WiFi module.

No permission required.

Community license

While the MDK-ARM is a commercial toolchain, a community license is available, that allows it to build and debug large projects. This version of the toolchain is to be used for learning projects and other noncommercial projects only.

Full instructions for obtaining and installing the community license are provided on the Tutorial Exercises download page shown below.

Tutorial exercises

All of the exercises in this book are provided as a software pack that can be downloaded from

https://github.com/DesignersGuide/IoT_Security_Examples

- **Download the latest version of the Elsevier.IoT_Device_Security.<version>. pack**
- **Once the pack has been downloaded double click on it and it will install using the pack installer utility.**

Exercise: Test project

This is a simple project that blinks the user RGB LED. It also writes to a console using the Instrumentation Trace debug channel rather than a hardware USART.

In The Pack Installer select the Boards tab and locate IoT_Device_Security

Now select the examples tab and load the first Example 1.1 Test project by pressing the copy button.

Select a suitable exercise directory and press the OK button (Fig. 3.2).

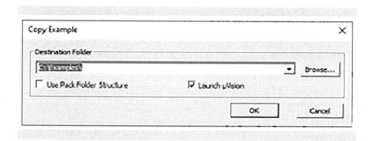

FIG. 3.2

Pack exercise copy button. The pack installer will copy the project from the pack installer repository. The original version is left unchanged.

This will copy the blinky project to your hard disk and start the Microvision IDE.

Connect a USB cable to the USB socket labelled Debug Link P6 and a PC USB socket.
Check Jumper J3 is set to the "Loc" position (default).

This connects the debugger and powers the board.

<to do> Install community license
Device support

The Core MDK-ARM toolchain does not include any support for specific microcontrollers. We can add support for specific devices by downloading and installing software packs that are stored in a cloud server. Fortunately, this is easy to do through a built-in pack installer utility.

Start the Microvision IDE from the desktop icon.
On the toolbar start the pack installer using the icon shown in Fig. 3.3 **or use project\manage\pack installer.**

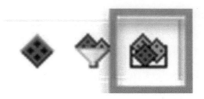

FIG. 3.3

The Microvision Pack installer icon. Within the Microvision IDE, press the pack installer icon.

No permission required.

When the pack installer utility starts it will connect to the cloud and update its list of software packs, this may take a few minutes.

When the pack installer is ready select the device tab (1) and navigate to the NXP/LPC55S69 tree (2) then select the LPC55S69JBD100 (3,4) (Fig. 3.4).

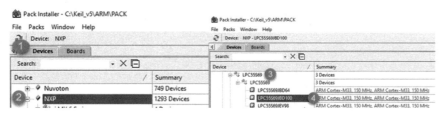

FIG. 3.4

Select the LPC55S69JBD100 microcontroller. In the devices tab, locate and select the NXP LPC55S69JBD100 microcontroller.

No permission required.

In the packs tab (4), install the LPC55S69DFP, device family pack (5), and the LPC55S69 XPRESSO board support pack (6) (Fig. 3.5).

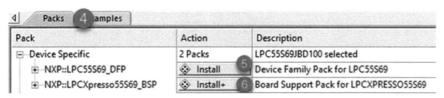

FIG. 3.5

Select the device support packs. In the packs tab, install the device support packs.

No permission required.

We also need to install the following packs that are located in the Pack installer/Packs tab/generic branch (Table 3.1).

Table 3.1 Required software packs.

Software pack	Description
ARM::mbedTLS	Cryptographic library for Cortex-M devices
ARM::mbedCrypto	Cryptographic Library for TrustZone Secure Partition
ARM:: CMSIS-Driver Validation	Test Suite for peripheral drivers based on the CMSIS-Driver specification
ARM::TF-M	Reference implementation of the PSA Trusted Firmware security services core files
Keil::ARM_Compiler	STDIO interface files for ARM compiler
Keil::LPC55S69xTFM_PF	Trusted Firmware platform files for the NXP LPC55S69 family
MDK-Packs::AWS_IoT_Device	Support files for AWS services
MDK-Packs::IoT Socket	Simple IP socket implementation
MDK-Packs::Paho_MQTT	Embedded MQTT client
MDK-Packs::CJSON	JSON data format parser
MDK-Packs::TinyCbor	CBOR data format parser

Install each of the packs listed in the table.

Additional utilities

In addition to the MDK-ARM toolchain, you will need a terminal emulator. While any should work, the exercises have been tested with Tera Term.

Download and install Tera Term using the URL below:
https://osdn.net/projects/ttssh2/releases/

The project workspace contains two projects. A fully configured project for reference and a shell project which we will build up to gain some experience with the IDE (Fig. 3.6).

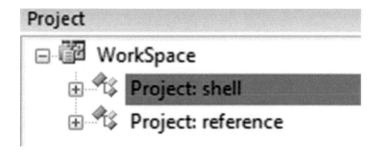

FIG. 3.6

Project workspace. The workspace contains working and prebuilt versions of the exercise project.

No permission required.

Highlight the Shell project right click and select "Set as Active Project" (Fig. 3.7).

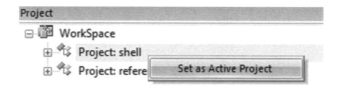

FIG. 3.7

Setting the active project. Select a project and right click to switch active projects.

No permission required.

The shell project is an empty project that has been created using the following steps:

Select project/new project.
Provide a project name.
Select the LPC55S69JD100 from the device database.

From this state we can start to expand the shell project by adding software components through a "Run Time Environment" (RTE) manager.
Open the RTE manager using the green diamond icon (dark gray in print version) on the Microvision toolbar or through Project/Manage/ Run Time Environment (Fig. 3.8).

FIG. 3.8

The run time manager toolbar icon. Open the run time manager from the Microvision IDE toolbar.

No permission required.

The RTE provides a tree of installed software components that can be added to a project by using the tick boxes in the selection (sel.) column. This dialog allows us to create and manage complex software platforms (Fig. 3.9).

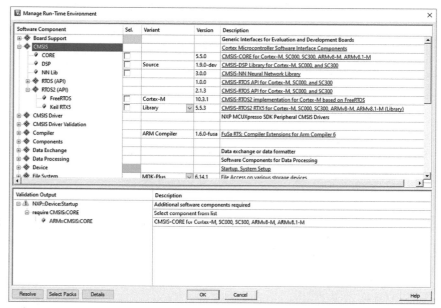

FIG. 3.9

The run time environment dialog. The run time environment dialog adds run time components and manages their dependent files.

When a selected component has all its necessary dependencies provided, the sel. tick box will appear green. If further options are required, it will appear orange. The validation output window will list the missing files and will show any options available to create a full project. To help this process, RTE also provides a resolve button that can be used to add missing dependencies as far as is possible for the tool-chain. Any remaining selections then need to be resolved by the developer. So, for example, you may need to select which low-level peripheral is going to be used with a particular software component.

In the RTE select Board Support::SDK Project Template::Project Template.
The template must be set to lpcxpresso55S69 (1).
Press the resolve button to add the supporting components.
Add the following additional components (Fig. 3.10).

Device::SDK_Utilities::assert (2)
Device::SDK_Utilities::Serial Manager_uart (3)
Open the CMSIS branch and add the Core support
This sets a path to the CMSIS-Core support files, which are then included by the device header file.
Open the RTOS2 branch and select the Keil RTX5 (Fig. 3.11).

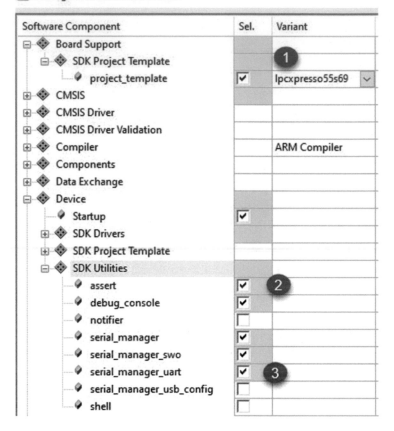

FIG. 3.10

RTE component selection. Add the core project components, dependency files may be added by pressing the resolve button.

No permission required.

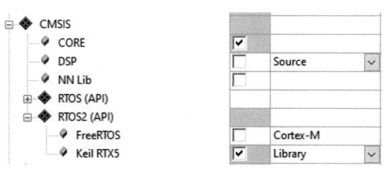

FIG. 3.11

Add the project components. In addition to the test framework, we must also add the CMSIS—Core and CMSIS RTOS2 components.

No permission required.

This adds a small footprint RTOS, which will be used in most of the examples in this book.

All the selected entries in the sel. Column should be green, if not use the validation window to resolve any missing components.

If this is not the case check the reference project for the correct settings.

Now click OK to add the components to the project.

The software components will be added to the project, as shown in Fig. 3.12.

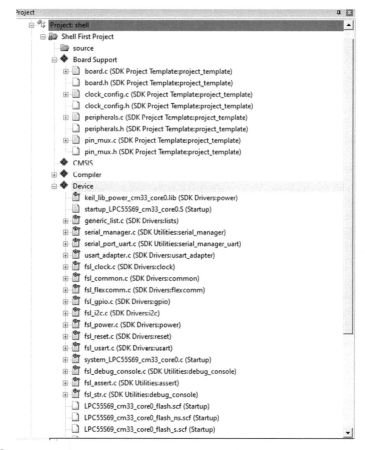

FIG. 3.12

Microvision project workspace. The RTE adds the board support and device driver library files to the project workspace.

No permission required.

In the project window, the component branches are shown with a green diamond (dark gray in print version) and the user source code branches are shown as a file folder.

Within the Software component branches, the source code is held in the pack repository as read-only files. The write protection is shown as a yellow key icon (light gray in print version).

Any configuration options are held in read/write header or source files which have _config as part of their name.

Most of the configuration files can be viewed through a configuration wizard, which is enabled through a tab that is located bottom left of the editor window (Fig. 3.13).

FIG. 3.13

Microvision project workspace. The RTE adds the board support and device driver library files to the project workspace.

No permission required.

The final image layout is controlled using a linker scatter file. These files have the extension .scf. Several scatter files are provided for different build configurations. In this project, we are using the LPC55S69_cm33_flash.scf, which defines a basic image layout for the internal flash memory.

Highlight the project root (Shell First Project), right click, and select "Options for Target" (Fig. 3.14).

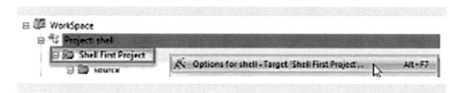

FIG. 3.14

Selecting the global project options. Select the root project, right click, and select "Options for Target" to open the global project options.

No permission required.

This view contains a set of dialogs that hold all the global project options.

Select the linker tab.

The default memory layout has been disabled, and instead, the linker will use our custom linker scatter file (Fig. 3.15).

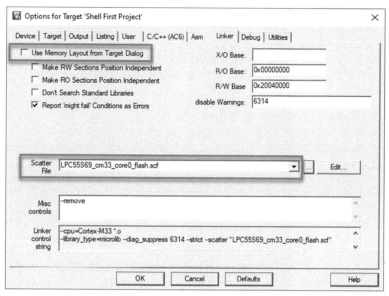

FIG. 3.15

Linker dialog. Disable the autogenerated linker script file (memory layout) and select instead use a linker script file.

Have a look through the other dialogs but for now don't change any options.

Click ok to close the options for target window.
Select the source folder.
Right click and select add existing file (Fig. 3.16).

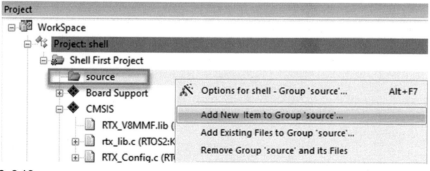

FIG. 3.16

Adding a project file. Select the source folder, right click, and select "Add existing file."

Navigate to the < example >/ directory.
Add the following "hello_world.c" file.
Click OK to finish.
Build the project using project/build Target (F7) or the toolbar icon.
Select debug/start|stop (Ctrl+F5) or the toolbar icon.

This will download the image to the target FLASH and run the code to main.
Select Debug run (F9) to Run the code.
Explore the debugger toolbar using the options shown below.
You can set a breakpoint by clicking on the dark gray boxes next to the source code (Fig. 3.17).

FIG. 3.17

Setting a breakpoint. To set a breakpoint click on a dark gray box in the editor margin.

No permission required.

A breakpoint is shown as a red dot (dark gray in print version).
The configuration of each peripheral is shown in the Peripheral/System Viewer menu (Fig. 3.18).

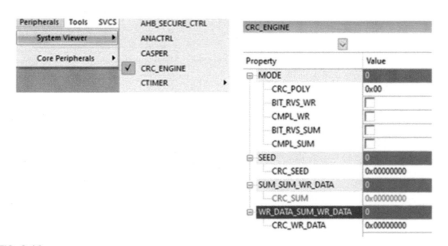

FIG. 3.18

Peripheral view window. The microcontroller peripherals are displayed in custom windows.

No permission required.

The state of the RTOS can be seen in a similar component viewer window.
Select the View\Watch Windows\RTX RTOS item (Fig. 3.19)

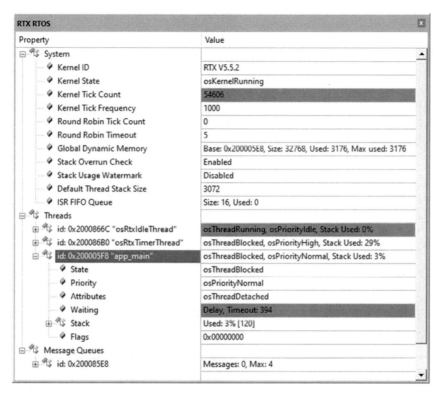

FIG. 3.19

Microvision project workspace. The RTE adds the board support and device driver library
files to the project workspace.

No permission required.

The code will also enable the debug "Serial Wire Out" SWO pin, which allows
the debugger to use the Instrumentation Trace and Data Watch Trace, which are part
of the Cortex-M Coresight debug architecture.
Start Tera Term
This will launch the new connection dialog.
Enable the Serial option and select the LPC-LinkII U Com Port
(Fig. 3.20)

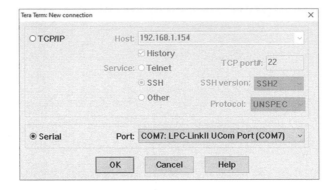

FIG. 3.20

Tera Term connection dialog. Enable the serial option and select the LPC-LinkII virtual serial port.

No permission required.

The Cortex-M33 debug architecture contains an "Instrumentation Trace." This provides a serial interface from the processor to a serial terminal via a virtual serial port created by the built-in debug hardware on the Xpresso evaluation board. Now within our code, STDIO used by printf and scanf will be redirected to the Tera Term console.

Select setup\serial port and set the baud rate to 115200 (Fig. 3.21)

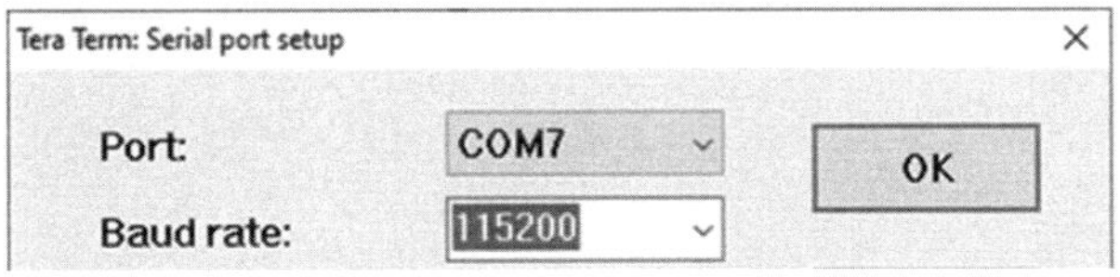

Tera Term: Serial port setup		✕
Port:	COM7 ⌄	OK
Baud rate:	115200 ⌄	

FIG. 3.21

Tera Term serial configuration. In the serial port menu, set the baud rate to 115200.

No permission required.

Return to the debugger reset the code and start the application code running. Observe the diagnostic messages printed to the terminal (Fig. 3.22).

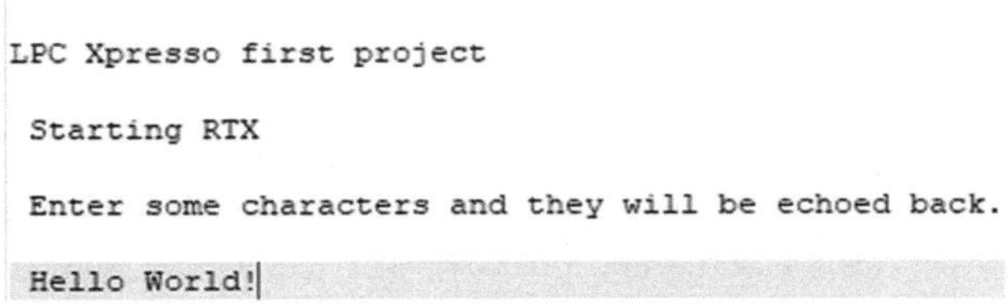

```
LPC Xpresso first project

Starting RTX

Enter some characters and they will be echoed back.

Hello World!|
```

FIG. 3.22

Microvision project workspace. The RTE adds the board support and device driver library files to the project workspace.

No permission required.

This will execute the code and display a startup message on the Tera Term console. You can now type characters within Tera Term and they will be echoed back the RGB LED is toggled on and off as each character is typed.

The default terminal window in Tera Term is white text on a black background. In this book, the display has been transposed to black text on white for better printing results.

This example should have familiarized you with the MDK-ARM toolchain and help prove out the hardware. Before we leave this exercise, it is worth noting one more thing:

How to get out of jail free

If you are experimenting with this board, you may do something that locks up the microcontroller preventing the debugger from connecting. Typically, this can occur if you add low power code or miss configure the processor clock tree.

If you get into this predicament, it is possible to erase the internal FLASH by holding down the ISP button and then powering the board. This will start the internal bootloader running rather than the FLASH code. You should then be able to connect the debugger and erase the FLASH memory. This will recover the board, and you can continue.

The LPC55S69 contains a PSACertified compliant secure boot ROM, and we will have a detailed look at this later. Needless to say, this technique does not work if the secure boot has been enabled. You have been warned!

CMSIS WiFi driver

The CMSIS WiFi driver is designed to provide a common interface to supported WiFi "System on Chip" SoC devices. Currently, the following devices are supported (Table 3.2).

Table 3.2 WiFi modules.

Device	Interface	Data bypass mode
ESP32	UART	No
ESP8266	UART	No
ISM43362	SPI	No
WizFi360	UART	No
QCA400x	UART/SPI	Yes

The CMSIS WiFi driver is a compound driver that uses a further CMSIS driver for low-level communication to the module. This will typically use an SPI or USART as the module interface (Fig. 3.23).

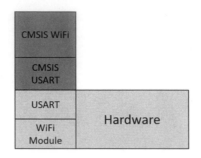

FIG. 3.23

CMSIS WiFi and USART drivers. The CMSIS WiFi driver is a compound driver that uses the CMSIS-USART driver to communicate with the WiFi module.

No permission required.

Each WiFi module contains its own TCP/IP stack. This allows the module to manage all network communications while providing a socket interface for the microcontroller. However, WiFi modules often have limitations in the size of IP packets they can send and receive. Many IoT devices only need to transfer relatively small amounts of data, so this is not usually a problem, but it is something to bear in mind when selecting a module. If the module supports "Data Bypass Mode," the onboard TCP/IP stack can be replaced by a TCP/IP stack such as LwIP or the Keil network component running on the application microcontroller. This removes many of the modules limitations and allows us to develop a wider range of more sophisticated network applications.

We can add WiFi support to our project through the run time environment manager. Since we are configuring two CMSIS drivers which are acting in concert, we need a methodical way of configuring and testing the drivers with minimal effort. Fortunately, the CMSIS WiFi driver is well supported within the CMSIS driver validation suite, and this provides an ideal way to bring up the driver for the first time.

Exercise adding WiFi support

In this exercise, we will set up a module that uses a UART interface and then have a look at the more complex configuration for a module with an SPI interface.

In the pack installer select Example 1.2 WiFi Module and press the copy button.

This is a multiproject workspace with a fully configured project for reference and a shell project, which we will use to add and test the CMSIS drivers.

Set the shell project to be the active project.
Open the manage run time environment and select the CMSIS Driver\ WiFi\ESP8266.

This module uses a UART interface, so we also need to add a CMSIS USART driver. In this case, we need to add support for a plain hardware USART, which is supported by the CMSIS Driver\USART(API)\flexcomm_usart_cmsis driver (Fig. 3.24).

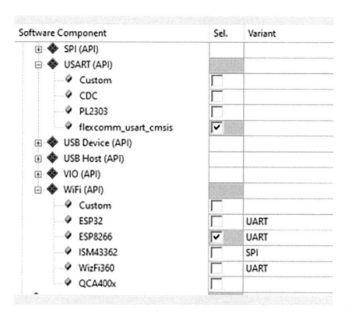

FIG. 3.24

Selecting the CMSIS drivers. Select the CMSIS USART and WiFi drivers in the Microvision RTE.

No permission required.

Next, we need to add to the CMSIS driver validation framework.

In the RTE, open the CMSIS Driver validation branch and select the framework and add the WiFi options.

If you have new or unknown hardware you could also add the USART validation tests (Fig. 3.25).

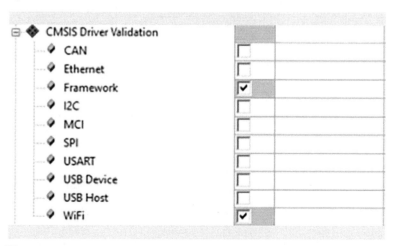

FIG. 3.25

CMSIS driver validation framework. Enable the CMSIS driver validation framework and the WiFi tests.

No permission required.

The validation framework is designed to run bare metal or with the CMSIS RTOS2. In this exercise, we will need to add the RTOS as well.

Add the RTX5 RTOS in CMSIS\RTOS2(API)\RTX.
Set the variant column to library (Fig. 3.11).

Depending on your installation, you may have several RTOS choices available. In this book, we are going to use the Keil RTX5 RTOS as this has a small footprint and native support for the CMSIS-RTOS2 API.

The validation framework sends test results to the debugger console window in either a text or XML format.
Resolve any dependencies and then click OK to add the driver files to your project.

Now we can use the configuration wizards to setup the CMSIS drivers and validation framework.

First, select the Device\RTE_Device.h file and enable the UART, which will be used to communicate with the WiFi module. As we are using the LPC55S69 expresso board, this will be UART 2.

Open device\RTE_Device.h and set RTE_USART2 to "1" as shown in Fig. 3.26.

```
#define RTE_USART0 0
#define RTE_USART0_DMA_EN 0
#define RTE_USART1 0
#define RTE_USART1_DMA_EN 0
#define RTE_USART2 1
#define RTE_USART2_DMA_EN 0
#define RTE_USART3 0
#define RTE_USART3_DMA_EN 0
#define RTE_USART4 0
#define RTE_USART4_DMA_EN 0
#define RTE_USART5 0
#define RTE_USART5_DMA_EN 0
#define RTE_USART6 0
#define RTE_USART6_DMA_EN 0
#define RTE_USART7 0
#define RTE_USART7_DMA_EN 0
```

FIG. 3.26

USART selection. USART 2 is used to communicate with the WiFi module.

Next select the CMSIS Driver\WiFi Config.h (Fig. 3.27).

FIG. 3.27

CMSIS WiFi configuration file. The CMSIS WiFi driver options are all in the module config.h file.

No permission required.

For initial testing, use the default settings, but we do need to adjust the USART driver number to match the hardware configuration on the Xpresso board. In this case, the USART driver value must be set to "2." We must also allocate 1024 bytes to the WiFi driver RTOS thread (Fig. 3.28).

ESP8266 WiFi Driver Configuration	
WiFi Driver Number (Driver_WiFi#)	0
Connect to hardware via Driver_USART#	2
Serial interface baudrate	115200
WiFi thread priority	osPriorityAboveNormal
WiFi thread stack size [bytes]	1024
Socket buffer block size	512
Socket buffer block count	8
Serial parser buffer block size	256
Serial parser buffer block count	8

FIG. 3.28

WiFi configuration wizard. Use the configuration wizard to select USART 2 and set the thread memory allocation to 1024 bytes.

No permission required.

The WiFi driver will configure the CMSIS USART driver so we have nothing further to do at the USART driver level.

To configure the validation environment, we need to setup the RTOS and debug components.

Select the CMSIS\RTX_Config.h file (Fig. 3.29).

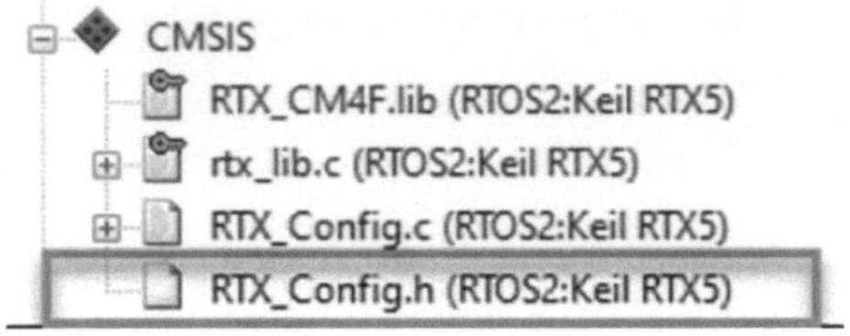

FIG. 3.29

The RTX RTOS configuration file. The RTX_Config.h file contains all the RTOS configuration options.

No permission required

Here, we must have a global memory pool of at least 8096 bytes and a default thread stack size to 2048 bytes (Fig. 3.30).

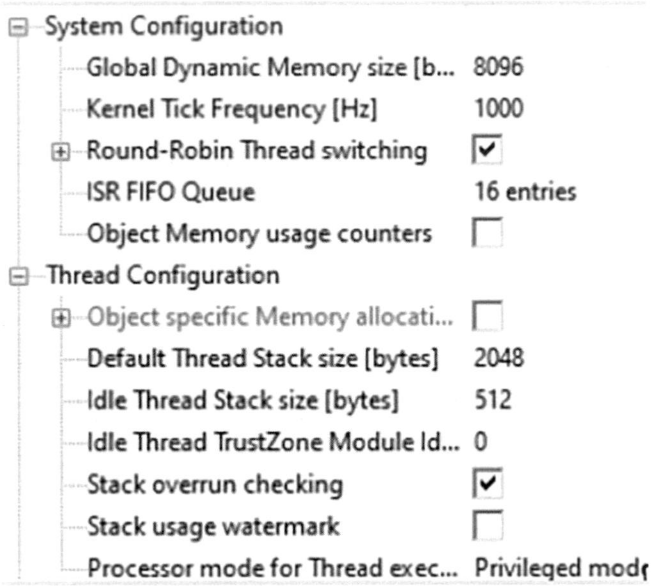

FIG. 3.30

RTX configuration wizard. Set the RTX configuration options using the wizard.

No permission required.

Now we can configure the validation framework in dv_config.h header. The first section allows us to set the global framework options. For this test, we can again use the defaults with the print output format set to XML for the final report.

Open CMSIS Driver Validation\DV_Config.h and select the wizard
Select an output format you want to work with either plain text or XML
(Fig. 3.31)

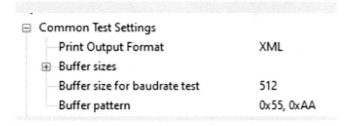

FIG. 3.31

CMSIS driver framework wizard. We can set the test report format in the validation framework wizard.

No permission required.

Open CMSIS Driver Validation\DV_WiFi_Config.h and select the wizard **The configuration\station section needs to be configured with the SSID, password, and security type of your WiFi access point** (Fig. 3.32).

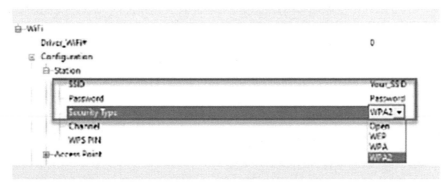

FIG. 3.32

CMSIS WiFi test suite configuration wizard. Set you WiFi network SSID password and security type.

No permission required.

During the validation tests, data packets will be sent to a "socket server" running on a network PC. The socket server is a dedicated executable that is designed to run in a Windows environment. The socket server is located in the following directory:

C:\Keil_v5\ARM\PACK\ARM\CMSIS-Driver_Validation\<version >\Tools\ SockServer\PC\Win

As this may change I have also included the socketserver executable in a folder within the current example. The socket server is an executable, which just needs to be started without any further configuration. However, you will need to create an exception rule in your firewall to allow a remote device to connect. Once started, its IP address will be displayed on the console screen (Fig. 3.33).

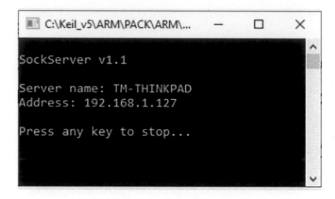

FIG. 3.33

Socket server interface. The socket server runs as a console application.

No permission required.

The socket server provides a number of testing services that are used by the CMSIS driver validation suite. Each service supports both TCP and UDP protocols (Table 3.3).

Table 3.3 Socket server protocols.

Service	Port	Description
Echo	7	Echo's back received data packets
Discard	19	Accepts remote socket connection
Chargen	19	Send continuous character stream
Assistant	5000	Connects to remote server socket

Start the socket server on a network PC.
Make a note of the PC IP address shown in the socket server console window
Then update the PC socket server IP address in the WiFi validation configuration header (Fig. 3.34).

FIG. 3.34

WiFi test suite configuration wizard. Set the socket server IP address in the DV_WiFi_Config.h configuration wizard.

No permission required.

The final section of the validation configuration wizard allows us to enable a wide range of tests for both the WiFi module features and communication. For initial testing, we can use the default test settings, and this will exercise most of the driver features (Fig. 3.35).

FIG. 3.35

Validation wizard default tests. Ensure that the default tests are enabled in the validation wizard.

No permission required.

Once the driver and test framework are configured we can invoke the test framework from main() as follows:

```
#include "cmsis_dv.h"
#include "cmsis_os2.h"
int main(void) {
SystemCoreClockUpdate();
osKernelInitialize ();
//app_initialize();
osKernelStart();    /* Start thread execution */
while(1);
}
```

This code is provided in a module main.c located in the project directory.

Open main.c in the project window to view the validation code.

Compared to a normal development project, there are a couple of settings that can be used to make this project a more efficient test environment. First, the project is configured to start the debugger after a build by setting the "Start debugging" option in the Options for target/User dialog (Fig. 3.36).

A script file has been added to the debugger dialog, and the script will execute when the debugger is started. This is very important as this "automates" the build and test loop, which can then be executed with a single button press (Fig. 3.37).

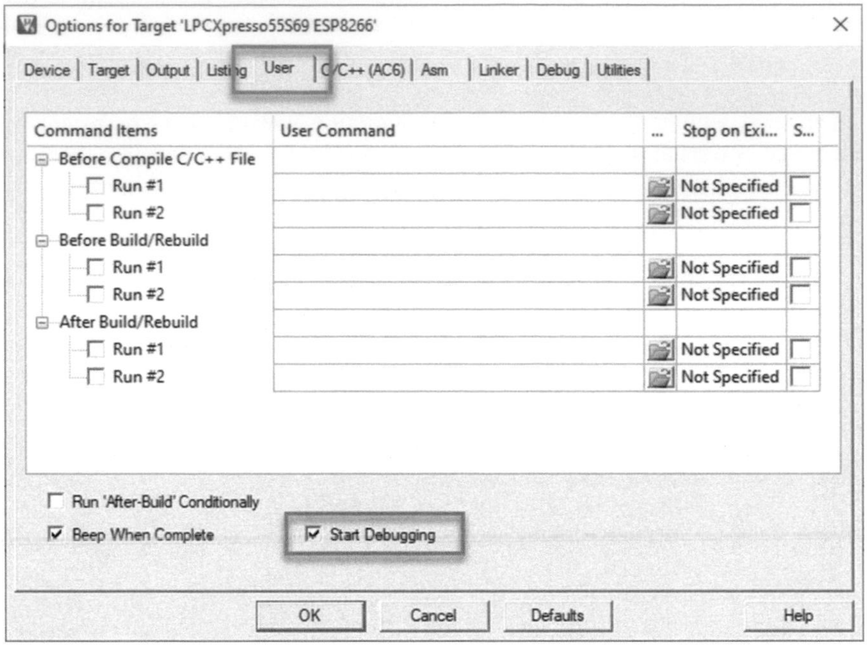

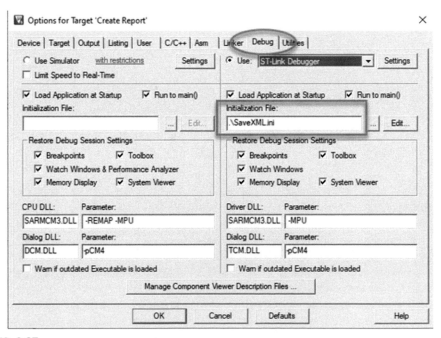

FIG. 3.36

Project global options user menu. The global project options can be set to start the debugger immediately after a project build.

No permission required.

FIG. 3.37

Global options debugger menu. Adding a debugger script file.

No permission required.

The script file controls execution of the test framework and logs the test results to a file in the project directory. When XML format is selected, a schema is also saved.

When using a standalone debug adapter such as Ulink or Jlink, the test results can be displayed in a console window in microvision. The SLOG command can be used to store the results in a file automatically.

```
G, cmsis_dv
//SLOG > TestReport\TestReport.xml
G, closeDebug
SLOG OFF
EXIT
```

Now build the project and execute the validation tests.

The validation tests report can be copied from the Tera Term console and saved to a file in the project directory. This file can then be viewed with a HTML browser (Fig. 3.38).

CMSIS-Driver WiFi Test Report

Mar 3 2020 14:09:53

Test Case	Details		Status
1	WIFI_SetOption_GetOption		Passed
2	WIFI_Scan		Passed
3	WIFI_Activate_Deactivate		Passed
4	WIFI_IsConnected		Passed
5	WIFI_GetNetInfo		Passed
6	WIFI_SocketCreate		Passed
7	WIFI_SocketBind		Passed
8	WIFI_SocketListen		Passed
9	WIFI_SocketAccept		Not executed
10	WIFI_SocketConnect		Not executed
11	WIFI_SocketRecv		Not executed
12	WIFI_SocketRecvFrom		Not executed
13	WIFI_SocketSend		Not executed
14	WIFI_SocketSendTo		Not executed
15	WIFI_SocketGetSockName		Passed
16	WIFI_SocketGetPeerName		Passed
17	WIFI_SocketGetOpt		Passed
18	WIFI_SocketSetOpt		Passed
19	WIFI_SocketClose		Passed
20	WIFI_SocketGetHostByName		Passed
21	WIFI_Ping		Passed
22	WIFI_Transfer_Fixed		Passed
23	WIFI_Transfer_Incremental		Passed
24	WIFI_Send_Fragmented		Passed
25	WIFI_Recv_Fragmented		Passed
26	WIFI_Test_Speed		Passed
27	WIFI_Concurrent_Socket		Passed
28	WIFI_Downstream_Rate DV_WIFI.c (8281): [INFO] Speed 87 KB/s DV_WIFI.c (8285): [FAILED] Execution timeout (2000 ms)	Less details	Failed
29	WIFI_Upstream_Rate DV_WIFI.c (8349): [INFO] Speed 61 KB/s	Less details	Passed

FIG. 3.38

WiFi test report. The final WiFi test report will show the results of the test suite.

SPI interface

If the WiFi module has an SPI interface, it will include a slave select line, which must be managed at the start and end of communication from the MCU. Since the SPI interface is synchronous, the module uses a "Data_Ready" line to signal the MCU that data are ready to be read from the WiFi module. The data ready line should be connected to an MCU GPIO pin that can generate an interrupt when the data ready line becomes active (Fig. 3.39).

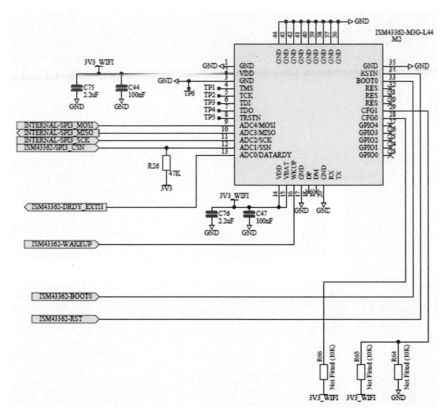

FIG. 3.39

WiFi module. Circuit diagram of a WiFi module with an SPI interface.

No permission required.

The driver for SPI based modules provides an extra hardware interface file that contains stub functions that allow these features to be managed by the MCU GPIO pins (Fig. 3.40).

FIG. 3.40

SPI hardware support file. A WiFi module with an SPI interface will have an additional hardware support file.

No permission required.

The MCU GPIO pin connected to the data ready line should be configured to trigger when the data ready line becomes active. Its interrupt function can then signal the driver that new data are ready using the function provided as shown below:

```
void GPIO_External_Interrupt(void){
      WiFi_ISM43362_Pin_DATARDY_IRQ();
      }
```

The hardware interface file contains stub functions to control the MCU GPIO pins connected to the reset line and slave select lines.

```
void WiFi_ISM43362_Pin_RSTN (uint8_t rstn) {
GPIO_WritePin(GPIOE,
                      GPIO_PIN_8,
                      rstn ? GPIO_PIN_RESET : GPIO_PIN_SET);
}
void WiFi_ISM43362_Pin_SSN (uint8_t ssn) {
GPIO_WritePin(GPIOE,
                      GPIO_PIN_0,
                      ssn ? GPIO_PIN_RESET : GPIO_PIN_SET);
}
uint8_t WiFi_ISM43362_Pin_DATARDY (void) {
  return (GPIO_ReadPin(GPIOE, GPIO_PIN_1) == GPIO_PIN_SET);
}
```

Once the hardware interface file is configured, you can test the driver as shown in the previous example.

Using the WiFi module

Once the WiFi driver has passed the validation tests, we can remove the validation framework and access the driver from our application code.

Open the RTE and remove the CMSIS validation framework options and click OK

In the project window, open main.c

Remove the validation header file

```
#include "cmsis_dv.h"
```

Remove the device validation new thread call

```
osThreadNew(cmsis_dv, NULL, NULL);
```

Uncomment the start of the application code

```
//app_initialize();
```

Open the file socket_startup.c

Enter your WiFi SSID and password into the #define strings in this file.

```
#define Your_SSID ""
#define Your_Password ""
```

The app_main thread will be used to first initialize and power up the WiFi module using the socket_startup() function

```
void socket_startup (void){
ARM_WIFI_CONFIG_t config;
Driver_WiFi0.Initialize (NULL);
Driver_WiFi0.PowerControl(ARM_POWER_FULL);
```

The code will then activate the WiFi module so that it attempts to connect to the network. If this is successful, we can run a main application that will be able to send and receive TCP/IP packets using the WiFi module.

```
config.pass= "Your_Password";
config.security = SECURITY_TYPE;
config.ch= 0U;
Driver_WiFi0.Activate(0U, &config);
if (Driver_WiFi0.IsConnected() == 0U) {
printf("WiFi network connection failed!\r\n");
} else {
  printf("WiFi network connection succeeded!\r\n");
}
  return 0; }
```

File system

The project also contains a port of the FATFS file system, which can be used to read and write files to an SD card that has been inserted into the SDIO socket on the evaluation board.

Once the WiFi module has been connected to the local network, the application code will initialize the file system and create a test file on the SD card.

Place an SD card in the card holder on the Xpresso evaluation board.

The code will now initialize the file system and create a test file on the SD card.

Remove the SD card, insert it in a card holder, and place it in your PC.

You should now be able to view and read the test file on your PC to check that the file system is working.

Conclusion

We now have our evaluation board set up with a WiFi interface to a local network that allows us to send and receive TCP packets through a socket interface. We can also build applications with a professional toolchain and debug them on the evaluation board. Over the next two chapters, we will look at building a secure communications channel that can be used by our IoT devices to communicate with a cloud server.

Cryptography—The basics

4

Introduction

This chapter will provide an introduction to current cryptographic algorithms that are used for secure communications and to secure stored data within an IoT node. Before we begin, it is important to lay down a few rules about developing a cryptographic system.

First, do not try to develop your own algorithm. While it may seem like a good idea to have your own patented algorithm it is highly unlikely you will get it right. It is also highly likely that someone will be able to break it and gain access to your system and/or data. Don't. Just don't. Stick to standard well-known algorithms that are under constant review by researchers. Any weaknesses or vulnerabilities will be found along with mitigations or migration to an improved algorithm. As a corollary to this rule, do not use a nonstandard algorithm provided by a third party. It is very likely that somebody's "secret sauce" will suffer from the same problems and should be treated as snake oil.

Secondly, do not try to code a standard algorithm. This may seem a bit extreme, particularly if you are a professional software developer. However, any code you do produce will only be used and reviewed by a small number of developers who are unlikely to be experienced cryptographers. Instead, use a standard library with a large user base whose source code is maintained and open for review. One of the guiding rules of cryptography is known as Kerkhoff's Principle, which states "The security of a cryptosystem must lie in the choice of its keys only; everything else (including the algorithm itself) should be considered public knowledge" or as Claude Shannon put it, "The enemy knows the system." Somewhat ironically secrecy about your software design and algorithms is ultimately the enemy of security; open discussion encourages better security.

Now that I have got that off my chest let's press on!

Table 4.1 defines acronyms for agencies and standards that are often quoted within microcontroller datasheets and user manuals.

Table 4.1 Security acronyms.

Acronym	
NSA	National Security Agency (United States)
NIST	National Institute of Science and Technology
FIPS	Federal Information Processing Standards
PKCS	Public Key Cryptography Standards

Acronyms of commonly quoted standards and agencies.

mbedTLS

The mbedTLS cryptographic library is a component of the mbedOS IoT operating system developed by Arm but is available as a stand-alone modular library. mbedTLS library was originally a commercial product developed by a Canadian company called Polar. Arm purchased Polar and the mbedTLS library in 2011 and released mbedTLS as a free-to-use resource for commercial and noncommercial projects. mbedTLS is provided under an Apache v2.0 noncontributory license. Due to its prominence as part of Arm's IoT firmware, mbedTLS is subject to a lot of research and scrutiny. The mbedTLS library is maintained under continued development with regular updates along with security alerts to notify you of discovered vulnerabilities and patches. A security center is maintained on the Trusted Firmware website.

https://developer.trustedfirmware.org/w/mbed-tls/security-center/.

If you use mbedTLS in a project, you should also join the mbedTLS security alerts mailing list.

There is an additional cryptographic library called mbedCrypto, which is derived from mbedTLS. The mbedCrypto library is designed to run as a security service as part of the PSA Trusted Firmware. We will see how to use mbedCrypto in the second half of this book.

Exercise: Install and verify mbedTLS

The mbedTLS source code can be downloaded from gitHub or installed as a software pack as shown below.

If you have not done so already, open the pack installer, select the Packs tab, and install the generic::mbedTLS software pack (Fig. 4.1).

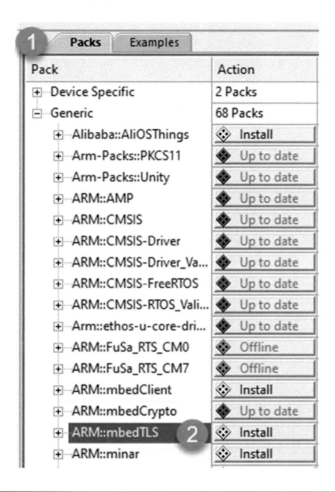

FIG. 4.1

mbedTLS software pack. Installing the mbedTLS software pack.

Once installed, our first mbedTLS project will build the library with its self-test option enabled so that we can verify its operation on our target hardware.

Open the pack installer select project 4.1 and press the copy button.

This is a fully configured project with the mbedTLS source code modules added. The mbedTls library is designed as a very modular library so it can be compiled with the minimal functionality required for a given project.

Open the file mbedTLS_Config.h. (Fig. 4.2).

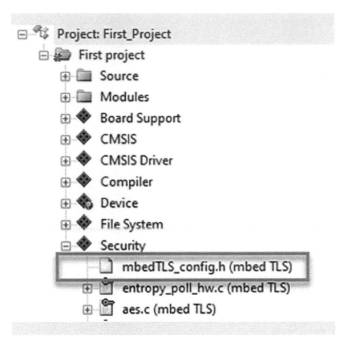

FIG. 4.2

mbedTLS configuration file.

No permission required.

The config file contains all the configuration switches used to select the features and modules within the mbedTLS library. The config file is divided into three sections (Table 4.2).

Table 4.2 mbedTLS configuration options.

Configuration section	Description
System support	Defines the system resources available to the library
Feature support	Configures features within a cryptographic algorithm
Modules	Enables a module containing a given cryptographic algorithm

In the current project, all of the cryptographic algorithms are enabled but the SSL (TLS) protocol is disabled. The **MBEDTLS_SELF_TEST** option is enabled so we can ensure that all the supported algorithms can be run on our hardware.

Build the project and start the debugger.
Place a formatted SD card in the evaluation board card holder.
Start Tera Term and connect to the virtual serial port at 115200 baud.
Run the code and the self-test results will be printed to the console window
(Fig. 4.3).

```
ENTROPY test: failed

PBKDF2 (SHA1) #0: passed
PBKDF2 (SHA1) #1: passed
PBKDF2 (SHA1) #2: passed
PBKDF2 (SHA1) #3: passed
PBKDF2 (SHA1) #4: passed
PBKDF2 (SHA1) #5: passed


Executed 26 test suites

[ 1 tests FAIL ]
```

FIG. 4.3

mbedTLS self-test results.

No permission required.

Now when you run the code, the self-test functions for each algorithm will execute and the results will be printed to the debugger console window.

The self-test functions execute a test suite of 26 test groups that cover the algorithms in the library. The set of tests for the random number generator will fail as this algorithm requires further configuration. We will fix this later. The project also creates a large file called "Hello_big.txt" on the evaluation board SD card. Keep this file as we will use it in future projects.

Open the RTE.
Click on the mbedTLS documentation link (Fig. 4.4).

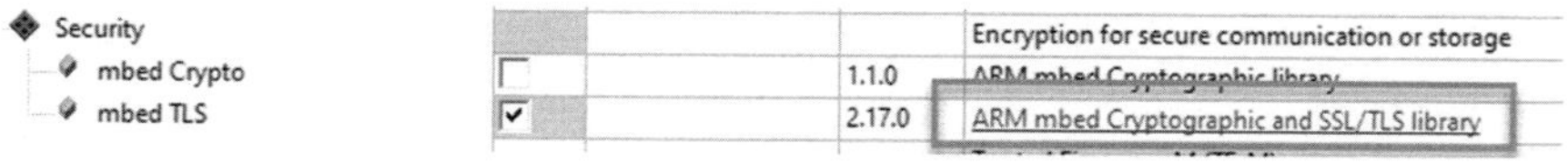

◆ Security			Encryption for secure communication or storage
◊ mbed Crypto	☐	1.1.0	ARM mbed Cryptographic library
◊ mbed TLS	☑	2.17.0	ARM mbed Cryptographic and SSL/TLS library

FIG. 4.4

mbedTLS library. The mbedTLS documentation is available from within the RTE.

No permission required.

The documentation is provided as a Doxygen file, and the main documentation is available in the "usage and description" section (Fig. 4.5).

FIG. 4.5

mbedTLS documentation. The mbedTLS configuration header has many #defines which are documented in the Usage and Description section of the documentation.

No permission required.

Very importantly and deserving of its own paragraph, the description of each configuration option is available in the documentation files/config.h page. This describes the purpose of each configuration #define and also any dependencies it requires.

The mbedTLS_config.h file also includes a check config file. This will report any configuration errors and give us a quick if slightly kludgie way to find the missing dependencies.

```
#include "mbedtls/check_config.h
```

Open mbedTLS_config.h and comment out the following option:

```
line 124 //#define MBEDTLS_AES_C
```

Rebuild the project.

The compiler will report that there is a missing dependency:

```
#error "MBEDTLS_CTR_DRBG_C defined, but not all prerequisites"
```

Click on the compiler error to locate the source code that caused it.

Here, we can see the possible missing #defines and can go back and enable the necessary options in the mbedTLS_config.h file.

```
#if defined(MBEDTLS_CTR_DRBG_C) && !defined(MBEDTLS_AES_C)
#error "MBEDTLS_CTR_DRBG_C defined, but not all prerequisites"
#endif
```

Information assurance

We want to use a cryptographic library to protect both the integrity of our IoT device and the data it produces or consumes. This is known as "information assurance" and it has four main pillars.

Confidentiality

The most obvious feature of our cryptographic library is to provide confidentiality of private information. Any data in our system must only be accessible to authorized individuals and must not be disclosed to unauthorized individuals.

Integrity

In addition to confidentiality, it is also necessary to validate the integrity of any data received from outside the bounds of our IoT node. This ensures that information and programs are only changed in a specified and authorized manner.

Availability

Any cryptographic system should work promptly and service must not be denied to authorized users.

Nonrepudiation and authentication

This feature of a cryptographic system allows us to prove both the integrity and the origin of the data. This means that we can prove who sent the message and that it has not been tampered with. It also means that the sender cannot deny (repudiate) that they are the originator.

Security services

It is the role of a cryptographic library to provide a range of security algorithms that achieve these information assurance aims. The scope of these security services is shown in Fig. 4.6.

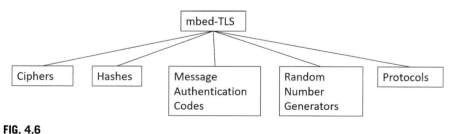

FIG. 4.6

mbedTLS services. Security services provided by the mbedTLS library.

Ciphers

Ciphers are used to ensure the confidentiality of information both when it is "in flight" during a communication session and when it is stored or "at rest" in the memory of a microcontroller.

Hashes

A cryptographic hash is used to validate the integrity of a block of data. You can pass data of arbitrary size into a hashing algorithm and it will return a (large) number called a Message Digest (MD) that is unique to that data. You can think of a Message Digest as a cryptographic checksum or fingerprint of the data.

Message authentication code (MAC)

A message authentication code (MAC) is like a hash in that it returns a unique number called a Tag, but this number depends on the input block of data and a password in the form of a numeric key. To regenerate the MAC Tag you need both the original data and the key. Thus, a MAC Tag can be used both to validate the data that have been received and also authenticate its origin to any member of a group that knows the key.

Authenticated encryption

In a communication protocol, we need to ensure the confidentiality and integrity of data in flight. It is common to encrypt a block of data with a cipher and also use a message authentication code so that a receiving station can validate its integrity and origin.

Random number generator (RNG)

A cryptographic system will also include a random number generator (RNG). This may come as a surprise as an RNG is vital to the successful performance of a cryptographic system. For example, encryption keys can be generated with random data, and the higher layer communication protocols require a stream of random numbers to establish a secure communication channel. The quality of your RNG is as important as the security of your cipher keys.

In this chapter, we are going to introduce each of the key services that provide the foundation for secure communication and see how they are supported in mbedTLS. Then in the next chapter, we will look at how to use these algorithms to establish a secure communication session.

Ciphers

We are all familiar with how a cipher works probably from using simple codes as children. The basic premise is simple—take our unencrypted text known as plain text and pass this through our cipher algorithm in combination with a cipher key. The output is then our encrypted text known as ciphertext. We can decrypt the ciphertext back to the plain text by running the ciphertext and the encryption key back through the cipher algorithm (Fig. 4.7).

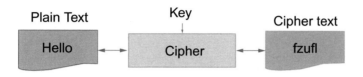

FIG. 4.7

Symmetric cipher. A symmetric cipher encrypts plain text to produce cipher text.

No permission required.

There are two main categories of cipher algorithm. These are symmetrical key and asymmetrical key algorithms. A symmetrical key cipher uses the same key to encrypt and decrypt the plain text. This means that the key must be known by both the sending and receiving station and must be shared by an initial secure channel. This makes it impossible to establish secure communications over an insecure channel such as the internet without having previously agreed on a cipher key through a separate secure channel. The second class of ciphers, known as asymmetrical ciphers, helps solve this problem. An asymmetrical cipher system has two keys: a public key and a private key. The public key is used for encryption and does not have to be kept secret; the private key is used for decryption and must be kept secret. In this chapter, we will look at symmetrical ciphers, and in the next chapter, we will look at asymmetrical ciphers and how to use them in a real system.

When considering a cipher system's security, a cipher is said to be "broken" when the ciphertext can be decrypted by an attack that exploits a weakness in the algorithm. If a cipher is not broken and you don't have access to the key, then the only way to decrypt the message is to try every key combination until you hit the correct key. This "brute force" approach can only be used successfully if the cipher key size is small enough to allow the resulting keyspace to be searched in a reasonable amount of time. As available computing power increases, we need to have larger key sizes to make brute force searches unfeasible.

Symmetrical ciphers

The family of symmetrical ciphers can split into two broad categories of streaming ciphers and block ciphers.

A streaming cipher encrypts one symbol at a time to create a stream of ciphertext that can then be decrypted symbol by symbol. A block cipher operates on a group of bytes to encrypt or decrypt multiple bytes at a time. While both types of cipher can be used to protect internet traffic, a block cipher works well with UPD and TCP packets.

Streaming ciphers

In a theoretical streaming cipher, each symbol will be a single bit. Each bit in the plain text stream will be combined with a bit from a random bitstream known as a keystream. The resulting stream of ciphertext can be decrypted by performing the same addition with a synchronized keystream (Fig. 4.8).

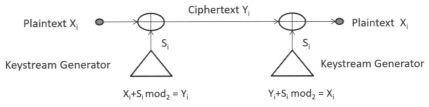

FIG. 4.8

Streaming cipher.

The process of combining the bitstream and the keystream is a mod2 addition which, when we look at the resulting truth table, can be performed by a single XOR gate (Fig. 4.9).

X	S	Y
0	0	0
0	1	1
1	0	1
1	1	0

= XOR

FIG. 4.9

mod2 operation. The truth table of a mod2 operation is a single XOR gate.

Therefore, a streaming cipher is potentially fast and simple to implement. The resulting encrypted bitstream provides a very high encryption level that is nigh on impossible to break. However, in practice, it is impossible to create a random keystream that never repeats itself and can be synchronized between the source and destination. There are a number of practical streaming ciphers that overcome these limitations. mbedTLS supports the ARC4 streaming cipher. This cipher was originally developed by Ron Rivest at the RSA Corporation and is called Rivest Cipher 4 (RC4). RC4 was sold as a commercial cipher. However, it was never patented, and at some point, the source code was posted on the internet. This gave rise to the Almost Rivest Cipher 4 (ARC4), which is now mostly considered to be in the public domain except, of course, by the RSA Corporation. While it is used in many commercial products and is included in mbedTLS, its legal basis is a bit of a gray area. Since the source code was posted, security researchers have found multiple vulnerabilities in ARC4, and it is considered an insecure algorithm. While it forms part of the WiFi security protocols WEP and WAP, its use was removed from TLS in 2015.

The ARC4 cipher generates a keystream from a pseudo-random bitstream generator. This consists of a secret internal state, which is an array of 256 bytes (Fig. 4.10).

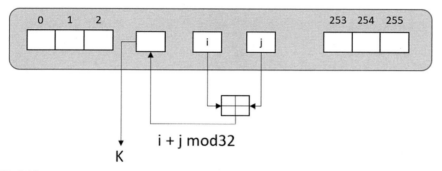

FIG. 4.10

ARC 4 state. The ARC4 cipher manipulates an internal state to create a pseudo-random bit stream.

No permission required.

The state array is initially filled with the values 0–255.

```
for (i - 0; i < 255; i++){
S[i] := i;
}
```

The state values are modified with an initial permutation shown below. The secret key has a length of between 1 and 256 bytes. The key should not be used for repeated sessions in a practical system. Instead, you must devise a protocol to derive a unique key for each session from a shared master key.

```
for(i = 0; i < 256; i++){
j = (j + S[i] + key[i % keylength]) % 256
swap values of S[i] and S[j]
}
```

The keystream value K is then produced by the following pseudo-random process.

```
i = 0,j = 0;//Act as indexes into the state
n = 0;
```

```
for( n=0;n<plaintextSizeBytes;n++){
i = (i + 1) % 256
j = (j + S[i]) % 256 swap values of S[i] and S[j]
K = S[(S[i] + S[j]) % 256]
cipherText[n] = K ^ plaintext[n]
}
```

Exercise: ARC4

This exercise configures mbedTLS to use the ARC4 cipher and then encrypts and decrypts the Hello_Big.txt file, which was created in the first exercise. Table 4.3 provides a summary of the mbedTLS ARC4 functions.

Table 4.3 ARC4 functions.

Function	Description
mbedtls_arc4_crypt	Encrypt/decrypt data for a given context
mbedtls_arc4_free	Clear the ARC4 context
mbedtls_arc4_init	Initialize the ARC4 context
mbedtls_arc4_setup	Setup the encryption key

mbedTLS ARC.

Open the pack installer, select Project 4.2 and press the copy button.

In this exercise, we will encrypt the hello_big.txt file 1000 times and then decrypt it back to the original plain text. This is a standard way to "stress test" the implementation of any encryption algorithm.

Open main.c

The file access and encryption routine is held in the ARC4_crypt() function.

```
ARC4_crypt("HelloBig.txt","ARC4.txt");
ARC4_crypt("ARC4.txt","HelloNew.txt");
```

Because the ARC4 cipher is performing an XOR with a random bit stream we can use the same function to encrypt and decrypt the data in our file.

When using an algorithm in mbedTLS, you first need to declare a context variable to hold the working values for a given instance. Within the ARC4_crypt() function, we declare and initialize an ARC4 context and then setup the cipher key.

```
static const unsigned char arc4_test_key[8] ={ 0x01, 0x23, 0x45,
0x67, 0x89, 0xAB, 0xCD, 0xEF };
mbedtls_arc4_context ctx;
mbedtls_arc4_init( &ctx );
mbedtls_arc4_setup( &ctx,arc4_test_key, 8 );// Add the key
```

Here, we are storing the key in the source code, which is exactly the wrong thing to do! We will look at a hardware-based key store in Chapter 11 and key management in Chapter 13. Now we can call the main encrypt/decrypt function.

```
mbedtls_arc4_crypt( &ctx, dataCount, ibuf, obuf );
```

Run the code.

This will encrypt the hello big file 1000 times and then decrypt it 1000 times before checking that the final decrypted file is the same as the original.

Block cipher

A block cipher is a second form of cipher, which operates over a group of bytes. A block cipher algorithm uses two tactics to achieve a strong level of encryption. These tactics are confusion (which substitutes one symbol for another) and diffusion (which spreads one plain text symbol over many ciphertext symbols). Changing one bit in the plaintext of a block cipher can change up to 50% of the ciphertext bits.

Data Encryption Standard (DES)

The Data Encryption Standard (DES) is a block cipher and was introduced by NIST in 1974. It has a 56-bit key size that makes it vulnerable to brute force attacks with current computing power, so while DES is still in use and is part of the TLS cipher suite, the DES cipher is not recommended for use new in designs. So while it is best to consider DES as deprecated it is still widely used. So, we can use it as a starting point to see how a modern cipher is structured (Fig. 4.11).

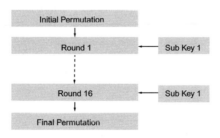

FIG. 4.11

DES encryption rounds.

No permission required.

   Block ciphers perform an encryption algorithm on a block of data. This is termed an "encryption round." The resulting encrypted block of data will then be run through further encryption rounds. In the DES algorithm, there will be up to sixteen rounds. Each encryption round has its own encryption key known as a subkey. The subkeys are derived from the initial encryption key, which is 56 bits long plus an additional 8 bits of parity. In block ciphers, the algorithm used to derive the subkeys is known as the key schedule (Fig. 4.12).

   The DES algorithm has a Feistel structure (named after its designer) (Fig. 4.13), where the 64 bits of input data are split into two 32 bit words. The lower word is fed through the encryption algorithm, and the output is then XORed with the upper word.

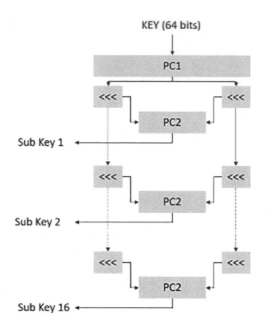

FIG. 4.12

DES key schedule.

No permission required.

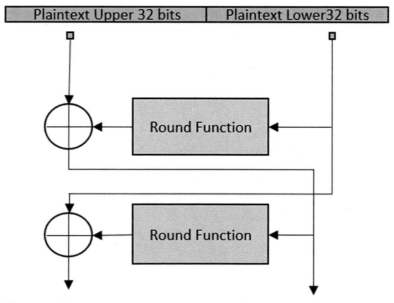

FIG. 4.13

Feistal structure. The DES cipher is constructed using a Feistal structure.

No permission required.

Since the encryption algorithm's output will be a pseudo-random transform, the XOR operation is a further layer of encryption. The resulting encrypted word is passed to the next encryption round, where it is again passed into the encryption algorithm. The original lower word is passed into the next round and becomes the upper word. The DES encryption function is shown in Fig. 4.14.

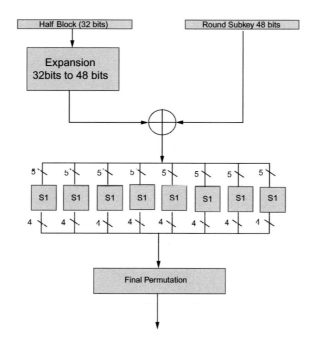

FIG. 4.14

The DES round function mixes the half packet data with the subkey and performs substitution and permutation operations.

No permission required.

Here, the 32-bit word block is passed through an expansion function where it is extended to 48 bits. The expanded data is then XORed with a 48-bit round subkey. The DES algorithm then provides confusion by splitting the 48-bit word into eight groups of six bits. Each six-bit group looks up a four-bit symbol in a dedicated substitution box or S box. Each S box performs a nonlinear transformation of the input data to create a 32-bit output word. This word's data are then diffused by a final permutation before they are XORed with the upper 32-bit word and passed to the next round. Repeat for a total of 16 rounds.

As stated at the beginning of this section, DES is considered an insecure algorithm, and there have been several demonstrations of brute-forcing key discovery. In 2006, an FPGA-based system called COPACABANA was developed, which took 7 days to find the key for an encrypted message. Since then, the time taken to brute force DES has fallen dramatically.

Double encryption

At first sight, using two layers of encryption would seem like an easy way to increase the security of a cipher with a small keyspace. If the key length is k, a brute force attack would be required to try every possible key until the correct one was found. This would take a maximum of 2^k steps. If we used two layers of encryption, you might expect an attacker would have to try every possible combination of keys until the right pair was found, taking a maximum of 2^{2k} steps. Sadly this is not the case, provided the attacker has access to a portion of the plaintext and matching ciphertext. They can use a technique called a "meet in the middle" attack, as shown in Fig. 4.15.

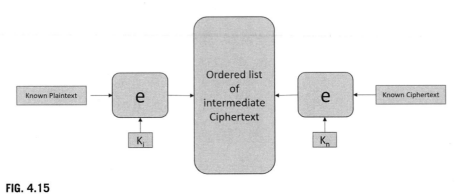

FIG. 4.15

Meet in the middle attack on double layer encryption.

No permission required.

First, the attacker would encrypt the known plaintext with every key to produce an intermediate list of ordered ciphertext; this would take 2^k steps. Next, they would take ciphertext and decrypt it with k_0, then check if the resulting plaintext matches any entry in the intermediate ciphertext table. If there is no match, we increment the key and try again until a match is found. This process takes a total of $2^k + 2^k$ or 2^{k+1}, the equivalent of increasing the key size by just one bit.

Triple DES

While two layers of encryption does not provide much of a security improvement, adding a third gives us significant benefits. An attacker using the meet in the middle attack would have to calculate the lookup table after either the first or second encryption layer. In either situation, they would be faced with $2^k \times 2^k$ steps of encryption to generate the lookup table or the same number of decryption steps to test keys against the lookup table. This is why three runs of the DES cipher are used to extend its key size. Because of the meet in the middle attack, the effective key length is 2k or 112 bits, not the expected 3k (Fig. 4.16).

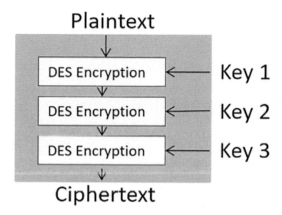

FIG. 4.16

Triple DES runs the DES algorithm three times with separate keys.

No permission required.

In a practical implementation the middle layer may be a decryption layer so that:

$$y = e_{k3}\left(e_{k2}^{-1}\left(e_{k1}(x)\right)\right)$$

If we use three different keys we have 3DES but if K1 = K2 then we are back to standard DES:

$$y = e_{k3}(x)$$

This approach is known as Encrypt Decrypt Encrypt or EDE.

DES-X

Another approach to strengthening the DES algorithm is key whitening. Here, we use three keys. The first key is XORed with the data. The resulting block is then passed through the DES algorithm, which uses the second key. The third key is XORed with the DES output packet as shown in Fig. 4.17.

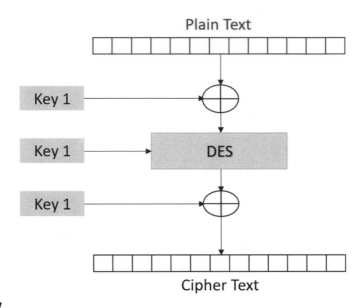

Plain Text

Key 1

Key 1

DES

Key 1

Cipher Text

FIG. 4.17

Key whitening. Increasing the strength of a block cipher with key whitening.

No permission required.

This approach is much faster than 3DES and has an apparently larger key size. Key1 and Key3 are the input data block's size, which is 64 bits. This gives a total size of the key material of 119 bits. However, the overall security strength can be as low as 88 bits if an attacker has access to the multiple plaintext and ciphertext pairs for cryptoanalysis.

Exercise: DES and triple DES

This exercise will use the DES and 3DES algorithms to encrypt and decrypt the hello_big.txt file that was generated in the first exercise.

Open the pack installer, select project 4.3 and press the copy button.

In main.c, we are calling a the function DES_Crypt() to encrypt and decrypt the helloBig.txt file. If you need it, a copy of the file is included in the exercise directory.

```
DES_crypt("HelloBig.txt","DES.txt",encrypt);
DES_crypt("DES.txt","DESPlain.txt",decrypt);
```

Inside the DES_Crypt() function, we first create the DES context and initialize it. The set of 3DES keys are then provided for further encryption or decryption.

```
static const unsigned char des3_test_keys[24] =
```

```
{
    0x01, 0x23, 0x45, 0x67, 0x89, 0xAB, 0xCD, 0xEF,
    0x23, 0x45, 0x67, 0x89, 0xAB, 0xCD, 0xEF, 0x01,
    0x45, 0x67, 0x89, 0xAB, 0xCD, 0xEF, 0x01, 0x23
};
mbedtls_des_context ctx;
    mbedtls_des_init( &ctx );
    mbedtls_des_setkey_enc( &ctx, des3_test_keys );
    mbedtls_des_setkey_dec( &ctx, des3_test_keys );
```

Once the keys have been provisioned we can encrypt/decrypt with the DES or3DES functions:

```
mbedtls_des_crypt_ecb( &ctx, ibuf, obuf );
```

Before leaving the function the context must be released:

```
mbedtls_des_free( &ctx );
```

Build the code.
Start the debugger and run the code.
Examine the resulting files generated on the SD card.

Advanced Encryption Standard (AES)

Today, the Advanced Encryption Standard (AES) is the algorithm of choice for most applications. It is also implemented in most hardware accelerators found within today's microcontrollers. The algorithm has no known vulnerabilities, and the only way for an attacker to decrypt a message is to try every encryption key. Unless you are the owner of a swanky new quantum computer a brute force attack on this scale would take many years.

Like other symmetrical ciphers, the AES algorithm is performed as a set of rounds depending on key size, which may be 128, 192, 256, or 512 bits.

Each round is comprised of four operations called layers that encrypt the data block using diffusion and confusion techniques to achieve a high-security level (Table 4.4 and Fig. 4.18).

Table 4.4 AES encryption rounds vs key size.

Key size in bits	Encryption rounds
128	10
192	12
256	14

The number of encryption rounds varies with key size.

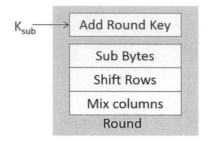

FIG. 4.18

AES round. Each round of the AES algorithm performs four operations.

Finite fields

Much of the mathematics in each layer of the AES cipher relies on finite field arithmetic. While you do not need to understand finite field math to get an appreciation of the AES, you are likely to see it mentioned in any further reading about cryptographic algorithms. A finite field also called a Galois field (GF()). This is a set of elements in a modulo ring where the number of elements is equal to a prime number. The smallest finite field is $GF(2) = \{0,1\}$ or as we know it a "bit." As we saw with the streaming cipher GF(2), modulo math maps to Boolean logic gates where an addition becomes an XOR and multiply is an AND operation. We can also create an "extension field," which is an array of GF(2) fields. For example, $GF(2^8)$ is an array of 8 GF(2) fields or, as we know it, a byte. We can then perform arithmetic operations on each of the GF(2) fields, which maps to bitwise Boolean logic. This allows us to use finite field math to design and verify our cipher and then efficiently implement it using logic gates.

AES algorithm

The AES algorithm accepts an input block of data that is 16 bytes long. The plaintext data are arranged as a four by four matrix for the algorithm. The data matrix is known as the algorithm state (Fig. 4.19).

$A_{0,0}$	$A_{0,1}$	$A_{0,2}$	$A_{0,3}$
$A_{1,0}$	$A_{1,1}$	$A_{1,2}$	$A_{1,3}$
$A_{2,0}$	$A_{2,1}$	$A_{2,2}$	$A_{2,3}$
$A_{3,0}$	$A_{3,1}$	$A_{3,2}$	$A_{3,3}$

FIG. 4.19

AES input state matrix. The input data block is arranged as a state matrix.

The first layer of each round is a confusion layer. It performs a byte orientated substitution similar to the S-Box in the DES algorithm (Fig. 4.20).

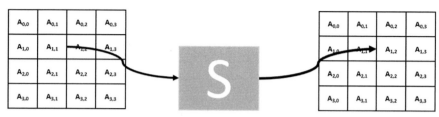

FIG. 4.20

The AES substitution round uses two standardized S-Boxes.

No permission required.

The DES algorithm has a different S Box for each round. Each of these substitution boxes is essentially filled with random values. In the AES algorithm, one pair (encrypt and decrypt) of S-Boxes (Fig. 4.21) are used for all rounds, and the values are carefully selected to perform a two-step mathematical process. The first step uses a GF(2) inversion to perform a highly nonlinear transform, while the second step removes the algebraic structure of the transform through an "Affine" transform (a column multiplication of fixed constants), making the ciphertext more resistant to cryptoanalysis.

AES S-Box

	00	01	02	03	04	05	06	07	08	09	0a	0b	0c	0d	0e	0f
00	63	7c	77	7b	f2	6b	6f	c5	30	01	67	2b	fe	d7	ab	76
10	ca	82	c9	7d	fa	59	47	f0	ad	d4	a2	af	9c	a4	72	c0
20	b7	fd	93	26	36	3f	f7	cc	34	a5	e5	f1	71	d8	31	15
30	04	c7	23	c3	18	96	05	9a	07	12	80	e2	eb	27	b2	75
40	09	83	2c	1a	1b	6e	5a	a0	52	3b	d6	b3	29	e3	2f	84
50	53	d1	00	ed	20	fc	b1	5b	6a	cb	be	39	4a	4c	58	cf
60	d0	ef	aa	fb	43	4d	33	85	45	f9	02	7f	50	3c	9f	a8
70	51	a3	40	8f	92	9d	38	f5	bc	b6	da	21	10	ff	f3	d2
80	cd	0c	13	ec	5f	97	44	17	c4	a7	7e	3d	64	5d	19	73
90	60	81	4f	dc	22	2a	90	88	46	ee	b8	14	de	5e	0b	db
a0	e0	32	3a	0a	49	06	24	5c	c2	d3	ac	62	91	95	e4	79
b0	e7	c8	37	6d	8d	d5	4e	a9	6c	56	f4	ea	65	7a	ae	08
c0	ba	78	25	2e	1c	a6	b4	c6	e8	dd	74	1f	4b	bd	8b	8a
d0	70	3e	b5	66	48	03	f6	0e	61	35	57	b9	86	c1	1d	9e
e0	e1	f8	98	11	69	d9	8e	94	9b	1e	87	e9	ce	55	28	df
f0	8c	a1	89	0d	bf	e6	42	68	41	99	2d	0f	b0	54	bb	16

Inverse S-Box

	00	01	02	03	04	05	06	07	08	09	0a	0b	0c	0d	0e	0f
00	52	09	6a	d5	30	36	a5	38	bf	40	a3	9e	81	f3	d7	fb
10	7c	e3	39	82	9b	2f	ff	87	34	8e	43	44	c4	de	e9	cb
20	54	7b	94	32	a6	c2	23	3d	ee	4c	95	0b	42	fa	c3	4e
30	08	2e	a1	66	28	d9	24	b2	76	5b	a2	49	6d	8b	d1	25
40	72	f8	f6	64	86	68	98	16	d4	a4	5c	cc	5d	65	b6	92
50	6c	70	48	50	fd	ed	b9	da	5e	15	46	57	a7	8d	9d	84
60	90	d8	ab	00	8c	bc	d3	0a	f7	e4	58	05	b8	b3	45	06
70	d0	2c	1e	8f	ca	3f	0f	02	c1	af	bd	03	01	13	8a	6b
80	3a	91	11	41	4f	67	dc	ea	97	f2	cf	ce	f0	b4	e6	73
90	96	ac	74	22	e7	ad	35	85	e2	f9	37	e8	1c	75	df	6e
a0	47	f1	1a	71	1d	29	c5	89	6f	b7	62	0e	aa	18	be	1b
b0	fc	56	3e	4b	c6	d2	79	20	9a	db	c0	fe	78	cd	5a	f4
c0	1f	dd	a8	33	88	07	c7	31	b1	12	10	59	27	80	ec	5f
d0	60	51	7f	a9	19	b5	4a	0d	2d	e5	7a	9f	93	c9	9c	ef
e0	a0	e0	3b	4d	ae	2a	f5	b0	c8	eb	bb	3c	83	53	99	61
f0	17	2b	04	7e	ba	77	d6	26	e1	69	14	63	55	21	0c	7d

FIG. 4.21

AES substitution boxes. AES s-box and inverse s-box.

No permission required.

There are two S-Boxes: one for encryption and an inverse box used for decryption. In a practical algorithm, the boxes can be stored as lookup tables or calculated on the fly.

The next two layers, shift rows and mix columns are used to provide diffusion of the state matrix data.

The second layer performs a shift rows operation. Each row of the state matrix is rotated by a different number of places. The first row is left in place while each subsequent row is shifted by 1, 2, and 3 places, respectively (Fig. 4.22).

$A_{0,0}$	$A_{0,1}$	$A_{0,2}$	$A_{0,3}$
$A_{1,0}$	$A_{1,1}$	$A_{1,2}$	$A_{1,3}$
$A_{2,0}$	$A_{2,1}$	$A_{2,2}$	$A_{2,3}$
$A_{3,0}$	$A_{3,1}$	$A_{3,2}$	$A_{3,3}$

No shift
<< 1
<< 2
<< 3

$A_{0,0}$	$A_{0,1}$	$A_{0,2}$	$A_{0,3}$
$A_{1,0}$	$A_{1,1}$	$A_{1,2}$	$A_{1,3}$
$A_{2,0}$	$A_{2,1}$	$A_{2,2}$	$A_{2,3}$
$A_{3,0}$	$A_{3,1}$	$A_{3,2}$	$A_{3,3}$

FIG. 4.22

AES shift rows. The shift rows layer rotates the data in the state matrix.

No permission required.

The second diffusion layer is the mix columns layer. Here, each column of the state matrix is treated as a vector and is multiplied by a 4×4 matrix of fixed terms to give a resulting output vector results column (Fig. 4.23).

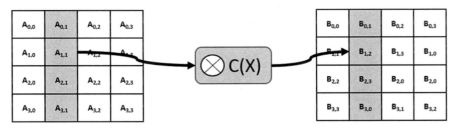

FIG. 4.23

AES mix columns. The second diffusion layer mixes the state matrix columns.

No permission required.

This ensures that every input byte influences four output bytes, and after only three rounds, every byte of the resulting state matrix depends on all 16 plaintext bytes. If you change one of the plaintext bytes, roughly 50% of the final cyphertext will change.

The final layer adds the round key for the next round of operations. Each byte of the round key is XORed with the matching byte of the state matrix (Fig. 4.24).

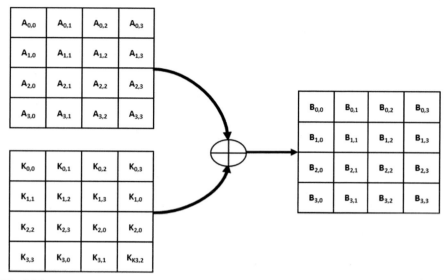

FIG. 4.24

AES add key. The sub for the next round is XORcd with thc data state matrix.

Like the DES algorithm, the AES cipher derives a set of round keys from the original input key. We need to derive one subkey for each round plus one key for an initial add key operation. A 128 bit AES has 10 rounds and requires 11 subkeys (Fig. 4.25).

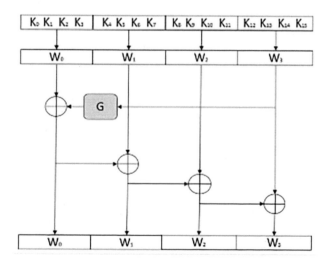

FIG. 4.25

The AES key schedule derives a subkey for each round.

The key schedule generates the round keys for each layer. The input key is considered as a set of 32-bit words arranged in four groups. High-order words are passed through a round function (G) and then XORed with the low order group. Each group is XOR'ed with its neighboring higher-order group in turn. At the end of this process, we have our round subkey. This subkey is used as an input to the same algorithm to generate the next round subkey.

The key schedule round function performs a wordwise rotate, followed by a substitution box and a final XOR of a round constant (Fig. 4.26).

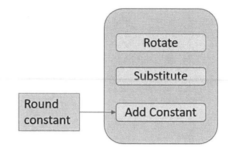

FIG. 4.26

AES key schedule round function.

No permission required.

The mbedTLS library supports the AES cipher with a set of functions shown in Table 4.5.

Table 4.5 mbedTLS AES functions.

Function	Description
mbedtls_aes_crypt_cbc	Encrypt/decrypt in cipher block chaining mode
mbedtls_aes_crypt_cfb128	Encrypt/decrypt in cipher feedback mode 128 bits
mbedtls_aes_crypt_cfb8	Encrypt/decrypt in cipher feedback mode 8 bits
mbedtls_aes_crypt_ctr	Encrypt/decrypt in counter mode
mbedtls_aes_crypt_ecb	**Encrypt/decrypt in electronic code book mode**
mbedtls_aes_decrypt	**Decryption function (internal)**
mbedtls_aes_encrypt	**Encryption function (internal)**
mbedtls_aes_free	**Free the context**
mbedtls_aes_init	**Initialize the context**
mbedtls_aes_setkey_dec	**Set the decryption key—126,192,256,512 bits**
mbedtls_aes_setkey_enc	**Set the encryption key—126,256,512 bits**

The AES cipher can be optimized for your application through a number of defines in the feature section of the mbedTLS_config.h file. Once the cipher is enabled, there are two key switches that define if the S-Boxes are implemented as lookup tables or calculated on the fly (Table 4.6).

Table 4.6 mbedTLS AES configuration options.

Configuration option	Type	Description
MBEDTLS_AES_C	Module	Enable use of the AES cipher
MBEDTLS_AES_ROM_TABLES	Feature	Use lookup tables in ROM
MBEDTLS_AES_FEWER_TABLES	Feature	Calculates the smaller AES tables during runtime to minimize RAM usage (save 6K RAM)

The mbedTLS configuration header allows you to define how the AES algorithm is implemented.

Exercise: Advanced Encryption Standard

In this exercise we will again encrypt the helloBig.txt file, this time using the AES algorithm.

> **Open the pack installer, select Project 4.4 and press the copy button.**
> **Open Thread.c**

In the AESencrypt() function, we declare an array and initialize it with our key value that no one will ever guess.

```
unsigned char key[32];
memset( key, 0, 32 );
```

Then we declare and initialize the context and set the key for both encryption and decryption.

```
mbedtls_aes_context ctx;
mbedtls_aes_init( &ctx );
mbedtls_aes_setkey_enc( &ctx,key,256);
fileIn = fopen("HelloBig.txt","r");
fileOut = fopen("HelloAES.txt","w");
while (fread(bufIn,1,16,fileIn)> 0)
{
mbedtls_aes_crypt_ecb( &ctx,
                                    MBEDTLS_AES_ENCRYPT,
                                    bufIn,
                                    bufOut );
fwrite(bufOut,1,16,fileOut);
memset(bufIn,0,16);
}
```

Decryption follows a similar process.

> **Build the code.**
> **Start the debugger and run the code.**

This will perform our standard test of encrypting 1000 times and then decrypting back to the original.

Streaming block ciphers

At the time of writing, the AES is the gold standard for commercial-grade encryption. If the AES algorithm is correctly implemented, there is no published method to break the encrypted ciphertext except by a brute force attack. If correctly implemented, AES is secure against an attack by an adversary with bounded computing power. However, we still have to be careful with a real-world implementation. At its core, a cipher is a translation from plain text to a pseudo-random ciphertext. If you put in the same text pattern, you will get the same ciphertext out. This can cause some information about the plain text to "leak" from the ciphertext. For example, if we encode data that has large areas of repeated values, then a shadow of this data will be visible in the ciphertext and may help an adversary to gain an insight into the contents of the message (Fig. 4.27).

FIG. 4.27

ECB encoding weakness encrypting a stream of data in ECB mode will "leak" information. https://en.wikipedia.org › wiki/Block_cipher_mode_of_operation.

No permission required.

The use of a block cipher to simply encrypt data block after block is called an electronic code book (ECB) (Fig. 4.28).

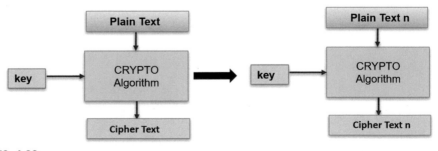

FIG. 4.28

Electronic code book encryption.

No permission required.

In practice, we would never use a cipher in this fashion. In the real world, a block cipher that is used to stream data or encrypt bulk data would require a chaining method to fully obscure the plaintext.

Chaining modes

The mbedTLS library supports three chaining modes, which can be used with the AES algorithm (Table 4.7).

Table 4.7 Block cipher chaining modes.

Chaining mode	Description
CBC	Cipher block chaining
CFB	Cipher feedback mode
CTR	Counter mode
GCM	Galios counter mode (see AEAD)

Cipher block chaining (CBC)

A commonly used chaining mode is called Cipher Block Chaining (CBC). We encrypt a block of data and then XOR the output ciphertext with the next plain text block before running the resulting block through the encryption algorithm. This process can then be continued for any number of plain text blocks. At the start of the process, the initial plain text block is XORed with a random block of data called the Initialization Vector (IV). The IV does not have to be kept secret and can be sent as plain text to the receiving station. In this scheme, each encrypted block is dependent on all of the preceding blocks (Fig. 4.29).

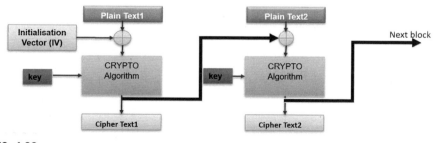

FIG. 4.29

Cipher block chaining XOR'es an encrypted block with the next block of plain text.

No permission required.

Cipher feedback mode

In cipher feedback mode, the previous block's ciphertext is fed into the symmetrical cipher (Fig. 4.30). This effectively creates a random block that is XORed with the next block of plaintext. Again, to start the process, we use a random Initialization Vector.

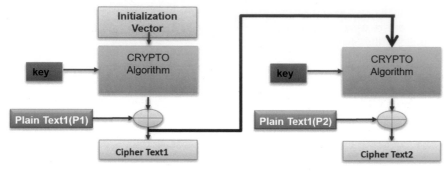

FIG. 4.30

Cipher feedback mode encrypts the ciphertext and then XOR's the output with the next plain text block.

No permission required.

Counter mode (CTR)

The final chaining mode supported in mbedTLS is counter mode (CTR). This mode's advantage is that multiple blocks may be encrypted in parallel (Fig. 4.31). This mode is particularly useful for achieving fast encryption in hardware accelerators.

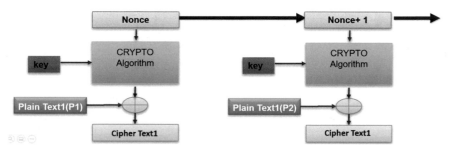

FIG. 4.31

Counter mode. AES counter mode uses a Number once (NONCE) in place of the chained cipher text.

No permission required.

In CTR mode, the IV is chosen to be smaller than the cipher block size and the remaining bitfield is used as a counter, which is incremented for each block. The counter value is known as a nonce or number once and should be unique for each session. The resulting value is encrypted before being XORed with the plaintext block. If the IV is known in advance, then the nonce encryption for each block can be calculated in advance. When using this mode, it is important to realize that if an IV is reused and an attacker has one of the plaintexts, it is possible to recreate the keystream and decrypt any further messages using the same IV.

Exercise: Chaining modes

Open the pack installer, select Project 4.5 and press the Copy button.
Open the file Thread.c

This example is based on the first AES example but this time we are using cipher block chaining to encrypt the helloBig.txt file.

This time we declare an initialization vector:

```
unsigned char vector[16] = {1,2,3,4,5,6,7,8,9,10,11,12,13,14,15,16};
```
In this example we will use cipher block chaining:

```
mbedtls_aes_crypt_cbc( &ctx,

                                            MBEDTLS_AES_ENCRYPT ,
                                            16,
                                            vector,
                                            bufIn,
                                            bufOut);
```

By changing the define to MBEDTLS_AES_DECRYPT the same function can be used for decryption.

Build the project and then run the code in the debugger.
Compare the ECB and CBC encrypted files for repeating patterns.

Cipher abstraction layer

While AES is the recommended cipher to use in a real-world system, the Transport Layer Security (TLS) protocol lists a range of ciphers that can be used during a communication session. In addition to DES and AES, mbedTLS provides a number of additional ciphers, so depending on your requirements and the server you are communicating with, you may need to include additional cipher support.

To support this range of ciphers, mbedTLS has a cipher abstraction layer (Table 4.8), which allows you to list the range of ciphers available and select a cipher to use.

Table 4.8 mbedTLS ciphers.

Cipher	Type	Description
ARC4	Streaming	Weak: do not use.
DES	Block	Obsolete: provided as legacy support.
3DES	Block	Slow.
AES	Block	Use this one!
Blowfish	Block	A contestant to be the AES algorithm. Developed by Bruce Schnier. You really should read his blog.
Camellia	Block	Developed by Mitsubishi and NTT of Japan. With a similar level of security to AES.
Cha Cha 20	Block	An alternative the AES designed to run more efficiently on a general purpose 32 bit processor.
XTEA	Block	eXtended Tiny Encryption Algorithm, requires minimal resources to implement.

mbedTLS supported ciphers.

A generic set of API calls then allow you to write code independent of the actual cipher in use. The function groups are outlined in Table 4.9.

Table 4.9 Cipher abstraction.

Abstract function group	Description
Initialize	Select a cipher and prepare it for use
Cleanup	Remove a cipher and cleanup its resources
Get cipher information	List the set of available ciphers and their feature sizes (key size, block size, context info, name, and type)
Set a Key	Set the encryption or decryption key and operating mode
Encrypt a message	Encrypt a message, includes subfunctions reset, update, and finish
Decrypt a message	Decrypt a message includes subfunctions reset, update, and finish

Exercise: Cipher abstraction layer

In this exercise, we will use the cipher abstraction layer to encrypt and decrypt the hello_big.txt file using the cipher abstraction layer.

In the pack installer select Exercise 4.6 and press the Copy button. Open main.c

The code provides two functions: abstractEncrypt() and abstractDecrypt().

Each function contains code based on the cipher abstraction layer and the actual algorithm to use is passed as part of the function call.

Examine the two abstraction functions.

First we create the context for the cipher and also a cipher_info object to hold the underlying cipher features:

```
const mbedtls_cipher_info_t *cipher_info;
mbedtls_cipher_context_t cipher_ctx;
```

Next we can initialize the cipher context and list the available ciphers:

```
mbedtls_cipher_init( &cipher_ctx );
list = mbedtls_cipher_list();
```

We can now use a text string to select an available cipher and set the context to use the selected cipher:

```
cipher_info = mbedtls_cipher_info_from_string( "AES-128-CBC" );
mbedtls_cipher_setup( &cipher_ctx, cipher_info);
```

The cipher can now be readied for encryption or decryption with an appropriate key and if available, a message digest (we will look at this class of algorithm in the next section).

```
mbedtls_cipher_setkey( &cipher_ctx,
                                    digest,
                                    cipher_info->key_bitlen,
                                    MBEDTLS_ENCRYPT);
```

We must also set the IV and get the plaintext block size:

```
mbedtls_cipher_set_iv( &cipher_ctx, IV, 16 );
mbedtls_cipher_get_block_size( &cipher_ctx );
```

Now we can encrypt the data by resetting the cipher and using the cipher update function to stream blocks of data:

```
mbedtls_cipher_reset( &cipher_ctx );
mbedtls_cipher_update( &cipher_ctx,
                                    buffer,
                                    ilen,
                                    output,
                                    &olen );
```

We can write our final block with the finish function:

```
mbedtls_cipher_finish( &cipher_ctx, output, &olen );
```

When we have finished using the cipher we can wipe the memory. Here, the key is wiped but all objects must be cleared:

```
mbedtls_platform_zeroize( key, sizeof( key ) );
```

Finally the context is released:

```
mbedtls_cipher_free( &cipher_ctx );
```

Run the code so that it creates files that are encrypted and then decrypted using each supported algorithm.
Examine the SD card and the generated files.

Hash functions

A cryptographic hash function is an algorithm that takes an arbitrary block of data and calculates a fixed-size string called a message digest (MD). A hash is a form of one-way encryption in that, given the plain text, you can recreate the message digest, but if you only have the message digest, there is no way to recreate the original plain text (Fig. 4.32).

FIG. 4.32

Hash overview. A Hash algorithm creates a unique fixed length string from a block of arbitrary data.

The typical usage of a Hash is to validate a block of data's integrity. If we receive a block of data (plain text or ciphertext) and a message digest, we can recreate the message digest from the received data. If it matches the received message digest, we know that the received data are genuine and have not been tampered with. However, there are problems with this. We can select from an infinite variety of arbitrary input data to generate a message digest, but we only have a finite number of message digest values. So, it follows that different input data can generate the same message digest value. This is known as a collision. When designing a hashing algorithm, we need to ensure that the algorithm is computationally efficient and collision-resistant (Table 4.10).

Table 4.10 Hash collisions.

Hash collisions	Description
Preimage Resistance	Given a hash Z it is infeasible to calculate the plain text X
Second Preimage Resistance	Given plaintext X1 we cannot find X2 such that $h(x1) = h(x2)$
Collision Resistance	If X1 != X2 then we should not find that $h(x1) = h(x2)$

This is harder than it may initially seem because of a probability theorem called The Birthday Paradox. This theorem is concerned with the probability of finding two people in a group who share the same birthday (a collision). If we include the 29th of February, there are a possible 366 birthdays. With a sample population of 367, we can be 100% sure of at least one shared birthday. Surprisingly, we can be 99.9% sure of a shared birthday with just 70 people and 50% sure with just 23 people (Fig. 4.33).

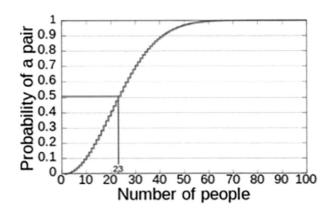

FIG. 4.33

Birthday Paradox. https://en.wikipedia.org/wiki/birthday_problem. Rajkiran G.

No permission required.

This is a problem for our theoretical hashing algorithm. The birthday paradox means that the number of inputs required to get a collision is roughly equal to the number of output values' square root. We need our hashing algorithm to output message-digest bit size of 2X bits for a security level of X bits.

Like ciphers, there are many hashing algorithms, both dedicated algorithms and hashing systems designed from other cryptographic algorithms, principally block ciphers (Fig. 4.34).

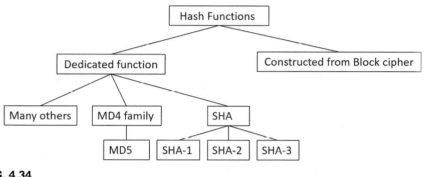

FIG. 4.34

Hash algorithms

The most widely used hash algorithms are the original message digest (MD) family developed by Ron Rivest at The RSA Corporation and the Secure Hash Algorithm (SHA), which is maintained as a FIPS standard.

Message digest 5 (MD5)

The MD5 hash algorithm is widely used for image verification and is part of the TLS protocol. However, it is now considered very insecure, and engineering collisions can be done in seconds, even with a low spec PC. For some applications of hashes, this is not a problem. For example, we do not need collision resistance for key generation or password storage. For the purposes of this book, MD5 should be considered deprecated.

Secure Hashing Algorithm (SHA)

The Secure Hash Algorithms (SHA) were developed by the NSA and . They are the family of algorithms recommended by the Federal Information Processing Standards. The SHA-1 algorithm is widely used, but both Google and Microsoft have demonstrated that it is possible to engineer collisions. It is recommended to use SHA-2 in new designs.

To understand how the SHA works, we can first examine the SHA-1 algorithm. The SHA family of hashes is based on an algorithm called a Merkle-Damgard construct shown in Fig. 4.35. The algorithm accepts message data in blocks of 512 bits and will

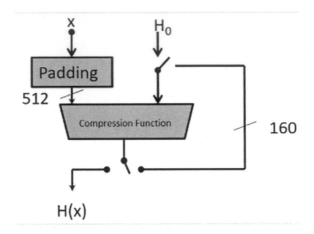

FIG. 4.35

SHA-1 algorithm.

support a total message size of up to 2^{64} bits. This is somewhat like a block cipher, but the message data x is applied in place of the key where it is stretched into a set of round keys' w0–w80. In place of the plaintext, the hash algorithm accepts the previously calculated message digest H. In the first pass, a set of standard round constants H_0 is used in place of the output hash. When the final message block has been processed, the resulting message digest H(x) will be output as a fixed length of 160 bits.

Before the message data are passed into the SHA-1 compression function, they are first preprocessed. The input block of data is split into chunks of 512 bits and input into the algorithm in turn. The final data packet will typically be less than 512 bits and must be padded by adding a logic 1s to the end of the message string. Then, extend any unused bits with logic zero. Finally, the length of the message data is written at the end of the packet, as shown in Fig. 4.36.

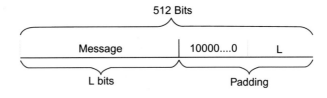

FIG. 4.36

SHA-1 padding.

The SHA algorithm consists of 80 rounds of processing, which are split into 4 stages of 20 rounds. The input block of 512 bits is first fed into a message schedule, which stretches the data into 80 subwords of 32 bits, one for each round, as shown in Fig. 4.37.

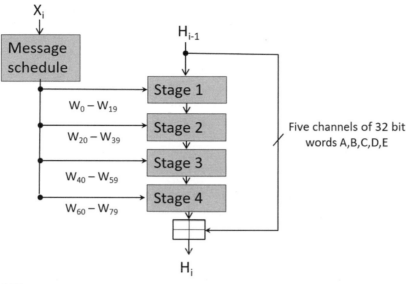

FIG. 4.37

SHA-1 rounds structure.

Each of the 80 rounds are processed in turn. The first stage takes the previous hash result (or the initial round constants H0) and applies a set of logical operations in a generalized Feistel structure, as shown in Fig. 4.38. The round word W_t and a stage constant K_t provide the round data input. Each stage has a dedicated round function F, which performs a further set of logical operations.

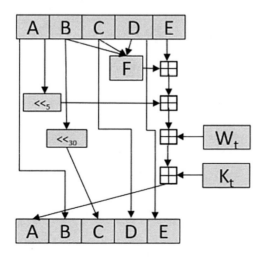

FIG. 4.38

SHA-1 round.

Once the round has completed, constants (A–E) will be passed to the next round. After the final round, the round constants will be fed back to round zero, and the next block of message data will be processed. When all of the message data has been processed, the final round constants will be output as the calculated message digest.

The general form of the SHA-2 algorithm is the same as SHA-1 but with a more complex round function and an expanded set of round constants. The SHA-2 algorithm provides hashing algorithms with different sizes of input message block and output message digest. Consequently, each SHA-2 algorithm is named after its blocksize as follows SHA-244, SHA-256, SHA-384, and SHA-512.

Salt

When designing a cryptosystem using hashes, it is always important to consider the input vector space's size. If your input data have a known length and a limited character set, you may be vulnerable to adversaries precalculating lookup tables, which can be used to reverse the hash. For example, it is common to store user passwords as Hashes. If an adversary acquires the password message-digest, they cannot decrypt the hash to find the password. They are faced with selecting a password generating its message digest, and checking if it matches the target message digest. However, poorly designed passwords can have a limited character set, leading to a small range of possible user passwords. This allows an adversary to develop a precalculated hash table known as a rainbow table as a test for commonly used passwords. To prevent this style of attack, we can add a "salt" to our input data. The salt is a string of random numbers that completely change the hash's output value. The salt can be stored in plain text alongside the resulting message digest. This makes a rainbow table useless, and if you use a different salt for each password, then two users with the same password will have different message digests.

The input data can be directly combined with the salt:

$$\text{Salted MD} = H(\text{password} + \text{salt})$$

Or added to a message digest of the input data:

$$\text{Salted MD} = H(H(\text{password}) + \text{salt})$$

Exercise: SHA-2 hash

In this exercise, we will compute the SHA-2 hash of the HelloBig.txt file using the mbedTLS library and compare this to an SHA-2 Hash computed using a PC app.

Download and install the HashCalc utility from the link below:
https://www.slavasoft.com/hashcalc/
In the pack installer select Exercise 4.7 and press the Copy button.
Make sure the SD card is in the evaluation board and contains the helloBig. txt file.
Build the program and start the debugger.
Run the code.

In the calculateHash function, we prepare the hash algorithm by declaring and initializing the SHA-256 algorithm and then call the start function:

```
mbedtls_sha256_context ctx;
mbedtls_sha256_init( &ctx );
mbedtls_sha256_starts( &ctx,0 );
```

The main function loop opens the helloBig file and reads 512 byte chunks of the data, which are fed into the SHA algorithm using the sha256_update() function:

```
file = fopen("HelloBig.txt","r");
if(file != NULL) {
while(!feof(file)){
memset(imageBlock,0x0,512);
wordsRead = fread(&imageBlock,
                            sizeof(unsigned char),
                            512,
                            file);
mbedtls_sha256_update( &ctx,
                            (const unsigned char *)imageBlock,
                                    wordsRead );
}
```

When we reach the end of the file, the sha256_finish() function is called to calculate the final hash value and then the context is released:

```
mbedtls_sha256_finish( &ctx, sha256sum );
mbedtls_sha256_free( &ctx );
printf(" Calculation finished.\n");
fclose(file);
```

The code then prints the hash value to the debug console screen (Fig. 4.39).

Place the SD card in your PC and start the HASH CALC app.

```
nitializing and mounting enabled drives...
Drive M0 ready!
Done!

Opening hellobig.txt and calculating hash
Calculation finished.
Hash Algorithm used is SHA256
Calculated HASH is FE 63 CD 0C 10 1D E2 08 C8 F4 80 C1 1B CB 4C 24 8E 2B B2 12 8E 92 2C 80 58 A4 E1 19 7C 53 2B D0
```

FIG. 4.39

Result of the Hash calculation.

Select the HelloBig.txt file.
Check the SHA256 box and make sure the HMAC box is unchecked.
Press the Calculate button and compare the PC calculated hash to the value in the debugger console window.

Since both hashes match we can be sure that the file has not been modified as we plugged the card into the PC. Note the message digest values shown may differ from the ones created by your file.

Message authentication code (MAC)

A message authentication code (MAC) performs a similar operation to a hashing algorithm. However, unlike a hash, a MAC has two inputs: a block of arbitrary data and a secret key.

The MAC algorithm will combine the two inputs to produce a fixed-length output string called a MAC TAG, which is unique to the two input values. In order to recreate the MAC TAG, you must have both the data and the key. A MAC can validate the integrity of the data and help to authenticate the sender as its MAC TAG can only be generated by someone who knows the key (Fig. 4.40).

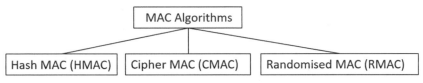

FIG. 4.40

Message authentication code. Different algorithms can be used to create a MAC function.

No permission required.

A MAC algorithm can be developed from existing cipher or hash algorithms. A newer standard not supported by mbedTLS allows a MAC algorithm to be developed from a random number generator.

Hash-based MAC

At first sight, it should be easy to create a MAC algorithm from a hash algorithm. All you would have to do is concatenate the data block with the secret key and run the result through the hash algorithm.

$$\text{HMAC} = \text{H}\left(\text{key} \parallel \text{message}\right) \text{or HMAC} = \left(\text{message} \parallel \text{key}\right)$$

The output message digest can only be reproduced by someone who has both the data block and the key. Unfortunately, this approach has a number of vulnerabilities and cannot be used.

Creating a MAC from a hash algorithm requires a more rigorous method of combining the key and data block. To create the MAC algorithm, we need two arrays of 64 bytes, which act as processing buffers. The first of these arrays is called the i_pad (inner pad), and the second is called the o_pad (outer pad). At the start of the process, both of these arrays are filled with a standard byte pattern and then XORed with the MAC key (Fig. 4.41).

FIG. 4.41

HMAC i_pad and o_pad.

```
i_key_pad = (0x36 x blocksize) ^ key
o_key_pad = (0x5C x blocksize) ^ key
```

Where the block size is the same length as the underlying hash message digest, if the input key is longer than the block size, we can shorten it by taking its hash which will give a message digest equal to the blocksize.

To calculate the MAC tag first the i_key pad array is appended to the beginning of the message data and its hash is calculated to give md_ipad.

```
md_ipad= H(i_key_pad ‖ message)
```

The o_key_pad is then concatenated with the md_ipad. The resulting data block is hashed again to give the final MAC TAG.

```
HMAC = H(o_key_pad ‖ md_ipad)
```

Within mbedTLS MAC functions are derived using hash and cipher functions and accessed through an abstraction layer.

Hash abstraction layer

Like the cipher module mbedTLS provides an abstraction layer that has a standard API for hash and MAC functions (Table 4.11).

Table 4.11 Hash abstraction.

Abstraction function group	Description
Get Hash Information	Lists a description of the available Hash and MAC functions and their features.
Calculate HASH	Functions used to calculate the HASH, reset, start, update, and finish
Calculate HMAC	Functions used to calculate the HMAC, reset, start, update, and finish

Exercise: HASH and MAC abstraction layer

This exercise demonstrates calculating a HMAC using the mbedTLS abstraction layer.

In the pack installer select Exercise 4.8 and press the Copy button.
Build the project and start the debugger.

We create and initialize the context for the message digest abstraction layer and an information object to hold the selected HMAC algorithm:

```
mbedtls_md_info_t *md_info;
mbedtls_md_context_t ctx_md;
mbedtls_md_init( &ctx_md );
```

Then select the hash algorithm to use as a basis for the HMAC:

```
md_info = mbedtls_md_info_from_string("SHA256" );
```

The abstraction layer allows us to setup the SHA-256 Hash:

```
ret = mbedtls_md_setup( &ctx_md, md_info, 1 );
```

Then call functions to set the key which is set to ten ASCII "1" characters:

```
mbedtls_md_hmac_starts( &ctx_md, key, keylen );
```

We can then process the test vector and produce a result:

```
mbedtls_md_hmac_update( &ctx_md,
                                    testVector,
                                    sizeof(testVector)
                                    );
mbedtls_md_hmac_finish( &ctx_md, outputHMAC );
```

We can then print the computed tag outputHMAC to the debugger console window.

Place the SD card in your pc and this calculate the MAC using the hashcalc app. This time check the HMAC box, set the Key Format to text string and enter ten numeral "1" as the key (Fig. 4.42).
Press the calculate button and check the two HMAC's match. The tag value may be different from the one shown in the illistration.

Authenticated encryption

It is a common requirement to both encrypt a message and generate its MAC to provide confidentiality and proof of integrity and the ability to authenticate the origin of the message. We can use a block cipher and MAC to do this in a variety of ways:

Encrypt then Mac (EtM)
In this scheme, the plain text is first encrypted and then a MAC is created from the ciphertext. Separate keys must be used for the encryption and MAC algorithms. The ciphertext and MAC are sent alongside each other. This method provides the highest level of security and is used in the IPSec protocol and more recently TLS.
Encrypt and MAC (E&M)
The E&M Scheme uses a single key. A MAC is created from the plaintext, the plaintext is then encrypted without the MAC, and the two are sent alongside each other. This has lower security than EtM and is used in applications such as Secure Shell (SSH).

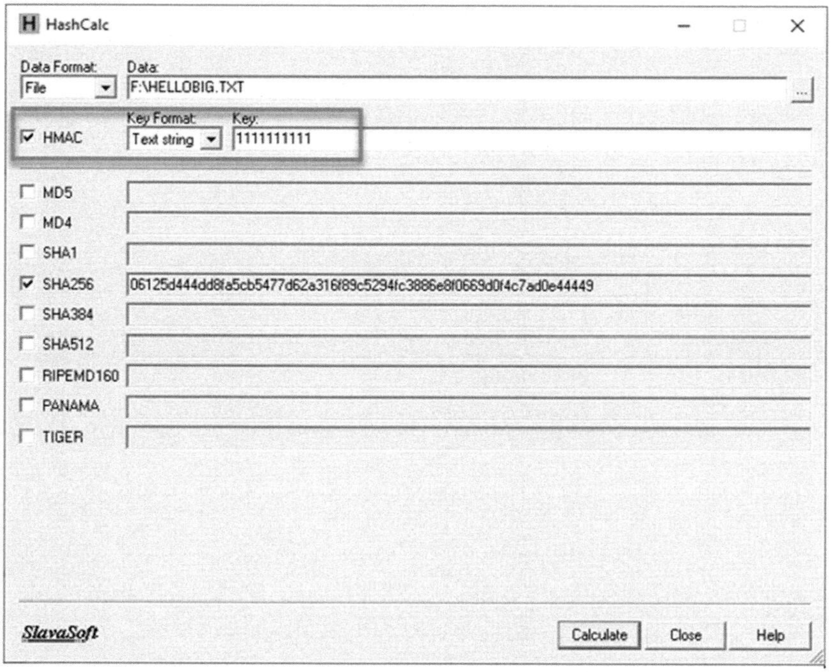

FIG. 4.42

Recalculate the MAC with HashCalc.

MAC then Encrypt (MtE)

A MAC of the plaintext is calculated, and then the plaintext and the MAC are encrypted together. A single key is used for both operations. This is the default method used by the TLS protocol.

Authenticated Encryption with Associated Data (AEAD)

When we are sending communication packets, we need the payload to be encrypted while the packet header will be sent as plaintext. However, we also need to ensure integrity and authentication for the whole packet to prevent an attacker from substituting the ciphertext with previously recorded valid ciphertext. AEAD is a technique that allows us to encrypt a block of data and generate a MAC over the encrypted block plus and additional block of associated data. In our case, this allows us to encrypt the packet payload and then generate a MAC over the payload and the plaintext header, which is the associated data. This binds the ciphertext to the packet frame. The most efficient way to implement this scheme is a chaining mode based on finite field math called Galois counter mode (GCM) (Fig. 4.43).

CGM uses AES to encrypt the plaintext using counter mode(CTR) chaining, where the cipher must have a minimum block size of 128 bits. The starting counter

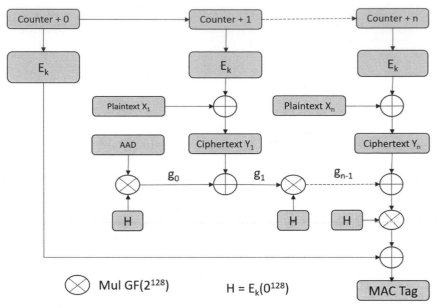

FIG. 4.43

Galois counter mode.

value is derived from the initial IV and a constant data item such as a serial number. We can encrypt blocks of data using the cipher Ek():

$$y_i = x_i E_k \left(CTR_i \right)$$

If we know the IV in advance it is possible to pre calculate the counter values $E_k(CTR_i)$.

It also computes a Hash based on the plaintext and the associated data which will be the unencrypted packet payload and header data.

We can generate the MAC tag by first calculating using $GF(2^{128})$ multiplication:

$$g_i = \left(g_{i-1} \oplus y_i \right) X H$$

where:

g_{i-1} = the previous tag block
y_i = the current encrypted block
$H = E_k(0^{128})$ and is known as the Hash subkey
Where 0^{128} an all zero input vector to the encryption cipher $E_k()$.
To get things rolling, we need an initial g_0 block and this is calculated using the associated data.
g_0 = AAD X H

Where AAD is the associated data that is held as plaintext, for our purposes, this will typically be the TCP/IP packed header.

The final MAC tab is generated by:

$$T = \left(g_n \; X \, H \right) \oplus E_k \; \left(CT \, R_0 \right)$$

where g_n is the final intermediate tag calculation.

AES-GCM is a very fast and efficient algorithm for encrypting streaming data and generating a MAC tag. It can be implemented on low-cost resource-constrained microcontrollers. However, as noted at the beginning of this section, you must be very careful to use a fresh IV for each session, or the resulting ciphertext will be vulnerable to cryptoanalysis. A variant of AES-GCM is called AES-GCM-SIV, where SIV stands for Synthetic Initialization Vector. This algorithm is designed to be misuse resistant in the event of an IV NONCE being reused. Currently, this mode is not supported in mbedTLS.

Exercise: AEAD in mbedTLS

The mbedTLS library provides support for AES-GCM as shown in Table 4.12.

Table 4.12 mbedTLS AEAD functions.

Function	Description
mbedtls_gcm_auth_decrypt	GCM Authenticated Decryption
mbedtls_gcm_crypt_and_tag	GCM Encryption/Decryption and Authentication
mbedtls_gcm_finish	Wraps up the stream and generates the tag
mbedtls_gcm_free	Free the context
mbedtls_gcm_init	Initializes the context
mbedtls_gcm_setkey	Sets the key
mbedtls_gcm_starts	GCM Stream start function
mbedtls_gcm_update	GCM Update function

In the pack installer select Exercise 4.8 and press the Copy button. Open main.c

We first declare the AEAD context and the cipher ID:

```
mbedtls_gcm_context ctx;
mbedtls_cipher_id_t cipher = MBEDTLS_CIPHER_ID_AES;
```

An array with the additional data is also created:

```
unsigned char associatedData[20] =
{0x31,0x32,0x33,......};
```

We next initialize the AEAD context then set the key and the underlying cipher:

```
mbedtls_gcm_init( &ctx );
mbedtls_gcm_setkey( &ctx,
                           cipher,
                           key,
                           KEY_SIZE_BITS );
```

Next start the first round of encryption with the IV and additional data:

```
mbedtls_gcm_starts( &ctx,
                           MBEDTLS_GCM_ENCRYPT,
                 vector,
                 sizeof(vector),
                 associatedData,
                 sizeof(associatedData) );
```

We can now encrypt further blocks of data.

```
mbedtls_gcm_update( &ctx,
                           bytesRead,
                           pt
                           inBuf,
                           outbuf );
```

Once all the data has been encrypted we can finish off by creating the MAC tag:

```
mbedtls_gcm_finish( &ctx, tag_buf, 16 );
```

and then release the context.

```
mbedtls_gcm_free( &ctx );
```

Build the project and download to the debugger.
Run the project.

The code will encrypt a file of data and store the cipher text along with the Additional Authentication Data in plain text.

The project will also decrypt the and recreate the MAC tag so it can be compared to the original.

Random numbers

In the preceding sections, we have seen a need for random numbers to be used as Initialization Vectors and NONCE numbers. Ideally, we will also generate cipher and MAC keys by a random process. In the next chapter, we will look at secure communications protocols which have further uses for random numbers. In real-world cryptosystems, a cryptographically strong RNG is an essential component and cornerstone of our system's security. Any weakness in the RNG would create predictability and lead to an adversary being able to access confidential data or subvert your entire system. You should consider that the RNG in your system is as important as the security of your cryptographic keys.

Entropy

In cryptography, the term entropy is a measure of uncertainty of a random variable. In information theory, the information content H_x of a value x, which has a probability Pr[x] of occurring is given by:

$$H_x = -\log 2 \big(Pr[x] \big)$$

Then, the entropy of a random source is the expected information content of its output symbol:

$$H(X) = \Sigma_x \, Pr[x] H_x$$

This gives us the expected uncertainty of x measured in bits. In practice, this will mean that the entropy of a string may be less than its total bit length. Low entropy data are well structured and easily guessable, for example, seed data based on time and date values. The important thing to remember when choosing a random source is the number of bits of entropy available. A 128-bit key generated from a source with 20 bits of entropy is only as good as a 20-bit key.

Random number generation

Random number generators come in two types: a true random number generator (TRNG) and a pseudo-random number generator (PRNG). In a typical system, a PRNG is implemented using an algorithm called a deterministic random bitstream generator (DRBG). In systems that need a high bandwidth of random numbers, it is necessary to use the output of a TRNG as seed data for the DRBG. The TRNG data is stored in a buffer called an Entropy Pool. This allows us to gather true random data during quiet periods. Values in the Entropy Pool can be accessed as required by the DRBG and expanded into an unpredictable bitstream (Fig. 4.44).

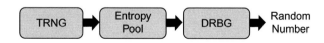

FIG. 4.44

Random number generator subsystem.

No permission required.

True random number generator (TRNG)

A typical "plain old microcontroller" does not contain a TRNG, and various approaches have been developed to create sources of random data. Typically, these use noise from analogue conversions or random timing sources, but these all risk being subverted by an attacker. However, new microcontrollers designed to be used as IoT devices will incorporate a TRNG as part of their security assistive structure. In Chapter 11, we will look at a Cortex-M33 based microcontroller that contains a FIPS-certified RNG.

Entropy Pool

The mbedTLS library provides functions to create an Entropy Pool in the micro-controller heap space. We can also specify one or more entropy sources that can be used to gather random data into the pool using the functions shown in Table 4.13. The Entropy Pool then acts as a buffer to supply true random data to a deterministic random bitstream generator (DRBG).

Table 4.13 mbedTLS Entropy Pool functions.

Function	Description
mbedtls_entropy_add_source	Add an entropy source to poll
mbedtls_entropy_free	Free the context
mbedtls_entropy_func	Retrieve entropy from the accumulator
mbedtls_entropy_gather	Trigger an extra gather pool for the accumulator
mbedtls_entropy_init	Initialize the context
mbedtls_entropy_update_manual	Add data to the accumulator manually
mbedtls_entropy_update_seed_file	Read and update a seed file
mbedtls_entropy_write_seed_file	Write a seed file

Deterministic random bitstream generator (DRBG)

Random numbers are used for many purposes outside of cryptography, for example, simulation and modeling. Here pseudo-random number generators are used to create fast streams of random data. However, within a cryptographic system, we need the same stream of random data, but additionally, it needs to be unpredictable. If an attacker knows a random value or values created by our system, it should not be possible to calculate future values or values in the past, provided that the initial seed value is secret. For our purposes, we must use a subset of pseudo-random number generators, which are cryptographically strong pseudo-random number generator. These are known as deterministic random bitstream generators (DRBG).

Testing for randomness

Once we have set up our random generator, how do we know it is working correctly? Fortunately, there are a number of test suits available that can be used to analyze a bitstream to determine if it is actually random. An open-source test suite is published by NIST and can be accessed via the link below:

https://nvlpubs.nist.gov/nistpubs/Legacy/SP/nistspecialpublication800-22r1a.pdf.

The NIST test suite provides fifteen statistical tests to analyze a random bitstream. The test suite uses a Chi-Squared test to provide a confidence level that the bitstream is truly random.

Exercise: Random generation

In this exercise, we will configure the TRNG within the LPC55S69 microcontroller and also add an Entropy Pool to feed a DRBG. We will then use a test from the NIST test suite to check for randomness.

In the pack installer select Exercise 4.9 and press the Copy button. open main.c

We can initialize an entropy pool and add an entropy source, ideally a true Random number generator provided by the microcontroller.

```
RNG_Init(RNG);  //MCU driver function
mbedtls_entropy_init( &entropy );
mbedtls_entropy-_add_source( &entropy,
      entropy_source,    //callback for entropy gathering
      NULL,
      RANDOM_BLOCK_SIZE,
      MBEDTLS_ENTROPY_SOURCE_ SOURCE);
```

The entropy callback function is used to collect a block of random data defined by RANDOM_BLOCK_SIZE to add to the entropy pool.

```
int entropy_source( void *data,
                    unsigned char *output,
                    ize_t len,
                    size_t *olen ){
uint32_t index;
((void) data);
  RNG_GetRandomData(RNG, output,len);
  *olen = len;
  return( 0 );
}
```

Now we can initialize the DRBG and add the entropy pool. The mbedtls_entropy_func( ) function is used to gather entropy from the pool.

```
mbedtls_hmac_drbg_init( &ctx );
mbedtls_hmac_drbg_seed( &ctx,
                          md_info,mbedtls_entropy_func,
                          (void *)&entropy,NULL, 0 ) ;
```

It is also possible to enable prediction resistance; this will cause the DRBG to reseed itself for every call to acquire random data.

```
mbedtls_hmac_drbg_set_prediction_resistance( &ctx,
                          MBEDTLS_HMAC_DRBG_PR_ON );
```

Once the DRBG is configured we can use it as a source of random data.

```
mbedtls_hmac_drbg_random( &ctx, buf, OUTPUT_LEN ) ;
```

Once we have some random data we can use the NIST Frequency test to analyze the bitstream. Here we are looking for a random mix of ones and zeros. The frequency test uses a statistical method called a Chi-Squared test to give a confidence that the bitstream is random.

```
Frequency(OUTPUT_LEN);
```

When we are finished with the DRBG we must free the context

```
mbedtls_hmac_drbg_free( &ctx );
```

Run the code.
The results of the Chi Squared test will be displayed in the terminal window. The NIST test suite provides a battery of tests which should be used in addition to the Frequency test to gain a confidence that you have a good source of Random values.

Managing keys

This is your big problem. We must be able to create, store, rotate, and put keys beyond use. Ideally, they must be unique to a device and be immutably bound to that device.

At the beginning of this chapter, we saw from Kerchoffs Law that our system's security depends on keeping the cipher keys secret. These are critical assets that must be protected to prevent our system from being compromised. This is a real challenge for a practical IoT system where they will be a fleet of devices distributed over a wide area and open to both software and physical attacks.

Just adding encrypted communication and storing the keys in FLASH memory or worse in the actual source code is a job done badly. Unfortunately, this was and still is a widely used practice in current IoT devices. In the second half of this book, we will look at the PSA Security Model that defines a software architecture that is resistant to malicious attacks. This includes the Arm Trusted Firmware to protect device secrets from a network attack. We will also look at hardware approaches to key storage within the LPC55S69 assistive security peripherals.

Creating keys

Ideally, when we generate an encryption key, it should be created within the IoT device and never be exported from the device. It should be created using a cryptographically strong random data source to avoid users selecting a weak key or password. Some keys cannot be created in the system, so we will also have to provide a well-defined key provisioning system. Above all, we want to try and avoid any common or global keys that would allow an attacker to "break once use many." In our IoT device, we will have a range of keys that are used for different functions (Table 4.14).

Table 4.14 Types of cryptographic keys.

Key name	Abbreviation	Description
Data Encryption Key	DEK	Encrypts data in a communication channel
Transmission Encryption Key	TEK	Encrypts the communication channel
Master Encryption Key	MEK	A master secret that can be used to derive fresh keys
Storage Encryption Key	SEK	Encrypts data at rest
Key Encryption Key	KEK	A key used to encrypt (wrap) other keys in a system. May also be called a wrapping key
Root of Trust Key	$RoTK_{pub}$	A public key used to validate the signature of an image. Anchored to a device by a hash stored in immutable memory

Storing keys

We can store all of our encryption keys in a file that is secured by the Key Encryption Key (KEK). This now gives us a single secret, which is the key to the kingdom. This now needs to be secured against two main types of attack: a software attack where an adversary can use a software vulnerability to steal secrets from our system, or a physical attack where an adversary has direct access to our device and can tamper with the hardware to extract the executable image and secrets.

We can mitigate against software attacks in two complementary ways. First, we can develop our firmware to have no software vulnerabilities (aka bugs), which can be used by an attacker. Since this is very difficult to do, the second is to architect our code to isolate the security functions from the main application code. This is a chief concern of the PSA Security Model and the purpose of the Cortex-M33 TrustZone security peripheral.

Microcontrollers designed for use as IoT devices will generally have an assistive security structure that includes a secure key store and defenses against hardware tampering. We will have a closer look at the type of features provided by such a device in Chapter 11.

Using keys

Once we have created a key, it must only be used for the cryptographic process for which it was created as it is bound to the device and cryptographic service. Ideally, this will be enforced by a policy within the key storage system. It is also important that most keys have a fixed lifetime known as the crypto period. When this expires, the key must be changed or "rotated." This can be done by using the initial key provisioning process or by keeping a master key from which we can create fresh keys using a key derivation function. A typical device will have a range of keys that are "bound" to a specific function and a device with both a usage policy and a fixed lifetime. When a key reaches the end of its life, it must be destroyed and "put beyond use" to prevent its reuse.

Key derivation functions (KDF)

In some cases, a user may need to provide a password from which we derive a strong encryption key. User passwords have a relatively small keyspace, so it is necessary to provide a salt to prevent the use of lookup tables, as discussed earlier in this chapter. The mbedTLS library provides some standard key derivation functions, which are defined in PKCS-5. This standard describes two derivation functions, one based on a hashing algorithm and one based on a cipher (Table 4.15).

Table 4.15 PKCS-5 key derivation functions.

Function	Description
mbedtls_pkcs5_pbes2	Key derivation using block cipher
mbedtls_pkcs5_pbkdf2_hmac	Key derivation using HMAC

Exercise: KDF

In this exercise, we will use the mbedTLS KDF functions to generate a set of encryption keys from a password string and a salt.

In the pack installer select Exercise 4.10 and press the Copy button. open main.c

The code declares strings for the password and the salt, and an array for the key:

```
unsigned char password[32] = "password"; //well of course
unsigned char salt[40] = "saltSALTsaltSALTsaltSALTsaltSALTsalt";
unsigned char key[64];
```

Next, we declare and initialize the context:

```
mbedtls_md_context_t sha1_ctx;
mbedtls_md_info_t *info_sha1;
mbedtls_md_init( &sha1_ctx );
```

We need to select the hashing algorithm to use with the KDF
```
info_sha1 = mbedtls_md_info_from_type( MBEDTLS_MD_SHA2 );
```
Then we can generate a key using the HMAC KDF function:

```
mbedtls_pkcs5_pbkdf2_hmac( &sha1_ctx,

                                          password,
                                          plen,
                                          salt,
                                          slen,
                                          it_cnt,
                                          key_len,
                                          key );
```

Build the project then start the debugger and run the code.
The generated key will be displayed in the console window.

Conclusion

In this chapter, we have looked at a range of cryptographic algorithms used to provide data confidentiality, integrity, and assurance. For the most part, these are symmetrical algorithms where any associated key is used for both the encryption and decryption process. This is fine for local data storage and a trivial communication system where a key can be easily agreed by both the sending and receiving stations. In the next chapter, we will look at how to establish secure communication over an insecure channel, where an adversary can watch and read all our message data. To make this work, we need a new family of asymmetrical algorithms and a wider supporting infrastructure.

Cryptography—Secure communications

5

Introduction

As we saw in the last chapter, a modern block cipher will allow two stations to communicate in private across an insecure channel. If both stations are able to agree on a secret key in advance through a secure channel, then establishing an encrypted channel can be straight forward although as we will see later, it is not without its problems. However, in many systems, the use of a "preshared key" is impractical. This means that a session key must be agreed between both stations over the insecure channel. This is a nontrivial problem that is addressed by the Transport Layer Security (TLS) protocol (Fig. 5.1).

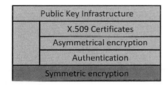

FIG. 5.1

Public key infrastructure. In addition to asymmetric encryption the TLS protocol defines a broad public key infrastructure.

No permission required.

If we want to communicate with a new station, we need to agree on a session key to be used by a symmetrical cipher. Now we are faced with having to transfer a secret between the two stations with an adversary watching. In this chapter, we will see how this can be achieved with the second class of ciphers called asymmetrical ciphers. We will then have a look at how the broader TLS protocol builds a practical solution to this key distribution problem.

Asymmetric ciphers

Unlike a symmetrical cipher, a generic asymmetric cipher has two keys. The first is a freely distributed public key, which is used to encrypt data but cannot be used to decrypt any message. The second key is the private key that the owning entity must

Designing Secure IoT Devices with the Arm Platform Security Architecture and Cortex-M33
https://doi.org/10.1016/B978-0-12-821469-5.00010-7

keep secret. The private key is used to decrypt messages that have been encrypted by the public key (Fig. 5.2).

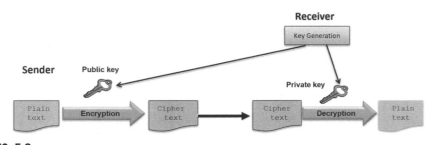

FIG. 5.2

Public key cryptography. Asymmetrical encryption algorithms have two keys. A public key for encryption and a private key used for decryption.

No permission required.

Apart from the number of keys, there are several big differences between symmetrical and asymmetrical ciphers. First, unlike a symmetrical cipher, we cannot just randomly select encryption keys. In an asymmetrical system, the key pair has to be calculated. While this is only done once, it can be time-consuming, especially if done within the microcontroller. Second, a typical asymmetrical cipher requires a very large key size to achieve the same level of security as a symmetrical cipher. An asymmetrical cipher key will need to be 3072 bits to achieve the same security level as a 128 bit AES cipher and should not be smaller than 2048 bits. This also means that asymmetrical ciphers are much slower to compute than symmetrical ciphers. In a practical system, they are only used to transfer small amounts of data, such as keying material for symmetrical ciphers. Finally, the use of very large keys means that asymmetrical ciphers use very large numbers, which cannot be represented with standard "C" variable types. An asymmetrical cipher will need a dedicated big number library that uses multiprecision integers (MPI) that can support the range of values required. There are a number of asymmetrical cryptosystems in existence, but the majority of communication systems use one of two algorithms; either the RSA cryptosystem or the Diffie Hellman Key Exchange. In this section, we will look at both the RSA and Diffie Hellman systems.

RSA

The RSA algorithm was developed by Ron **R**ivest, Adi **S**hamir, and Leonard **A**dleman in 1977. Today, it is the most popular asymmetric algorithm, being used in around 90% of systems. The RSA algorithm is based on the "integer factorization problem." While it is easy to multiply two primes together, it is very time-consuming to factor a large number into its constituent primes. This allows us to create a one-way function that is easy to compute, but the resulting product is hard to factorize.

The mathematical RSA identity is shown below:

$$\left(m^e\right)^d \bmod n = m$$

From this, we can derive functions to encrypt and decrypt the plain text:

$$m^e \bmod n = c$$

$$c^d \bmod n = m$$

m Plain text message
d private key
e & n public key
c is the ciphertext

Here, we can see that the encryption and decryption function is identical. We just need to use the appropriate values for each operation.

The size of the public modulus n is important for two reasons. First, the values for the plaintext n and cyphertext c must be within the integer ring (the modulus) defined by n. Secondly the maximum bit size of the message is equal to the bitsize of n. Finally, the public and private key values e and d must also exist within the integer ring defined by n. For our cryptosystem to be secure, n must contain many key pairs to be invulnerable to brute force attacks. In ever-increasing computing power and advances in factorizing algorithms, a safe value for n needs to be a minimum of 2048 bits.

Unlike a symmetrical cipher, we cannot just pick an encryption key at random. Since the public and private keys are related, they have to be calculated.

RSA key generation uses the following algorithm:

First we select two large primes p and q
We can then calculate $n = p.q$
Next calculate $\varphi(n) = (p-1).(q-1)$ which is known as the Totient
Now we must select e such that it is a prime less than $\varphi(n) - 1$
Now $d.e = \bmod \varphi(n)$
Hence $d = e^{-1} \bmod \varphi(n)$

We can select values for p and q using a random number generator then test to see if the numbers are prime. Two methods to do this are the Millar Raban primality test and the Fermat primality test as shown in Fig. 5.3.

FIG. 5.3

Primality test. A primality test is used to determine if a random number is prime.

No permission required.

We now have to select e, the public exponent. Again, this must be prime and within the cyclic group defined by "n." This gives us an opportunity to improve the performance of the RSA algorithm. Here, we can select the value 65537. This value is useful because it is prime and is $2^{16}+1$ or Hexadecimal 10001. This improves the RSA encryption algorithm's performance by reducing the number of multiplies. While "e" can be a relatively small value, "d" the private key is the same bit size as n (2048 bit), so decryption is many times slower.

Exercise: RSA small numbers

This exercise demonstrates using the mbedTLS big number library to implement a demonstration version of the RSA algorithm. The values used in this example are very small and give a weak cipher, which should not be used in any real application.

In the Pack Installer and select Exercise 5.1.

The bignum library is enabled in mbedTLS_config.h

```
#define MBEDTLS_BIGNUM_C
```

The example code declares a set of multiprecision integer to be used for the RSA values:

```
mbedtls_mpi P, E, N,Q,D,M,C, X;
```

Each value is initialized and Prime values are loaded into P,Q,E and M:

```
void initLargeNum(void)
```

We can then compute the RSA key pair with void computeKeys(void)

This is done by first calculation the Totient:

```
mbedtls_mpi_mul_mpi( &N, &P, &Q );
mbedtls_mpi_sub_int(&Q, &Q, 1 );
mbedtls_mpi_sub_int(&P, &P, 1 );
mbedtls_mpi_mul_mpi( &L, &P, &Q );
```

We can then derive the key pair using an inverse modulus calculation, which is part of the bignum library:

```
mbedtls_mpi_inv_mod( &D, &E, &L );
```

Once the key pair has been calculated, we can use two functions to encrypt and decrypt plain text:

```
void computeRSA(void){
mbedtls_mpi_exp_mod( &X, &C, &D, &N, NULL );
}
void computeMessage(void){
mbedtls_mpi_exp_mod( &C, &M, &E, &N, NULL );
}
```

As you can see, the encrypt and decrypt functions contain the same "mod a log" code but the type of operation depends on which key you use.

Build the code and start the debugger.
Start the Tera Term console.

Examine the functions, then run the code.
Observe the output in the Tera Term console (Fig. 5.4).

```
Private modulus 2F7E09

Plaintext message 55

Encrypted message 272149


Totient 3460F8
public exponent 010001
Public modulus 34721F
Private modulus 2F7E09

Plaintext message 55

Encrypted message 272149

Decrypted plaintext 55
```

FIG. 5.4

RSA results. The exercise calculations and results are shown in the console window.

No permission required.

Malleability

In the last exercise, we used the "school book" version of RSA. Even if we used large numbers, this is not a fully fledged cryptosystem. The core RSA algorithm is malleable. In other words, the cypher text can be modified by an attacker, and it will still decrypt to a meaningful value. We can see this by attacking our previous example if we take an integer S and apply this to the cypher text c.

$$S^e \cdot c$$

Then, when we decrypt

$$\left(S^e \cdot c\right)^d = S \cdot m \bmod_n$$

If S = 2, an attacker has managed to double the value of m and the receiving station will accept this as valid data.

Exercise: RSA malleability

Go back to the project in exercise 5.1.
Uncomment the schoolBookAttack() function in main.c.

Here, we are taking the value "2" and raising it to the power of the public exponent e and then multiplying the cyphertext:

```
void schoolBookAttack (void){
mbedtls_mpi S;
```

```
mbedtls_mpi_init( &S );
mbedtls_mpi_read_string( &S, 16,"00002" );
mbedtls_mpi_exp_mod( &S, &S, &E, &N, NULL );
mbedtls_mpi_mul_mpi( &C, &C, &S );
}
```

Build the code and rerun the example (Fig. 5.5).

```
Totient 3460F8
public exponent 010001
Public modulus 34721F
Private modulus 2F7E09

Plaintext message 55

Encrypted message 272149

Decrypted plaintext AA
```

FIG. 5.5

RSA malleability results. The results of the malleability attack are shown in the console window.

No permission required.

The attacker has successfully modified the encrypted message from 0x55 to double its value 0xAA. There has been a banking error in your favor.

RSA padding

We can overcome this malleability weakness by adding a padding scheme to the plaintext data. There are a number of different padding schemes, but the idea is to place a pattern alongside the plaintext prior to encryption. When we decrypt, we can check the padding to detect any manipulation of the cyphertext. This has the effect of armoring the ciphertext to make it resistant to any malleability attacks.

PKCS 1_1.5

The original form of padding for the RSA cryptosystem was described in the PKCS1_1.5 document published by the RSA corporation. In this scheme, the total plaintext size is defined by the modulus n. The start of the plaintext contains the padding as a header followed by the data. The header starts with two bytes that define the block padding scheme. For PKCS1_1.5 the header value is set to 0x02. The remainder of the header is filled with random data until the start of the message data with a null byte delimiter between the random values and the message data. There must be a minimum of eight bytes of random data. The format is shown in Fig. 5.6.

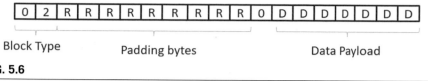

FIG. 5.6

PKCS_1 1.5 padding. The PKCS_1 1.5 padding completes the RSA crypto system.

No permission required.

While this scheme is still widely used it is subject to a number of protocol attacks, most notably one called Bleichenbacher's Attack.

Optimal Asymmetric Encryption Padding

A more up-to-date alternative to PKCS1_1.5 padding is Optimal Asymmetric Encryption Padding (OAEP). This scheme creates a padded header and encoded message packet but requires much more computation than PKCS1_1.5.

The scheme consists of a two-byte block type field the same as PKCS1_1.5, which for OAEP is set to 0x0000. This is followed by a masked seed field and then the encoded message.

The OAEP encoding uses a Mask Generation Function (MGF()). In most systems, this will be a hashing algorithm, typically SHA-1.

The OAEP padding is calculated as follows:

N is the size of the modulus n in bytes
H is the size of the Hash message digest in bytes
L is a custom label if not defined it will be a string on NUL bytes
M is the message data
PS is a string of NULL bytes. The length of PS is N - 2H -2
Now:
Data Block DB = Hash(L)‖PS ‖0x01 ‖M
dbMask = MGF(seed,N-H-1)
maskedDB = DB ^ dbmasked
then:
seedMask = MGF(maskedDB,H)
maskedSeed = seed ^ seedMask
and:
Encoded Message EM = 0x00 ‖maskedSeed ‖maskedDB as shown in Fig. 5.7

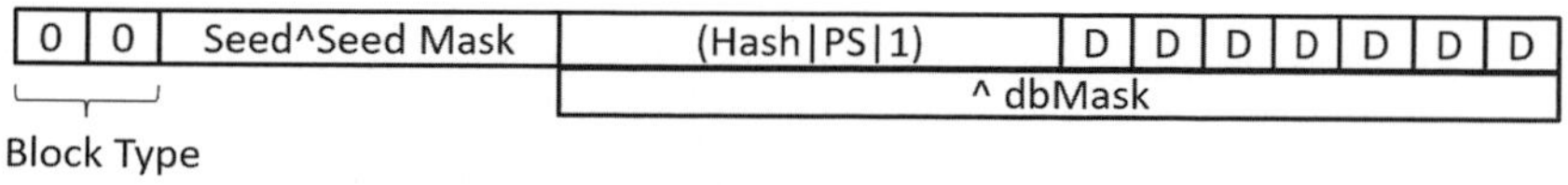

0	0	Seed^Seed Mask	(Hash|PS|1)	D	D	D	D	D	D	D
			^ dbMask							

Block Type

FIG. 5.7

Optimal Asymmetric Encryption Padding (OAEP). The OAEP scheme solves some weaknesses within PKCS_1 1.5.

No permission required.

When using the RSA cipher, the padding scheme is not an option. It must be used to create a working cryptosystem. There are no exceptions.

The RSA functions provided by mbedTLS are shown in Table 5.1, and we will use these functions in the next exercise.

Table 5.1 RSA functions.

Function	Description
mbedtls_rsa_check_privkey	Check a private key for validity
mbedtls_rsa_check_pub_priv	Check a key pair for validity
mbedtls_rsa_check_pubkey	Check a public key for validity
mbedtls_rsa_copy	Copy a context
mbedtls_rsa_free	Free the context
mbedtls_rsa_gen_key	Generate a key pair
mbedtls_rsa_init	Initialize the context
mbedtls_rsa_pkcs1_decrypt	Decrypt with PKCS 1 padding
mbedtls_rsa_pkcs1_encrypt	Encrypt with PKCS 1 padding
mbedtls_rsa_rsaes_oaep_decrypt	Decrypt with PKCS 1 OAEP padding
mbedtls_rsa_rsaes_oaep_encrypt	Encrypt with PKCS 1 OAEP padding
mbedtls_rsa_rsaes_pkcs1_v15_decrypt	Decrypt with PKCS 1.5 padding
mbedtls_rsa_rsaes_pkcs1_v15_encrypt	Encrypt with PKCS 1.5 padding
mbedtls_rsa_set_padding	Set the context padding

Exercise: mbedTLS RSA key generation and cipher

In this exercise, we will generate a pair of RSA keys and then use them to encrypt and decrypt a symmetrical encryption key. The keys will be stored in keyfiles within the evaluation boards file system.

In the Pack Installer and select Exercise 5.2.

To generate the RSA keys, we create a context for the RSA cipher along with contexts for a random number generator and entropy pool.

```
mbedtls_rsa_context rsa;
mbedtls_entropy_context entropy;
mbedtls_ctr_drbg_context ctr_drbg;
```

The example code will initialize the RNG and open files to store the public and private keys.

Then we can initialize the RSA cipher with its context and our choice of padding system.

```
mbedtls_rsa_init( &rsa, MBEDTLS_RSA_PKCS_V15, 0 );
```

We can generate the RSA keys with a single function call. This uses random values to search for suitable primes. A weakness in our RNG implementation would result in predictability, which could be exploited by an adversary.

```
mbedtls_rsa_gen_key( &rsa,
            mbedtls_ctr_drbg_random,
                                &ctr_drbg,
                                KEY_SIZE,EXPONENT )
```

The definitions used in the function call define the required bit size for the private key and the value to be used for the public exponent "e."

```
#define KEY_SIZE 2048
#define EXPONENT 6557
```

Once generated we can check both keys:

```
mbedtls_rsa_check_pubkey( &rsa )
 mbedtls_rsa_check_privkey( &rsa )
```

and then use the public key to encrypt an array holding some plain text such as a symmetric cipher encryption key.

```
mbedtls_rsa_pkcs1_encrypt( &rsa,
                mbedtls_ctr_drbg_random,
                                NULL,
                                MBEDTLS_RSA_PUBLIC,
                                PT_LEN,
                                rsa_plaintext,
                                rsa_ciphertext )
```

We can then decrypt the cipher text with the private key and check it matches the original plaintext.

```
mbedtls_rsa_pkcs1_decrypt( &rsa,
                mbedtls_ctr_drbg_random,
                                NULL, MBEDTLS_RSA_PRIVATE,
                                &len,
                                rsa_ciphertext,
                                rsa_decrypted,
                                sizeof(rsa_decrypted) );
```

Run the code and observe the diagnostic messages displayed on the terminal.
Also make a note of the time taken to run the example. We will compare RSA to other algorithms later in this chapter.

RSA problems

One inherent problem with RSA is that if the private key is ever compromised, an adversary will be able to decode any previous and future messages that have been encrypted with the public key. There is a second public-key cryptosystem that avoids this problem and provides "perfect forward secrecy."

The Diffie Hellman (DH) Key agreement system

Like RSA, the Diffie Hellman (DH) system is based on a mathematical one-way function. While RSA is based on the integer factorization problem, DH is based on the discrete logarithm problem. That is, exponentiation can be used to create a one-way function, and that exponentiation is commutative.

$$K = \left(\alpha^x \right)^y = \left(\alpha^y \right)^x \equiv \left(\alpha^x \right)^y \mod p$$

DH uses this identity to create a key exchange protocol. To set up, we need to select a large prime p, then both stations with a large integer alpha to be our domain parameters, which are public values. The value of alpha must be within the cyclic group (modulus integer ring) of p-2.

At the beginning of communication, the master station shares its domain parameters. Then both stations select a session private key, which is a second integer within the cyclic group of p-2. They then both compute their respective public key:

$$K_{pr} = \text{element in cyclic group of p-2}$$

$$K_{pub} = \alpha^{K_{pr}} \mod p$$

Both sides can now exchange their public keys and can compute a shared secret as follows:

$$\left(K_{pub,B} \right)^{K_{pr,A}} = K_{AB} = \left(K_{pub,A} \right)^{K_{pr,B}}$$

The DH algorithm is not a cryptosystem like RSA. It is used to agree on a shared secret which will be different for every set of domain and session parameters. This means that if any station's private key is compromised, it will be of no use in recalculating the shared secret of other sessions, hence the concept of perfect forward secrecy.

Exercise: DH small numbers

This exercise demonstrates using the mbedTLS big number library to implement a demonstration version of the DH algorithm. Like the RSA, small numbers exercise, the values used in this example are very small and give a weak cipher which should not be used in any real application.

In the Pack Installer and select Exercise 5.3.
Open Main.c

The code initializes a set of MPI numbers and initializes the domain values Alpha and P along with private key values for two stations a and b.

```
mbedtls_mpi_init( &Pub_A );
mbedtls_mpi_init( &Pub_B );
mbedtls_mpi_init( &a );
mbedtls_mpi_init( &b );
```

```
mbedtls_mpi_init( &Alpha );
mbedtls_mpi_init( &P );
mbedtls_mpi_init( &Secret_A );
mbedtls_mpi_init( &Secret_B );
mbedtls_mpi_read_string( &P, 16,"0001D" );
mbedtls_mpi_read_string( &Alpha, 16,"00002");
mbedtls_mpi_read_string( &a, 16,"00005");
mbedtls_mpi_read_string( &b, 16,"0000C");
```

Using the domain values, we can then compute the public key for each station.

```
mbedtls_mpi_exp_mod( &Pub_A, &Alpha, &a, &P, NULL );
mbedtls_mpi_exp_mod( &Pub_B, &Alpha, &b, &P, NULL );
```

By exchanging public keys each station can now compute the shared secret.

```
mbedtls_mpi_exp_mod( &Secret_A, &Pub_B, &a, &P, NULL );
mbedtls_mpi_exp_mod( &Secret_B, &Pub_A, &b, &P, NULL );
```

Build the code.
Start the debugger and run the code (Fig. 5.8).

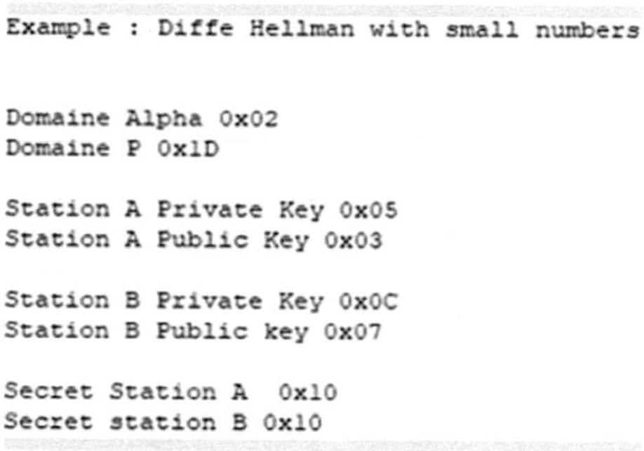

```
Example : Diffe Hellman with small numbers


Domaine Alpha 0x02
Domaine P 0x1D

Station A Private Key 0x05
Station A Public Key 0x03

Station B Private Key 0x0C
Station B Public key 0x07

Secret Station A   0x10
Secret station B 0x10
```

FIG. 5.8

Console display of DH key agreement. The DH key agreement process will be displayed in the debugger console window.

No permission required.

The results of each calculation are displayed in the debugger console window.

In a practical system, the initial value for the prime p is chosen using a random number generator and one of the prime verifying algorithms we saw with the RSA algorithm. The integers used to compute the public keys should also be selected using a random number generator to prevent the selection of weak values which an adversary could guess (Table 5.2).

Table 5.2 DH functions.

Function	Description
mbedtls_dhm_calc_secret	Derive and export the shared secret
mbedtls_dhm_free	Free the context
mbedtls_dhm_init	Initialize the context
mbedtls_dhm_make_params	Setup and write the key server parameters
mbedtls_dhm_make_public	Create private value and export public value
mbedtls_dhm_read_params	Read the key server exchange parameters
mbedtls_dhm_read_public	Read the peer's public value

Exercise: Diffie Hellman Key agreement

In this exercise, we will configure the evaluation board as a server and allow the PC to connect over a WiFi connection. A client on the PC will then request the DH domain parameters along with its public key. The client will use these values to calculate its public key and will then send this to the server. Both the server and client will calculate a shared secret. The server will use the shared secret to encrypt a text message which is sent to the client for decryption.

In the Pack Installer select Exercise 5.4.
Set the server project as the active project.

The embedded node is designed to run as a server with the address 192.168.0.10. You may need to adjust this to work with your WiFi network. When the PC client starts it will ask you to input the server address.

In the server we first declare the necessary contexts for the DH, AES ciphers and random number generator. We then initialize them as well as starting the local file system.

```
mbedtls_dhm_context dhm;
mbedtls_aes_context aes;
mbedtls_dhm_init( &dhm );
 mbedtls_aes_init( &aes );
```

The full example code initializes the filesystem, networking, and random number generator before loading the servers DH parameters from the embedded file system.

```
f = fopen( "dh_prime.txt", "rb" ) ) == NULL )
mbedtls_mpi_read_file( &dhm.P, 16, f )
mbedtls_mpi_read_file( &dhm.G, 16, f )
fclose( f );
```

We then calculate the session DH parameters and extract the public parameters into a buffer ready to be sent over the network.

```
mbedtls_dhm_make_params( &dhm,
            (int) mbedtls_mpi_size( &dhm.P ),
                                    buf,
```

```
                                  &n,
                                  mbedtls_ctr_drbg_random,
                                  &ctr_drbg )
```

The server then opens a network port and waits for a remote connection.

The client connects to the server then sends its DH public parameter. Next, the client will reply with its public parameter.

The server can then load the local context with the clients public DP parameters and calculate the shared secret.

```
mbedtls_dhm_read_public( &dhm, buf, dhm.len );
mbedtls_dhm_calc_secret( &dhm,
                buf,
                                  sizeof( buf ),
                                  &n,
                                  mbcdtls_ctr_drbg_random,
                                  &ctr_drbg );
```

Once we have the shared secret, it can be used as the encryption key to wrap the plaintext reply.

```
mbedtls_aes_setkey_enc( &aes, buf, 256 );
memcpy( buf, PLAINTEXT, 16 );
mbedtls_aes_crypt_ecb( &aes, MBEDTLS_AFS_ENCRYPT,buf,buf );
```

The server will then send the encrypted packet back to the client.

The client-side follows a similar set of API calls to generate the session DH parameters and exchange public values with the server. The major difference is that it creates an ephemeral session key pair and shares the public values with the server.

```
mbedtls_dhm_make_public( &dhm,
                (int) dhm.len,
                                  buf,
                                  n,
                                  mbedtls_ctr_drbg_random,
                                  &ctr_drbg )
```

Once the client has received the servers' public values, it is able to calculate the same shared secret as the server. When the ciphertext packet arrives from the server, it can use the shared secret to decrypt the message back to the original plaintext.

In the server project copy the DH_prime.txt file from the PC_app folder to the SD card and place this into the evaluation board.
Build the server project and start the debugger.
Run the server code so it is waiting for a connection.
Open a Windows command window and run the dh_client executable located in the PC_app folder (Fig. 5.9).

FIG. 5.9

DH Key agreement over a network. The PC application and the embedded node negotiate a shared secret over the local WiFi network.

No permission required.

The two stations will display their progress as they negotiate a secure connection.

Like RSA, the DH algorithm uses very large numbers and needs the use of the mbedTLS "big number library." However, unlike RSA, the DH algorithm can be implemented with a different style of number line which greatly improves its performance.

Elliptic curve cryptography

So far, all of our asymmetric ciphers are based on the "integer factorization problem" or the "discrete logarithm problem" and a standard (linear) number line. In order to get a good level of security, we need to use very large numbers. This, in turn, results in a large amount of compute time. However, it is also possible to build a discrete logarithm problem by using an alternative number line and arithmetic based on elliptic curves. If you have been brought up on a diet of engineering math, this all looks a bit arbitrary; if you want to take a deeper look at the underlying math, I have listed a number of open source books in the bibliography. Everyone needs an obscure hobby.

Elliptic curve cryptography replaces our standard linear number line with a curve based on the identity.

$$y^2 \equiv x^3 + a.x + b$$

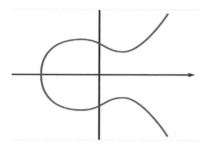

FIG. 5.10

Elliptic curve. A textbook elliptic curve which is symmetrical around the X-axis.

No permission required.

We can plot the curve as a set of real numbers, which gives us the textbook curve, as shown in Fig. 5.10. An important feature of an EC curve is that it is symmetrical about the X axis.

For cryptographic use, we want to create a finite field Chapter 4. We first need to create an integer ring, which can be done by adding a modulus operation. If we make p a prime, we can create a cyclic group in which each element is known as a primitive element.

$$y^2 \equiv x^3 + a.x + b \bmod_p$$

Addition

While doing algebraic operations on a curve may seem a bit odd, it is possible to perform addition of two points as shown in Fig. 5.11.

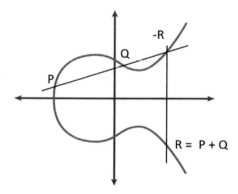

FIG. 5.11

Elliptic curve addition. Elliptic curve addition is performed by bisecting the curve and then reflecting over the X-axis.

No permission required.

To add two points, P and Q, we bisect them with a line and extend this line until it cuts the curve at a third point. If we then reflect this point across the X-axis, we get a result R = (P + Q).

Point doubling

We can also calculate P + P by extending the tangent of point P until it cuts the curve at a new point. Again this point is reflected across the x-axis to give us a result of 2P, as shown in Fig. 5.12.

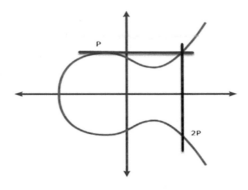

FIG. 5.12

Elliptic curve point doubling. Point doubling takes a tangent and then reflects across the X-axis.

No permission required.

Group element

For our integer ring to become a cyclic group we also need a neutral element φ such that

$$P + \varphi = P$$

On a standard number line, the neutral element would be zero, but on our elliptic curve, it is not clear what we can use. In practice, we can define a point at "plus" infinity along the Y-axis as the neutral element. So we can consider φ to be asymtotic to each point on our curve

$$P + (-P) = \varphi$$

If we use our point addition method to calculate − P it turns out that the inverse of P is its mirror across the X-axis as shown in Fig. 5.13.

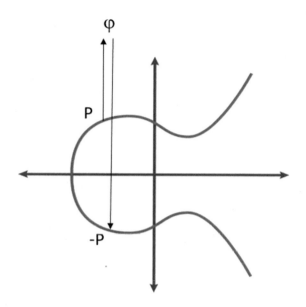

FIG. 5.13

Elliptic curve inversion. A modular inversion is calculated by a reflection across the X-axis.

No permission required.

To create a discrete logarithmic problem on an elliptic curve, we use another property of elliptic curve addition: adding a point P to itself is the equivalent of raising P by a power on a linear number line.

So in effect:

$$P^d = T$$

is expressed as

$$(P + P + P + P + P) = T$$

Addition *d* times
Which can written as

$$dP = T$$

We can then take our base point P and calculate its powers and use these as the basis for a discrete logarithm problem. As we will see in the next exercise, the public key is T and d is the private key.

To create an elliptic curve cryptosystem, we need to define a suitable curve (not easy). In practice, the EC curves supported by mbedTLS come from NIST, the Internet Engineering Task Force or the original researcher, Neil Koblitz. It should be noted that because of their underlying structure, the NIST curves have a higher performance than the IETF Brainpool curves (Table 5.3).

Table 5.3 mbedTLS elliptic curves.

mbedTLS EC curve	Description
MBEDTLS_ECP_DP_NONE	
MBEDTLS_ECP_DP_SECP192R1	192-bits NIST curve
MBEDTLS_ECP_DP_SECP224R1	224-bits NIST curve
MBEDTLS_ECP_DP_SECP256R1	256-bits NIST curve
MBEDTLS_ECP_DP_SECP384R1	384-bits NIST curve
MBEDTLS_ECP_DP_SECP521R1	521-bits NIST curve
MBEDTLS_ECP_DP_BP256R1	256-bits Brainpool curve
MBEDTLS_ECP_DP_BP384R1	384-bits Brainpool curve
MBEDTLS_ECP_DP_BP512R1	512-bits Brainpool curve
MBEDTLS_ECP_DP_CURVE25519	Curve25519
MBEDTLS_ECP_DP_SECP192K1	192-bits "Koblitz" curve
MBEDTLS_ECP_DP_SECP224K1	224-bits "Koblitz" curve
MBEDTLS_ECP_DP_SECP256K1	256-bits "Koblitz" curve

Exercise: Elliptic Curve Diffie Hellman

In this exercise, we replace the standard DH algorithm with the elliptic curve version and compute the server and client keys and shared secret. In the elliptic curve version of the DH algorithm, the public and private keys are points on the elliptic curve. In the code below, the values in the ECDH context are as follows:

- grpThe elliptic curve to use
- QThe public key
- Qpthe peer public key
- dThe private key
- Xa coordinate on the elliptic curve
- zThe shared secret

In the Pack Installer select Exercise 5.5.
Build the project then download it using the debugger

The project has code that first creates and initializes a context for both the client and server stages:

```
mbedtls_ecdh_context ctx_cli, ctx_srv;
mbedtls_ecdh_init( &ctx_cli );
 mbedtls_ecdh_init( &ctx_srv );
```

The next few function calls are symmetrical for both the client and server here we will look at the client version.

For the client we first load the common elliptic curve.

```
mbedtls_ecp_group_load( &ctx_cli.grp,
          MBEDTLS_ECP_DP_CURVE25519 );
```

We can then generate the public and private keys using a random number as a seed.

```
mbedtls_ecdh_gen_public( &ctx_cli.grp,
                 &ctx_cli.d,
                                        &ctx_cli.Q,
                                        mbedtls_ctr_drbg_random,
                                        &ctr_drbg );
```

The public key MPI is then exported as a binary string to be shared with the server code.

```
unsigned char cli_to_srv[32];
mbedtls_mpi_write_binary( &ctx_cli.Q.X, cli_to_srv, 32 );
```

The public key can then be read by the peer, in this case the server.

```
mbedtls mpi read_binary( &ctx_srv.Qp.X, cli_to_srv, 32 )
```

This process is repeated by the server code.

Once the public keys have been exchanged both the server and the client can compute a shared secret z.

```
mbedtls_ecdh_compute_shared( &ctx_srv.grp,
                 &ctx_srv.z,
                                        &ctx_srv.Qp,
                                        &ctx_srv.d,
                                        mbedtls_ctr_drbg_random,
                                        &ctr_drbg );
```

Run the code and the process will be printed to the console window

Both the server and client will calculate the same shared secret. This exercise is comparable to Exercise 5.2, which uses RSA. Here we can see that the EC version is much faster.

Message signing

In the last chapter, we saw how to calculate Message Authentication Code (MAC), which can be used to authenticate data through the use of a password. This password has to be shared through a secure channel between all stations that need to communicate.

Unfortunately, this is not a practical approach if we try to establish secure communications between different stations over a public internet connection. Fortunately, we can use public-key cryptography to authenticate data through a digital signing technique.

RSA signing

The RSA approach to signing data is very straight forward and elegant. If we want to sign a message to authenticate it as originating from us, we go through the following

2-step process. First, compute the hash of the plain text we want to sign. Second, we encrypt the hash using the RSA algorithm, but we use our private key. The resulting ciphertext is the signature of our plaintext. We can send the plaintext and signature to any other station along with our public key. The receiving station can authenticate the plain text by decrypting the signature using our public key. This will reveal the per calculated hash of the plaintext. They can now compute the hash of the plaintext, which should match the signature hash. If this is the case, we have confirmed the integrity of the plaintext and also its origin, as the signature could only have been created with our private key (Fig. 5.14).

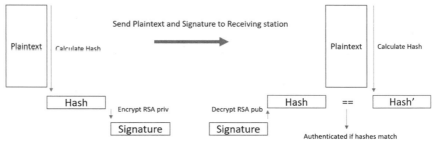

FIG. 5.14

RSA signing digital data. RSA can be used to sign data by taking its hash and then encrypting using the private key.

No permission required.

In practice, the process is slightly more difficult as we have to add padding to the signature to prevent an existential attack. Like the RSA encryption and decryption functions, the different padding strategies are directly implemented by the mbedTLS signing API calls.

Exercise: RSA signature

In this exercise we will calculate and verify the signature of a file of plaintext data using the RSA algorithm.

In the Pack Installer select Exercise 5.6
Open main.c

At the start of the code, we define each of the RSA public and private key numbers as an ASCII string:

```
#define RSA_N "9292758453063D803DD603D5E777D788" \
        "8ED1D5BF35786190FA2F23EBC0848AEA" \
        ...............
        "5E94BB77B07507233A0BC7BAC8F90F79"
```

We then define a multiprecision integer and initialize it along with the RSA context:

```
mbedtls_mpi K;
mbedtls_mpi_init( &K );
mbedtls_rsa_init( &rsa, MBEDTLS_RSA_PKCS_V15, 0 );
```

We can then set the RSA public and private keys by reading in each MPI number:

```
MBEDTLS_MPI_CHK( mbedtls_mpi_read_string( &K, 16, RSA_N ) );
MBEDTLS_MPI_CHK( mbedtls_rsa_import( &rsa,
                        &K,
                                            NULL,
                                            NULL,
                                            NULL,
                                            NULL ) );
```

To create the signature, we first calculate the HASH of the plaintext file:

```
mbedtls_sha1_ret( rsa_plaintext, PT_LEN, sha1sum )
```

Then, we compute the signature using the private key and use the pkcs1 padding scheme:

```
mbedtls_rsa_pkcs1_sign( &rsa,
                                            myrand,
                                            NULL,
                                            MBEDTLS_RSA_PRIVATE,
                                            MBEDTLS_MD_SHA1,
                                            0,
                                            sha1sum_0,
                                            rsa_ciphertext );
```

Once the signature has been computed, a receiving station can recompute the hash and then verify the integrity of the plaintext using the sending stations public key:

```
mbedtls_rsa_pkcs1_verify( &rsa,
                                            NULL,
                                            NULL,
                                            MBEDTLS_RSA_PUBLIC,
                                            MBEDTLS_MD_SHA1,
                                            0,
                                            sha1sum_1,
                                            rsa_ciphertext );
```

Build the project.
Place the SD card with the helloBig.txt file into the evaluation board.
Run the code to generate and verify the signature.

Elliptic Curve Digital Signature Algorithm

An alternative to signing messages with RSA is the Digital Signature Algorithm, which is a NIST standard FIPS 128 - 3.

The ECDSA algorithm is more complex than RSA and has separate sign and verify algorithms. The ECDSA algorithm can also be implemented using elliptic curve cryptography, which is becoming more widely used for small embedded systems.

To sign a message, we need to select and compute a range of variables as shown in Table 5.4.

Table 5.4 ECDSA parameters.

Parameter	Description
CURVE	An elliptic curve
p	Modulus or CURVE
a b	Coefficients of CURVE
A	A point which generates a cyclic group of prime order q
d	A random integer in the range $0 < d < q$
B	Computed as dA
Public key k_{pub}	p,a,b,A,B
Private key k_{pr}	D
Random ephemeral session key k_e	Where $0 < k_e < q$
x	The message

Key generation

To compute a set of keys for ECDSA, we need to select a random integer d and compute $B = dA$. This will now give us the two keys, as shown in Table 5.4. This process is much faster than generating an RSA key pair.

ECDSA signing

Signing a message follows the same approach as RSA. We first need to calculate a hash of the data to be signed. The ECDSA algorithm is certified for use with the SHA-1 and SHA-2 algorithms. Once the hash is calculated, we can calculate the final ECDSA signature. The "C" pseudo code is shown below:

$$R = k_e A$$

$$r = xR$$

$$s = \left(\text{hash}(x) + d.r \right) k_e^{-1} \% q$$

where r and s are the signature.

ECDSA verification

We can then verify the signature with the following calculations:

$$w = s^{-1} \bmod q$$
$$z = \text{hash}(\text{ message })\text{sizeof}(q)$$
$$u_1 = (zw)\bmod q$$
$$u_2 = (rw)\bmod q$$
$$P = u_1 A + u_2 B$$

If x_p is the x coordinate of P, the signature is valid if $x_p = r \bmod q$

Exercise: ECDSA

In this exercise, we will generate an ECDSA key pair and then compute and verify an ECDSA signature.

In the Pack Installer, select Exercise 5.7

We can first select an elliptic curve from our library.

```
#define ECPARAMS MBEDTLS_ECP_DP_SECP192R1
```

Then create a context for the signing and verifying algorithms and initialize.

```
mbedtls_ecdsa_context ctx_sign, ctx_verify;
mbedtls_ecdsa_init( &ctx_sign );
mbedtls_ecdsa_init( &ctx_verify );
```

In addition, we must create a random number generator so that we can generate a key pair.

```
mbedtls_ecdsa_genkey( &ctx_sign,
              ECPARAMS,
                                   mbedtls_ctr_drbg_random,
                                   &ctr_drbg );
```

Before calculating the signature we must first calculate the message hash.

```
unsigned char hash[] == {0xFa,0xce,0x33......};
```

Now we can calculate the signature.

```
unsigned char sig[512];
mbedtls_ecdsa_write_signature( &ctx_sign,
            MBEDTLS_MD_SHA256,
                                 hash,
                                 sizeof( hash ),
                                 sig,
                                 &sig_len,
                                 mbedtls_ctr_drbg_random,
                                 &ctr_drbg );
```

Now we have the signature we can verify it is correct. Our receiving station must setup the same elliptic curve and also copy the signing public key.

&

Now we can verify the signature:

```
mbedtls_ecdsa_read_signature( &ctx_verify,
                    hash,
                                            sizeof( hash ),
                                            sig,
                                            sig_len );
```

Run the code and the results will be printed to the console window.

You will also see that the process of key generation, signing, and verification is significantly faster than the RSA examples.

Using asymmetrical ciphers

If we can give our public key to anyone, this enables them to encrypt and send a message that can only be decrypted using our private key. At first sight, it would appear possible to exchange keying material for a symmetrical cipher through a simple request and reply protocol similar to our DH key agreement exercise above. Unfortunately, this naïve use of asymmetrical encryption is prone to many attacks, not least of these being a "Man in the Middle" attack.

Man in the Middle

If we have two stations trying to establish a secure communication channel, they are traditionally called "Bob" and "Alice." There is a possibility that a malicious third party can intercept their messages, traditionally called "Mallory" (Fig. 5.15).

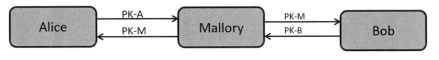

FIG. 5.15

Man in the Middle attack. A Man in the Middle attack allows "Mallory" to intercept communication between Alice and Bob.

No permission required.

In this scenario, when Alice tries to send her public key to Bob, it can be intercepted by Mallory, who substitutes his public key and sends it on to Bob. If Bob tries to send his public key to Alice, Mallory is again able to capture Bob's key and again send his public key to Alice. If Bob or Alice use Mallory's public key to encrypt a message, Mallory will be able to intercept it and decrypt it with his private key and then re-encrypt it with the relevant public key before retransmitting the message.

This allows Mallory to read all messages sent between Alice and Bob without either of them being aware of the interception.

Public key infrastructure

In order to prevent a "Man in the Middle" and similar attacks, asymmetrical ciphers are used within a scheme called the public key infrastructure (PKI). This scheme allows two stations to securely exchange public keys. The PKI rests on having a trusted third party called a certificate authority (CA) (Fig. 5.16).

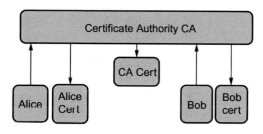

FIG. 5.16

Certificate authority. A certificate authority is a trusted 3rd party who signs certificates for Alice and Bob.

No permission required.

Before they can communicate, Alice and Bob must send their public keys and credentials, including the name of their station. This can be a URL, hostname, or even an IP address. The certificate authority will then create a certificate that contains this information in a standard format. The data in the certificate are signed by the private key of the certificate authority and then returned to their owners. The certificate authority also publishes its own certificate, which contains its public key. The CA's certificate is available to everyone, and it typically stored within all the participating stations. When Alice and Bob want to establish a secure channel, they can exchange their station certificates. When they receive a certificate, they can ensure its authenticity by using the certificate authorities public key extracted from the CA certificate to validate the signature of the received certificate. Once we have validated the received certificate, we have the public key of the station we want to communicate with. Since the certificate also contains credentials such as a URL or hostname, it is bound to its originating station. Thus, we can be sure that a malicious certificate has not been substituted by a Man in the Middle.

X.509 certificates

The certificates used in this scheme are held in a format called X.509. In addition to the senders' public key, the certificate contains a subject field that identifies its origin. This includes the sender's name and location along with a field called the "common name." The common name field is a text string and does not have a well-defined format. In fact, you can really put just about anything in here as it is just tested for equality by the receiving station. In practice, it will contain either a hostname or a URL. You could put in a raw IP address, but this is considered bad practice and should be avoided (Fig. 5.17).

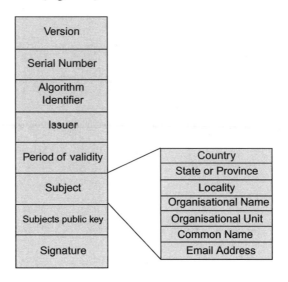

FIG. 5.17

X.509 certificate. An X.509 certificate is an structured array of data encoded using ASN.1 notation and signed by the CA private key.

No permission required.

The X.509 certificate contains additional fields for the X.509 version, a certificate serial number, the issuing certificate authority, and its period of validity as a start and end date. The certificate also contains fields that define the algorithms used to sign the certificate. In order to sign the certificate, the certificate authority will calculate a hash of the certificate fields and then calculate the signature of the certificate by encrypting the hash using an asymmetrical cipher and the certificate authorities private key.

Certificate validation

Every station in our system will have the CA's certificate and hence the CA's public key. When we receive a new certificate, we can extract the calculated hash value from its signature using the CA's public key. Next, we can calculate the certificate's hash and compare it to the signature hash. If the two match, then the certificate is valid. To fully trust it, we would next check its period of validity and whether the common name contains the hostname or URL of the station we are trying to communicate with. If we are satisfied with all of this information, then we can start to communicate with the remote station using its public key stored in the certificate.

Certificate lifetime

The mbedTLS library supports certificates being stored in a standard file system and allows them to be stored as arrays in FLASH memory. The "Period of Validity" field in the X.509 certificate gives every certificate a fixed lifetime and an expiration date. If you are designing a system where each node will have a long lifetime, you will likely have to update the certificates held in the IoT device. Since the CA certificate is public information, it does not need to be held in secure storage. This would allow you to either update the certificate directly if it is held in the file system or do a firmware update if the certificate is stored in FLASH as part of the application image.

Certificate revocation list

While a certificate will naturally expire and have to be replaced, it is likely that at some point, we will need to forcibly remove the rights of a node to connect to our system. The Transport Layer Security (TLS) protocol supports two methods of doing this. The first is a certificate revocation list (CRL). Here we can maintain a list of device certificates that are no longer allowed to join our system. The CRL is loaded by the server and acts as a blacklist of prohibited devices. In the broader internet, the certificate authority will maintain a CRL, which can be periodically downloaded to ensure that no revoked device can connect to the server. While CRLs are widely supported, a newer revocation method called online certificate status protocol (OCSP) is becoming the preferred method of checking the status of a certificate. The online certificate status protocol allows a node to directly query the current status of a certificate with the CA before allowing it to connect.

Certificate encoding

An X.509 certificate is a collection of strings and arrays that can be held as a C object. However, to enable data interchange between many diverse systems, we need to define a standard interchange format. The encoding rules for digital certificates are defined by a telecoms standard called Abstract Syntax Notation One or ASN.1. The ASN.1 standard is defined by the International Telecommunication Union and is an interface description language that is widely used in telecoms and computer networking systems. The ASN.1 standard defines a set of Basic Encoding Rules (BER), which provide a flexible system for encoding data. There is also a subset of rules called the Distinguished Encoding Rules (DER), which define an "unequivocal transfer syntax" or one way to encode and decode a given set of data. An X.509

certificate is encoded using the ASN.1 format with DER encoding. The output of this encoding will be a block of binary data. A certificate may be further encoded into a base 64 format which encodes the binary data as ASCII characters. This ASCII format was originally developed to send binary data as email attachments and is known as Privacy Enhanced Mail or PEM. When we store a certificate, it will either be in a binary format (.der) or an ASCII format (.pem), but either format contains the same information. The ASN.1 format can be described as fiendishly complicated, but fortunately, we do not need to work with it directly. We can use mbedTLS and other tools to generate and parse X.509 certificates.

Certificate authority selection

On the broader internet, there are many clients in the form of PCs, tablets, and mobile phones that want to connect to secure web servers. In this situation, we need the CA to be a trusted third party who can provide certificates to public websites and have their certificate stored in general users' devices. However, if you are going to design a closed system that only contains your own servers and devices, it is possible and usually desirable to be your own certificate authority. This creates a "walled garden" where only authenticated devices can connect to the server. Most commercial IoT cloud systems act as their own CA.

We can further improve the security of the system by issuing certificates to devices. In this case, the server and device exchange and validate each other's certificates. This form of mutual authentication provides a higher level of security and should be used for IoT systems whenever possible. We will set up both server authentication and mutual server/device authentication as we look at the TLS protocol. If you are using a commercial cloud system it should enforce mutual authentication.

Certificate chain

In the real world one, CA does not rule them all. There are a small number of root CA's who may sign the certificates for a regional or industry CA. This local CA can, in turn, sign an end-entity certificate. This creates a chain of certificates or certificate path. If you are working with a cloud server or commercial certificate authority, you may be issued a single certificate or a chain of certificates. In the case of a certificate chain, you will need to parse each certificate until you find one you can trust. This is fully managed by the mbedTLS library, so you don't need to develop any further code to parse the certificate chain.

Exercise: Creating X.509 certificates

In this exercise, we will look at how to create a set of X.509 certificates which are used to validate the credentials of both servers and clients. We will use XCA, which is an open-source tool to create the certificates. XCA has a graphical user interface which is useful when learning.

> **Download and install the XCA application.**
> https://hohnstaedt.de/xca/
> **In the Pack Installer select Exercise 5.8.**
> **Start the XCA program.**
> **Select File\open database and select the database in the Exercise 5.8 Creating X509 Certificates\XCA DB directory.**
> **Enter the database password, which is of course, "password."**

The database contains three templates, which we can use to create a set of certificates for our network of IoT devices and servers.

Certificate authority

First we will create a "certificate authority" certificate, which will be used to sign the server and client certificates.

> **In the templates tab select the "Certificate Authority" template, right click and select "Create Certificate"** (Fig. 5.18).

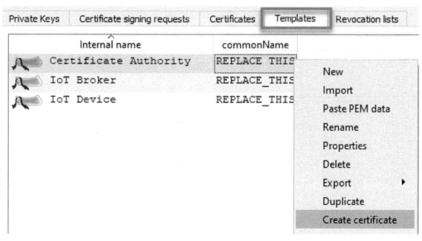

FIG. 5.18

XCA user interface. Create a root certificate authority.

No permission required.

Select the source tab This certificate will be our "Root of Trust" and, as such, will be self-signed. The algorithm used to sign the certificate is SHA256. This is the current minimum standard you should use to sign a certificate (Fig. 5.19).

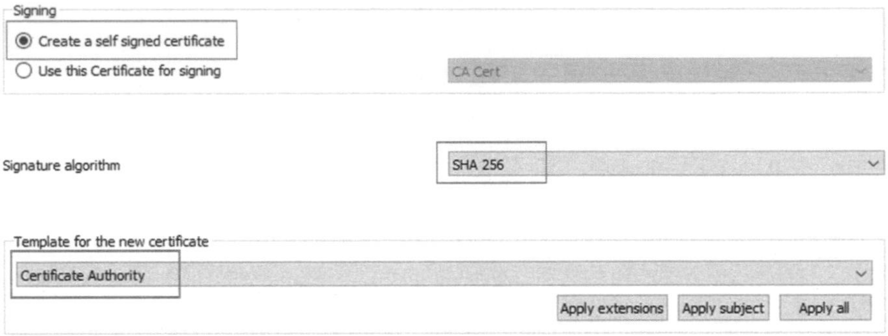

FIG. 5.19

Create the CA certificate. Select the signing algorithm. Use SHA256 and a minimum.

No permission required.

Select the subject tab (Fig. 5.20).

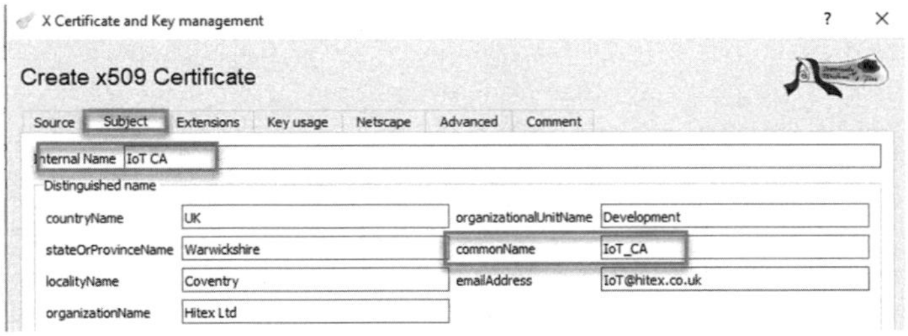

FIG. 5.20

Certificate subject. Set the certificate common name to IoT_CA.

No permission required.

Enter an internal name and a common name. These can be different, but in this case, I have used IoT_CA. The template has set the other distinguished name fields, but you can change them to match your needs.

Select the Extensions tab (Fig. 5.21).

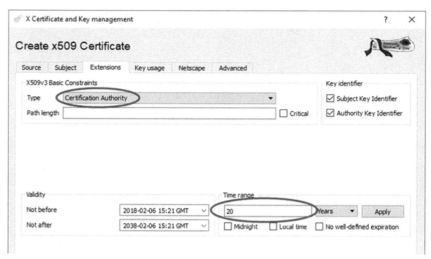

FIG. 5.21

Certificate extensions. Here, we can set the certificate as a CA cert and also define its lifetime.

No permission required.

Here, the type of certificate is configured as "certificate authority" and there is a default time range of 20 years.

Select the Key Usage tab.

This dialog allows you to limit the properties of the certificate. By leaving everything blank, we are not adding any restrictions to our basic certificate. Once you have a working system, you can experiment with these fields.

Go back to the subject tab (Fig. 5.22).

FIG. 5.22

Generate key. Once we have defined the certificate we can generate the key pair.

No permission required.

Press the create button to generate the key (Fig. 5.23).

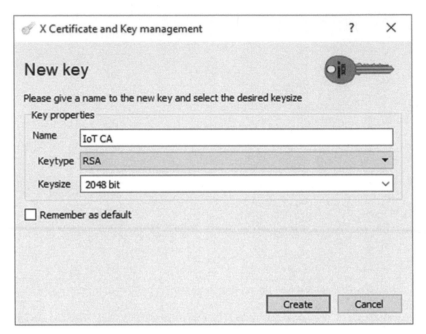

FIG. 5.23

Generate key size and type. Next we select the key type and size.

No permission required.

Here, we will generate a 2048 bit RSA key

Finally, press OK on the subject dialog to create the certificate.

The new certificate and key can be viewed in the certificates window (Fig. 5.24).

FIG. 5.24

Root certificate. Once the certificate is generated, it will be shown as a root certificate.

No permission required.

and the private keys window (Fig. 5.25).

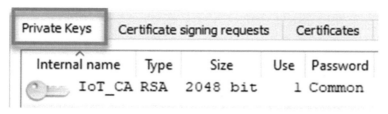

FIG. 5.25

Generated private key. The private key icon is displayed, but its value is hidden until it is exported.

No permission required.

The certificate authorities private key is securely held in the XCA database and must always be kept secret as it is used to sign the server and client certificates.

Server certificate

Go back to the templates tab and this time select the "broker" template and create a new certificate (Fig. 5.26).

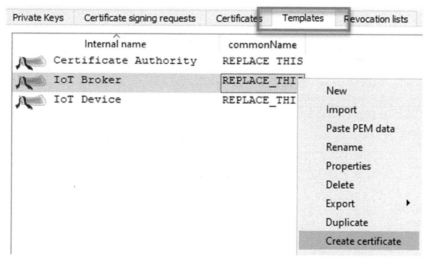

FIG. 5.26

Server certificate. Create a new certificate using the broker (IoT server) template.

No permission required.

Here we are using the term Broker as another name for Server. We will see the role of a "broker" in the next chapter.

In the source tab select the IoT_CA certificate as the signing source (Fig. 5.27).

FIG. 5.27

Signing the server certificate. The server certificate is signed by the CA private key.

No permission required.

Select the subject tab (Fig. 5.28) and set the common name to IoT_Broker

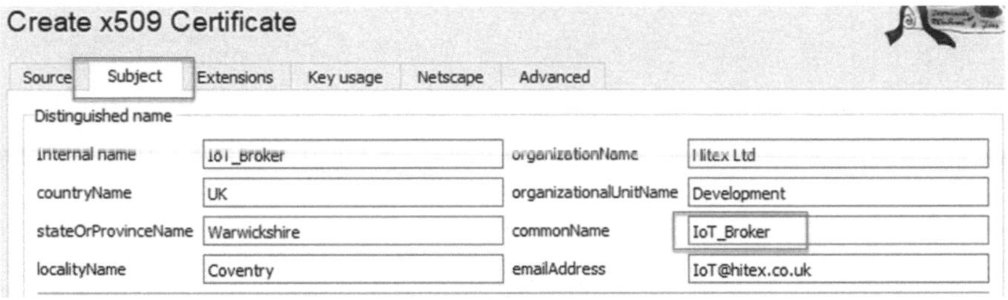

FIG. 5.28

Server subject. The server subject dialog sets the common name to IoT_Broker.

No permission required.

Select the extensions tab (Fig. 5.29) and set the certificate type to end entity.

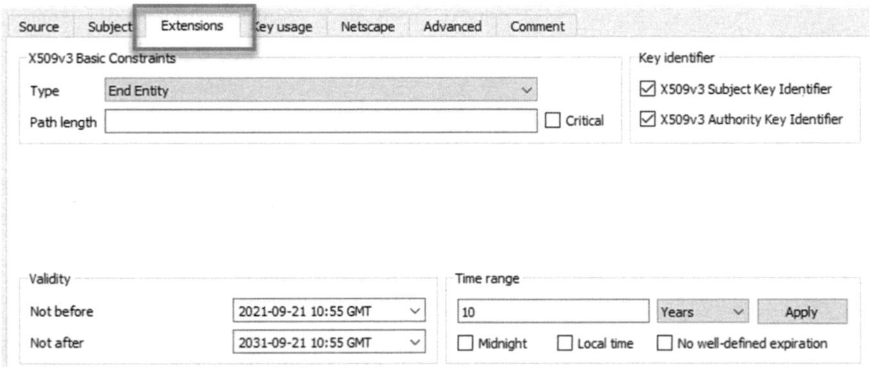

FIG. 5.29

Certificate extensions dialog. Here, we can set the certificate type to End entity and also set a lifetime.

No permission required.

This time the type of certificate is set to "End Entity" and the life time of the certificate is limited to 10 years.

Return to the subject tab and create the key and certificate as we did for the "certificate authority" certificate.

Device certificate

Now we are going to repeat the process one more time to create a device certificate. This will then give us all the certificate and keys we need to build a secure networked system.

In the templates tab select the device template, right click and select "Create Certificate" (Fig. 5.30).

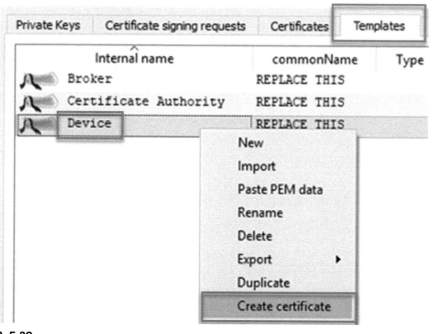

FIG. 5.30

Create Certificate. Create a new certificate using the device template.

No permission required.

In the source field, we must again use the IoT_CA certificate for signing (Fig. 5.31).

Signing		
○ Create a self signed certificate with the serial	1	
◉ Use this Certificate for signing	IoT_CA	▾

FIG. 5.31

Certificate signing. The device certificate is signed by the root CA private key.

No permission required.

Select the subject dialog.
Fill out the internal and common name fields with your selected device name (Fig. 5.32).

Source	Subject	Extensions	Key usage	Netscape	Advanced

Distinguished name

Internal name	IoT_Device	organizationName	Hitex Ltd
countryName	UK	organizationalUnitName	Development
stateOrProvinceName	Warwickshire	commonName	IoT_Device
localityName	Coventry	emailAddress	IoT@hitex.co.uk

FIG. 5.32

Device certificate subject. The device certificate common name is set to IoT_Device.

No permission required.

Here, I have used IoT_Device for the common name.
Select the certificates window (Fig. 5.33).

Internal name	commonName	CA	Serial	Expiry date	CRL Expiration
IoT_CA	IoT_CA	Yes	01	2038-02-06	
IoT_Broker	IoT_Broker	No	02	2028-02-06	
IoT_Device	IoT_Device		03	2028-02-06	

FIG. 5.33

Final certificates. The XCA workspace shows the certificates and their hierarchy.

No permission required.

Now in the certificate window, we can see the certificate hierarchy. The IoT_CA certificate is our "Root of Trust," and it has signed both the broker and the device certificates. If you have the IoT_CA certificate installed, it can be used to check the signature of either the broker or the device certificate and authenticate the data in the certificate.

Select each certificate, right click and select export to file (Fig. 5.34).

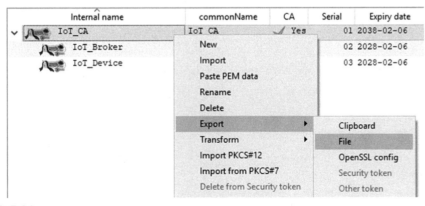

FIG. 5.34

Certificate export. Select a certificate and open the export certificate dialog.

No permission required.

The certificate information is encoded in "Abstract Syntax Notation 1" (ASIN1) using the "Distinguished Encoding Rules" (DER). Here, the heavy lifting is done for us by XCA. When we save the certificate, the binary data is further transformed into a format called "Privacy Enhanced Mail" (PEM), which is base64 encoded binary with a short additional header.

Leave the export format as PEM and press OK (Fig. 5.35).

FIG. 5.35

Certificate export dialog. Expert the certificates in PEM format.

No permission required.

Select the Private Keys dialog.

Now we have three keys stored. We need to export the server and device keys so they can be stored in their respective devices. The certificate authority key must never be exposed outside of the XCA database (Fig. 5.36).

Private Keys	Certificate signing requests	Certificates	Templates	Revocation lists

Internal name	Type	Size	Use	Password
IoT_Broker	RSA	2048 bit	1	Common
IoT_CA	RSA	2048 bit	1	Common
IoT_Device	RSA	2048 bit	1	Common

FIG. 5.36

Certificate keys database. The keys database allows us to manage the private keys.

No permission required.

Select the IoT Server key right click and select export to file and save it in a PEM format. Repeat this for the device key

Now in our certs directory, we should have five files: three certificates and two key files (Fig. 5.37). We will use these certificates for server and device authentication later in this chapter.

IoT_Broker

IoT_Broker

IoT_CA

IoT_Device

IoT_Device

FIG. 5.37

The network credentials. We now have a collection of certificates and private keys.

No permission required.

Certificate and key storage

mbedTLS provides functions to load certificates and keys from static arrays stored in the microcontroller flash memory or from an embedded file system (Table 5.5). The certificates and keys can be stored in DER or PEM format. Keys can be exported and stored in a standard keyfile format that provides password-based encryption with symmetrical ciphers. As we will see in later chapters, the PSA Trusted Firmware creates a Secure Internal Storage volume to hold device secrets. In addition, a Cortex-M33 based microcontroller designed to be an IoT device is likely to provide a key store mechanism, and we will also look at these features in the coming chapters.

Table 5.5 Certificate and key storage.

Function	Description
mbedtls_x509_crt_parse()	Load a certificate from an array
mbedtls_x509_crt_parse_file()	Load a certificate from a filesystem
mbedtls_pk_parse_key()	Load a key from an array with optional password
mbedtls_pk_parse_keyfile()	Load a key from a filesystem stored as a keyfile with optional password

Exercise: Parsing X.509 certificates and keys

Here, we will look at how to load and parse stored certificates within our embedded microcontroller using the standard mbedTLS functions.

Open the pack installer, select project 5.9 and press the Copy button.
Open main.c

As usual, we start by declaring the necessary contexts that we will need in this example.

Here, we have a context for a certificate authority and a client certificate. We also have a public key context to load our private key.

```
mbedtls_x509_crt cacert;
mbedtls_x509_crt clicert;
mbedtls_pk_context pkey;
mbedtls_x509_crt_init( &clicert );
```

We can then parse anX.509 certificate.

```
mbedtls_x509_crt_parse( &clicert,
                (const unsigned char *) mbedtls_test_cli_crt,
                mbedtls_test_cli_crt_len );
```

Since this information is public information, we do not need to store it securely. It can be placed in the microcontroller flash memory as a "C" array.

```
#define TEST_CA_CRT_EC\
"-----BEGIN CERTIFICATE-----\r\n"\
"MIICUjCCAdegAwIBAgIJAMFD4n5iQ8zoMAoGCCqGSM49BAMCMD4xCzAJBgNVB
AYT\r\n"\
"Ak5MMREwDwYDVQQKEwhQb2xhc1NTTDEcMBoGA1UEAxMTUG9sYXJzc2wgVGVzd
CBF\r\n"\

.............................. ..

"uCjn8pwUOkABXK8Mss9OfzCfCEOtIA==\r\n"\
"-----END CERTIFICATE-----\r\n"
```

Alternatively, the certificate can be stored in the embedded file system and loaded from a file.

```
mbedtls_x509_crt_parse_file (&cacert,"iot_ca.crt");
```

Once the certificates are loaded, we can verify the validity of the certificates.

```
ret = mbedtls_x509_crt_verify( &clicert,
                    &cacert,
                    NULL,
                    NULL,
                    &flags,
                    NULL,
                    NULL );
```

Similarly, an RSA private key can be loaded directly from an array stored in flash memory.

```
mbedtls_pk_parse_key( &pkey,
              (const unsigned char *) mbedtls_test_srv_key,
              mbedtls_test_srv_key_len,
              NULL,
              0 );
```

or loaded from a keyfile:

```
int mbedtls_pk_parse_keyfile(&pkey,&keyfile,&password);
```

Once loaded we can test the RSA keys:

```
mbedtls_pk_verify
```

Build the code and start the debugger.

The code will parse the certificates and display their details to the tera term console window.

Putting it all together

Over the last two chapters, we have looked at the essential cryptographic algorithms and the public key infrastructure. We can now look at how to establish a secure communications channel across the internet with the Transport Layer Security (TLS).

The TLS protocol is designed to be encapsulated in Transport Control Protocol packets, which in turn ride inside an Internet Protocol packet to provide a reliable streaming communications channel (Fig. 5.38).

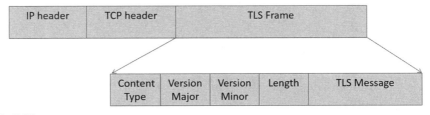

FIG. 5.38

TCP\IP packet structure. The TLS packet rides inside the TCP frame.

No permission required.

The TLS packet consists of the actual message data prefixed by a header that contains the protocol version, the length of the message data in bytes, and the content type, which is a code for the type of TLS packet being sent (Table 5.6).

Table 5.6 TLS content type.

Content type	Type
20	Change cipher spec
21	Alert
22	Handshake
23	Application
24	Heartbeat

When a TLS connection is established, further encrypted packets will be sent in application frames. If there is an error or if the connection needs to be shut down, an Alert frame will be sent. If you are sending infrequent message application packets but need to keep the connection from timing out, it is possible to send a heartbeat frame. When the connection is first negotiated, the server and client exchange a list of available ciphers. During a communication session, it is possible to switch ciphers suites by sending a change cipher spec message. A TLS session will always start with an initial handshake where the client and server authenticate each other and establish a shared secret which can then be used as the basis for a symmetrical encryption key.

The handshake packet has a further code that denotes the handshake content type for each stage of the TLS handshake (Table 5.7).

Table 5.7 Handshake types.

Message type	Description
0	Hello Request
1	Client Hello
2	Server Hello
4	New Session Ticket
11	Certificate
12	Server Key Exchange
13	Certificate Request
14	Server Hello Done
15	Certificate Verify
16	Client Key Exchange
20	Finished

At the start of a TLS session, both the client and server will have the CA certificate. In the case of a system that is setup for server authentication, the server will have its own certificate, which has been signed by the CA, and it will also have its own private key (Fig. 5.39).

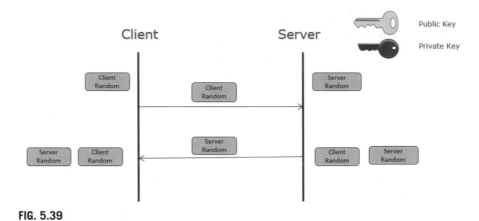

FIG. 5.39

TLS client hello. The TLS handshake starts with a client hello message to the server.

No permission required.

At the start of the TLS handshake, the client will send a client hello message to the server. The client hello message from the client to the server will contain a random number which is sent in plain text along with a session ID, a list of cipher suites, and compression methods. The cipher suites are predefined groups of asymmetrical and symmetrical ciphers along with hash and MAC algorithms. A small sample set of these cipher suites is shown in Table 5.8.

Table 5.8 Cipher suite.

ID	Cipher suite (key exchange, signing, cipher, hash)
0x2F	TLS_ECDHE_RSA_WITH_AES_128_GCM_SHA256
0x30	TLS_ECDHE_RSA_WITH_AES_256_GCM_SHA384
0x67	TLS_DHE_RSA_WITH_AES_128_CBC_SHA256
0x69	TLS_DHE_RSA_WITH_AES_256_CBC_SHA256

The server will reply with its own server hello message that also contains a random number again sent in plain text.

The server will next send its X.509 certificate which can be verified by the client using the public key in the CA certificate (Fig. 5.40).

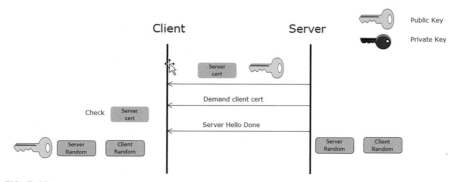

FIG. 5.40

TLS server certificate. The server sends its certificate for verification using the CA certificate stored in the device.

No permission required.

Once the certificate has been validated, it tells the client to authenticate its origin through the certificate common name. In the case of a website, the common name will be a URL that should match the address that the client is expecting to connect to. It is less clear what to use for an IoT device common name. Typical choices are the device IP address or its internal hostname. The certificate also provides the client with the servers' public key.

Next, the client will generate another random number called a premaster secret, and this is again sent to the server, but this time, it is encrypted and hashed using the servers public key (Fig. 5.41).

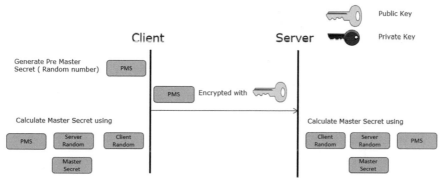

FIG. 5.41

Pre master secret exchange. The device sends an encrypted pre master secret to the server.

No permission required.

Now both the server and client have two agreed random numbers which have been sent in plain text and a further random number that has been exchanged in secret. Using these numbers, we can create a master secret which will be the basis for our symmetrical encryption key. The master secret is derived through a special pseudo-random function (Fig. 5.42).

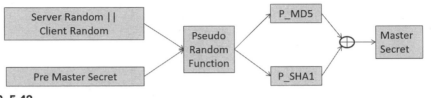

FIG. 5.42

Master secret generation. The random and premaster secrets are used to generate a master secret.

No permission required.

The two plain text random numbers are concatenated together and passed into the pseudo-random function along with the premaster secret. The output value from the pseudo-random function is then hashed using both an MD5 and an SHA-1 hash algorithm. The two message digests are finally added together modulo32 to provide the final master secret.

Once both sides have agreed on a master secret, the client will send a change cipher spec message to select a cipher suite followed by a finish handshake message. The server will reply with a matching change cipher spec and finish message (Fig. 5.43).

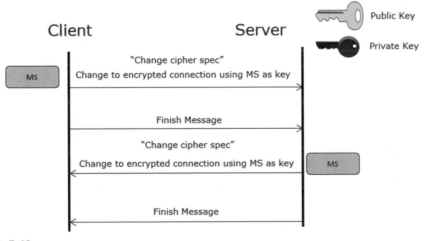

FIG. 5.43

End of the TLS handshake. The TLS handshake ends with a change cipher spec to select the active cipher suite.

No permission required.

Now both sides will switch to encrypted communication using the chosen cipher suite with the master secret as the agreed key. Your session data will be encrypted with a MAC tag and placed in a TLS application frame (Fig. 5.44).

Content Type	Version Major	Version Minor	Length	Application Data	MAC

FIG. 5.44

Encrypted and MACed frame. The master secret is used to encrypt and MAC streaming data.

No permission required.

Now both the server and the client have established a secure communication channel, and all further data packets will be encrypted. If an error occurs, either end can send an alert frame to notify its partner that there is a problem. The alert frame has an alert level field that can be set to a warning level or fatal level and a description field with 31 codes to describe the alert condition (Fig. 5.45). In practice, if an alert frame is sent, the session will usually terminate. An alert frame is also used to end a TLS session.

Content Type - 21	Version Major	Version Minor	Length	Level	Description	MAC

FIG. 5.45

TLS alert frame. A TLS alert frame is used to signal errors and also finish a session.

No permission required.

Establishing a TLS connection

We can create both a server and client with the mbedTLS library. To create a secure server, we first need to declare and initialize contexts for the SSL configuration and the SSL operating layer.

TLS server

```
mbedtls_ssl_context ssl;
mbedtls_ssl_config conf;
mbedtls_ssl_config conf;
mbedtls_ssl_context ssl;
```

We also need to declare and initialize contexts for entropy, random, public key, X509 certificate, and network components in a similar fashion.

At the start of the example code, the server has to load the CA certificate and the servers' certificate. At this point, we could also load a certificate revocation list.

```
mbedtls_x509_crt_parse( &srvcert,
            (const unsigned char *) mbedtls_test_srv_crt,
            mbedtls_test_srv_crt_len );
```

```
mbedtls_x509_crt_parse( &srvcert,
            (const unsigned char *)
            mbedtls_test_cas_pem,
            mbedtls_test_cas_pem);
```

Next we can load the server private key.

```
mbedtls_pk_parse_key( &pkey,
            (const unsigned char *) mbedtls_test_srv_key,
            mbedtls_test_srv_key_len,
            NULL,
            0 );
```

Now we can bind an IP port to the TCP protocol.

```
mbedtls_net_bind( &listen_fd,
            NULL,
                                        "4433",
                                        MBEDTLS_NET_PROTO_TCP ) )
```

Our next step is to setup the ssl-config context with its default settings and to act as a server.

```
mbedtls_ssl_config_defaults( &conf,
                MBEDTLS_SSL_IS_SERVER,
                                        MBEDTLS_SSL_TRANSPORT_STREAM,
                                        MBEDTLS_SSL_PRESET_DEFAULT )
```

Then we can configure and add a random number generator.

```
mbedtls_ctr_drbg_seed( &ctr_drbg, mbedtls_entropy_func,
                &entropy,
                                        (const unsigned char *) pers,
                                        strlen( pers ) ) ) != 0 )
mbedtls_ssl_conf_rng( &conf,
                mbedtls_ctr_drbg_random,
                                        &ctr_drbg );
```

The TLS stack is instrumented to produce debug messages as it executes. The SSL Config context can be passed a user callback function to manage these messages. Normally, it can be written to a debug UART or the ITM, but it is also possible to log the debug data to a file.

```
mbedtls_ssl_conf_dbg( &conf, my_debug, stdout );
```

During runtime, the callback function is passed the debug message, which consists of a debug code, the file, and line of origin and an informational text string.

```
static void my_debug( void *ctx,
            int level,
                                        const char *file,
```

```
                                              int line,
                                              const char *str )
```

There are five levels of debug message and we can dynamically control the message threshold level (Table 5.9).

Table 5.9 Debug message level.

Threshold level	Description
0	None
1	Error
2	State Change
3	Informational
4	Verbose

```
    mbedtls_debug_set_threshold( DEBUG_LEVEL );
```
Next we can add the certificates to the ssl configuration context.
```
    mbedtls_ssl_conf_ca_chain( &conf, srvcert.next, NULL );
```
Once the configuration structure is fully populated we can configure the working ssl context.
```
    mbedtls_ssl_setup( &ssl, &conf );
```
The mbedTLS library can be connected to the underlying transport by defining the send and receive callback functions.

```
    mbedtls_ssl_set_bio( &ssl,
               &client_fd,

                                              mbedtls_net_send,
                                              mbedtls_net_recv,
                                              NULL );
```

Both the send and receive functions are designed to map onto a typical BSD sockets interface.

```
    int mbedtls_net_send( void *ctx,
                   const unsigned

                                              char *buf,
                                              size_t len )
    {
       send (SOCK(ctx), (const char *)buf, len, 0);
    }
    int mbedtls_net_recv (void *ctx,
                   unsigned char *buf,

                                              size_t len)
    {
       recv (SOCK(ctx), (char *)buf, len, 0);
    }
```

Once all this is configured we can accept connections from clients.

```
mbedtls_net_accept( &listen_fd, &client_fd, NULL, 0, NULL );
```

When a client accepts, we can process the TLS handshake to establish a secure connection.

```
mbedtls_ssl_handshake( &ssl )
```

If the handshake is successful, we can now read and write plaintext application packets to and from the TLS library.

```
mbedtls_ssl_write(&ssl, buf, len));
mbedtls_ssl_read(&ssl, buf, len);
```

If an error or other condition causes the server to shutdown, it must release each of the contexts.

```
mbedtls_ssl_free( &ssl );
mbedtls_ssl_config_free( &conf );
```

TLS client

The Client code follows a very similar process, but there are a few key differences. The SSL_configuration context is set to be a client:

```
mbedtls_ssl_config_defaults( &conf,
                    MBEDTLS_SSL_IS_CLIENT,
                                  MBEDTLS_SSL_TRANSPORT_STREAM,
                                  MBEDTLS_SSL_PRESET_DEFAULT ) ;
```

During the SSL configuration, we need to set the authentication mode. This will tell the stack how to proceed if verification of the certificate fails. In the example code, VERIFY_OPTIONAL is used so that we will always establish a connection when using test certificates (Table 5.10).

Table 5.10 Authentication mode.

Authentication mode	Description
MBEDTLS_SSL_VERIFY_NONE	No certificate verification is required
MBEDTLS_SSL_VERIFY_OPTIONAL	Verify the certificate but continue if verification fails
MBEDTLS_SSL_VERIFY_REQUIRED	Verify the certificate and abort if verification fails

```
mbedtls_ssl_conf_authmode( &conf,
              MBEDTLS_SSL_VERIFY_OPTIONAL );
```

We must also set the hostname of the server. This must match the Common Name on the servers X.509 certificate. While the certificate is public information, only the server has the matching private key.

```
mbedtls_ssl_set_hostname( &ssl, "mbed Test Server 1" );
```

Once the SSL context is configured, we can connect to the server and perform the handshake.

```
mbedtls_net_connect( &server_fd,
                SERVER_NAME,
                                            SERVER_PORT,
                                            MBEDTLS_NET_PROTO_TCP );
mbedtls_ssl_handshake( &ssl );
```

Once we have finished the handshake, we can verify the certificate.

```
result = mbedtls_ssl_get_verify_result( &ssl );
```

If everything is OK, we can start to communicate to the server using the same ssl_read and write functions.

When the client has finished its session, we must close the TLS session and then free the contexts.

```
mbedtls_ssl_close_notify( &ssl );
```

Exercise: TLS server authentication

This exercise will configure the evaluation board as a client and use a PC server application based on mbedTLS as the server. This will give us a simple local network that can be used to test and experiment with x.509 certificates and the mbedTLS networking API.

Open the pack installer, select project 5.10 and press the copy button

The exercise directory contains an mbedTLS client project for the LPC55S69 evaluation board. This example uses the mbedTLS test certificates, which are provided as header files. **The certificates will fail verification in a couple of ways which is useful to see.**

Open and build the MDK-Arm project.
Start the debugger and run the code.

When the device connects to the WiFi Network, it will print out its IP address to the console window.

Make a note of the IP address and press the user button to continue.

The debugger console window will show the TLS connection initializing and then waiting for a connection (Fig. 5.46).

```
 . Loading the server cert. and key... ok
 . Bind on https://localhost:4433/ ... ok
 . Seeding the random number generator... ok
 . Setting up the SSL data.... ok
 . Waiting for a remote connection ...
```

FIG. 5.46

Console diagnostic messages. The TLS handshake session will be displayed as diagnostic messages within the tera term console window.

No permission required.

Now start a web browser and connect to the evaluation boards IP address and port 4433 using the following syntaxhttps://192.168.0.10**: 4433**

The HTTPS is important as it tells the browser to establish a secure connection. The browser will report a bad certificate, but you can force it to proceed. It will connect to the evaluation board, and a HTML message will be sent to the browser (Fig. 5.47). The CA certificate has not been installed within the browser, we have just used the browser to show that the certificate is faulty.

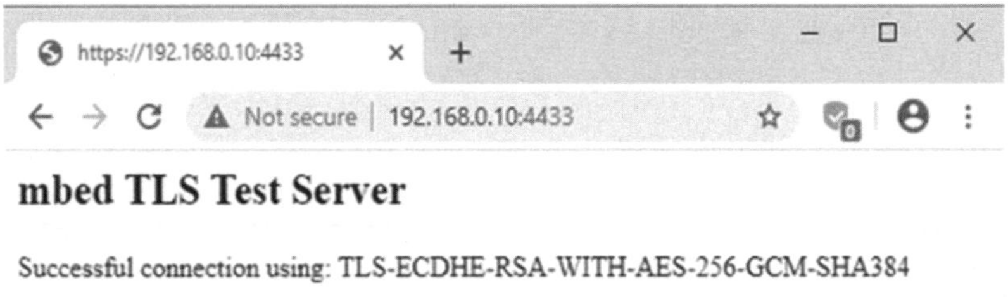

mbed TLS Test Server

Successful connection using: TLS-ECDHE-RSA-WITH-AES-256-GCM-SHA384

FIG. 5.47

Web browser connected to the evaluation board. A web browser will establish a connection to the evaluation board but will encounter some problems.

No permission required.

In Explorer navigate to the project sub directory < project >\PC_Client\ Now start the ssl_client.exe.

This will connect to the same port and display more detailed diagnostic messages.

Again we can see that the certificate has failed. Two reasons are given: first, the Common Name is wrong, and second, the certificate has been signed an unacceptable hash, in this case, a deprecated SHA-1 algorithm was used (Fig. 5.48).

```
. Verifying peer X.509 Certificate... failed
! The certificate common name(CN) does not match the expected CN
! The certificate is signed with an unacceptable hash

>Write to server: 18 bytes written
```

FIG. 5.48

ssl_client console screen. The ssl_client will find the same problems with the X.509 certificate and print diagnostic messages.

No permission required.

If the authentication mode is changed to "verification required" then the communication session would be terminated when the handshake fails.

```
mbedtls_ssl_conf_authmode( &conf,
            MBEDTLS_SSL_VERIFY_REQUIRED);
```

Server and client authentication

So far, we have looked at a standard TLS handshake which is typically used when a web browser establishes a secure connection to a website. This system has the attraction that the client only needs to hold the CA certificate, which is public information and can have a long lifetime. However, for an IoT system, we really need to go a bit further and use a client certificate that will allow the server to authenticate the client. This mutual authentication provides a much higher level of security and can remove the need for a further sign-on password. However, it does mean that the client has to be provisioned with its own individual certificate and private key.

In such a system, the server will demand a client certificate once it has sent its certificate. Once the client has validated the server certificate, it will send its certificate to the server. The server will validate the client certificate and reply with a hash of all the existing handshake messages signed with the client's public key (Fig. 5.49).

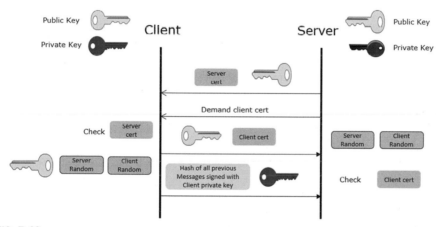

FIG. 5.49

TLS handshake with client certificate. The server can authenticate the client by requesting its certificate.

No permission required.

In our existing server code, we can force the server to authenticate the client by setting an authentication mode:

```
mbedtls_ssl_conf_authmode( &conf,
                 MBEDTLS_SSL_VERIFY_REQUIRED );
```

The server will now request and validate the client certificate as part of the TLS handshake.

On the client side, in addition to the CA certificate, we need to load the client certificate:

```
ret = mbedtls_x509_crt_parse( &clicert,
                  (const unsigned char *) mbedtls_test_cli_crt,
                                  mbedtls_test_cli_crt_len );
```

Along with the client private key which must also be added to the TLS configuration context.

```
ret = mbedtls_pk_parse_key( &pkey,
               (const unsigned char *) mbedtls_test_cli_key,
                                  mbedtls_test_cli_key_len,
                                       NULL,
                                       0 );
ret = mbedtls_ssl_conf_own_cert( &conf, &clicert, &pkey ) ;
```

Exercise: TLS server and client authentication

In this exercise, we will configure our network client and server to perform mutual authentication. The code is basically the same as the last example but has been extended to provision the client with a device certificate and private key. The server is configured to request the device certificate, which will be validated by the servers CA certificate.

In this exercise you can use the certificates created in exercise 5.9 or use the ones provided in the project directories.
Open the pack installer, select project 5.11 and press the copy button.
In explorer navigate to the subdirectory < project >\PC_Server

Copy the CA and broker certificates created in project 5.9 plus the broker private key to the PC_Server directory or use the existing files.

Start the tls_server.exe project.
In explorer navigate to the < project >\Embedded Client\certs.
Copy the IoT_Device.crt certificate and IoT_Device.pem keyfile on to the SD card. Again use the existing files or the ones created in exercise 5.9
Place the SD card back into the Xpresso board.
Open the project in < project >\Embedded Client\project.
Examine main.c
Build the project and download.
Run the code.
Examine the debug console window.

This will establish a secure connection which mutually authenticates both the Server and the Client.

Conclusion

In the last two chapters, we have covered the main encryption algorithms that you are likely to need when developing an IoT device. While the focus here has been on secure communication, the same algorithms are used to provide protection for data at rest and also to sign and verify device images to establish trust in the integrity of a device's firmware. To finish the communication section, the next chapter will introduce protocols and data formats commonly used with IoT devices. We will also look at connecting our device to both a local server and a commercial cloud server.

IoT networking and data formats

6

Introduction

So far, we have looked at establishing a secure communications channel between an embedded device and a server. To build an IoT platform, we need two further things: a communication protocol to transfer data and an encoding format to provide a message schema. This chapter will look at the current dominant communication protocol used by IoT devices. This is the Message Queued Telemetry Protocol (MQTT) originally developed by IBM and now an ISO standard. MQTT has been widely adopted by commercial IoT services to become one of the key protocols used by constrained IoT devices to transfer data to a cloud server and other IoT devices. We will also look at some commonly used data encoding formats that allow you to develop a flexible message schema.

We will begin with a broad overview of the MQTT and then do some hands-on examples to have a deeper look at how the protocol works. Developing network applications can be complicated because many different elements are involved: the embedded node, the communications protocol, and the remote server. It is not always clear why a system is not working or even where the fault lies. It can often feel like debugging squared. Through this chapter, we will build up the system in incremental steps as a way of testing that each additional new layer works. This helps to build confidence in the overall system and makes it easy to trap errors early. In the hands-on exercises, we will start with PC-based tools to send and receive unencrypted messages. We can then add an embedded node and then check this works correctly. To create a fully functional system, we can then add TLS encryption and use the PC client to test our X.509 certificates. This will ensure we have the network credentials correct before adding encryption to the embedded node. By the end of the chapter, we will have set up an IoT system using components on a local network. This can then be used as a platform for future experiments.

Message queued telemetry transport (MQTT)

MQTT is a communications protocol originally developed by IBM that has now been adopted as an ISO/OASIS standard. Currently, MQTT is the most widely used and supported communications protocol for small IoT devices. MQTT is designed to be

Designing Secure IoT Devices with the Arm Platform Security Architecture and Cortex-M33
https://doi.org/10.1016/B978-0-12-821469-5.00008-9

a light-weight protocol for small, constrained devices with a low software footprint. It is widely supported with free-to-use tools and software libraries for both PCs and embedded nodes. MQTT is royalty-free for use within commercial and noncommercial products.

MQTT architecture

The MQTT protocol is a client-server architecture. A typical system will consist of a cloud-based server, which is called a Broker (Fig. 6.1). Each IoT device is a client of the Broker and can send and receive messages to and from the Broker.

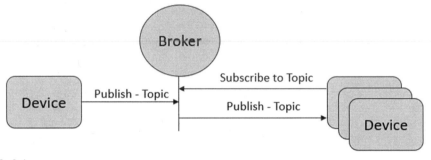

FIG. 6.1

MQTT broker.

No permission required.

MQTT uses a publish and subscribe communications model. Each client can connect to the Broker and subscribe to a particular message known as a Topic. Any client may connect to the Broker and publish new data to any Topic. When the data within a Topic is updated, a message with the new data will be broadcast to any and all clients that are subscribed to that Topic. In this case, clients may be other IoT devices. Additionally, a typical Broker will also provide an HTTPS socket interface for services and REST-based applications. MQTT Brokers are designed to support several thousand IoT devices allowing you to build a large scale system very easily. Most commercial IoT services will support MQTT with regional servers to provide a global network infrastructure.

Message topics

When an MQTT client connects to a Broker, it can publish a message Topic. The Broker does not need to be preconfigured with a list of available Topic messages. A new Topic will automatically be added to the Broker database when first published by a client (Fig. 6.2). A message Topic will also be created if any client subscribes to it and it is not currently in the Broker database.

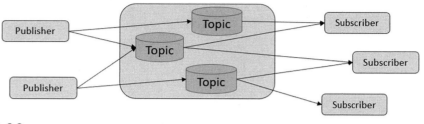

FIG. 6.2

Message broker database. The MQTT Broker maintains a database of topics which can be created on demand.

No permission required.

A Topic consists of a message header followed by the message data. A Topic is a form of addressing that creates a message hierarchy similar to the folder structure within a file system. A typical Topic header is shown below:

weather/uk/cities/london

It is also worth noting that adding a final forward slash creates a different Topic:

weather/uk/cities/london/

Each Topic header is a UTF-8 string that consists of a number of user-defined levels delimited by Topic separators in the form of a forward slash (/). Our message data will then follow the Topic header. The message data can be in any arbitrary format, but it is common to use a standard data interchange format such as JAVA Script Object Notation (JSON) and more recently, Concise Binary Object Representation (CBOR).

Topic subscription

Any client can subscribe to any topic, whether a publishing node has created it or not. If you subscribe to a nonexisting Topic, the Broker will be forced to create it. When a client subscribes to a topic, it is possible to use a range of wildcards to receive groups of messages. The hash (#) character can be used to receive all messages below the topic level elements in the header.

Weather/uk/#will receive all weather messages for UK locations.
We can also use the plus character (+) to substitute for any name in a given topic level.
Weather/+/cities/+ would subscribe to all countries and all cities.

Quality of service

Each message Topic will also be assigned Quality of Service (QoS). The QoS defines the delivery effort between the client and the Broker. The MQTT protocol defines three QoS levels. Level zero relies on the network transport layer to make a best-effort attempt to deliver the message but does not guarantee that it will be delivered. If you select QoS level one, the MQTT protocol does guarantee delivery, but the message may be received more than once, while QoS level two guarantees that a message will be delivered exactly once with no duplicates (Table 6.1).

Table 6.1 Quality of service levels.

QoS level	Message delivery	Delivery semantics	Delivery guarantees
0	≤ 1	At most once	Best effort. No guarantee
1	≥ 1	At least once	Guarantees delivery. Duplicates possible
2	$= 1$	Exactly once	Guarantees delivery. No duplicates

When you are defining message QoS Levels, it is important to realize that the QoS Level is defined by both the publishing client and the subscribing client (Fig. 6.3).

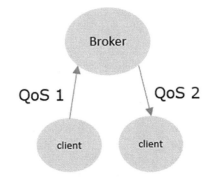

FIG. 6.3

Quality of service.

No permission required.

Thus a client could publish a message at QoS Level 1 where a message may be delivered to the Broker with possible duplicates. A separate client could subscribe to the same Topic with a QoS Level 2 and expect a single update without duplicated messages.

Retained topics

It is also possible for a client to publish a message topic to the Broker and define it as a "retained message." This will cause the Broker to store the message along with its QoS. When a new client subscribes to the message topic or an existing subscribed client reconnects to the Broker, the stored message will be immediately sent to the subscribing client. This is very useful when communicating with low power nodes that may frequently connect and disconnect to a network.

Heartbeat

When a client connects to a server, it defines a "keep-alive period" in seconds. Then during normal operation, the client must send at least one message during the keep-alive period. If the node is a subscriber-only, it must send a PINGREQ message and receive a PINGACK back from the Broker. If the Broker does not receive any communication from a client in one and a half times the keep-alive period, it must disconnect the client. Similarly, the client must disconnect from the Broker if it does not receive any messages and the keep-alive period is exceeded.

Last will and testament

When a client connects to a Broker it can publish a "last will and testament" message. This is a normal MQTT message that any other client can subscribe to. However, the published message is stored until the Broker determines that it has lost communication with the client. When this happens the last will and testament message will be sent to all the subscribed clients. The Broker will determine it has lost communication with the client if the keep-alive period is exceeded and it has not received a disconnect message.

Methods

The MQTT protocol is encapsulated within a network transport. This is normally a TCP message which provides for guaranteed delivery. Since the MQTT protocol is designed to support resource constrained devices, a relatively small number of methods support the connect/disconnect, publish, and subscribe model (Table 6.2).

Table 6.2 MQTT methods.

MQTT message	4 bit code	Description
CONNECT	1	Client request to connect to server
CONNACK	2	Connect acknowledge
PUBLISH	3	Publish message
PUBACK	4	Publish acknowledge
PUBREC	5	Publish received (Assured delivery part 1)
PUBREL	6	Publish received (Assured delivery part 2)
PUBCOMP	7	Publish complete
SUBSCRIBE	8	Client subscribe request
SUBACK	9	Unsubscribe acknowledge
UNSUBSCRIBE	10	Client unsubscribe request
UNSUBACK	11	Unsubscribe acknowledge
PINGREC	12	PING request
PINGRESP	13	PING response
DISCONNECT	14	Client disconnect

Exercise: PC broker and client

In this section, we will install an MQTT Broker on a development PC along with a test client. We can then check both the Broker and client's operation before we move to design an embedded node. This also allows us to generate and test X.509 certificates before using them with an IoT device. We will use the popular Eclipse Mosquitto Broker and a widely used client called MQTT.fx for these examples.

Download both applications from the links in Table 6.3.

Table 6.3 MQTT applications.

Application	URL	Description
Mosquitto	https://mosquitto.org/download/	MQTT broker
MQTT.fx	http://mqttfx.jensd.de/index.php/download	MQTT PC client

Installing the Mosquitto Broker

This tutorial assumes you have installed the Mosquitto Broker as a window service by following the default installation settings. Depending on the version of the Mosquitto server, you may also need to install OpenSSL for supporting dll files.

In the pack installer copy Exercise 6.1.

This exercise contains an embedded MQTT project that we will use in the next section along with a directory called utilities, which contains some X.509 certificates and a configuration file for the Mosquitto broker.

Copy the mosquitto.conf file to c:\program files(x86)\mosquitto directory. Copy the certificates from the utilities folder to a new folder c:\certs or use the certificates created in Exercise 5.8

You must use the c:\certs directory or change the paths in the Mosquitto configuration file.

In the windows search box type services and open the services control app (Fig. 6.4).

FIG. 6.4

Windows services. Launch windows services.

No permission required.

Locate the Mosquitto service and restart it to load the new configuration file.

If the Mosquitto Broker does not restart it will most likely be an error in the configuration file, probably failing to load the certificates (Fig. 6.5).

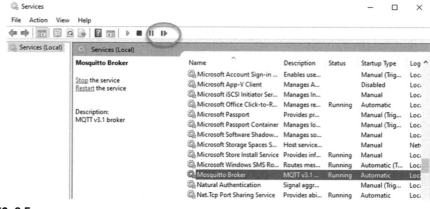

FIG. 6.5

Windows services panel. Restarting the broker in the windows services panel

No permission required.

This configuration file will enable three ports on the server, which we can use for testing (Table 6.4).

Table 6.4 Mosquitto MQTT ports.

Port	Service
1883	MQTT unencrypted communication
8883	MQTT with TLS protocol. Broker authentication
8884	MQTT with TLS protocol. Broker and device authentication

Once the Mosquitto Broker is running with the new configuration file, we can connect to it with the MQTT.fx client.

Start MQTT.fx
Select and press the paper sheet icon (1) on the far left side (Fig. 6.6).

FIG. 6.6

Create a new connection. Create a new connection using the default setup.

No permission required.

This will set the broker address as the local host (127.0.0.1) and the plain text port (1883).

The settings button (2) will allow you to define your own profile.

Next press the Connect button (Fig. 6.7).

FIG. 6.7

Connect to the local broker. Connect to the local broker.

No permission required.

This will connect you to the Broker. When this happens, the gray circle (3) will turn green to show the connection and an open padlock will show that the connection is unencrypted.

Next we can subscribe to a Topic. This can be "made up" as we do not need to do any configuration within the Broker (Fig. 6.8).

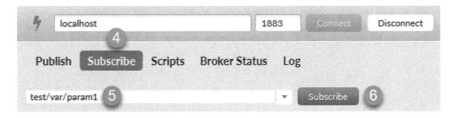

FIG. 6.8

MQTT.fx topic subscription. Once we have connected, it is possible to subscribe to an arbitrary topic.

No permission required.

Select the Subscribe menu (4).
Enter a Topic (5) and press the second Subscribe button (6).

Here, I have used test/var/param1 but you could use anything, just avoid a slash at the start or end of the topic.

Now select the Publish menu (7) (Fig. 6.9).

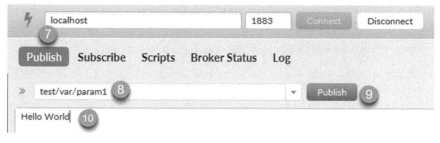

FIG. 6.9

MQTT.fx publish. Publish a topic with MQTT.fx.

No permission required.

Add the same Topic string (8).
Enter a message in the payload box (9) and then press Publish (10).

This will publish the message to the Broker where it will be echoed to any client which has subscribed to the same Topic (Fig. 6.10).

FIG. 6.10

MQTT subscribed messages.

No permission required.

Now that we have a working broker and client, we can add an MQTT client to our WiFi example and connect to the local broker. The Keil pack system provides a set of cloud connectors for commercial IoT cloud systems, including a plain MQTT broker.

The MQTT Paho client is part of the eclipse project and is designed to integrate to any network stack that provides a socket-type interface.

Exercise: Embedded MQTT client

In this example, we will connect an embedded client to our local Mosquitto client running on your PC and then to a cloud server. For the local connection, you will need to create a rule or exception within your PC firewall to allow a remote client to connect.

Open the microVision project that was copied in Example 6.1

This is a multiproject workspace. The exercise project is our WiFi example and the second project is a working solution.

Now add the Paho MQTT client using the microVision RTE.

Open the RTE and select the following components:
IoT Client::MQTTClient-C
IoT Utility::MQTTPacket
SocketAPI::WiFi (Fig. 6.11)

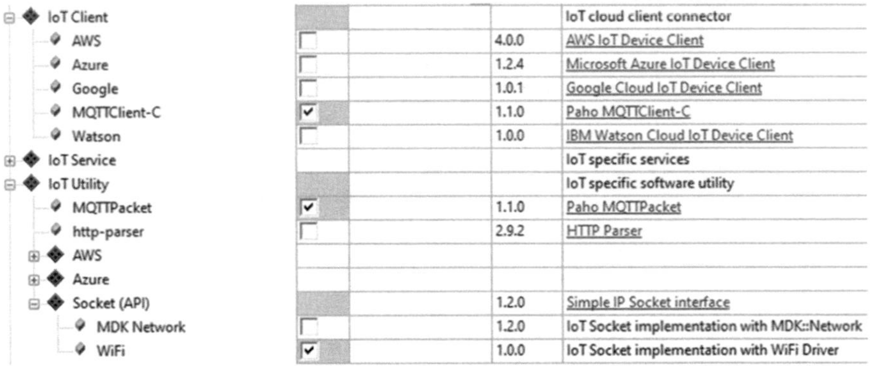

⊟ ◆ IoT Client				IoT cloud client connector
— ◊ AWS	☐		4.0.0	AWS IoT Device Client
— ◊ Azure	☐		1.2.4	Microsoft Azure IoT Device Client
— ◊ Google	☐		1.0.1	Google Cloud IoT Device Client
— ◊ MQTTClient-C	☑		1.1.0	Paho MQTTClient-C
— ◊ Watson	☐		1.0.0	IBM Watson Cloud IoT Device Client
⊞ ◆ IoT Service				IoT specific services
⊟ ◆ IoT Utility				IoT specific software utility
— ◊ MQTTPacket	☑		1.1.0	Paho MQTTPacket
— ◊ http-parser	☐		2.9.2	HTTP Parser
⊞ ◆ AWS				
⊞ ◆ Azure				
⊟ ◆ Socket (API)			1.2.0	Simple IP Socket interface
— ◊ MDK Network	☐		1.2.0	IoT Socket implementation with MDK::Network
— ◊ WiFi	☑		1.0.0	IoT Socket implementation with WiFi Driver

FIG. 6.11

Add an MQTT client via the RTE. Add the Paho MQTT client and packet via the RTE.

No permission required.

Click OK to add the files to the project.
In socket_startup.c, **update the code to set the SSID name for your network and its password.**

```
#define SSID""
#define PASSWORD ""
#define SECURITY_TYPE ARM_WIFI_SECURITY_WPA2
```

Once the device is connected to the WiFi network, it will invoke a function called MQTTEcho_Test(). This code is provided as a standard template.

Select the source Group 1 folder, right click and select Add New.
Select user code template/IoT Client::MQTT Echo (Fig. 6.12).

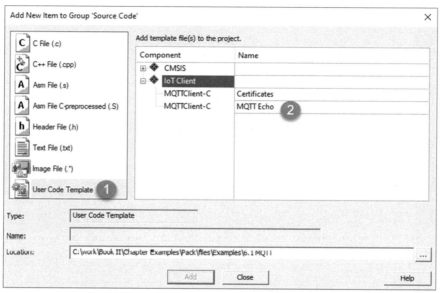

FIG. 6.12

Echo client template. Add the echo client template.

Now click Add.

As its name implies, this will add example code to add a simple echo test similar to the one we just performed with the PC client.

Open MQTT_Echo.c.
Go to line 11 and change the server name to the IP address of your PC.

```
//#define SERVER_NAME "mqtt.eclipse.org"
#define SERVER_NAME "192.168.0.127"
```

The address mqtt.eclipse.org is the address of a public test server.

Once we have tested a local connection to the PC, we can set the server address to use the eclipse server and test against a public cloud server:

```
#define SERVER_PORT 1883
MQTTClient client;
Network network;
MQTTPacket_connectData connectData = MQTTPacket_connectData_initializer;
NetworkInit(&network);
MQTTClientInit(&client, &network, 30000, sendbuf, sizeof(sendbuf),
             readbuf, sizeof(readbuf));
```

```
NetworkConnect(&network, SERVER_NAME, SERVER_PORT);
connectData.MQTTVersion = 3;
connectData.clientID.cstring = "MDK_sample";
MQTTConnect(&client, &connectData);
```

Once a WiFi connection is established, the echo code will create a network and client instance and then connect to the Broker using the unencrypted port 1883.

Once connected, it will subscribe to a collection of topics using the # wildcard.

The subscription function defines a callback function *void messageArrived (MessageData* data)* which will be triggered when a matching message is received:

```
MQTTSubscribe(&client, "MDK/sample/#", QOS2, messageArrived);
```

The messageArrived callback function is passed a pointer to a message data structure:

```
typedef struct MessageData
{
  MQTTMessage* message;
  MQTTString* topicName;
} MessageData;
```

This in turn contains structures for the message topic and the message payload:

```
typedef struct MQTTMessage
{
  enum QoS qos;
  unsigned char retained;
  unsigned char dup;
  unsigned short id;
  void *payload;
  size_t payloadlen;
} MQTTMessage;

  typedef struct
{
  char* cstring;
  MQTTLenString lenstring;
} MQTTString;
```

Once we have subscribed to the message topics, we can create a message payload: MQTTMessage message;

```
char payload[30];
message.qos = QOS1;
message.retained = 0;
message.payload = payload;
message.payloadlen = strlen(payload);
```

And then publish the message as the Topic "MDK/sample/a"

```
MQTTPublish(&client, "MDK/sample/a", &message);
```

The example code publishes ten messages and then disconnects. We can provide a delay between each message by using a dedicated delay function provided by the MQTT client function:

```
MQTTYield(&client, 1000);
```

Unlike an osDelay function this will suspend the thread for 1000 mSec while still allowing for MQTT messages to be received.

When all of the messages have been published, we will disconnect from the Broker and network:

```
NetworkDisconnect(&network);
```

Start the MQTT.fx client connect to the Broker as before.
Subscribe to MDK/samplc/#.
Build the project and start the debugger.
Start Tera Term and connect to the virtual serial port.
Run the code.

You should see the arrival of each message in the debugger and the MQTT.fx client (Fig. 6.13).

```
onnecting to WiFi ...
WiFi network connection succeeded!
MQTT Connected
Message arrived on topic MDK/sample/a: message number 1
Message arrived on topic MDK/sample/a: message number 2
Message arrived on topic MDK/sample/a: message number 3
Message arrived on topic MDK/sample/a: message number 4
Message arrived on topic MDK/sample/a: message number 5
Message arrived on topic MDK/sample/a: message number 6
Message arrived on topic MDK/sample/a: message number 7
Message arrived on topic MDK/sample/a: message number 8
Message arrived on topic MDK/sample/a: message number 9
Message arrived on topic MDK/sample/a: message number 10
MQTT Disconnected
```

FIG. 6.13

MQTT session progress.

No permission required.

If not check your PC firewall settings.

Retained messages

When we publish a message, it is possible to set the retained option. This will keep the last topic payload within the Broker. When a client subscribes to the topic, the retained payload will immediately be sent.

Disconnect the MQTT.fx client from the Broker.
Go to line 70 in mqtt_echo.c and set the retained value.

```
message.retained = 1;
```

Build the code.
Start the debugger and run the code.
Wait until the embedded client has sent the messages and disconnected.
Now connect the MQTT.fx client and subscribe to MDK/sample/#.

You will be immediately sent the last message published to this Topic (Fig. 6.14).

FIG. 6.14

The retained message is sent when a new client is connected.

No permission required.

Connection object

When we established a connection to the Broker the connection parameters were passed in the variable connectData which was initialized with its default settings.

```
MQTTPacket_connectData connectData = MQTTPacket_connectData_initializer;
```

MQTTPacket_connectData is a structure that contains the elements shown in Table 6.5.

Keep alive interval

The connection object allows us to set a keep-alive interval in seconds. The client must send a message to the Broker within one and a half times this period, or the Broker will disconnect the client. If the client does not have a valid message to send, it can send a PINGREQ message to the Broker. In this case, the client should monitor the Broker's PINGRESP reply. If this does not arrive in a timely fashion, the client

Table 6.5 Connection object.

Variable	Type	Description
struct_id[4]	char	Must be set to M,Q,T,C
struct_version	int	Version of this structure. Must be "0"
MQTTVersion	unsigned char	Version of MQTT to be used. 3 = 3.1 4 = 3.1.1
clientID	MQTT string	A custom ASCII string for your device
keepAliveInterval	unsigned short	Keep alive interval in seconds
Cleansession	unsigned char	A no persistent connection where no subscriptions are stored
willFlag	unsigned char	Last will and testament available
Will	MQTTPacket_willOptions	Last will and testament message
username	MQTTString	Broker user name if required
password	MQTTString	Broker password if required

should disconnect from the network. This mechanism can be disabled if the keep-alive interval is set to zero. If the keep-alive interval is enabled, it can be used in conjunction with the client last will and testament.

Last will and testament

When we connect to a server it is possible to define the Last Will and Testament (LWT) of a client device.

This message will be sent to all clients that are subscribed to the LWT topic if the publishing client does not disconnect gracefully. For example, it may run out of battery power and shutdown without performing a network disconnect. This will leave the Broker connection open, but the keep-alive will fail. If this or a similar failure occurs, the Broker will send the LWT message.

We can define a LWT message in the connection object. The will value should be set to logic "1," and the message can be defined in the "will" object (Table 6.6).

Table 6.6 Last will and testament object.

Variable	Type	Description
struct_id	Char	Eyecatcher string "WQCT"
struct_version	Int	Structure version
topicName	MQTTString	Topic to use for LWT message
Message	MQTTString	LWT message data
Retained	unsigned char	Set to "1" if message is retained
QoS	unsigned char	Set required QoS

Enter the following code on line 12 of mqtt_echo.c after the definition of connectData.
MQTTPacket_connectData connectData = MQTTPacket_connectData_initializer;

```
connectData.keepAliveInterval = 10;
connectData.willFlag = 1;
MQTTString topic = MQTTString_initializer;
topic.cstring = "MDK/LWT";
connectData.will.topicName = topic;
MQTTString message = MQTTString_initializer;
message.cstring = "Bye";
connectData.will.message = message;
```

Build the code and start the debugger.
Set a breakpoint on the MQTTYeild() function line 78 of MQTTEcho.c (Fig. 6.15).

```
76
77 ⊟#if !defined(MQTT_TASK)
78 |     if ((rc = MQTTYield(&client, 1000)) != 0)
79         printf("Return code from yield is %d\n", rc);
80 ⊦#endif
81     }
```

FIG. 6.15

MQTTYeild() breakpoint. Set a breakpoint on the MQTTyeild().

No permission required.

Connect the MQTT.fx client and subscribe to MDK/LWT.
Run the embedded code.

The client will connect to the Broker and define the LWT and a keep-alive interval of ten seconds. It will then subscribe and publish a message as before. When it hits the breakpoint, no further messages will be sent. When one and a half times the keep-alive interval (fifteen seconds) has passed, the LWT will be sent to the subscribed client.

Remove the breakpoint.
Reset the embedded client and run again.

This time the code runs to completion and the LWT message is sent when the net-workDisconnect function is called. We have disconnected from the network without disconnecting from the Broker.
Add the following line of code before the networkDisconnect function.

```
MQTTDisconnect(&client);
NetworkDisconnect(&network);
```

Rebuild the code and run again.
This time the embedded code will run to completion without sending the LWT. In this example, we have added an MQTT client, connected to a Broker and been able to publish and subscribe to MQTT messages. We have also explored the keep-alive interval and the LWT message. However, all of this communication has been in plain text. In the next section, we will look at how to add the TLS protocol.

Exercise: TLS encryption

We are going to add the TLS security in two stages. First, we will set up a system that authenticates the server but let any client connect. Next, we will set up the TSL security to authenticate both the server and client.

In the Mosquitto program directory, locate and open the mosquitto.conf file.

The configuration file allows you to define multiple active MQTT ports. Each port is defined as a listener.

Our first encrypted port is defined in the Broker configuration file as port 8883, and this is the default setting in the mosquitto config file.

```
listener 8883
```

In the security section we define the CA certificate, the Broker certificate and the Broker private key.

```
cafile C:\certs\iot_ca.crt
# Path to the PEM encoded server certificate.
certfile C:\certs\iot_broker.crt
# Path to the PEM encoded keyfile.
keyfile C:\certs\iot_broker.pcm
```

We can first test that the certificates are setup correctly with the MQTT.fx client.

Start the MQTT.fx client.
Make sure the connection list view is selected (1).
Now press the settings icon (2).
Now configure the TLS settings (Fig. 6.16).

FIG. 6.16

MQTT.fx TSL settings. Set a connection profile in MQTT.fx and enable the TLS support.

Set the profile name to localTLS.
Enter your PC IP address (or use localhost).
Set the Broker port to 8883.
Next select the SSL/TLS menu.
Select CA certificate file and select the IoT_CA.crt.
Then press OK to accept the settings.
In the main dialog select the localTLS profile and press connect.

This should now negotiate a secure connection to the Broker.

You can further test the connection by subscribing and publishing Topics as before.

Now that we have established that the secure port on the Broker is working and the CA certificate is correct we can add the mbedTLS library to the embedded client and establish a secure embedded connection.

In the pack installer copy project 6.2.
This is a multiproject workspace with a working project and a reference project.
Set the working project as the active project.
Open the RTE and add the Security/mbedTLS component (Fig. 6.17).

FIG. 6.17

Add the mbedTLS library using the RTE.

No permission required.

In the project directory there is a preconfigured version of the mbedTLS_Conf.h file. This is setup with the necessary options for the TLS protocol.

Copy this file to the < project >/RTE/security folder.

The mqtt_echo.c template code is designed to support a secure connection if the following define is declared at a project level.

```
#define MQTT_MBEDTLS
```

Open the option for target/C/C++ tab and enter the define (Fig. 6.18).

The define will cause the embedded client to connect to the encrypted port with a secure version of the network connect function:

```
#define SERVER_PORT 8883
NetworkConnectTLS(&network, SERVER_NAME, SERVER_PORT, &tlscert)
```

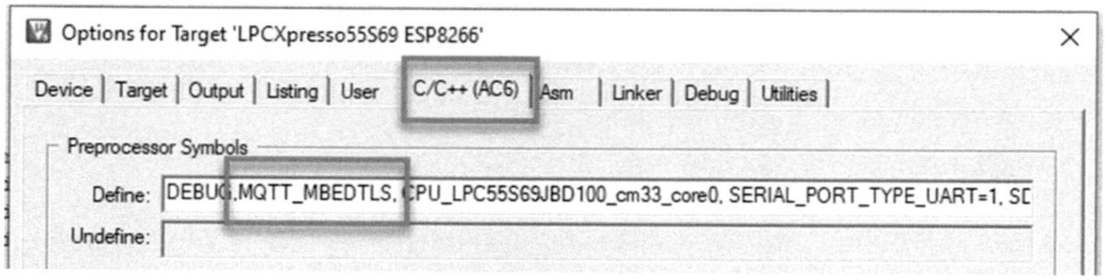

FIG. 6.18

Enable encrypted communication by setting the mbedTLS #define.

Here, we need to provide the Certificate Authority certificate, the default is an array called tlscert[].

```
#if (MQTT_MBEDTLS != 0)
#include "certificates.h"
#endif
```

A template header file is provided for you to add the Broker CA cert. In this example, a preconfigured version is located in the project directory:

Open the certificates.h file in the project directory.

The Broker CA certificate is held in const char array and formatted as shown below:

```
static const char CA_Cert[] =
"-----BEGIN CERTIFICATE-----\n"
"MIIE1DCCA3ygAwIBAgIBAIANBgkqhkiG9w0BAQsFADCBkjELMAkGA1UEBhMCVUsx" \
...............
"1Do2MazGz+kKBHKdOYtsWaOxVhLOkOjS\n" \
"-----END CERTIFICATE-----\n" \
;
```

Build the project.
Start the debugger and run the code.

The embedded client will now connect to the encrypted TLS port and send the same set of MQTT messages, but this time they will be sent over an encrypted channel.

In this example, we are authenticating the server and allowing any client to connect. The Broker has an additional listening channel on port 8884. This port has the same security options as 8883, but we have enabled the additional option "requires_certificate true." The security settings in the Mosquitto configuration file are as follows:

```
cafile C:\certs\iot_ca.crt
certfile C:\certs\iot_broker.crt
keyfile C:\certs\iot_broker.pem
require_certificate true
```

This will force the Broker to authenticate the client. As before we can test the certificates in mqtt.fx by configuring a new profile for client authentication:

Start MQTT.fx and open the settings dialog.
Create a new profile as before.
This time use the port number to 8884.
In the TLS menu, add the certificates and device private key in the self-signed certificates section (Fig. 6.19).

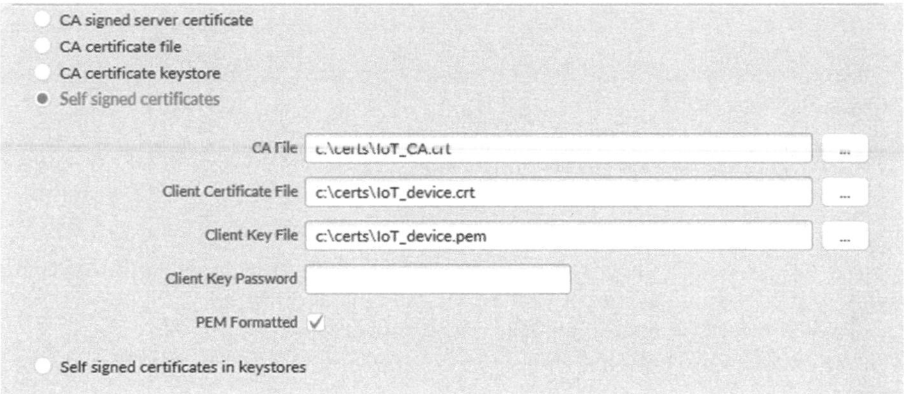

○ CA signed server certificate
○ CA certificate file
○ CA certificate keystore
● Self signed certificates

CA File	c:\certs\IoT_CA.crt
Client Certificate File	c:\certs\IoT_device.crt
Client Key File	c:\certs\IoT_device.pem
Client Key Password	
PEM Formatted	✓

○ Self signed certificates in keystores

FIG. 6.19

MQTT.fx client server authentication.

No permission required.

Click OK to save the profile.
In the main dialog click connect.

This will now establish a secure connection which authenticates both the client and Broker.

Open the embedded client example.

The certificate.h is preconfigured with the client certificate and key.
These are defined in two additional arrays:

```
static const char ClientCert[];
static const char ClientKey[];
```

Open mqtt_echo.c

We need first switch the port to 8884 so we connect to the mutual authentication port:

```
Line 14#define SERVER_PORT 8884
```

And then provide the additional certificate and key.

```
Line 30 TLScert tlscert = {(char *)CA_Cert,
                           (char *) ClientCert,
                           (char *) ClientKey};
```

Rebuild the project.
Start the debugger and run the code.

This will now establish mutually authenticated secure connection with the Broker and allow us to transfer data between the IoT device and the Broker.

Data formats

So far, we have used ASCII stings as the payload within our MQTT message. In a practical system, we will need to exchange more complex data between IoT devices and the Broker. This is often done by creating a protocol schema that defines the content and representation of the payload data to be transferred. Both ends of the communication pipe have to agree and implement this protocol. Any changes or extensions to the message must be carefully managed to prevent breaking the schema. However, there are a couple of widely used data interchange formats that make this process much easier and have parser components that are available for a wide range of platforms and programming languages. The two formats that we will look at in this section are JavaScript Object Notation (JSON) and Concise Binary Object Representation (CBOR).

JavaScript Object Notation

Put simply, JSON is a syntax for storing and exchanging data between different computing systems. There are three big advantages to using JSON. First, it is easy to adopt and use. Second, JSON is text-based, making it human-readable and intuitive to understand. Third, it is schema-less, in that the parser will format the message as a set of labels and data which the receiver can interpret without a detailed knowledge of the message structure. This allows you to develop reliable communication packets where the content is evolving over time. The JSON format has achieved widespread adoption, particularly in IoT networks and system configuration files.

JSON object

A JSON object is an ASCII string enclosed by curly braces and contains a set of key/value pairs. A key is a label for the following data. It is encoded as an ASCII string enclosed by double-quotes. There are various data types that can be used as values and we will look at these below but for example, a quote enclosed string is a valid value, an example is shown below:

{"key_0": "value_0"}

Table 6.7 JSON data types.

Type	Description	
String	Unicode characters enclosed by double quotes (")	"location" : "office",
Number	Double precision floating point in Java Script format	"number" : 210.3,
Boolean	True or false	"alarm" : true ,
Null	No value to assign	"zone" : null,
Object	An unordered set of name value pairs	{ "temperature" : 20, "humidity" : 40, }
Array	An ordered collection of values	record : ["1","2","3"],

We can add other key value pairs by using a comma (,) as a delimiter.

The following data types are available within a JSON Object (Table 6.7).

Exercise: JSON encoding

This example will encode and decode some sample data into a JSON string and send this as the payload of our MQTT message. As we are subscribed to the same message, we can receive and decode the JSON data back to usable variables.

In the pack installer copy project 6.3.

Open the RTE and select the Data exchange:JSON::cJSON component.

cJSON is a lightweight JSON parser that can be used to encode and decode JSON objects.

Open the json_test.c file.

This module contains functions to serialize and deserialize some example application data.

The serialize function first creates some dummy data values for typical process values of temperature, pressure and humidity. We then create the JSON object and JSON variables for each data value. The cJSON type is a structure with elements to store each JSON type and a linked list to chain successive elements together. We also create a char pointer, which is used to store the resulting JSON serialized string:

```
char *serialize() {
int temperature = 23, pressure = 1000, humidity = 40;
cJSON *Jobject, *Jtemperature, *Jpressure, *Jhumidity ;
static char *J_string = NULL;
................
```

Next we can create the JSON object then create and initialize each JSON value:

```
Jobject = cJSON_CreateObject();
Jtemperature = cJSON_CreateNumber(temperature);
Jpressure = cJSON_CreateNumber(pressure);
Jhumidity = cJSON_CreateNumber(humidity);
```

Then we can assemble the JSON object and serialize it to the string:

```
cJSON_AddItemToObject(Jobject, "temperature", Jtemperature);
cJSON_AddItemToObject(Jobject, "pressure", Jpressure);
cJSON_AddItemToObject(Jobject, "humidity", Jhumidity);
J_string = cJSON_PrintUnformatted(Jobject);
cJSON_Delete(Jobject);
```

The function returns the formatted string, which is used as the payload for the MQTT message.

Run the code so that it sends the formatted message.
Observe the received message in MQTT.fx.

We can now deserialize the string back to usable data.

In the deserialize function, we create a JSON object and then parse the received string to a JSON object.

```
int deserialize(const char * const Jstring){
const cJSON *jnum = NULL;
cJSON *Jobject = cJSON_Parse(Jstring);
```

We can then extract the value for each element into a cJSON number:

```
jnum = cJSON_GetObjectItemCaseSensitive(Jobject, "temperature");
```

We can then test for the type of data and if a value is present. If all is good we can extract the value into a variable:

```
if (cJSON_IsNumber(jnum) && (jnum->valueint != NULL))
    printf("Temperature - %i\n", jnum->valueint);
```

JSON arrays

JSON also allows us to declare arrays of JSON types. An array obeys the same rules as a key value pair while the value is a collection of comma delimited JSON types enclosed by square brackets:

```
{"locations":[ "office", "Meeting_1", "Kitchen" ]}
```

We can extend our serialize() function to add an array.
Uncomment the function JSON_ARRAY()
This function contains code to create and populate a JSON array:

```
cJSON *Jarray = cJSON_CreateArray();
cJSON_AddItemToObject(Jobject, "Locations", Jarray);
```

Next we can create some JSON values:

```
cJSON *location_0 = cJSON_CreateString("Office");
cJSON *location_1= cJSON_CreateString("Meeting_1");
```

```
cJSON *location_2 = cJSON_CreateString("Kitchen");
```

and then add them to the array:

```
cJSON_AddItemToArray(Jarray, location_0);
cJSON_AddItemToArray(Jarray, location_1);
cJSON_AddItemToArray(Jarray, location_2);
```

In the deserialize function, we can create cJSON variables for the JSON array and the locations:

```
cJSON *Jarray, *location[3];
int index;
```

We can now load read the JSON array within the JSON object and then loop through the stored values and extract the location strings:

```
Jarray = cJSON_GetObjectItemCaseSensitive(Jobject,
                                          "Locations");

for(index = 0; index < 3; index++) {
   location[index] = cJSON_GetArrayItem(Jarray,index);
    if (!cJSON_IsString(location[index]) ||
        location[index]->valuestring != NULL)
         printf("Location - %s\n", location[index]->valuestring);
    }
```

Rebuild and rerun the code.

You can observe the received message in mqtt.fx and the decoded values in the debugger console window.

Nested JSON objects

It is also possible to have a JSON object within a JSON object. This follows the same rules as a key-value pair, but the value is a self-contained JSON object. While this may look a bit like an array, we are storing key: value pairs. This allows us to search within a secondary JSON object without having to know much about its actual structure. In a real-world system, this becomes a powerful technique.

```
{"office":{ "temperature":23, "pressure":1000, "humidity":40}}
```

In the code uncomment the function Nested_JSON_Object();

We create our JSON object as before and then add a further JSON object:

```
Jsub_object = cJSON_CreateObject();
cJSON_AddItemToObject(Jobject, "office", Jsub_object);
```

We can then populate the nested object with key/value pairs:

```
cJSON_AddItemToObject(Jsub_object, "temperature", Jtemperature);
cJSON_AddItemToObject(Jsub_object, "pressure", Jpressure);
cJSON_AddItemToObject(Jsub_object, "humidity", Jhumidity);
```

if we receive a nested object it is possible to search for the sub object and then extract values from it:

```
Jsub_object = cJSON_GetObjectItemCaseSensitive(Jobject, "office");
cJSON *Jtemp = cJSON_GetObjectItemCaseSensitive(Jsub_object,
                                                "temperature");
if (cJSON_IsNumber(Jtemp) && (Jtemp->valueint != NULL)){
    printf("Office Temperature - %i\n", Jtemp->valueint);
}
```

Rebuild and rerun the code.

You can observe the received message in mqtt.fx and the decoded values in the debugger console window.

Concise binary object representation

While JSON is widely used to encode IoT data, it is designed to transport values encoded as ASCII strings. In many cases, we want to transport large amounts of binary data such as encryption keys and even firmware updates. The only way to do this with JSON is to base 64 encode the data. This significantly increases the complexity and bulk of our data packets. To efficiently transfer data in a binary encoded form, we can use a different encoding format called Concise Binary Object Representation (CBOR). While there are other encoding schemes available such as ASIN.1, BSON and Message Pack, CBOR is becoming more widely used for IoT because a typical encoder/decoder requires minimal resources so that it will run on very limited devices. CBOR is also based on the JSON data model and like JSON, you can easily adapt and extend the message schema without risking breaking the whole communication scheme.

There are a number of open-source CBOR encoders available. The one currently used as part of the Platform Security Architecture firmware is QCBOR. This implementation is optimized for speed and code size.

The CBOR data format describes how to encode different data types as a serialized byte string. Each data item is preceded by a header byte which defines the encoded data type (Fig. 6.20).

The header byte is split into two fields the top three bits is the major type field while the lower five bits is the additional information field.

The major type field describes the data item following the header byte. The current CBOR standard defines seven data types which are encoded as follows (Table 6.8).

Each data type will use the additional information field to fully describe the data item while the data value is held in adjacent bytes (Table 6.9).

FIG. 6.20

CBOR header. The CBOR header byte is divided into type and additional fields.

No permission required.

Table 6.8 CBOR major types.

CBOR major type	Encoded value
0	Unsigned integer
1	Negative integer
2	Byte string
3	Text string
4	Array of data items
5	Map of key/value pairs
6	Semantic tag
7	Floating point

Table 6.9 Additional field encoding.

Additional data value	Description
0–23	Simple value (value 0..23)
24	Simple value (value 32..255 in following byte)
25	IEEE 754 Half-Precision Float (16 bits follow)
26	IEEE 754 Single-Precision Float (32 bits follow)
27	IEEE 754 Double-Precision Float (64 bits follow)
28–30	Unassigned
31	"break" stop code for indefinite-length items

Integer encoding

To encode an unsigned integer the major type field will be set to zero. If the value in the integer is in the range 0–23, it will be directly encoded in the additional information field. If the integer value is greater than 23, the remaining values in the additional information field 24–27 specify the number of bytes (1–4 following the header byte which are used to hold the unsigned integer value.

Exercise: CBOR encoding

In the pack installer copy Exercise 6.4.
In microVision open the RTE.
Add the QCBOR encoder/decoder (Fig. 6.21).

Open main.c.
This file contains examples of how to encode/decode the CBOR major types.
We can use QBOR to encode three bytes as shown below:
First include the QCBOR header:

```
#include "qcbor.h"
int main(void) {
```

FIG. 6.21

Select the QCBOR encoder/decoder.

No permission required.

Next create a context for this CBOR serialization and a structure which contains a pointer to the serialized object and its length:

```
QCBOREncodeContext EC;
UsefulBufC Encoded;
```

Now create some input data items and a buffer to hold the final serialized string:

```
uint8_t data_A = 0x10, data_B = 0x55; pBuf[300];
uint16_t data_C - 0xAA55;
```

In the code, we must first initialize the encoder with the context and output buffer:

```
QCBOREncode Init(&EC, UsefulBuf_FROM_BYTF_ARRAY(pBuf));
```

Now we can encode each unsigned integer. Although the encoder function produces an optimized string for each word size up to uint64_t:

```
QCBOREncode_AddUInt64(&EC, data_A);
QCBOREncode_AddUInt64(&EC, data_B);
QCBOREncode_AddUInt64(&EC, data_C);
```

Finally, the encoder can be exited. The encoded structure contains a pointer to the serialized pBUF array and the length of the CBOR string:

```
QCBOREncode_Finish(&EC, &Encoded));
```

This will generate the serialized string shown in Table 6.10.
The CBOR string can now be decoded.

Table 6.10 Encoding.

Encoding	Description
0x10	Header uint8_t directly encoded
0x18	Header uint8_t with one byte following
0x55	Data
0x19	Header uint16_t with two bytes following
0xAA	Data
0x55	Data

First create our data items and the CBOR context:

```
uint8_t decode_A;uint8_t decode_B;uint16_t decode_C;
QCBORDecodeContext DC;
```

Then create a CBOR item which is used to hold the initial decoded value and initialize the decoder with the previously encoded byte string:

```
QCBORItem Item;
QCBORDecode_Init(&DC, Encoded, QCBOR_DECODE_MODE_NORMAL);
```

We can now read each item in turn:

```
QCBORDecode_GetNext(&DC, &Item);
```

Once an item has been read, we can query the data type and then read the data value:

```
if(Item.uDataType == QCBOR_TYPE_UINT64) {
  decode_A = Item.val.uint64;
}
QCBORDecode_GetNext(&DC, &Item);
if(Item.uDataType == QCBOR_TYPE_UINT64) {
  decode_B = Item.val.uint64;
 }
QCBORDecode_GetNext(&DC, &Item);
if(Item.uDataType == QCBOR_TYPE_UINT64) {
  decode_C = Item.val.uint64;
}
```

Once the full string has been parsed, we can exit the decoder and release the context:

```
QCBORDecode_Finish(&DC)
```

It is also possible to encode signed integer using a mix of major type 0 and 1 items:

```
 int8_t data_A = -0x10, data_B = 0x55;
int16_t data_C = -0xAA55;
QCBOREncode_AddInt64(&EC, data_A);
QCBOREncode_AddInt64(&EC, data_B);
QCBOREncode_AddInt64(&EC, data_C);
```

Which encodes to (Table 6.11).

Table 6.11 CBOR decoding.

Byte value	Decoding
0x2F	Major type zero.
0x18	Major type zero with one byte to follow
0x55	Data
0x39	Major type one with two bytes to follow
0xAA	Data
0x54	Data

We can decode the serialized data the same way, but this time, we can test for a signed value and read the signed integer tag:

```
if(Item.uDataType == QCBOR_TYPE_INT64) {
  decode_C = Item.val.int64;
}
```

It is also possible to store text strings byte strings and arrays in a similar fashion:

```
QCBOREncode_OpenArray(&EC);
QCBOREncode_AddUInt64(&EC, 451);
QCBOREncode_AddUInt64(&EC, 331);
QCBOREncode_CloseArray(&EC);
```

This encodes as a set bytes of plus an initial header that with the major type set to array and the number of elements is held in the additional data field (Table 6.12).

Table 6.12 Array encoding.

Encoding	Description
0x82	Header declares an array with two items
0x19	Header for first item
0x01	Data
0xC3	Data
0x19	Header for second item
0x01	Data
0x4B	Data

We can also encode text and byte strings:

```
QCBOREncode_Init(&EC, UsefulBuf_FROM_BYTE_ARRAY(nBuf));
QCBOREncode_AddText(&EC,
      UsefulBuf_FROM_SZ_LITERAL("bar bar foo bar"));
QCBOREncode_AddSZString(&EC, "oof\n");
```

When decoded the item structure will provide a pointer and length of the string data:

```
QCBORDecode_GetNext(&DC, &Item);
if(Item.uDataType == QCBOR_TYPE_TEXT_STRING ) {
  bufPtr = (uint8_t *) Item.val.string.ptr;
  size = Item.val.string.len;
}
```

Byte and text strings

CBOR is also able to store strings of data and text. For fixed-length strings, the length of the string is stored as an integer at the beginning of the string using the Type 0 integer rules (Table 6.13).

Two types of string are defined: a byte string (Type 2), which contains binary data, and a text string, which holds a human readable ASCII string (Type 3).

Table 6.13 Byte string encoding.

CBOR value	Type	Additional	Description
0x83	Type 2	3	Array of three elements
0x19 0x12C	Type 0	2	uint16_t = 300
0x18, 0x64	Type 0	1	uint8_t = 100
0x15	Type 0	Direct encoding	uint8_t = 21

Array of data items

We can also store arrays of integers using the same approach as byte arrays. However, the array size is defined as the number of objects, not the number of bytes.

Array of maps

The CBOR data format also supports the storage of maps. Here, maps are tables of key-value pairs which equate to objects in JSON. The first item is the key and the second is the value. Like a data item array, the array's size is the number of map pairs, not the overall number of bytes (Table 6.14).

Table 6.14 Map encoding.

JSON encoding	CBOR encoding	CBOR description
{	A3	Map with three items
"name" : "map1"	64 6E616D65	Text with 4 items "name"
	64 6D617031	Text with 4 items "map1"
"type":"number",	64 74797065	Text with 4 items "type"
	66 6E756D626572	Text with 6 items "number"
"value": 1	65 76616C7565	Text with 5 items "value"
}	01	Unsigned int 1
Encoding = 40	Encoding = 30 bytes	

Indefinite arrays, strings, and maps

CBOR can also handle arrays, strings and maps of variable length. In this case, an array is opened without defining the number of data items. Data items can be added as normal. When all of the current data has been written, the array is closed by writing a data item encoded as a major type 7 plus a break character as the data value (Table 6.15).

Table 6.15 Indefinite array encoding.

JSON encoding	CBOR encoding	Description
[	0x9F	Indefinite Array of bytes
—		
0x17,	0x17	Unsigned 0x17 encoded as one byte
0x18,	0x18 0x18	Unsigned 0x18 encoded as header plus data
0x1F,	0x18 0x1F	Unsigned 0x1F encoded as data
]	0xFF	Header Type 7 + Break 0xE0 | 0x1F

Semantic tags

In addition to providing the header for standard data types, CBOR provides support for semantic tabs. A tag is header type 6 and contains a single value. This is used as a hint to the decoder to describe a custom format for the following encoded bytes.

This allows us to use tabs to extend CBOR encoding types in a number of useful ways. To start with, we can use tags to create additional data items. The tag is placed immediately before the custom data to provide a self-described blob of binary data. The decoder may understand the tag, or it can be passed to a higher layer for decoding. The CBOR standard defines a number of tags and unassigned ranges for extension a small selection is shown in Table 6.16.

Table 6.16 Semantic tags.

Tag value	Tag semantics	Data encoded as
0	Standard date/time string ie 2021-11-12T23:20:50.52Z	UTF-8 string
1	Epoch-based date/time, number of seconds from 1970-01-01T00:00Z	Multiple
2	Positive bignum	Byte string
3	Negative bignum	Byte string
4	Decimal fraction	Array
5	Bigfloat	Array

To encode a positive bignum value the encoder will first write the tag value 0x02 followed by a byte stream, which holds the value of the bignum (Table 6.17).

The decoder will then return the tab and an integer array, which can then be used to initialize an MPI value.

In addition to the tags defined in the CBOR specification (RFC 7049), the range of tags has been extended and maintained in an IANA registry. The draft list of tags is available from:

Table 6.17 Tag encoding.

Bignum value	CBOR encoding	Description
0x111111111111111111 11111111111	0xC2	Semantic tag 2 positive Bignum
	0x4F	Size of 15 bytes
	0x111111111111111111 11111111111	Byte string value for the bignum

https://www.iana.org/assignments/cbor-tags/cbor-tags.xhtml

We can use these tags to improve an encoded CBOR stream's efficiency. For example, if we need to encode an array of 32-bit floating-point values. In a standard encoding, each float will be stored with a header followed by 4 bytes. By using a tag, we can define a much terser encoding. We can use a tag to declare a float array followed by the byte values of the IEEE754 floating-point number. In the IANA registry, a 32-bit float array is defined by tab 81 follower by a byte string. This allows us to store our array as a single tag followed by a binary blob where each float value is stored as four bytes.

Conclusion

In this chapter, we have looked at using JSON and CBOR to encode application data that will ride within an MQTT packet. However, the uses for both of these data formats are much more widespread. As we will see in the next chapter, JSON is often used to hold configuration information and is used to define the options within an IoT cloud platform. Additional standards such as JSON Object Signing and Encryption (JOSE) and CBOR Object Signing and Encryption (COSE) are used to create web tokens that form the basis of the Entity Attestation Token (EAT), which is used to prove the identity and capabilities of an IoT device.

Using an IoT cloud service

7

Introduction

In this chapter, we are going to connect our IoT device to a cloud server and see how to integrate the IoT data with some typical backend services that are often required for IoT applications. While cloud development is not really the focus of this book, this chapter is intended to get you started with a basic platform from which to build a fully fledged system. Initially, there are two choices: we could create a cloud computing instance and develop our own system from scratch, or we can use a cloud service that provides a set of ready-made services. We are going to explore the latter, though a guide to developing your own system is listed in the Bibliography. Unless you are an expert in cloud servers (or know one), the best option is to use an existing IoT cloud service. The most popular choices are shown in Table 7.1.

Table 7.1 Cloud services.

Cloud service	URL
Amazon Web Services	https://aws.amazon.com/iot/
Google Cloud	https://cloud.google.com/iot-core/
IBM Watson	https://www.ibm.com/cloud/watson-iot-platform
Microsoft Azure	https://azure.microsoft.com/en-gb/services/iot-hub/

Commercial IoT cloud services.

By far, the most widely used of these servers is Amazon Web Services (AWS). We will look at connecting our devices to AWS and exploring some of the key backend services it has to offer.

AWS account

The first thing we need to do is setup an AWS account. You can do this by following the instructions in the link below:

aws.amazon.com/free.

This will give you free access for 1 year to many of the services provided by AWS. There are some bandwidth and time limits to the free tier so please check the restrictions here:

https://aws.amazon.com/free/?all-free-tier.sort-by=item.additionalFields. SortRank&all-free-tier.sort-order=asc.

AWS IoT

All of the above cloud services provide an MQTT broker with a secure TLS port. This allows our devices to transfer data into the cloud service. Once in the cloud, we need a range of services to store and manage the data so that it is accessible to a front end application (Table 7.2).

Table 7.2 Cloud backend services.

Service	Description
Database	Persistent storage for large IoT datasets
Rules engine	Transform, augment, filter, and route data received from a device to another AWS service
Analytics	Store, analyze data, transform data at scale
Logging	Event process and error messages

Common services provided by an IoT cloud platform.

The AWS IoT service provides a secure MQTT server that can be connected to a vast range of highly scalable backend services. In addition, AWS provides a set of dedicated IoT services, as shown in Table 7.3, which we will also look at in this chapter.

Table 7.3 AWS IoT services.

Service	Description
Device defender	Cloud and device security monitoring
Device shadow	Cloud-based twin. Maintains last known state of offline devices
Device jobs	Processes lists of commands for selected groups of devices

Connect a device

Within the AWS IoT system, IoT devices are known as "Things." So to connect our first device, we must first register it as a Thing within the AWS IoT platform. This will create a set of custom credentials in the form of a device certificate, private key, and AWS CA certificate. In this section, we will go through this process for an individual device and test the credentials with the MQTT.fx client before deploying them to a real device.

Open a browser and go to https://aws.amazon.com/ then select "Sign into the console."
Log into AWS and select the Services console (Fig. 7.1).

FIG. 7.1

AWS console.

No permission required.

From the Services console select IoT Core (Fig. 7.2).

FIG. 7.2

IoT Core.

No permission required.

The IoT Core page provides a set of configuration resources to register and manage our IoT Things (Fig. 7.3).

FIG. 7.3

AWS IoT Core services dialog.

No permission required.

Create a connection policy

Before we connect our first Thing, we need to create a connection policy. This is a set of rules described by a JSON object that defines what type of Things can connect and what MQTT methods are available to them.

In the sidebar, select "Secure" item and then select Policies (Fig. 7.4).

FIG. 7.4

Thing Policies. Select the "Thing Policies" menu item.

No permission required.

Press the Create button in the top right hand corner of the screen to start defining a new policy (Fig. 7.5).

FIG. 7.5

Create a Thing. Press the Create button to start creating a new IoT Thing.

No permission required.

To begin with we will define a policy that does not place any limits on what clients can connect and what they can do.

Enter a policy name and set Action to IoT:* (Fig. 7.6).

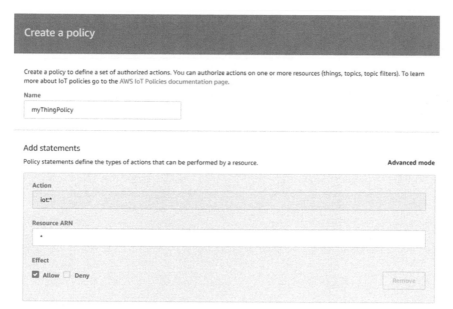

FIG. 7.6

Define a Policy to define the IoT "Thing" access rights.

No permission required.

This will allow access to every MQTT method.

We can allow any type of client to connect by setting the Resource ARN field to * and also check the "Allow" box.
If you now click on Advanced Mode, you can view and edit the JSON policy descriptor.

```
{
"Version": "2012-10-17",
"Statement": [
{
  "Effect": "Allow",
  "Action": "iot:*",
  "Resource": [
  "*"
 ]
 }
}
```

Now press the Create button to define the policy.
Now we can add an actual Thing.
On the sidebar expand the Manage section and select Things (Fig. 7.7).

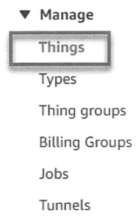

FIG. 7.7

Select the Thing Menu. From the sidebar select the Thing Menu.

No permission required.

In the Things menu, press the local Create button to start the process (top right of screen) (Fig. 7.5).
The menu allows us to enroll a fleet of devices or a single Thing. This time we only want to add a single device.

Select the Create a single Thing option (Fig. 7.8).

Register a single AWS IoT thing
Create a thing in your registry   Create a single thing

FIG. 7.8

Register a Single Thing.

No permission required.

AWS provides additional options to register and preregister a full fleet of devices so you can easily commission a fleet of real world devices.

Now select a name for your device (Fig. 7.9).

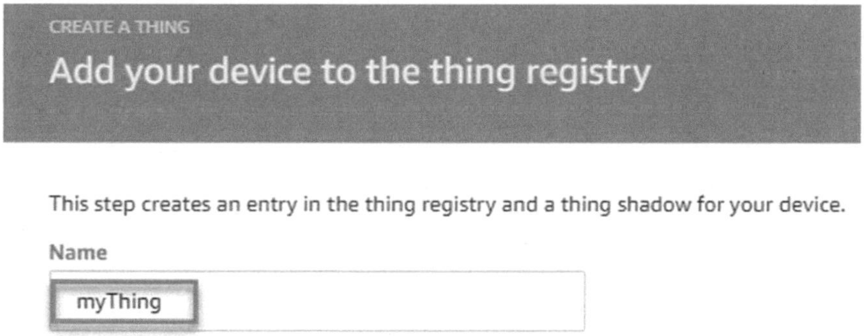

CREATE A THING
Add your device to the thing registry

This step creates an entry in the thing registry and a thing shadow for your device.

Name

myThing

FIG. 7.9

Thing registry. Select a name for your device and add it to a thing registry of active devices.

No permission required.

This menu also has further options to set a Thing Type and Thing Group. We do not need these initially, but they are useful for searching, identifying, and managing devices within a real system.

Once you have set the device name press the Next button.

Now we can create the device certificate and key pair. Again, there are a number of options here but we will let AWS do all the work.

Select the One click certificate creation (Fig. 7.10).

CREATE A THING
Add a certificate for your thing   STEP 2/3

A certificate is used to authenticate your device's connection to AWS IoT.

One-click certificate creation (recommended)
This will generate a certificate, public key, and private key using AWS IoT's certificate authority.   Create certificate

FIG. 7.10

Create certificate. Create the TLS X.509 Certificates for your device.

No permission required.

AWS allows you to use your own certificates, in which case you have to upload a CA certificate, or you can generate one with a certificate signing request by providing your own private key.

Once the certificate has been created, you should download the certificate and key pair (1) along with the AWS root CA certificate (2). You also need to activate the credentials (3), and then finally, we need to attach our connection policy (4) (Fig. 7.11).

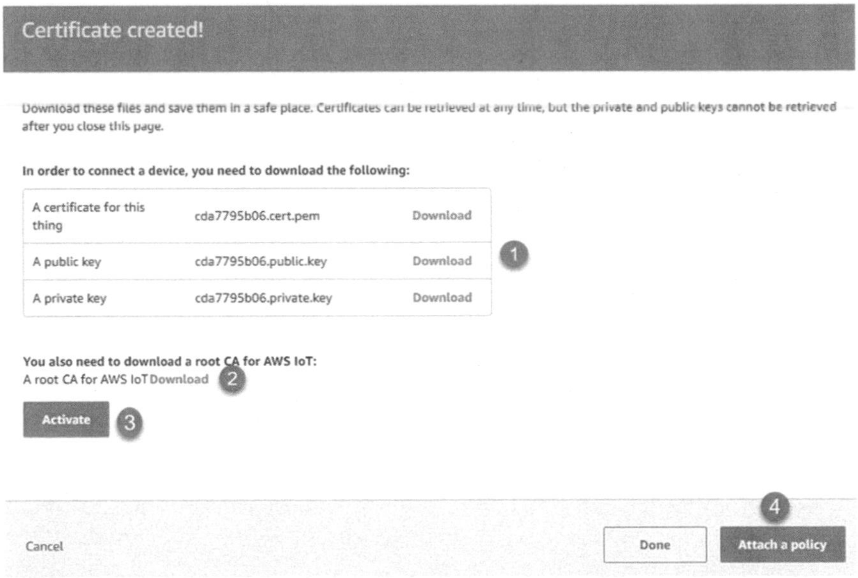

FIG. 7.11

Certificate created. Download the device certificates and the AWS CA certificate.

No permission required.

Each device can have its own policy depending on its overall system role. Here we can allow our devices to perform any action and access any resource. You can attach an existing policy or create a new device policy.

Press the "Create New Policy" button.
Set the Action field to "iot:*" and the resource field to "*" (Fig. 7.12).

Create a policy

Create a policy to define a set of authorized actions. You can authorize actions on one or more resources (things, topics, topic filters). To learn more about IoT policies go to the AWS IoT Policies documentation page.

Name

myThingPolicy

Add statements

Policy statements define the types of actions that can be performed by a resource.   **Advanced mode**

Action

iot:*

Resource ARN

.

Effect

☑ Allow ☐ Deny

Remove

FIG. 7.12

Device policy. Set the device policy to allow all MQTT operations.

No permission required.

Now that we have created our first device we can try an initial test using a built in MQTT client. This will ensure the AWS MQTT broker is working correctly.

From the sidebar select the test option (Fig. 7.13).

▶ **Defend**

▶ **Act**

Test

FIG. 7.13

Test the Thing configuration. Select the Test item from the lower left sidebar.

No permission required.

This option is at the end of the sidebar menu so you may need to scroll down.

This allows us to subscribe to an MQTT topic. For testing we can create any topic we like (Fig. 7.14).

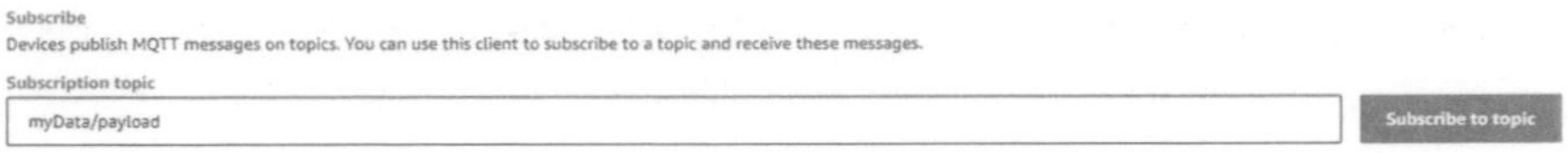

Subscribe
Devices publish MQTT messages on topics. You can use this client to subscribe to a topic and receive these messages.
Subscription topic

| myData/payload | | Subscribe to topic |

FIG. 7.14

Subscribe to an MQTT test topic.

No permission required.

Once we have subscribed, the menu will update to give us a publish option with a predefined message in JSON format.

Press the Publish button. The message will be sent to the MQTT broker and is then echoed back to appear on the screen with a timestamp.

Next we can try to connect an external client. But first we need to know the IP address of our MQTT broker instance.

In the sidebar, select the Settings option which is at the bottom (Fig. 7.15).

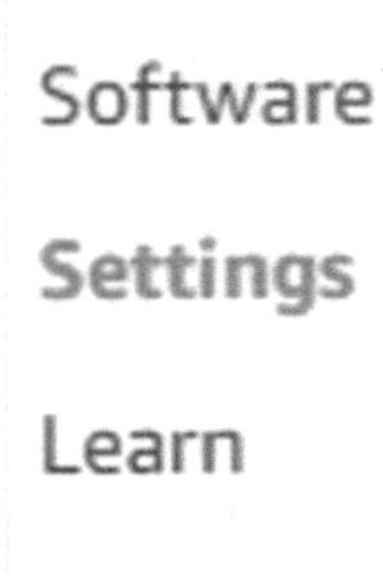

Software

Settings

Learn

FIG. 7.15

Sidebar Settings menu item. From the sidebar select the Settings item.

No permission required.

This will give us the address of the endpoint which we can use to publish and subscribe MQTT messages.

Copy the endpoint address (Fig. 7.16).

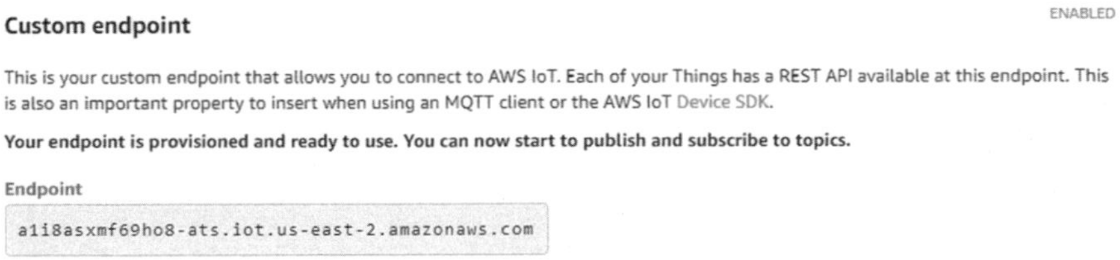

Custom endpoint   ENABLED

This is your custom endpoint that allows you to connect to AWS IoT. Each of your Things has a REST API available at this endpoint. This is also an important property to insert when using an MQTT client or the AWS IoT Device SDK.

Your endpoint is provisioned and ready to use. You can now start to publish and subscribe to topics.

Endpoint

| a118asxmf69ho8-ats.iot.us-east-2.amazonaws.com |

FIG. 7.16

Broker endpoint address. Copy your AWS MQTT Broker endpoint address.

No permission required.

The same menu controls the system logging features. Ignore this for now and we will come back to it later.

Now start the MQTT.FX client and create a new profile (Fig. 7.17).

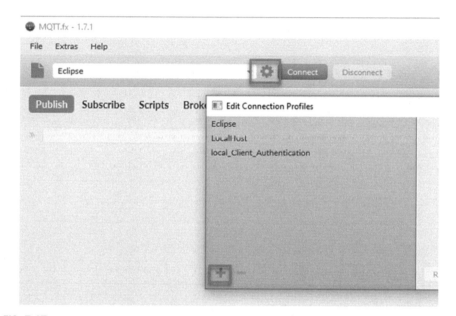

FIG. 7.17

MQTT.fx client. Start the MQTT.fx client and open the new profile menu.

No permission required.

Open the settings using the "cog" icon on the toolbar.
Add a new profile using the + button at the bottom of the Edit connection profile dialog.
Setup the connection as shown in Fig. 7.18.

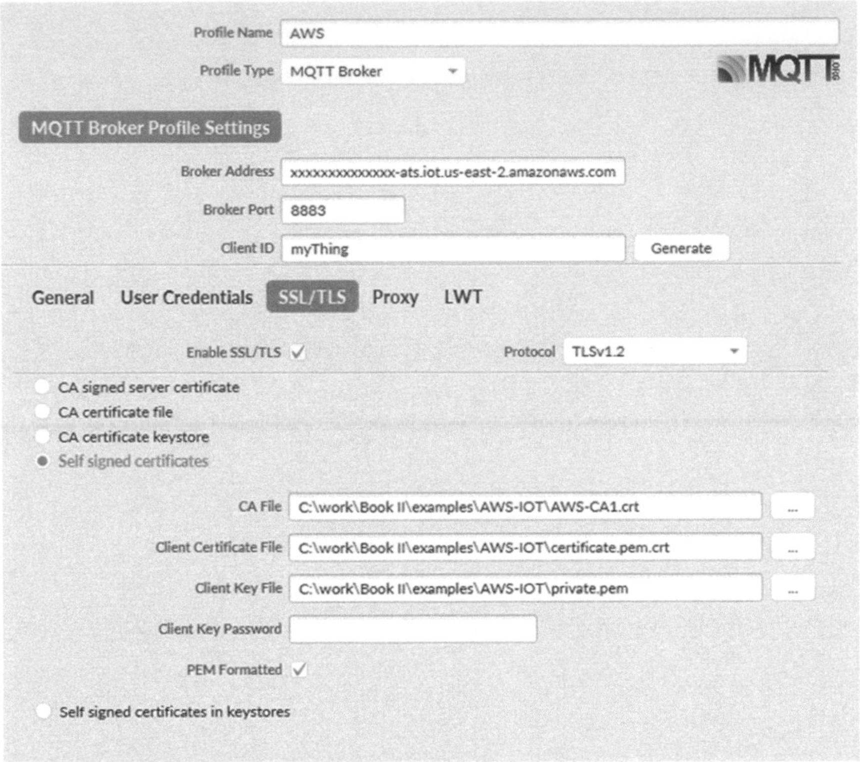

FIG. 7.18

MQTT.fx profile settings. Configure the MQTT.fx profile settings with the AWS MQTT broker endpoint and your device certificates.

No permission required.

Use the endpoint address as the connection address.
The broker port must be 8883 for the MQTT encrypted connection.
To install the security credential select Self Signed Certificates.
Add the AWS CA certificate along with the Thing certificate and Private Key.
Also make sure the PEM format box is checked.
Now click OK to save the AWS profile.

If you press the Connect button on the main toolbar we will connect to our instance of the AWS MQTT broker.

Once the connection is established, you can subscribe and publish to a topic.
Use MQTT.fx to publish a few messages and then go back to the IoT Core console and select Monitor in the sidebar (Fig. 7.19).

AWS IoT

FIG. 7.19

Select the Monitor menu. From the sidebar select the Monitor menu.

No permission required.

This provides us with a set of graphs and gauges, which present the current status of our system (Fig. 7.20).

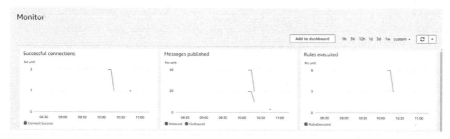

FIG. 7.20

AWS Monitor display. The monitor screen contains a graphical display of you networks activity.

No permission required.

Once you have successfully proved your connection to the AWS IoT broker using the PC client, we can connect an embedded device.

Go to the pack installer and select Exercise 7.1
Open Source Code\socket_startup.c and add your WiFi SSID and WiFi Password using the #defines shown below:

```
#define SSID""
#define PASSWORD""
#define SECURITY_TYPE ARM_WIFI_SECURITY_WPA2
```

Open IoT Client\IoT_Config.h
Set the broker address using the define shown below:

```
#define IOT_DEMO_SERVER""
```

The server port is set to 443, which is normally HTTPS only. However, the AWS server provides multiple protocols on this port by using a TLS extension called Application Layer Protocol Negotiation (ALPN), which allows this port to also provide the MQTT protocol.

This file contains array definitions to hold the device TLS credentials.

Open the AWS CA certificate, device certificate, and device private key files in the microvision editor.

Copy the contents of each credential into the matching arrays.

The "C" formatting is shown below and you can also use the mbedTLS Certs.c file for reference:

```
#define IOT_DEMO_ROOT_CA "-----BEGIN CERTIFICATE-----\r\n" \
"MIIDQTCCAimgAwIBAgITBmyfz5m/jAo54vB4ikPmljZbyjANBgkqhkiG9w0BA
QsF\r\n" \
"ADA5MQswCQYDVQQGEwJVUzEChMGQW1hem9uMRkwFwYDVQQDExBBbWF6\r\n" \
"5MsI+yMRQ+hDKXJioaldXgjUkK642M4UwtBV8ob2xJNDd2ZhwLnoQdeXeGADb
kpy\r\n" \
"-----END CERTIFICATE-----\r\n"
```

This example does not need a username or password.

Build the project and download it into the Xpresso board.

The code will connect to the AWS broker and send the following topics at one second intervals where the data is provided by incrementing counters.

my/process

my/time

You can monitor the topics in the iotCore\test screen or you can connect the MQTT.fx client and subscribe to the topics.

To use MQTT.fx you will need to register a new Thing to generate a second set of credentials.

Run the embedded code.

The embedded code will publish the my/process and my/time topics at one second intervals and they will be visible in the MQTT.fx client and the AWS test screen.

Adding the Dynamo DB database

Our IoT network will be capable of generating vast amounts of data which we will need to store and process in the cloud service. AWS provides a range of database options for different applications. In order to store our data, we will use the dynamoDB database as it has a very fast millisecond update time, which makes it ideal for an IoT application. However, it is limited to a table size of 400 kB. In this section, we will look at using the DynamoDB to store our data in two ways: first, we will store it as a table of process data and then look at creating a time-series database that adds a date and timestamp for each entry.

Go back to the services console and select the Database: DynamoDB
(Fig. 7.21)

FIG. 7.21

The services console database options. Select the Dynamo DB from the services console.

No permission required.

Here, we will create two database tables one for the process data and one for the time series data.

In the DynamoDB dialog press the create table button (Fig. 7.22)

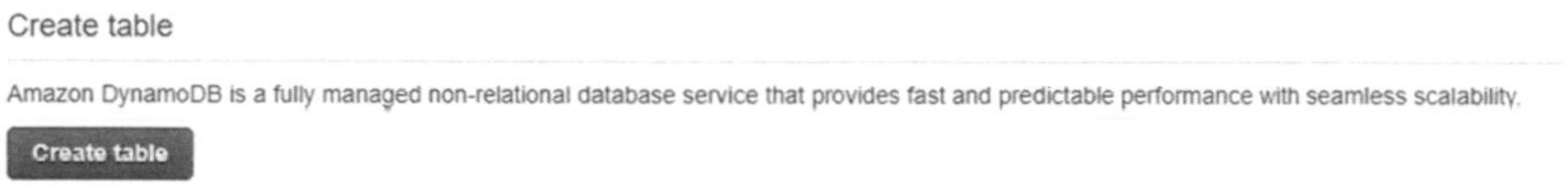

Create table

Amazon DynamoDB is a fully managed non-relational database service that provides fast and predictable performance with seamless scalability.

Create table

FIG. 7.22

Now create a Dynamo DB table.

No permission required.

When we first create a database we only need to define the primary and secondary sort keys. When we add records additional fields will be created as required.

First give your database a name. I have used "ordered_table" (Fig. 7.23)

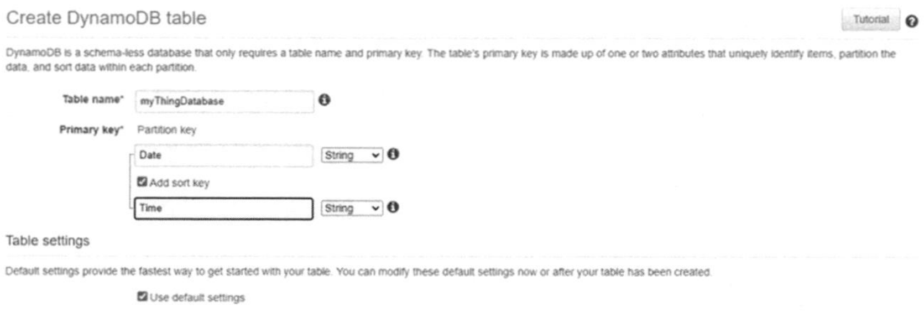

Create DynamoDB table   Tutorial   ?

DynamoDB is a schema-less database that only requires a table name and primary key. The table's primary key is made up of one or two attributes that uniquely identify items, partition the data, and sort data within each partition.

Table name*	myThingDatabase	ⓘ
Primary key*	Partition key	
	Date	String ⌄ ⓘ
	☑ Add sort key	
	Time	String ⌄ ⓘ

Table settings

Default settings provide the fastest way to get started with your table. You can modify these default settings now or after your table has been created.

☑ Use default settings

FIG. 7.23

Create a Dynamo database. Define the database primary and secondary search keys.

No permission required.

Set the Primary key to "row," tick the Add Sort Key box and name this as "col."
Make sure the Use default settings box is ticked and then click Create.
Now repeat this process to create a second table called time_series
Set the primary key to "date" and the secondary key to "time."

Now we have created two test databases as shown in Fig. 7.24.

FIG. 7.24

Test databases. You should now have two Dynamo database tables.

No permission required.

Action rules

We now have to connect together our IoT Things and the two new databases. This is done through a sophisticated rules engine that can be used to trigger actions within the cloud system. Here we will create two rules which will be triggered by selected MQTT messages. Once triggered, they will process the topic payload, which must be formatted as a JSON object.

Go back to the IoT core console.
Expand the Act section and select rules (Fig. 7.25).

FIG. 7.25

Select the rules engine. From the IoT Core sidebar select the Act rules engine.

No permission required.

Now press the Create button to define a rule with an associated action. First give the rule a name. In this case I have used "Process" (Fig. 7.26).

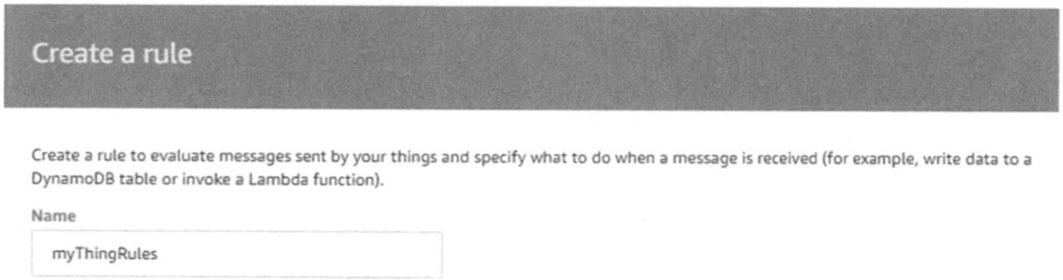

Create a rule

Create a rule to evaluate messages sent by your things and specify what to do when a message is received (for example, write data to a DynamoDB table or invoke a Lambda function).

Name

myThingRules

FIG. 7.26

Create a rule. To create a rule first provide a suitable name.

No permission required.

Now we can define a trigger condition. This uses a SQL query to examine the JSON payload, with definitions for conditions and filters. For our first example, we can define a simple query that stores the received messages sent to the topic my/process.

Edit the SQL query so it matches the following string SELECT sensor1 FROM 'my/process' (Fig. 7.27).

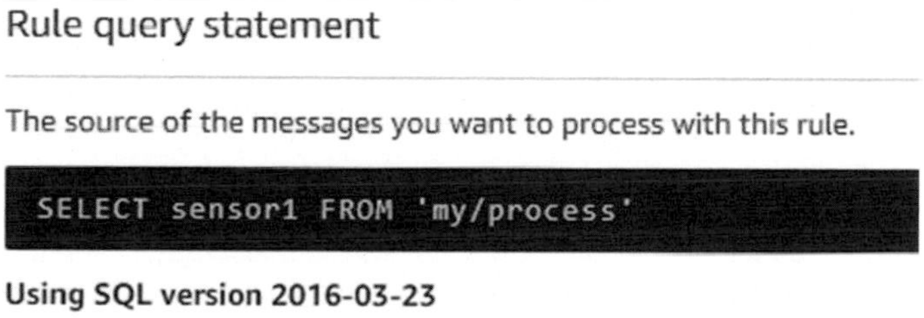

Rule query statement

The source of the messages you want to process with this rule.

`SELECT sensor1 FROM 'my/process'`

Using SQL version 2016-03-23

FIG. 7.27

Define a SQL query to extract a JSON field from the MQTT topic payload.

No permission required.

This rule will be triggered when the topic my/process is received. It will also filter the payload so that only the sensor1 record is stored.

Press the "Add an action" button.
Select the Insert message in DynamoDB table (Fig. 7.28).

FIG. 7.28

Rule action. Select an action to insert a message into the DB table.

No permission required.

Use the drop down to select the process DynamoDB that we created earlier (Fig. 7.29).

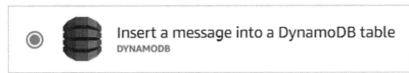

FIG. 7.29

Action database selection. Select the time_series database table.

No permission required.

Now we can format how the MQTT message payload is mapped to the database fields (Fig. 7.30).

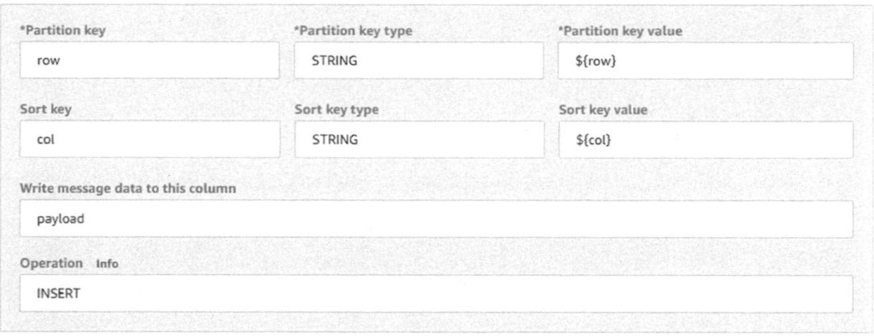

*Partition key	*Partition key type	*Partition key value
row	STRING	${row}

Sort key	Sort key type	Sort key value
col	STRING	${col}

Write message data to this column

payload

Operation Info

INSERT

FIG. 7.30

Topic payload to database mapping. Now we can map the topic JSON fields to the database partition and sort key fields.

Once we select the database, the partition and sort key fields will be automatically populated. We can now define the data source to populate the database fields when the message is received.

Set Partition Key Value to {row}

Make sure you use "{" here as a simple "(" will also be accepted but the query will not work.

Set Sort Key Value to {col}

This will extract the row and col values from each received JSON message and enter them into the partition and sort database fields.

Set the "write message data to this column" to payload.

This will place the filtered sensor1 data into a new database field called payload.

Press the "Create Role" button and call the new role processRole.
Press Create Rule.

In MQTT.fx select the publish screen.

Set up the topic as my/process.
Set the payload as follows:

{ "row" : "1", "col" : "1", "sensor1" : "20", "sensor2" : "30" }
Now publish a message.

It is useful to subscribe to the my/process topic in MQTT.fx. You can then check that the JSON formatting is correct by using is built in parser.

Change the row and col values and publish a second message.
Go to dynamoDB and the tables view.
Select the process table and then select the items tab.

You will now see the two sensor1 records in the database (Fig. 7.31).

FIG. 7.31

View the table Items. Select the process table and view the inserted Items.

No permission required.

Setting the Time Series rule

We can now create a second rule to process a new topic my/time which will add timestamped sensor data to the time series database.

Go to the IoT Core : ACT : Rules dialog.
Press the Create button to add a new rule. This time call it "time_series"
(Fig. 7.32).

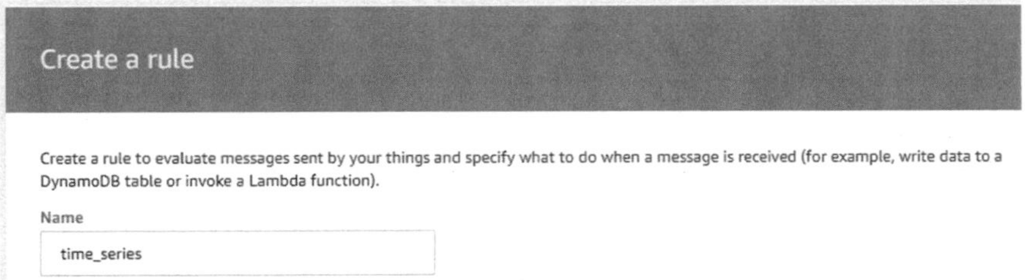

FIG. 7.32

Time series rule. Create a new rule for the time series topic.

No permission required.

This time we will use a wild card to copy the full message payload into the database record.

Edit the SQL query as shown below (Fig. 7.33)

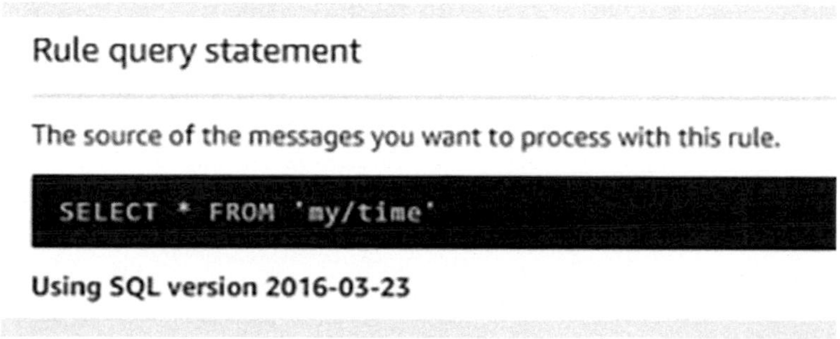

Rule query statement

The source of the messages you want to process with this rule.

```
SELECT * FROM 'my/time'
```

Using SQL version 2016-03-23

FIG. 7.33

time_series SQL query. An SQL query is used to extract the full payload from the my/time topic.

No permission required.

SELECT * FROM 'my/time'

Now press the "Add Action" button and again select "Insert message into a dynamo DB table."

When we setup the database the primary key was set to date and the sort key was set to time.

Here we can use a local timestamp for each of the key values.

Partition key value : ${parse_time("yyyy.MM.dd", timestamp()) }
Sort key value : ${parse_time("HH:mm:ss", timestamp())}

We also need to define a message column for the data, and in this case, it is just called payload.
We must also define the SQL operation, which in this case is INSERT.

Now to make the rule active we create a role that allows the IoT Core to access the database.

Press the "Create Role" button and provide a role name such as "timeRole."

The finished screen is shown below in Fig. 7.34.

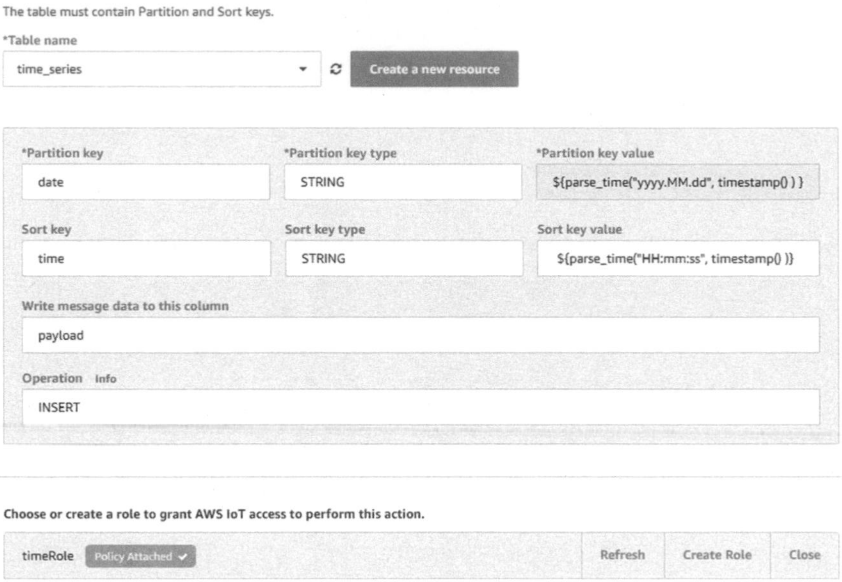

The table must contain Partition and Sort keys.

*Table name

| time_series | ▾ | ⟳ | Create a new resource |

*Partition key	*Partition key type	*Partition key value
date	STRING	${parse_time("yyyy.MM.dd", timestamp()) }

Sort key	Sort key type	Sort key value
time	STRING	${parse_time("HH:mm:ss", timestamp())}

Write message data to this column

| payload |

Operation Info

| INSERT |

Choose or create a role to grant AWS IoT access to perform this action.

| timeRole Policy Attached ✔ | | Refresh | Create Role | Close |

FIG. 7.34

Define the topic to database mapping. Use the timestamp function to populate each record with a data and time in the partition and sort key fields.

No permission required.

Testing the Time Series database

To test if our system is working go back to the MQTT.fx client and publish a message to a topic which begins with my/time (Fig. 7.35).

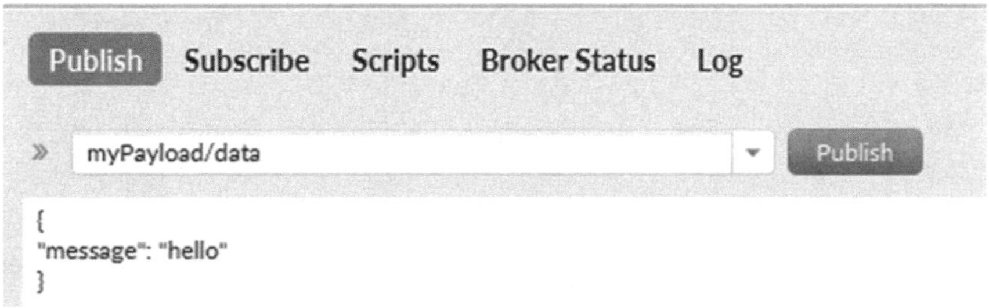

| **Publish** | Subscribe | Scripts | Broker Status | Log |

| » | myPayload/data | ▾ | Publish |

```
{
"message": "hello"
}
```

FIG. 7.35

IoT to database test message. Publish a my/time topic to test the ACT rule.

No permission required.

We can now send our JSON data packet but without the row and col records:

```
{
"sensor1" : "20",
"sensor2" : "30"
}
```

Publish this message a few times from the MQTT.fx client.
Go back to the DynamoDB console.
In the sidebar select "Tables" (Fig. 7.36) **and then select the time_series**
table.

FIG. 7.36

DynamoDB sidebar. From the DynamoDB sidebar select the tables option.

No permission required.

Select the Items tab and you should see our recent messages added to the
database (Fig. 7.37).

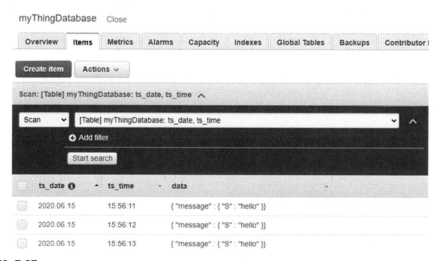

FIG. 7.37

Dynamo table with IoT data. View the time_series table populated with timestamped IoT
data.

No permission required.

Go back to the embedded example we setup at the beginning of this chapter and re-run the code.

This will generate the process and time series messages at one second intervals to populate the two databases.

IoT analytics

Another way to capture our data is with the IoT analytics service. The analytics service can be used to capture vast amounts of data into an AWS Simple Storage Service (S3). S3 provides virtually limitless inexpensive storage, making it ideal for storing and analyzing huge IoT datasets.

In order to feed our MQTT messages into an S3 volume, we must create a channel that acts as a temporary storage pipeline for the data. The channel data are then processed before they are stored in the S3 volume. Fortunately, there is a setup wizard, which we can use to create an initial analytics system.

Go to the services console.
Select IoT analytics (Fig. 7.38).

FIG. 7.38

IoT Analytics. Select the IoT Analytics item from the services Internet of things console.

No permission required.

The analytics console provides a quick setup wizard, which will create each stage of the analytics process automatically.

Enter a prefix name for the analytics resource such as myThingAnalytics.

By entering a topic, we can narrow the scope of message data that will reach the S3 bucket.

For this example, set the topic to my/time to capture the sensor messages for the previous time series database (Fig. 7.39).

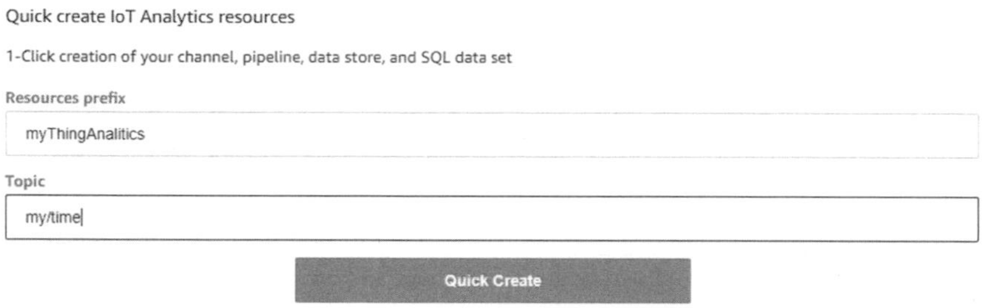

Quick create IoT Analytics resources

1-Click creation of your channel, pipeline, data store, and SQL data set

Resources prefix

myThingAnalitics

Topic

my/time

Quick Create

FIG. 7.39

Analytics setup dialog. In the setup wizard define a prefix and topic for your analytics configuration.

No permission required.

Press the Quick Create button and the wizard will setup each stage of the analytics system (Fig. 7.40).

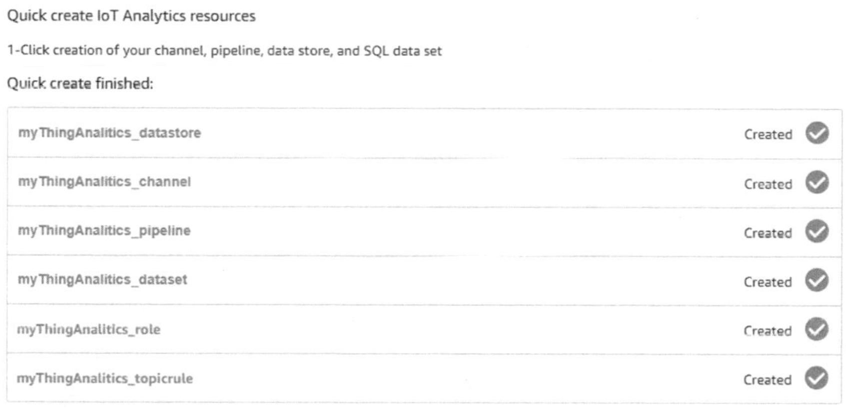

Quick create IoT Analytics resources

1-Click creation of your channel, pipeline, data store, and SQL data set

Quick create finished:

myThingAnalitics_datastore	Created ✓
myThingAnalitics_channel	Created ✓
myThingAnalitics_pipeline	Created ✓
myThingAnalitics_dataset	Created ✓
myThingAnalitics_role	Created ✓
myThingAnalitics_topicrule	Created ✓

FIG. 7.40

IoT analytics wizard. The wizard automates creation of an analytics pipeline.

No permission required.

We now need to change the default setup to extract the message data that we are actually interested in.

On the sidebar, select the Pipeline screen and click on the newly generated pipeline (Fig. 7.41).

Channels

Pipelines

Data stores

☐ **Name**

☐ mything_pipeline

FIG. 7.41

Analytics pipeline. Select the analytics pipeline and open its dialog.

No permission required.

In the pipeline view, click the Activities Edit link (Fig. 7.42).

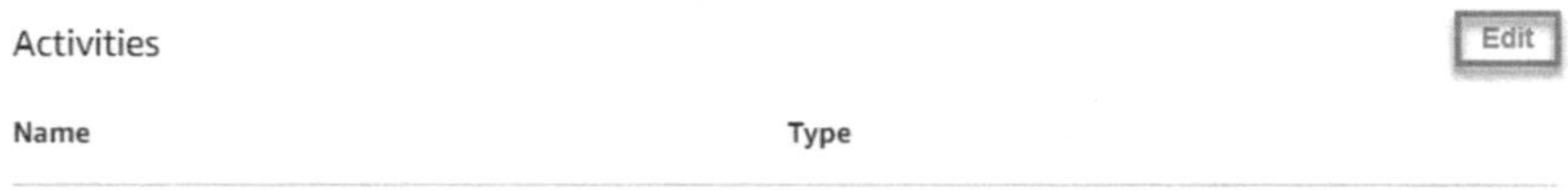

Activities   Edit

Name   Type

FIG. 7.42

Analytics pipeline activities section. Select the pipeline activities edit item.

No permission required.

Here, we can enter the JSON keys that we are interested in extracting from our messages.

In this example, we are going to send the sensor message.

```
{
"sensor1" : 20,
"sensor2" : 30
}
```

In the attributes box enter sensor1 as the first key and set the value to zero. Change the type from string to number.
Press the add new button.
Add a second attribute the same way but this time set the key to sensor2 (Fig. 7.43).

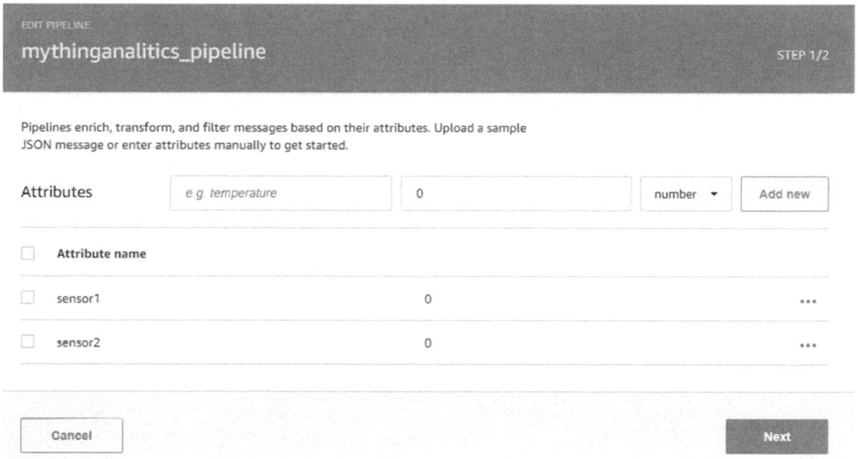

FIG. 7.43

Configure the pipeline attributes. The attribute fields select the topic JSON fields and convert the value to a number.

No permission required.

Once you have entered both attributes press the "Next" button.

The pipeline stage can preprocess data before they are placed into the S3 bucket. This allows us to automatically transform and clean the data before they are stored. For now, we will just store the raw data (Fig. 7.44).

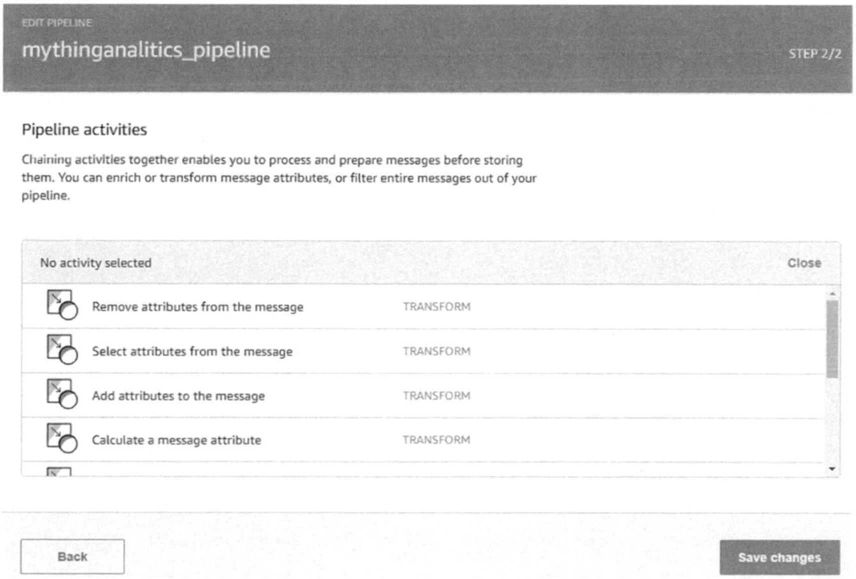

FIG. 7.44

Activities transforms. Additional methods may be used to transform the data before they are stored in the S3 bucket.

No permission required.

Press the "Save Changes" button.
Our analytics engine is now active.

Start the LPC55S69 Xpresso board so that it connects and sends the sensor message.
Go back to the Analytics screen and open the dataset screen.

The initial details panel shows the dataset SQL query.
In the top left corner, select the Actions drop down and select the Run now option to execute the query (Fig. 7.45).

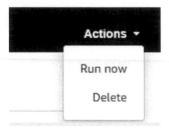

FIG. 7.45

Run the analytics query. Run the analytics rules to process data stored in the pipeline.

No permission required.

This will give you a preview of the processed data.
Now select the Content screen (Fig. 7.46).

Most recent version

▼ 12/02/2021, 11:03:47   d963cbd9-7fae-4416-bc04-3277290b5ee7   ● Succeeded   1226 ms   Delete

162a7945-fc82-43c9-81d6-e4ccf121230b.csv   Download

Result preview

sensor1	sensor2	_dt
20	30	2021-02-12 00:00:00.000
20	30	2021-02-12 00:00:00.000

FIG. 7.46

Analytics dataset. The transformed data are stored in an S3 table.

No permission required.

This will give you a view of the processed data along with an option to download a CSV file for offline processing.

Logs

An essential component of a large-scale IoT system is a logging mechanism. We need to be able to visualize the current state of our system and be able to spot malfunctions and intrusions.

We can enable the AWS logging system and then create a set of dashboards that display activity within different elements of the system. We can also customize and extend the logging messages to suit the needs of our system.

Go to the IoT Core screen.
Select the Settings option.
In the Logging section, click the "Edit" button.
Now provide a role name and set the logging level.
There are four logging levels. For this exercise select the info level
(Fig. 7.47).

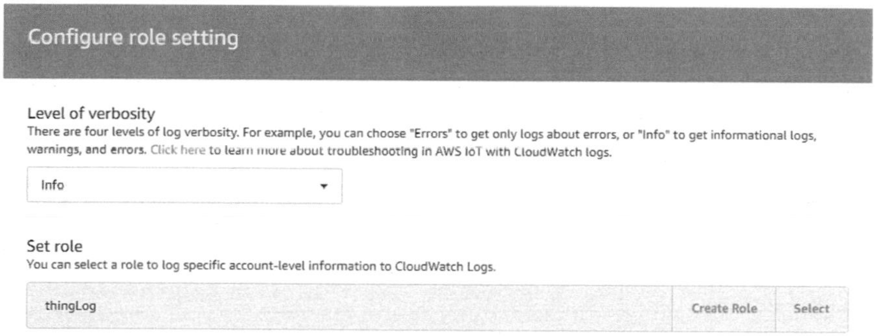

Configure role setting

Level of verbosity
There are four levels of log verbosity. For example, you can choose "Errors" to get only logs about errors, or "Info" to get informational logs, warnings, and errors. Click here to learn more about troubleshooting in AWS IoT with CloudWatch logs.

Info

Set role
You can select a role to log specific account-level information to CloudWatch Logs.

thingLog   Create Role   Select

FIG. 7.47

Set the logging verbosity. Adjust the logging verbosity level to "info."

No permission required.

Now go to the Services screen and select the Management & Governance: CloudWatch Service.

The CloudWatch Service provides a visualization for all the different service logs within AWS.

In the sidebar, select the Log groups option.
Within the log groups select the AWSIoTLogsV2.
This will display our IoT message activity.
Expand an entry to see the trail of messages processing within the existing system.
In the sidebar select logs: insights.
Use the dropdown box at the top to select the log group (Fig. 7.48).

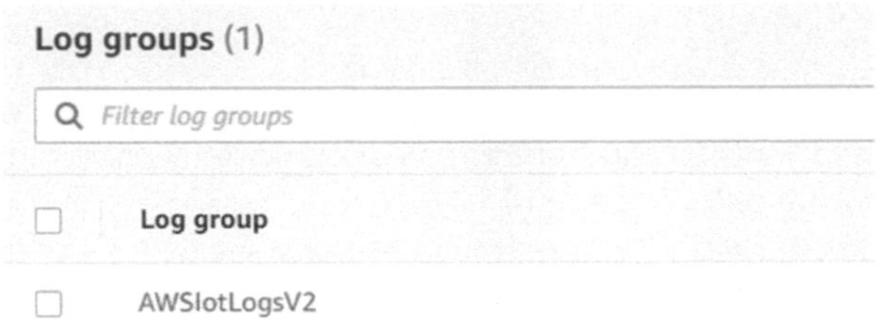

Log groups (1)

Q *Filter log groups*

☐   **Log group**

☐   AWSIotLogsV2

FIG. 7.48

Select run query. Select the AWSIoTLogsV2 log group.

No permission required.

Select Run Query to generate the visualization (Fig. 7.49).

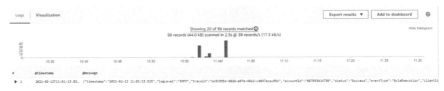

FIG. 7.49

Log visualization. Activity on your network can be viewed as a set of visualizations

No permission required.

Lambda

The AWS Lambda service allows you to execute code in response to events within any AWS service. A wide range of programming languages are supported including Python. Execution of Lambda code is serverless. In effect, Lambda allows you to easily integrate your custom code into AWS services without the need to provision and maintain a dedicated server.

Device services

The AWS platform also provides a set of unique services, which can be added to your device to extend its capabilities and monitor its current state. The optional services are device defender, device shadow, and device jobs.

Device defender

The IoT Core service includes a security profiling service that is used to monitor the behavior of your devices. You can set rules so that if a device behaves abnormally, it will cause a violation, which will be reported as an alarm. These alarms can be recorded in the cloud watch logs and may also generate a message such as an email or SMS to a relevant manager.

Go to the IoTCore screen, expand the Defend : Detect branch and select the Security Profiles option.
Now press the "Create" button and select "Create rule-based anomaly detection" to define a profile (Fig. 7.50).

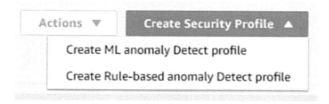

FIG. 7.50

Security profile types. You can create a rules based security profile a Machine learning profile or both.

No permission required.

The second option, "Create an ML anomaly detection profile," allows you to enable a set of connection rules, which will use Machine Learning to create a set of rules that will learn the normal activity of your devices and be able to spot anomalous behavior. It is possible to enable both types of anomaly detection to test, which is most suitable for your network.

Enter a profile name.
Define a profile using the option boxes below (Fig. 7.51).

Name		Description (optional)	
myThingDefense		An optional short description	

Behaviors
Specify how your device should behave. You can use cloud-side metrics without a device agent deployed learn more ↗
Note: once created, behavior names cannot be edited. ⑦

Name ⑦	Metric ⑦	Dimension (optional) ⑦	Dimension operator ⑦	...
messages	Messages received	Not set	Not set	

Check type ⑦	Operator ⑦	Value	Duration ⑦
Absolute value ▼	Less than ▼	5	5 minutes ▼

Datapoints to alarm ⑦	Datapoints to clear ⑦
1	1

FIG. 7.51

Defining a rule-based profile. Create rules to define the allowed activities.

No permission required.

When using this menu, it is important to realize that you define a behavior that your device should follow. Here, we have defined a behavior called messages, which are used to monitor received messages. We define our system behavior to receive less than five messages within a five-minute window.

The dimension option allows us to monitor a specific MQTT topic or range of topics by using wildcards.

Click the "Next" button.

This jumps to a screen which allows us to define a messaging alert if the rule is violated.

Press the "Next" button.

We finally need to define a range of things, which will have their behavior monitored.

Tick the "All Things" box and press the "Next" button.

This will take us to a final review page.

When you are happy press the "Save" button.
Now go back the MDK-Arm debugger and re-run the embedded example.

This will send a block of messages which will violate the device security profile.

When you have run the embedded code go back to the IoT Core screen and select the Detect : Alarms screen.
The violations screen will now display a breach of the security policy
(Fig. 7.52).

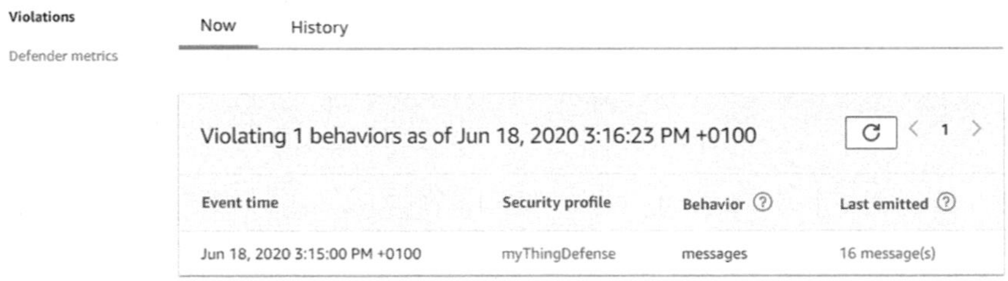

Violations	Now	History			
Defender metrics					

Violating 1 behaviors as of Jun 18, 2020 3:16:23 PM +0100   ↻ ‹ 1 ›

Event time	Security profile	Behavior ⑦	Last emitted ⑦
Jun 18, 2020 3:15:00 PM +0100	myThingDefense	messages	16 message(s)

FIG. 7.52

Security violations. Security alarms are shown when a security policy is breached.

No permission required.

We can also add an agent to our application that reports additional metrics to the IoT Core platform. These are used to monitor device behavior and will identify anomalous activity. The device defender is a self-contained agent, which collects communication information during runtime. When the device connects, it will send a report to the defender service.

Go to the pack installer and select Exercise 7.2 and press the "Copy" button.
Open the RTE and expand the IoT service AWS branch.
Select the common and device defender components (Fig. 7.53).

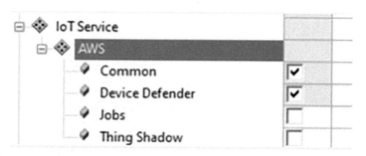

FIG. 7.53

AWS components in the MDK-Arm. Select the AWS common framework and device defender support in the RTE.

No permission required.

This example extends our previous project by using the device defender to monitor the device communications activity. When the device connects, we will send a report using a topic reserved for the device defender.
Open the file device defender.c.
The following header file is added to import the device defender API.
#include "aws_iot_defender.h".
We first need to initialize the defender metrics:

```
metricsInitStatus = IotMetrics_Init();
```

Then define the metrics to be used on this device:

```
AwsIotDefender_SetMetrics( AWS_IOT_DEFENDER_METRICS_TCP_
CONNECTIONS, AWS_IOT_DEFENDER_METRICS_ALL );
```

Then set a publish interval in seconds; the minimum period is 300 seconds.

```
AwsIotDefender_SetPeriod( DEFENDER_PUBLISH_INTERVAL );
```

When the device connects, we can setup the defender info context and start the device defender:

```
startInfo.pClientIdentifier = pIdentifier;
startInfo.clientIdentifierLength = ( uint16_t ) strlen( pIdentifier );
startInfo.callback = callback;
startInfo.mqttConnection = mqttConnection;
defenderResult = AwsIotDefender_Start( &startInfo );
```

When we disconnect from the device, we must stop the defender and clean up the metrics:

```
AwsIotDefender_Stop();
IotMetrics_Cleanup();
```

Build the project and download it to the evaluation board.

As the code runs, it will now maintain a device defender activity log and send this to the broker periodically or as the device connects.

Device shadow service

The device shadow service is used to store the state of selected device topics in the cloud server. This allows an external app to read the last known state of its topics from the device shadow, even if the device is not connected. It is also possible for an app to update the device shadow, then when a device reconnects, it can query the shadow and synchronize any changes to its internal state.

The state is stored as a set of JSON objects, which has the following basic structure:

```
{
"desired": {
"welcome": "aws-iot"
},
"reported": {
"welcome": "aws-iot"
}
}
```

Changes to a device's state from an App will be stored in the desired section while updates from the device will be stored in the reported section.

There are two types of shadow: a "classic" shadow document, which will contain all of the supported topics, and a "named" shadow, which will hold a subset of MQTT Topics. The topic prefixes for both types are shown in Table 7.4.

Table 7.4 Shadow topic prefix.

Topic prefix	Description
$aws/things/thingName/shadow	Unnamed (classic) Shadow
$aws/things/thingName/shadow/name/shadowName	Named Shadow

We can update the device shadow through a set of reserved MQTT Topics shown in Table 7.5.

Table 7.5 Shadow topics.

Topic	Description
/get	Publishes an empty message to this topic to get the device's shadow
/get/accepted	Publishes a response shadow document to this topic when returning the device's shadow
/get/rejected	Publishes an error response document to this topic when it cannot return the device's shadow
/update	Publishes a request state document to this topic to update the device's shadow
/update/delta	Published a response state document to this topic when it accepts a change for the device's shadow, and the request state document contains different values for desired and reported states
/update/accepted	Publishes a response state document to this topic when it accepts a change for the device's shadow
/update/documents	Publishes a state document to this topic whenever an update to the shadow is successfully performed
/update/rejected	Publishes an error response document to this topic when it rejects a change for the device's shadow
/delete	To delete a device's shadow, publish an empty message to the delete topic
/delete/accepted	Publishes a message to this topic when a device's shadow is deleted
/delete/rejected	Publishes an error response document to this topic when it cannot delete the device's shadow

Device shadow

From the AWS IOT menu select "Manage Things" and select your device. From the device menu select "Shadow" and then "Classic shadow."

This will display the default JSON document.

**Open MQTT.FX and connect to the AWS IOT gateway.
Set the publish topic to "$aws/things/<your thing name>/shadow/update"
Set the payload to:**

```
{
 "state":{
 "reported":{
powerState : "on",
 "P4.1" : "set"
}
}
}
```

Now publish the data.

This will update the document stored on the server with the state of the real world device.

Conclusion

In this chapter, we have established a secure connection from our device to a commercial IoT cloud platform and explored some of its backend services. From here, you will be able to explore further using the many tutorials available from the AWS documentation. However, we have stored some key secrets as arrays in the unprotected flash memory. Here they are very vulnerable to both software and hardware tampering. In the remaining chapters, we will look at how to design our device to both securely store secrets and to be resistant against a software attack.

Software attacks and threat modeling

Introduction

This chapter will consider how a small embedded system may be attacked by exploiting software "loopholes" in your application code. Many of the techniques described in this chapter are routinely used to "hack" large computer systems, which feature standard operating systems and standard software packages. It may seem fanciful that a small embedded system with few resources running bespoke code can be attacked in the same way, and historically, this has indeed been true. With the explosive growth of IoT systems that deploy vast fleets of devices with a common codebase, IoT devices are becoming a worthwhile target. It is highly likely that through your career, you have mainly been concerned with writing code that functions correctly, which is enough of a challenge in its own right. However, for an IoT or any internet-connected device, we need to write code that is both functional and secure. To meet this objective, we must consider how an attacker may attempt to subvert our code to gain access to privileged information or simply to stop it from functioning correctly. It is only fairly recently that developing secure code has become an issue for small embedded systems and is still not widely understood. Progress has also been limited because most "plain old microcontrollers" simply do not have the hardware design capable of protecting against software and hardware intrusion. This is changing with the introduction of microcontroller's based on the Cortex-M33 CPU, which have both large amounts of FLASH and SRAM memory coupled with extensive assistive security peripherals. However, as our device hardware becomes more capable, we have seen a matching increase in software complexity, with larger codebases and increasing use of third-party software components such as RTOS and communication libraries. All of this complexity gives more potential opportunities for an attacker. This chapter will look at the most common forms of software attack and then consider ways to minimize an attackers options by writing secure code and introducing a process to identify and mitigate threats to our devices.

Before looking at the most common secure coding issues, we need to understand how to categorize threats against our IoT devices.

Security flaw

A software defect that poses a potential security risk. This is really a software bug that was not exposed by functional software testing. However, if the system is misused, the security flaw will cause it to behave unexpectedly, creating a security vulnerability.

Designing Secure IoT Devices with the Arm Platform Security Architecture and Cortex-M33
https://doi.org/10.1016/B978-0-12-821469-5.00004-1

Security vulnerability

A set of conditions that allow an attacker to violate an explicit or implicit security policy. For example, this may involve an attacker providing an out of bounds input, which causes a device to expose some privileged data.

Security exploit

A technique that takes advantage of a security vulnerability to violate an explicit or implicit security policy. Once an adversary has discovered a security flaw and vulnerability, they can then develop a set of actions to systematically attack your system. A skilful adversary will also combine several vulnerabilities in a coordinated attack.

Threats

A threat can be defined as a motivated adversary capable of exploiting a vulnerability. An adversary's motivation may be to create a "denial of service" by causing the system to crash. They may also desire to subvert your system's functionality or access confidential information held by your system.

An adversary's capabilities may range from a highly skilled hacker employed by a nation-state to criminal gangs or even curious kids playing with the internet. We should also make an assumption that techniques developed by a highly skilled adversary will tend to propagate over time. This will happen as a wider understanding propagates and advanced software tools become more freely available. In other words, what a few skilful hackers can do today will trickle down to "script kiddies" in the near future to become a routine problem, and we can be sure that tomorrow will bring something worse. This may seem overly pessimistic or alarmist, but unless you take measures to defend against potential attacks, the risk of a catastrophic attack will increase over time. While small microcontroller systems have not traditionally been the target of software attacks, this is a growing threat, and you should not be complacent.

Common security exploits and vulnerabilities

In this next section, we are going to look at a sample of common programming errors that create security flaws. However, we will start by looking at the most common forms of software attack that are used to exploit security flaws and vulnerabilities.

Buffer overflow

One of the most commonly occurring software exploits is known as a buffer overflow attack. This form of attack exploits both poor coding style and weakness in the C language itself. In C, a string is represented as an array of memory locations followed by a NULL terminator. As the C language does not have any inherent bounds checking, it is left up to the programmer to ensure that strings and arrays are handled correctly. Failure to correctly manage string buffers will leave your application open to a buffer overflow attack (Fig. 8.1).

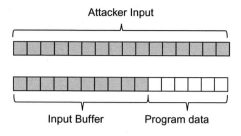

Attacker Input

Input Buffer   Program data

FIG. 8.1

Buffer overflow. An attacker can input data past the buffer bounds and corrupt program data.

No permission required.

To understand how a buffer overflow attack is performed, we need to consider the following scenario. In our application, we are receiving user commands over a UART. These are entered as ASCII characters and are read into a receive buffer before being processed by a command parser. The project will build correctly, and it compiles and links without any errors or warnings, and during testing, it performs correctly.

```c
int main (void) {
bool motorRunning = false;
 while(1) {
   printf("Enter command \n\r");
   motorRunning = IsStartMotor();
   if (motorRunning == true){
       break;
   }
   printf("Motor Halted \n\r");
 }
printf("Motor Running \n\r");
while(1);
}
char command[12];
bool Result;
char valid;
 bool IsStartMotor(void) {
 Result = false;
 gets(command);
 valid = strcmp(command, "motor start");
  if(valid == 0) {
   Result = true;
 }
 return (Result);
 }
```

If we look at the linker map file, we can see that the command buffer defined as global data and is assigned to the microcontroller SRAM. It is immediately followed by the "result" variable, which indicates if the command is true or false.

```
command        0x2007c000 Data    12 main_app.o(.bss)
  Result       0x2007c00c Data     1 main_app.o(.bss)
   valid       0x2007c00d Data     1 main_app.o(.bss)
```

This allows a malicious user to enter a string of characters that exceed the command array's bounds, which corrupts the result variable and potentially any other following data. In this example, an attacker can start the motor by simply entering more than 12 characters. The code is also using the gets() library function. This function accepts input until it receives a new line character (0x0A) or an End of File character (-1). While it is used to fill a buffer with user input in the form of an ASCII string, it will also accept the full range of binary values, including NULL and place these in the input buffer. There are other similar library functions that will potentially create security vulnerabilities, which we will look at later in this chapter. However, bear in mind that gets() is such a security risk it has been removed in the C99 standard.

Exercise: Buffer overflow

In the pack installer select Exercise 8.1 and press the Copy button.
Build and run the code.
In the terminal window enter the commands motor start.

This will check that the program works correctly.
Now try a buffer overflow by entering four additional characters.
This will set the result variable and cause our imaginary motor to start.

Add code to limit the number of input characters.
Add code to check that each character is within the ASCII character set.

Stack smashing

Before we look at a more sophisticated version of a buffer overflow attack, we need to understand how the thumb-2 instruction set implements a return from a function. As the thumb-2 instruction set does not contain a dedicated return instruction, the compiler uses several different approaches to affect a function call return.

Within a function, there may also be branches to an absolute address.
b. 0x899
Since the instruction and address are hardwired into the FLASH, this is not much use to us. A return may also be implemented by performing a branch exchange using the link register.
Bx lr
In this case, we are branching to the address held in the link register. If we can influence the value held in the link register, we can start to control the program's flow.

A third method is used when the called function will, in turn, call a second function. In this case, the link register contents must be protected, so on entry to the initial function, it will be pushed onto the stack.

PUSH lr

At the end of the function, the pop instruction is used to load the return address, which was in the link register directly into the program counter.

POP pc

This last method is useful to us, particularly when a buffer has been declared as a local variable. If we have declared an input buffer as a local variable, it will exist on the stack and will precede the values pushed on entry. Now, if we enter data that goes beyond the bounds of the command buffer, the stack frame will be corrupted, including the function return address as shown in Fig. 8.2.

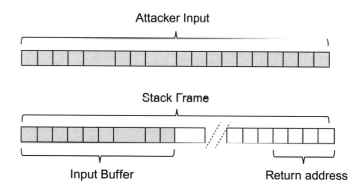

Attacker Input

Stack Frame

Input Buffer   Return address

FIG. 8.2

Stack smashing. Stack smashing uses a buffer overflow to modify stack values.

No permission required.

This makes it very easy to force the program to crash just by entering a long string of random characters. If we are a bit more cunning, it is possible to craft an input packet that modifies the return address so that the program jumps to a location where there is meaningful code. This is called an ARC attack because it changes the flow control resulting in a modified execution ARC of the program. We can also place arbitrary values into any other registers that have been pushed onto the stack. As these registers are typically used to pass parameters to a function, it is possible to make a function call by loading meaningful values into the saved register locations and then loading a function entry address in place of the existing return address.

Fortunately, this is a widely known technique and most compilers have "stack guard" options, which will defend against such an attack. The options for commonly used compilers are shown in Table 8.1.

Table 8.1 Stack guard.

Compiler	Stack guard switch	Description
Arm Compiler V6.xx and GCC compiler	-fno-stack-protector	Disable stack protection
	-fstack-protector	Enable stack protection for vulnerable functions with a local array of eight bytes or more
	-fstack-protector-all	Enable stack protection for all functions with a local array of eight bytes or more
	-fstack-protector-strong	Enable stack protection for all functions with any size of local variables
IAR	--stack-protection	Enable stack protection

Stack guard configuration options.

Once enabled, the stack guard places and monitors a pattern in the stack frame. The pattern, known as a cannery, is placed before the return address. Any attempt to modify the return address will corrupt the cannary pattern. The compiler will extend the return code at the end of the application function to check the cannary before using the return value. If the cannary has been corrupted, the application code will be notified through a callback function. We can also make things more difficult for an attacker by using a cannary pattern that includes NUL char and LF characters, which will cause library functions like strcpy() to terminate.

Exercise: Stack smashing

This exercise demonstrates a successful stack smashing attack, which causes an overflow of a buffer located on the stack. The attack can be detected by recompiling with the compiler stack protection switch enabled.

In these examples, the memory locations displayed in the debugger window may differ in the working example as a later compiler version may change the final code generation.

**In the pack installer select exercise 8.2 and press the copy button.
Open main.c.**

We have moved the command buffer to be a local variable in the isMotorStart() function.

```
bool IsStartMotor(void)
{
char command[12]; bool Result = true; char valid = 0x55;
 // gets(command);
memcpy(command,attack,30);
valid = strcmp(command, "motor start");
 if(valid == 0)
```

```
    {
     Result = 1;
    }
    return (Result);
}
```

We are also using memcpy() in place of gets() to load the attack vector, which is defined as an array. In this case, both the editor and compiler will provide a warning that we are exceeding the size of the command buffer.

```
    char attack[30] =
{1,2,3,4,5,6,7,8,9,10,11,12,13,14,15,16,0xB9,0x08,00,00};
```

Run the code to the memcpy() function.
Open the view memory window and set the address to the current stack pointer value, which is shown in the register window (Fig. 8.3).

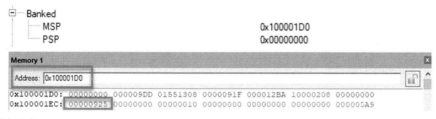

FIG. 8.3

Debugger memory view. Use the memory window to display the stack contents and locate the return address.

No permission required.

Here, we can see the current stack value, which has been pushed onto the stack.

Run the code to the isStartMotor() return command.

Here we can see that the return address has been modified. Fig. 8.4 The Thumb-2 instruction branches jump to an odd address and will execute the instruction at 0x000008B8. This location is the entry to a function that will print a suitable message. This is an ARC attack as we have changed the ARC (flow) of the program.

FIG. 8.4

Debugger memory view. The attack vector will modify the return address.

No permission required.

Start Tera Term and connect to the virtual comm port.
Run the code and view the message in the debug console (Fig. 8.5).

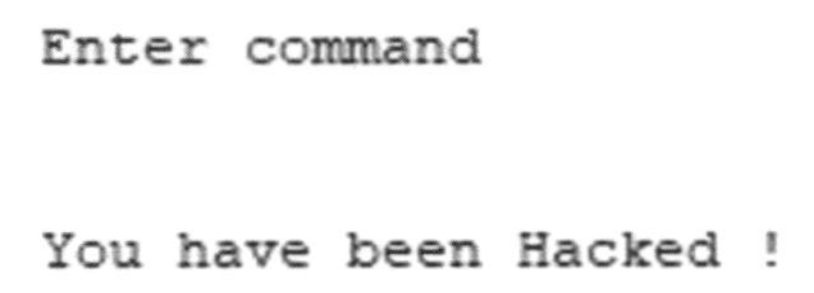

```
Enter command
```


```
You have been Hacked !
```

FIG. 8.5

Debugger console view. The compromised code will output a diagnostic message.

No permission required.

Exit the debugger.

The compiler provides protection against this type of attack in the form of a stack guard.

```
void *__stack_chk_guard = (void *)0xdeadbeef;
```

This places a stack guard canary into the stack frame, which is checks when the code modifies the stack. If the canary is not present or corrupted, the __stk_chk_fail() function is called.

```
void __stack_chk_fail(void){
  printf("Stack smashing detected.\n");
}
```

Uncomment the stack guard code at the start of main.
Open the options for target/compiler tab and add the -fstack-protector to the misc controls box (Fig. 8.6).

```
Misc      -fno-inline-functions -fstack-protector
Controls
```

FIG. 8.6

Compiler stack protector. Enable the stack protector in the compiler misc controls text box.

No permission required.

Build the code then start the debugger and run the code.

This time the stack smashing attempt will be detected and trapped.

Return orientated programming (ROP)

An ARC attack is an entry-level stack smashing exploit that is simply used to change the program flow to a new address. We can use stack smashing to create a more sophisticated technique that allows an adversary to chain together numerous stack smashing attacks. First, we need to disassemble the device code and find other POP instructions which are loading the program counter from the stack. Once we have located such an instruction, we can perform a stack smash to jump a few instructions before the new POP instruction. These instructions will execute and perform an operation such as loading a register or storing a value in memory. Once these instructions have executed we will reach the POP instruction. This will load the next return address from the attack vector stored on the stack. This address will be the start of the original gets() function. Now we are back where we started, and the attacker can load in the next attack vector (Fig. 8.7).

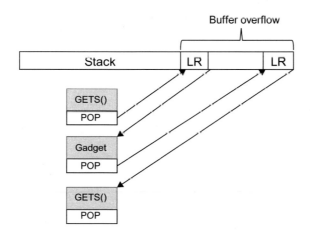

FIG. 8.7

ROP attack. A ROP attack can chain together useful "gadgets" to create a sophisticated exploit.

No permission required.

Now each of these gadgets only performs a simple operation but if an attacker can find a collection of gadgets they become an "attack instruction set."

Historically, this kind of attack has not been a concern for small embedded systems, which are largely running bespoke code. The effort of developing the exploit was far greater than any likely gains. However, with the growth of very large numbers of IoT nodes all using common components and RTOS, this is likely to change.

There is also the problem that most if not all Cortex-M and Cortex-M33 microcontrollers contain ROM code, which is installed by the Silicon Vendor (Fig. 8.8).

AHB port	Non-secure start address	Non-secure end address	Secure start address	Secure end address	Function [1]
0	0x0000 0000	0x0009 FFFF	0x1000 0000	0x1009 FFFF	Flash memory, on CM33 code bus. The last 17 pages (10 KB) are reserved on the 640 KB flash devices resulting in 630 KB internal flash memory
	0x0300 0000	0x0301 FFFF	0x1300 0000	0x1301 FFFF	Boot ROM, on CM33 code bus.
1	0x0400 0000	0x0400 7FFF	0x1400 0000	0x1400 7FFF	SRAM X on CM33 code bus, 32 KB. SRAMX_0 (0x1400 0000 to 0x1400 0FFF) and SRAMX_1 (0x1400 4000 to 0x1400 4FFF) are used for Casper (total 8 KB). If CPU retention used in power-down mode, SRAMX_2 (0x1400 6000 to 0x1400 65FF) is used (total 1.5 KB) by default in power API and this is user configurable within SRAMX_2 and SRAMX_3.

FIG. 8.8

Microcontroller system ROM. Most microcontrollers have immutable system code stored in a memory mapped ROM.

This code will be standard across a given family and could be searched by an attacker to build a standard library of gadgets for that device. For example, the following pair of instructions is located within the ROM of a popular Cortex-M microcontroller:

```
0x001007F8 6066    STR    r6,[r4,#0x04]
0x001007FA E8BD8FF8 POP
```

First, jump to the POP instruction and use this to load values into the registers R3 – R11 and load the PC to jump to the STR instruction, which will save the value in R6 into the memory location held by R4 + 4. The POP will again execute and can be used to return to the gets() instruction. This allows us to place an arbitrary value in an arbitrary memory location. Repeat this process enough times, and you can download arbitrary malware into the microcontroller RAM and then pass execution to it.

Armed with this and any other gadgets that can be found, the attacker would then only need to find a single loophole in your code to mount a sophisticated attack. Furthermore, a library of such gadgets becomes a hacker instruction set that can be packaged into a more sophisticated attack tool. Such a tool could, in theory, allow scripting of complex exploits by almost any adversary. While this would take a lot of initial effort by a skilled adversary, once such a directory of gadgets has been discovered, they can be packaged into a standard tool that would be widely available via the internet. This would be enough to subvert many existing IoT systems.

Exercise: ROP Gadgets

In this exercise, we will look at the mechanism of a ROP attack against a standard microcontroller.

In the pack installer select Exercise 8.3 and press the Copy button.
Build the program and start the debugger.

Here, we have the same example program, but this time, the attack string has been changed to perform a ROP attack. Again the gets() instruction has been replaced by the memcpy() function so that the attack vectors are stored in an array that is used to simulate the attacker input.

Set a breakpoint on the memcpy instruction.
Run the code so it hits the breakpoint.
Place the cursor display message array, right click and select "add to memory window."
Run the code so it goes through each attack vector.

On each iteration you will see the display message being modified until a new message is stored.

When the exploit has finished the new message will be printed in the console window.

Pointer issues

Once we have a useful vulnerability, obvious targets within the application code are C pointers. By modifying the pointer address, we can write values to arbitrary locations in the memory and in the case of function pointers, we can transfer execution to attacker-supplied code.

Some of the Cortex-A application processors provide hardware checking to prevent this kind of attack, but these are not available on Cortex-M processors. The main defense against pointer subversion is to prevent buffer overflow attacks. For pointers accessing very sensitive data or functions, it is possible to store an encrypted version of the pointer and decrypt them before use.

Integer vulnerabilities

While integers are the most commonly used program variable within our code, they also represent a source of many subtle vulnerabilities which an attacker can exploit. It is important to note here that if your testing consists of using data that conforms solely to expected values, then many of these issues may go undetected. An attacker is mainly interested in using out of range and unexpected values to provoke an anomalous result.

Wraparound

Unsigned integers do not overflow but simply wrap modulo their maximum value. If an unsigned value is incremented past its maximum value, it will wrap around to zero. Similarly, if we decrement an unsigned value below zero, it will wrap to its maximum value. This can be the source of many bugs and vulnerabilities. In the code below, if len is set to 1, then size will wrap to 0xFFFFFFFF and pass the test. When the memory is allocated, size is incremented and will again wrap to 0, causing unexpected behavior from the malloc() function.

```
void getBuffer(size_t len, char *src) {
size_t size;
if (len < 1000 ){
size = len - 2;
char *buffer = (char *)malloc(size);
  memcpy(buffer, src, size);
  }
}
```

Overflow

When signed integers are incremented past their maximum values (or decremented past their minimum values), they will overflow, causing a sign change as shown below.

```
short int test = 32767;
test++; // = -32767
```

Truncation

Another class of integer vulnerabilities may be caused by copying a value stored in one variable to another with a smaller range. In the code below, size is declared as a signed long but is copied into an unsigned short int. This results in a loss of the data stored in the upper bytes of size as it is copied to bufSize. This may result in not enough memory being allocated to buf, which will cause a buffer overflow in the heap space.

```
char *cpy_array(char *s, long size) {
unsigned short bufSize = size;
char *buf = (char *)malloc(bufSize);
if (buf) {
  memcpy(buf, s, size);
  return buf;
}
return NULL; }
```

Shift

When working with very constrained microcontrollers, it was a common practice to use the left shift operator as a fast way to perform a multiplication by a power of two. However, this is prone to error, and today's compilers will know to implement this kind of trick. Therefore, you should only use the shift operators for bit manipulation. In the code below the value 0x80000000 is shifted right by 24 bits resulting in 0xFFFFFF80 or -128. However, when passed to sprintf (), which requires an unsigned value, it equates to 4294967168. As the results buffer is too small to store this string, only the top four digits will be stored.

```
int stringify = 0x80000000;
char buf[256];
sprintf(buf, "%u", stringify >> 24);
```

Conversion

Converting between signed and unsigned types is another bad practice that will often result in a vulnerability that may not be exposed by functional testing. In the code below, the size of a dynamic array is initialized by passing a signed value size. While this is checked for a maximum value, there is no test for a minimum. This would allow an adversary to pass a negative value. This would pass the check, and the memory allocation function would be called. However, malloc() takes an unsigned value, so the negative value in size would be converted to a large positive value. This would result in a large amount of the heap memory being allocated to the array, or the malloc() would fail. In either case, this could well cause our application to crash.

```
void initialize_array(int size){
if (size < MAX_ARRAY_SIZE)
{
array = malloc(size);
}
```

You should also be careful when using the char type for small values. Depending on the compiler, a char deceleration may be signed or unsigned. For this reason, always be explicit by using unsigned char or signed char.

Switch statements

A common programming error when using a switch statement is to accidentally omit a break statement at the end of a case. Since this is actually a valid use of C as it is possible to allow code to run through several cases, it would not be picked up by the compiler or linker. If undetected, such a bug can become a useful vulnerability for an attacker. You must ensure that every case within a switch statement is well formed: each case must be terminated by a break. Also, all of the cases in a switch statement must be used.

```
enum __colour {red,green,blue} //unused case
switch (colour){
red:
  i++; //missing break
green:
  i--;
break;
default:
break;
}
```

Like the misuse of integers, a static analyzer will provide a warning if a break is missing. If the static analyzer is also checking against a coding standard like MISRA C or Cert C, this will be reported as an error.

Integer mitigations

We can perform runtime mitigations by performing pre- and postchecks within functions before and after using data passed to functions. A compiler will provide a header limits.h, which provides standard defines for the maximum and minimum values for each data type. An example of a precheck for addition is shown below:

```
limits.h
```

for a calculation sum = sum + i

```
if (i > UINT_MAX - sum){
   too_big();
}
else
{
   sum += i;
}
```

while with a postcheck for addition we can test that a wraparound has not occurred:

```
if( sum < i )
{
//wraparound error
}
```

Compiler support: There are a couple of runtime traps that are useful for detecting arithmetic errors. By setting the compiler switch -ftrapv, an undefined instruction exception will be raised in the event of signed arithmetic overflow. It is also possible to generate a divide by zero exception by setting the DIV_ZERO bit in the Cortex Processor Configuration and Control Register.

Accessing memory

Another great source of security vulnerabilities are variadic functions which allow a variable number of arguments. Variadic functions such as printf() and scanf() directly handle user I/O and have a potential for misuse, which can create serious security loopholes. For example, we can use the printf () function to write a string to the standard IO.

```
char str[] = "Hello World";
printf(str);
```

While this is not good coding practice (that's the point), it will compile and run. If an adversary is able to manipulate the string to contain the standard printf() format codes, it is possible to view the contents of the microcontroller memory. For example, the following string will cause the printf () function to display the current stack values.

```
char str[] = "%04x %04x %04x %04x.%04x %04x %04x %04x\n\r";
```

This sort of attack is more of a problem on x86 processors. With a stack-based processor, it is possible to use format codes to make arbitrary writes to memory. Fortunately, the Arm Cortex-M RISC architecture is more resistant to this type of attack. However, you should be aware of it and sanitize input strings just in case.

Exercise: Variadic functions

This exercise demonstrates using STDIO library functions to view stack memory.

Open the pack installer and select Exercise 8.5 and press the Copy button.
Open the console window.
Open the stack window.
Run the code up to the printf() function.
Make a note of the current stack values.
Run the printf() function and compare the output to the values stored on the stack.

These are just a small sample of common software vulnerabilities that an attacker can exploit. The bibliography lists some books on secure coding, which are recommended for further reading.

Mitigation

Now that we have some understanding of the threats our IoT node is likely to face, we need to consider some mitigation methods and techniques. This can be considered at three levels: the development process, implementation, and verification.

Development process

Security training

Your development team should be trained to write secure code along with how to use and interpret any coding standard you are working to. They should also understand the basics of how to attack a computer system, including your own design.

Threat model

When designing your system, you must consider the potential threats against the system and produce a model of how an attacker may act. This will include a description of the available attack surface. Depending on the threat model, the attack surface may be the communication interfaces where a device can only be accessed remotely. It may include local buses and hardware tampering if the device is in a public location. We will have a look at threat modeling techniques later in this chapter.

Security requirements

When designing your system, security issues must be part of your initial requirements and become an integral part of the design from the beginning. It is not advisable to add security features to a design at a later stage. As we will see in the following chapters, as well as writing code securely, we also have to use a proven security model and software architecture. If this is not done at the outset, it will be virtually impossible to adopt later without a ground-up redesign of the system.

Security model

As we will see in the next chapter, the Arm PSA provides a template security model that our applications threat model and security requirement can feed into. The security model defines an abstract system architecture that can be implemented on any Cortex-M device to create an attack-resistant device. By being familiar with the PSA resources (firmware libraries and tools), you will minimize the cost of developing a secure device, be able to adopt a proven security model from the beginning of the project, and develop a device that complies with the current industry standards and regional laws.

Change management

During development, you must also implement a formal change management process so that any changes to the original design specification are considered against the security model. Our goal is to avoid hasty changes or short-term cludges that can compromise the overall design.

Peer review

During the design process, you must hold separate security reviews in addition to code reviews. Any significant findings will be used to update the threat and security model.

Expert validation

As we have seen in Chapter 3, the Arm PSA includes a certification process. You should consider meeting Level 1 certification as mandatory for all IoT device designs. By adopting the PSA certification process, you will be able to demonstrate a recognizable level of validation. If you are new to developing secure devices, you should also consider using an outside consultant to review your design and development process. If your IoT device contains high-value assets such as financial or medical information, you should consider formal testing by a security lab in order to gain Level 2 certification or above.

Functional safety standards

Functional Safety and Security are two sides of the same coin. Companies developing functional safety products have had to address all of the above points for many years. Safety standards for different industries are well developed and accompanied by documented formal processes. Many of the approaches used for functional safety can be adopted to develop secure devices. It is well worth reviewing a safety standard to find features worth adopting into your existing design process.

Implementation

Software architecture

We can go a long way to reducing software vulnerabilities by adopting a well-structured software architecture. As discussed in "Designers Guide to the Cortex-M Microcontrollers," we can structure our code as a series of software layers with the different functional elements designed as self-contained components, as shown in Fig. 8.9.

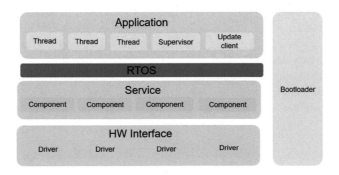

FIG. 8.9

Software architecture. Creating a standard component based architecture aids testing and code reuse.

No permission required.

In this scheme, the RTOS threads provide the application "business logic." The components provide the functional code required to drive a particular peripheral. The driver layer provides the low-level code and interrupts for each peripheral. As we will see in the following chapters, we should also isolate sensitive data and functions into a separate execution partition that is only accessed through a well-tested API.

Secure coding

Currently, the programming language of choice for a small microcontroller system is the C language. This is both a blessing and a curse as the ethos of the C language is "trust the programmer" and "don't get in the programmer's way." This has yielded an ideal language for small embedded systems, which provides unrestricted access to low-level hardware. Unfortunately, it is just these kinds of features that make C a basket case for both safety and security applications. A number of coding standards have been developed specifically for use in embedded systems. The most widely adopted standards are Cert-C, MISRA-C, and BARR-C. The CERT-C coding standard has been specifically designed to provide rules for secure coding in the C programming language. MISRA-C was originally developed for use in automotive safety-critical systems and has now been widely adopted for general embedded system use. The BARR-C coding standard was developed as a coding style guide with the aim to minimize coding errors (Table 8.2).

Table 8.2 Secure coding standards.

Standard	Description	URL
Cert-C	A general coding standard to improve the safety, reliability, and security of software systems using the C Programming language.	https://resources.sei.cmu.edu/downloads/secure-coding/assets/sei-cert-c-coding-standard-2016-v01.pdf
MISRA-C	Originally developed for the automotive industry, now widely adopted for general embedded systems use. The focus of MISRA-C is on safety critical systems.	https://www.misra.org.uk/Publications/tabid/57/Default.aspx
BARR-C	A style guide aimed at reducing coding defects. May be combined with the above standards.	https://barrgroup.com/embedded-systems/books/embedded-c-coding-standard

Fault injection hardening

A further defense against both software and hardware attacks is to add additional code to your project to make it harder for an attacker to manipulate your code without being detected. The Platform Security Architecture describes the following "Fault Injection Hardening" FIH techniques, which are recommended for your application code.

Control flow monitor

To catch malicious modification of the expected control flow. When an important portion of a program is executed, a flow monitor counter is incremented. The program moves to the next stage only if the accumulated flow monitor counter is equal to an expected value.

Default failure

The return value variable should always contain a value indicating failure. Changing its value to success is done only under one protected flow (preferably protected by double checks).

Complex constant

Replace Boolean values with complex constant values as these are more difficult for an attacker to modify.

Redundant variables and condition checks

To make branch condition attack harder it is recommended to check the relevant condition twice (it is better to have a random delay between the two comparisons).

Random delay

Some software and hardware attacks require very precise timing. Adding random delay to the code execution makes the timing of an attack much harder.

Loop integrity check

Ensure that a program loop has been fully executed. After a loop has executed, check the loop counter whether it indeed has the expected value.

Duplicated execution

Execute a critical step multiple times to prevent fault injection from skipping the step. To mitigate multiple consecutive fault injections, random delay can be inserted between duplicated executions.

Defense in depth

When designing your system architecture, you should assume that each security mechanism will be breached. This means that you should have multiple layers of security within your IoT device, so if one fails, the next will protect your device. This is the ethos adopted by the PSA security model, which will be covered in the remainder of this book.

Hardware

As we will see in the second half of his book, the Armv8-M architecture has hardware features that have been specifically added to enhance its ability to protect against software attack. Equally, the Silicon Vendors who have adopted Cortex-M33 processes have added their own security peripherals to build a Trusted Execution Environment around the processor. This has created a new generation of microcontrollers that surpass the limitation of a "plain old microcontroller" and are suited to build the Internet of Things.

Tool chain

The most important tool in any project is the compiler and linker. You must become thoroughly acquainted with all the compiler and linker switches that can be used to enforce the generation of secure code (Table 8.3). When developing for a secure project, the compiler should be configured to implement its strictest interpretation of your source code. The compiler warning level must be set to its highest level. All warnings should be treated as errors, and the "C" standard must be rigidly applied. Consider using a safety certified compiler.

Table 8.3 Arm compiler security options.

Compiler switch	Description
-fbracket-depth	Sets the limit for nested parentheses, brackets, and braces.
-ftrapv	Instructs the compiler to generate traps for signed arithmetic overflow on addition, subtraction, and multiplication operations.
-fwrap	Instructs the compiler to assume that signed arithmetic overflow of addition, subtraction, and multiplication, wraps using two's complement representation.
-mexecute-only	Generates execute-only code, and prevents the compiler from generating any data accesses to code sections.
-pedantic -pedantic-errors	Generate warnings (pedantic) or errors (pedantic-errors) if code violates strict ISO C and ISO C++.
-Werror	Turn warnings into errors.
-WAll	Show all warnings

Verification

Broadly speaking, there are two main techniques to verifying your source code. Static analysis will parse the code across modules for common programming errors and dynamic testing that will reveal functional errors. Your design workflow should use both techniques.

Metrics

Alongside a coding standard and static analyzers, you should also adopt a set of useful software metrics. These should be used to measure and manage the complexity of the source code. A useful metric is McCabe's Cyclomatic Complexity Metric. This analyses the C' source code of a function and calculates the number of paths through a function. Within a project, we can set a maximum value for the complexity of a function, and here a typical maximum complexity number is ten. Any function that exceeds this value should be rewritten or decomposed into a set of smaller functions. Since the McCabe's complexity number indicates the number of paths through a function, it is also a useful indication for the number of software tests required to achieve full coverage of a function.

Static analysis

In addition to the compiler warnings and errors, you should also use a static analyzer to check both the syntax and grammar of your source code (Table 8.4). A good static analyzer will do a project-wide analysis of your code that is far more exhaustive than the checks made by the compiler and linker. Many commercial static analysis tools can also be used to check compliance with the MISRA-C and CERT-C coding standards.

Table 8.4 Static analysis.

Static analyser	Company	URL
Coverity	Synopsys	https://www.synopsys.com/software-integrity/security-testing/static-analysis-sast.html
ECLAIR	Bugseng	https://www.bugseng.com/eclair
Parasoft C/C++ test	Parasoft	https://www.parasoft.com/solutions/development-testing/static-analysis/
PC-Lint	Gimpel	https://www.gimpel.com/
SPLINT	University of Virginia	https://splint.org/

Software testing

Adequate software testing is a vital part of any embedded project. It is even more important in an IoT project if we want to create a secure device. During the formal testing phase of your project, in addition to testing for functional accuracy, your test team will also need to consider additional tests that probe security issues revealed by your threat modeling exercise. When writing the code, you should also use a developer test framework to write a series of unit tests as you go along. In addition to locating bugs early in the development cycle, writing test cases for each function will force you to revisit and refactor the code. While this does add an overhead in developing your code, it does result in a significant improvement in code quality and is highly recommended. For more details of using a test framework see Designers Guide to Cortex-M Development (3rd edition).

Fuzzing

Fuzzing is a form of testing that passes random packets of data across a device's trust boundaries to find useful vulnerabilities or simply cause a malfunction in the device. In the case of a small IoT device, it may have a range of serial interfaces such as a USART, I2C, or SPI. Here we can fuzz these channels by sending a range of non-sense inputs in order to see how the device responds. A good fuzzing target is often a user interface. Even a simple UI will have a large "tree" of possible inputs. It is not uncommon for there to be many combinations that are unexpected by the developer. This makes a user interface a rich target for useful exploits.

Enhanced debug

The debug architecture of the Cortex-M33 processor includes an instruction trace unit called the Embedded Trace Macrocell (ETM). This is an optional feature that the silicon vendor can fit at the design stage. Typically, a suitable debug adapter will be used to stream every instruction executed by the Cortex-M33 to your PC's hard disk.

A suitably advanced debugger will provide performance analysis and code coverage analysis of the raw instruction trace. The performance analysis tool will allow you to see each function's maximum and minimum run time and the number of times it has executed. The code coverage analysis will help you to guarantee that all the code in your application has been executed as expected. Such trace tools are widely used during the development of safety-critical applications since they allow a deep analysis of code execution. If your target microcontroller is fitted with an ETM, you should consider using the instruction trace to monitor code coverage and perform timing analysis.

The Cortex-M33 processor also includes an Instrumentation trace that can act as a serial debug channel. This allows you to send error and information messages from your code to a console window via the debug channel. This should be used during development monitor code execution and reveal any run time faults as the code executes.

The IEEE top 10 secure coding practices

To conclude this section, here are the top 10 secure coding practices from The IEEE (Table 8.5)

Table 8.5 IEEE Top 10 secure coding practices.

Practice	Description
Validate input	Validate input from all untrusted data sources. Proper input validation can eliminate the vast majority of software vulnerabilities.
Heed compiler warnings	Compile code using the highest warning level available for your compiler and eliminate warnings by modifying the code. Use static and dynamic analysis tools to detect and eliminate additional security flaws.
Architect and design for security policies	Create a software architecture and design your software to implement and enforce security policies. For example, if your system requires different privileges at different times, consider dividing the system into distinct intercommunicating subsystems, each with an appropriate privilege set.
Keep it simple	Keep the design as simple and small as possible. Complex designs increase the likelihood that errors will be made in their implementation, configuration, and use. Additionally, the effort required to achieve an appropriate level of assurance increases dramatically as security mechanisms become more complex.
Default deny	Base access decisions on permission rather than exclusion. This means that, by default, access is denied and the protection scheme identifies conditions under which access is permitted.

Continued

Table 8.5 IEEE Top 10 secure coding practices—cont'd

Practice	Description
Adhere to the principle of least privilege	Every process should execute with the least set of privileges necessary to complete the job. Any elevated permission should only be accessed for the least amount of time required to complete the privileged task. This approach reduces the opportunities an attacker has to execute arbitrary code with elevated privileges.
Sanitize data sent to other systems	Sanitize all data passed to complex subsystems [C STR02-A] such as command shells, relational databases, and commercial off-the-shelf (COTS) components. Attackers may be able to invoke unused functionality in these components through the use of SQL, command, or other injection attacks. This is not necessarily an input validation problem because the complex subsystem being invoked does not understand the context in which the call is made. Because the calling process understands the context, it is responsible for sanitizing the data before invoking the subsystem.
Practice defense in depth	Manage risk with multiple defensive strategies, so that if one layer of defense turns out to be inadequate, another layer of defense can prevent a security flaw from becoming an exploitable vulnerability, and/or limit the consequences of a successful exploit. For example, combining secure programming techniques with secure runtime environments should reduce the likelihood that vulnerabilities remaining in the code at deployment time can be exploited in the operational environment.
Use effective quality assurance techniques	Good quality assurance techniques can be effective in identifying and eliminating vulnerabilities. Fuzz testing, penetration testing, and source code audits should all be incorporated as part of an effective quality assurance program. Independent security reviews can lead to more secure systems. External reviewers bring an independent perspective; for example, in identifying and correcting invalid assumptions.
Adopt a secure coding standard	Develop and/or apply a secure coding standard for your target development language and platform.

Threat modeling

As part of designing a secure IoT device, we have to add a new activity called Threat Modeling to our design process. When we Threat Model a system, we are examining the design to identify potential security weaknesses and propose suitable mitigations. Threat Modeling should also be carried out throughout your project's design cycle, so any changes that impact the model are caught and analyzed. Historically Threat Modeling has not been widely used in small embedded systems, so to start with, it can seem like a black art. In order to get proficient, you will need to practice using the techniques described below on existing or on imaginary (experimental) designs. It is also important to realize that Threat Modeling is a team sport and should involve all your development team members.

Where to start

In order to start thinking about security issues in an IoT system, a first step is to read through online IT and IoT attack libraries. An attack library is a categorized list of potential threats that have been used against existing systems. The first stop is the Open Web Application Security Project (OWASP). As well as listing security threats and vulnerabilities for IT systems, the OWASP website includes a specific section devoted to IoT threats. The OWASP IoT project maintains a list of the top threats against IoT devices and several categories of active threats.

https://wiki.owasp.org/index.php/
OWASP_Internet_of_Things_Project#tab=IoT_Top_10

Another useful attack library is the Common Attack Pattern Enumeration and Classification. This is a more general resource but useful none the less.

https://capec.mitre.org/data/index.html

Use these resources to develop a healthy and informed paranoia.

Threat modeling process

There are a wide range of approaches to Threat Modeling, and we will have a look through some techniques that are useful for an IoT system but first, I want to go over some approaches to analyzing and documenting the system. The 4+1 architectural view model outlines a set of four descriptions of a system taken from the view of different stakeholders. The additional +1 view is the possible use cases or scenarios that your device is intended for. By considering each view, we can build up documentation that fully describes the system and our device's role within it, as shown in Table 8.6.

Table 8.6 4+1 Architecture.

View	Description	Stakeholder
Logical	The functional requirements that describe the applications object model	Designers
Implementation	Describes the architectural layers of the application.	Programmers
Process	Describes the design's operation, concurrent threads and internal synchronization	Integrators
Deployment	Describes the mapping of the software onto the hardware and shows the system's interfaces to sensors and user input	Deployment managers
Use case	Describes the possible end uses of the system	All including end users

We can then analyze these descriptions through a five step process to develop our application threat model (Table 8.7).

Table 8.7 Threat modeling process.

Action	Description
Identify your Assets	Identify elements of your system an attacker will want to access
Model your system	Create a model of your system for analysis
Brainstorm the threats	Perform a group brainstorming session to identify the threats
Document the Threats	Assess the realistic threats from the brainstorming session and document them
Rate and rank each threat	Rate each threat and then rank them to create an actionable list

Threat modeling may be considered as a five stage process.

Identify assets

The first step in our threat modeling process is to identify the assets that make up our system. These are the elements that will be of most interest to an attacker, and protecting them will be a priority of your security model. Typical assets of a system include stored data (aka Data at Rest), user credentials, stored secrets such as encryption keys, biometric data, financial data, and location information. Once you have identified your assets, they should be documented and ranked in importance.

Create a system model

You should perform your Threat Modeling exercise very early in the project, ideally, before any code has been written. The final application may not be fully understood at this stage, but you will know its main objectives. Our next step is to create a system model as far as possible. This model will consist of all the available documentation from our architectural views that describes the system's objectives and use cases.

Brainstorm the threats

Once we have a system model, we can start to discover potential threats. This is best done as a group brainstorming session. Here all of the relevant stakeholders will examine the system model and propose potential threats. At this point, all threats should be added without judging if they are practical or not. During this session, the threats should be added to a mind map. After you have populated the mind map, you next go through each diagnosed threat and decide if it is really a practical threat. If it is actionable, it should be documented as a potential threat. This brainstorming process should be repeated through the development process alongside code reviews so that any design changes are fed into the security model.

Software bugs as threats

Our initial threat modeling process is concerned with finding avenues of attack that could be used by an adversary. During development and even after release, software bugs will be discovered. These must also be documented and rated for their security implications.

Threat modeling techniques

The purpose of Threat Modeling is to discover the security requirements for a given design so that a comprehensive security model can be developed. The Threat Modeling process will help to evaluate potential vulnerabilities and will often reveal issues that are not covered by the existing design process.

In this section, we will look at some standard methodologies that can be successfully used to produce a Threat Model for your application. It is very important to go through the Threat Modeling process at the beginning of the design process. You should also re-evaluate the Threat Model in the light of any changes to the design requirements.

Identify the threats

Now that we have a full description of the system, we can start to consider how an attacker may attempt to subvert it. We can first start by thinking who an attacker may be and what access they may have to the system. Are we only concerned with network attacks, or do we have to protect the hardware as well? In what environment does our system sit, and what opportunities does it present for an attacker? Who are our users, and how do they access the system? What is the lifecycle of the final product? How will it be manufactured, provisioned and on-boarded to the network? These sorts of questions will help build up a view of the possible "attack surfaces available to an adversary."

Once we have an understanding of our system assets and attack surfaces that give an adversary a possible loophole through which to compromise our system, we can begin to define trust boundaries within it. These are typically interfaces to the outside world but also include interfaces to local storage such as memory cards along with local peripherals such as an ADC or RTC, serial interfaces like I2C, SPI, and, of course, the CoreSight debug interface. As well as these hardware interfaces, you should also consider internal software trust boundaries. These will most likely be API interfaces to any third-party software components that are being used (Fig. 8.10).

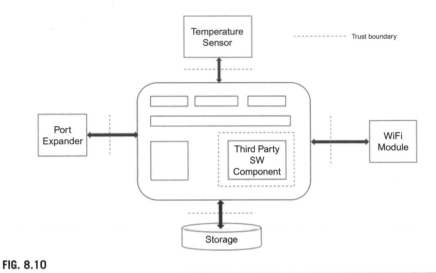

FIG. 8.10

Trust boundaries. A software design will have external and internal trust boundaries.

No permission required.

After you have defined the system model along with its attack surfaces and trust boundaries, we can start to analyze the system for threats. There are a number of Threat Modeling methodologies, but in this section, we will look at two of the most widely used approaches: the STRIDE method and Attack Trees.

STRIDE

The STRIDE method was developed by Adam Shostack at Microsoft as an acronym that can be used as a guide to identifying potential threats. Each letter in the STRIDE acronym describes a possible attack vector that may be used by an attacker. By considering each in turn, we can build a detailed description of threats against our devices. It is important to always remember that STRIDE is an acronym, not a taxonomy, and does not cover every possibility. Do not be blinkered by the process.

Spoofing

Spoofing is pretending to be something or someone other than yourself. Spoofing may be a technical process where an attacker's node or server pretends to be an authentic part of your system, or it can be a human who impersonates a user or administrator to gain confidential information.

Tampering

In an IoT, system tampering can be a physical attack on a node, or it may be an attempt to modify data within the system. Physical tampering may be an attempt to copy the devices firmware or locate a stored encryption key. Physical tampering may also include introducing faults and errors by manipulating a device's sensors.

Data tampering is an attempt to alter data at all levels within a system. This may be stored data such as a configuration file, run time data within application variables or network data where packets can be added or removed.

Repudiation

In most cases, an adversary will want to deny responsibility for any attack and may actively remove incriminating evidence as part of an exfiltration. Alternatively, a user may repudiate an action such as setting off an alarm or may cause an alarm through a genuine mistake. When we design a system, it is important to consider good authentication and logging so it is possible to manage repudiation claims effectively.

Information disclosure

Information disclosure is allowing an unauthorized individual to see data that they are not allowed to see. This may be the ability to extract useful information from log or error messages up to the ability to read an entire database or to compromise network communications. In an IoT system, security of the devices firmware through the entire product lifecycle (development, production, updating, and decommissioning) should also be considered.

Denial of service

A denial of service attack will typically prevent a node from reaching a resource it needs to perform correctly. This may mean flooding a node or server with packets so that it cannot process real data or a physical intervention such as severing a wireless connection using a Faraday shield.

Elevation of privilege

An elevation of privilege allows a user to perform an action that they are not allowed to do. In a typical IoT system, this is where a standard user is granted administrator rights and acquires access to manage the system.

STRIDE-based Tools
Elevation of privilege (E of P)

The STRIDE method has also been gamified in the form of a card game called "Elevation of Privilege." The E of P deck consists of a suite of cards for each class of thread. Within each suit each card represents a particular threat. You can download a pdf file with images of each card to print your own deck using the link below.

https://www.microsoft.com/en-gb/download/details.aspx?id=20303

The deck is used as follows. The cards are dealt out to each member of your development team. Play starts with the player holding the "3 of tampering." They can play any card that they consider to be a possible threat. If everyone else agrees, then this is accepted as a threat and recorded. The next player can play a card in the same suite. At the end of a round, the player who played the highest value card starts the next round. This is a simple, fast game that can be a fun way to creatively discover security threats to your system.

Security cards

Similar to E of P is a deck of cards called "Security Cards" that are intended for use in a brainstorming session. The deck consists of 42 cards split into four dimensions along with templates to make your own cards.

https://securitycards.cs.washington.edu/

The security cards deck is less of a game than E of P and more a way to guide your thinking to develop a threat model. For example, you can consider a particular aspect of your system and then sort the cards in order of relevance for that particular threat. You can also consider how several threats may be combined to successfully attack your system.

Threat modeling utilities

There are also some free to use graphical Threat Modeling tools. These allow you to draw a data flow diagram of your system, define trust boundaries and then categorize threats to each element using the STRIDE acronym.

Threat modeling tool

Microsoft provides a free to use tool called Threat Modeling Tool, which is based on the STRIDE process. This can be downloaded from the link below:

https://docs.microsoft.com/en-us/azure/security/develop/threat-modeling-tool

An introductory tutorial is available here:

https://docs.microsoft.com/en-us/azure/security/develop/
threat-modeling-tool-getting-started

OWASP threat dragon

The OWASP project has also provided a Threat Modeling tool called OWASP Threat Dragon. Like the Microsoft tool, Threat Dragon uses the STRIDE process. It provides a whiteboard environment and a minimal set of design objects. This allows you to draw a Data Flow Diagram (DFD) for any software system. Once you have described your system, it is possible to add trust boundaries to the DFD and then analyze and record threats to each element using the STRIDE system.

http://docs.threatdragon.org/#downloads

With an introductory tutorial here:

http://docs.threatdragon.org/#threat-model-diagrams

Pay particular attention on how to add data flow connections!

The simplicity of the Threat Dragon interface makes it quick, easy and intuitive to use. At the time of writing, it is still under active development, but it is still a very useful tool.

Attack trees

A second commonly used threat modeling method is the use of Attack Trees. This is a more abstract method of analyzing possible attacks and is a good way of capturing domain knowledge from team members and external experts who may not be experienced at software development. This makes Attack Trees a good compliment to the STRIDE method.

To develop an Attack tree first define an attackers objective and create this as a root node in a tree diagram as shown in Fig. 8.11.

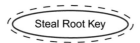

FIG. 8.11

Attack tree objective. Define an attacker objective as the goal of an attack tree.

No permission required.

Next, we can consider all the ways an attacker may achieve this goal. Each different method is added as a leaf node. We can first start with general categories and then drill down into specific methods (Fig. 8.12).

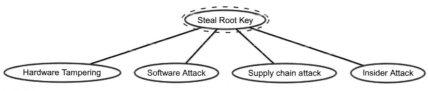

FIG. 8.12

Attack tree. Add a layer of possible attack methods.

No permission required.

We can then add further child nodes to each leaf node to represent the steps an attacker needs to achieve to reach the subgoal and then their eventual objective. In our current diagram, each subnode represents a different path, so each path is a logical OR. To allow us to model an attack that requires two or more steps to be taken in combination, any node can be a logical AND, which is represented as shown in Fig. 8.13.

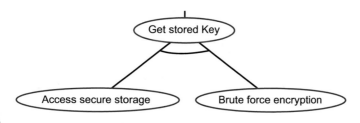

FIG. 8.13

Attack tree. Notation used to describe a combinational attack.

No permission required.

Once we have defined all the nodes in an Attack Tree, we can start to categorize each node to work out the threats to our system. We can first categorize each node against a realistic chance of success. Here, we can use a broad brush and define each node as possible or impossible. This is intended to prune the tree so we can concentrate on all the viable threats.

Next we can categorize each node using a set of domains to further quantify the potential threat faced. Commonly used threat domains are listed in Table 8.8.

Once each node has been populated with its domain values, we can use the tree

Table 8.8 Attack domains.

Domain	Values
Feasibility	Possible, impossible
Difficulty	Low, medium, high
Cost	Currency
Time	Hours, days, weeks
Skill level	Low, medium, high
Probability of success	Percentage

Attacker threat potentials can be assessed using different cost domains.

to evaluate each attack path and the cost of an attack in each domain. This could include things such as the least difficult, the cheapest or the highest probability of success. Building an Attack Tree is a group effort. You can create an Attack Tree and populate it with as many nodes as you can think of, then pass it to each member of your development team so they can expand it with any additional attacks that have not been considered. Once you have a finished tree, you can determine the biggest risks by analyzing the attack tree branches and their combined domain values the find the most viable threats.

The attack defense tool (ADTool)

The Attack Defense Tool is a free tool developed by the University of Luxembourg. The ADTool allows you to create attack trees and model the effect of different domain parameters to calculate the costs of an attack. The ADTool also extends the attack tree method by allowing you to add defensive countermeasures and model their effect.

Download and install the ADTool from:

https://satoss.uni.lu/members/piotr/adtool

A case study "Using attack–defense trees to analyze threats and countermeasures in an ATM" is also available here:

https://satoss.uni.lu/members/rolando/papers/FFGKST2016.pdf

Document the threats and bugs

As you discover threats to your system, it is important to document them systematically. You should have a standard template that records each threat both in summary and detail. Each threat should be assigned a name and threat number. If you are using Attack Trees, you should still document each threat separately, so you have one coherent system. During the development process, any discovered bugs must be assessed for their impact on security and then logged in in a similar way.

Rate the threats and bugs

As we go through the development cycle and repeat, the modeling process, new threats may emerge, along with software bugs that have an impact on device security. Our next step is to rate each issue and then rank them in order to prioritize development effort. How you assess each threat's severity depends on the system, you are designing. You can create your own scale, be it numeric (1-10), or labels (low, medium, high). There are several systems that are publicly available which you can adopt or adapt to your needs.

Attack tree rating

As we have seen in Attack Trees, if each node has been populated with a full set of threat categories, it has a rating system built-in. This can be used to analyze the impact of each threat.

Common vulnerability scoring system (CVSS)

The Common Vulnerability Scoring System (CVSS) uses eight metrics to calculate a severity score between 0.0 and 10.0. The first four metrics are concerned with defining the possibility of an attack exploit, as shown in Table 8.9.

Table 8.9 CVSS threat metrics.

Exploit	Metric
Attack vector	Network adjacent local physical
Attack complexity	High, low
Privileges required	High, low, none
User interaction	Required, none

We then have to define the impact of a successful exploit using four impact metrics, as shown in Table 8.10. Combining the exploit and impact values together will give us a base score.

Table 8.10 Impact metrics.

Impact	Metric
Scope changed	Changed, unchanged
Confidentiality	High, low, none
Integrity	High, low, none
Availability	High, low, none

Temporal score

Once we have a base score, we can consider how an attacker may be using a vulnerability and how difficult it may be to fix. This temporal score is derived from a further three metrics, as shown in Table 8.11.

Table 8.11 Temporal score.

Temporal metric	Values
Exploit code maturity	High, Exists, Proof of concept, Unproven, None
Remediation level	Official, Fix, Temporary, Fix, Workaround, None
Report confidence	Confirmed, Reasonable, Unknown

Environmental score

The environmental score allows us to provide modified values for the exploitability and impact values for different physical operating environments. It also provides a set of impact sub score modifiers that allow you to define the confidentiality, integrity, and availability requirements for a given environment.

Example CVSS calculator

To see how CVSS works, let us have a look at a practical example. In this exercise, we will calculate the threat to our IoT device from a software attack that is attempting to gain the device root key. This is a new style of attack that has recently been the subject of a research paper, and the exploit requires an attacker to have access to a local network. In order to calculate a CVSS score, we can use an online calculator, which is maintained by NIST.

> **Open a browser and connect to** https://nvd.nist.gov/vuln-metrics/cvss/v3-calculator

First, we can enter the base score metrics. For this attack, an adversary must have local network access, and as this is a research attack, the complexity is high. We also do not need any special privileges or need to trick a user into helping us. The initial base score settings are shown in Fig. 8.14.

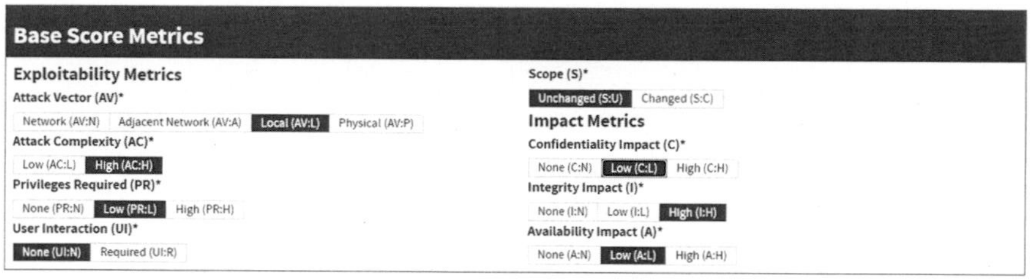

FIG. 8.14

CVSS initial base score settings. Enter your base score into the CVSS calculator.

No permission required.

Next, we can enter the temporal score. This is a proof of concept attack which has high complexity. We do not know how we can mitigate against it. We have only read about this attack as a possibility, so we do not know if it can be reproduced in the wild (Fig. 8.15).

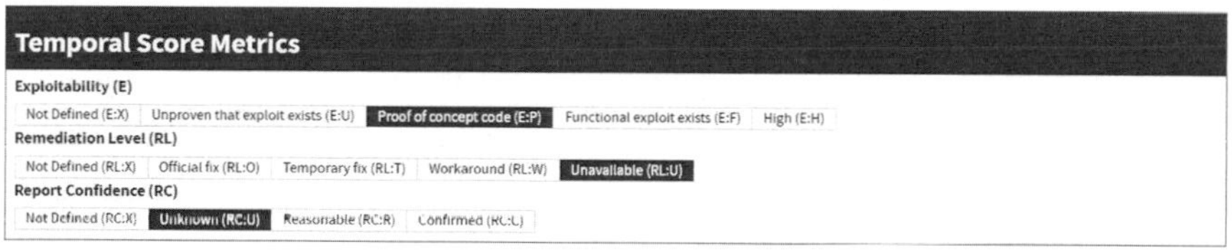

FIG. 8.15

Temporal calculator. The temporal calculator lets you define the maturity of a threat.

No permission required.

We can use the environmental score to adjust the base score for different types of user scenario. For example, access to the local network may be easy in a domestic or office environment. An industrial or factory network may be locked down much harder (Fig. 8.16).

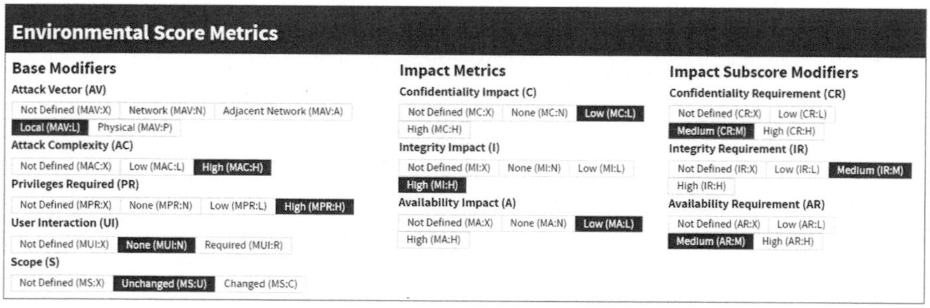

FIG. 8.16

Environmental calculator. Estimate the threats within the operating environment.

No permission required.

Once we have entered each of the scores, a result will be calculated, as shown in Fig. 8.17. Our base scores show that the base and impact of the attack are midrange, but the exploitability is low.

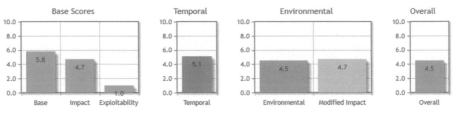

FIG. 8.17

CVSS threat calculated results. The CVSS calculator will display the calculated threat results.

No permission required.

DREAD

A similar rating system has the acronym DREAD, which stands for

Damage Potential **R**eproducibility **E**xploitability **A**ffected Users **D**iscoverability

Rather than use a calculator you estimate the threat by assigning a value between 0 and 10 then average the scores to get a final threat value.

Example DREAD rating

Using the attack from the previous example, we can calculate the DREAD rating as shown in Table 8.12.

Table 8.12 DREAD example.

Metric	Value	Comment
Damage potential	10	An attacker could compromise a device
Reproducibility	2	Difficult to reproduce and has only been done in a research environment
Exploitability	3	Requires custom tools and a high level of skill
Affected	2	Affects a single user
Discoverability	4	Not easy for attackers to discover but may change over time
Overall	4.1	Lower end of midrange threat

Mitigation

Our Threat Modeling process's final step is to define and develop suitable mitigations for each discovered threat. Each proposed mitigation should be added to the Threat Model documentation. We can then prioritize the development of each mitigation relative to the severity of the threat within our system. Depending on the severity of the threat, it may be necessary to consider providing "defense in depth" with several layers of mitigation.

In the next chapter, we will look at the PSA security model that provides a template that we can use to create a robust design that can counter many common threats. We can also feed in the results of our Threat Modeling exercise to produce a secure IoT device.

Example threat models

The Arm developer website contains a set of worked threat model examples. Download these from the link below and study their content.

https://developer.arm.com/architectures/security-architectures/
platform-security-architecture

Conclusion

In this chapter, we have looked at common security vulnerabilities that enable software attacks against your devices. We can develop a design process and coding practices that will limit the extent and impact of any software attacks against our devices, but this is really only a first line of defense. In the following chapters, we will look at the PSA Security Model and the software architecture it defines to add additional layers of defense to create a more robustly secure device.

Building a defense with the PSA security model

Introduction

In order to meet the threat of a software attack, the Platform Security Architecture (PSA Certified) defines an abstract security model that can be applied to any Cortex-M processor. This chapter will provide an introduction to the security model and its objectives. Then in the rest of this book, we will see how to implement this model using a Cortex-M33 microcontroller. The PSA security model defines 10 security goals required to create a robust IoT device, as shown in Table 9.1.

Table 9.1 PSA security model requirements.

Goal number	Requirement
1	All devices must be uniquely identifiable
2	All devices must support attestation
3	Application data and secrets must be bound to a given device and its security configuration
4	All devices must support a Secure Boot process to ensure that only authorized software can run on the device
5	Software isolation must always be provided
6	A secure update process must always be provided
7	All updates must be validated before being installed
8	A device must prevent unauthorized rollback of software updates
9	All devices must support a security life cycle and the current state of a device must be attestable
10	All devices must impediment a generic cryptographic service at the most trusted level of the system

The PSA security model defines 10 mandatory requirements.

In order to meet these goals the PSA security model defines four strategies:

Software architecture
Device lifecycle
Trusted security services
Secure Boot with a firmware update client.

While these are presented as abstract definitions in the security model, they provide a structure and terminology that is useful for implementing a real-world solution.

Software architecture

When we develop code for a microcontroller, we are used to developing a single application image that is built within a single IDE project. In contrast, the PSA security model defines a tier of processing environments, as shown in Fig. 9.1.

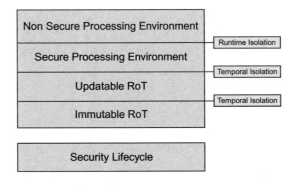

FIG. 9.1

PSA Certified processing environments. PSA Certified defines a tier of processing environments.

No permission required.

You can interpret "processing environment" to be a self-contained executable image and associated IDE subproject. This means that our final application will be constructed as a set of interdependent subprojects. During the boot stage, the aim of the security model is to establish a secure Root of Trust (RoT), which can be used to validate each of the executable software components within the device. The Root of Trust will also provide a unique immutable identity for the device. Once we are past the initial boot stage and the RoT is established, the microcontroller resources are divided into two execution environments or partitions, as shown in Fig. 9.2.

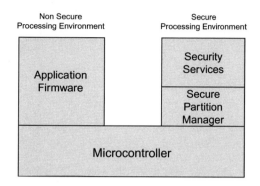

FIG. 9.2

Secure and nonsecure runtime partitions. The microcontroller resources are divided between a secure and nonsecure partitions.

No permission required.

The first partition creates an execution environment for the application code called the Non-Secure Processing Environment (NSPE). The second partition is a separate environment for the sensitive security functions called the Secure Processing Environment (SPE). The NSPE and the SPE are isolated from each other, so that code in the NSPE cannot see any data or code in the SPE. The NSPE can access SPE functions by using a well-defined API to make calls across the isolation boundary. In practical terms, the application code runs like a standard image and is assumed to be vulnerable to a software attack. However, all of the device secrets are located in the SPE. They are used only within the SPE and are never directly exposed to the NSPE. This allows the NSPE to pass data to the SPE where, for example, it may be encrypted using a provisioned secret key, and the encrypted data are then returned to the NSPE. If the NSPE does get compromised, there is still no way to access device secrets stored in the SPE.

The different processing environments that make up the security model are separated by either "temporal barriers" or "runtime isolation" through partitioning.

Temporal barrier

The PSA boot process consists of several stages. As each stage executes, it runs as a single-threaded application and then passes control to the next stage. This shift from one execution environment to another is termed a temporal barrier. The new processing stage cannot see the contents of the previous stage data except for a defined state which is passed across the temporal barrier. This state is a collection of measurements that consists of the device ID, image hashes, and firmware version numbers. In order to keep the overall code footprint low, software components that are used in the boot process may be reused by the main application code. In more familiar microcontroller scenarios, the initial boot stage consists of a ROM first-stage boot-loader, which passed control to a separate second-stage bootloader stored in FLASH memory.

Runtime isolation

After we have passed through the temporal barriers, the code will be divided into two different processing environments: the SPE and NSPE. The PSA security model requires that they are fully isolated from each other. The PSA security model suggests a number of different isolation methods. The most common methods used with a standard microcontroller are outlined below.

Secure element

A secure element is an additional standard device that contains firmware that can provide cryptographic services to the main processor and acts as a "vault" for device secrets and certificates. A secure element is often interfaced to a microcontroller via a serial interface such as SPI and has a well-defined protocol that defends against software attacks launched via a compromised host microcontroller. A distinguishing feature of a secure element is that it can run its own application software such as payment transactions.

Trusted Platform Module (TPM)

A TPM is very similar to a Secure Element, but it differs in that it cannot run its own applications and acts as a coprocessor to the host microcontroller to provide security services. A TPM can also be used to securely store values calculated by the host processor. For example, the TPM may store measurements (hashes) of images calculated during a Secure Boot process.

Dual core microcontroller

Both the Secure element and the Trusted Platform Module are additional external components and carry a cost in both silicon and board space. It is possible to implement separate processing environments using a dual-core microcontroller. Such devices often feature a Cortex-M4 or Cortex-M7 as the main processor, with a Cortex-M0 as the secondary processor. Using such a device would allow the Cortex-M4 to be used as the application processor while the Cortex-M0 is used as the security processor. For this approach to work, the system resources must be rigidly divided between the two processors. We would also need to define a message-passing protocol that allows communication between the two CPUs. While this does create a secure and Non-Secure Processing Environment, it has a large design overhead of a custom proprietary approach, which must be maintained along with the application code.

Trusted Execution Environment

We can create a Trusted Execution Environment within a single core microcontroller. In this model, the processor resources are divided to create a secure and nonsecure partition. This allows secure code to execute in isolation from the nonsecure partition and provide secure services to the main application boundary. Depending on the Cortex-M processor we are using, there are two main ways to create a Trusted Execution Environment.

Single core Armv6/7-M microcontroller

It is possible to implement a Trusted Execution Environment within an Armv7-M-based microcontroller using a mixture of hardware and software. In this scheme, the MPU would be used to manage an access policy across the regions, and a secure hypervisor or microVisor would be used to manage software calls across the partition.

Single core Armv8-M microcontroller

The latest generation of Cortex-M processors, Cortex-M23/33 and M55, features an optional security peripheral called TrustZone that allows you to define a Trusted Execution Environment at the hardware level. This approach allows us to easily implement the PSA security model on a single processor without large software overhead. In addition, microcontrollers that feature a Cortex-M33 processor and TrustZone will have additional hardware security assistive features, which support the implementation of the PSA security model.

PSA Execution environment

The tier of execution environments shown in Fig. 9.1 will execute a boot flow that establishes the Secure and Non-Secure Processing Environments. In practice, the processor will execute the different images as shown in Fig. 9.3. The immutable RoT is ideally established through a Secure Boot process (BL1) provided by the silicon vendor and preprogrammed into the microcontroller ROM when the device is manufactured. As the code is in the microcontroller ROM, it cannot be modified or updated and is, therefore, "immutable." When the Secure Bootloader finishes execution, it passes control to the updatable RoT, which is located in the microcontroller FLASH.

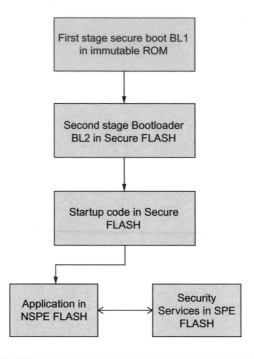

FIG. 9.3

The security model boot flow. As the microcontroller boots execution passes through several separate execution images.

No permission required.

The updatable RoT runs in two phases. The first phase runs as a single thread of execution, and depending on the capabilities of the microcontroller Secure Boot ROM, the updatable RoT may start with a second-stage bootloader (BL2), which is used to validate the SPE and NSPE images. The BL2 bootloader is also capable of managing any firmware updates that are pending. Once the BL2 bootloader has finished, it will pass execution to the SPE code. This is initially a single-threaded code that is used to prepare the device to run the main application. This involves creating the two runtime partitions to host the Non-Secure and Secure Processing Environments. Execution is then passed to the application code, which resides in the NSPE. All the sensitive code and data, such as cryptographic functions and encryption keys, are located in the SPE. As discussed earlier, the SPE will be a separate compute environment that provides a set of trusted secure services to the application code.

Immutable Root of Trust (RoT)

The Immutable RoT is the anchor for the identity and integrity of the device. It is implemented as the microcontroller Secure Boot ROM and will validate the updatable RoT to ensure that only authorized software can run on the device. This requires a RoT key pair to be generated. The private key is used to sign images while the RoT public key will be anchored in the device and used to validate images during boot. At the end of the Secure Boot process, the Immutable RoT will pass a Secure Boot record to the updatable RoT. If present, the second-stage bootloader will extend this boot record with software measurements of all the remaining execution images. The data in the boot record will be used to create an initial attestation record that allows a device to prove its identity to a validating server. The attestation record consists of a unique ID and software component measurements (image hash, version information) that are gathered by the immutable and updatable RoT. These values are formatted using the CBOR encoding rules to make an Entity Attestation Token. We will look at this further in Chapter 13.

Execution environment validation

The Secure Boot process will validate at least one execution environment, normally the second-stage bootloader BL2. The contents of this record are shown in Table 9.2.

Table 9.2 Component state.

State	Description
Version	The PSA Certified firmware version number
Signer identity	A signature generated by the device
Measurements	Execution image firmware version, size, and signatures

The PSA security model allows the device images to be validated as either one single image or a series of individual images, which are independently validated.

Single signer

The immutable RoT may be configured to validate all of the execution environments in the updatable RoT. In practice, this means that all of the code in the microcontroller FLASH will be signed by the RoT private key as one single image, as shown in Fig. 9.4.

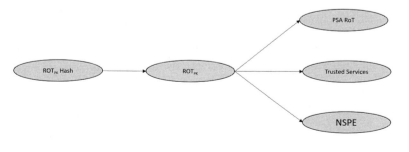

FIG. 9.4

Single signer model. The execution environments may be signed as a single image.

Multisigner

A more sophisticated approach is to create a "chain of trust" linked to the immutable RoT. In this scheme, the immutable RoT validates the first stage of the updatable RoT, which is typically the BL2 bootloader. The updatable RoT will then, in turn, validate each of the remaining execution environments with additional public key pairs, which are part of the second-stage bootloader BL2 (Fig. 9.5).

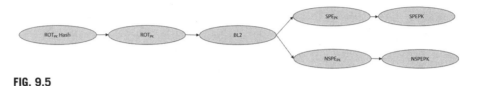

FIG. 9.5

Multisigner model. Each execution image may be individually signed.

This approach has two main advantages. First, it allows the secure and nonsecure partitions to be updated independently. Second, it allows different entities to sign the images or components that they provide.

Boot seed

The boot seed is a random 32-bit number that is regenerated on each boot and is used as a session ID. It is included as part of an initial attestation token to ensure that the token is not being reused from a previous session. Previous values of the boot seed are not recorded within our device, but it is assumed that the size of the number is enough to prevent it from accidental reuse.

Updatable Root of Trust (RoT)

The updatable RoT is subdivided into two execution stages. The first is a FLASH-based boot stage which begins execution once the microcontroller Secure Boot ROM has finished. This is a single-threaded code that is located in the microcontroller FLASH and is linked to start execution from the reset vector. The first code to execute will be a second-stage bootloader (BL2), which will update the NSPE and SPE if any new images are available. The BL2 bootloader is also used to validate the existing execution environments, as discussed earlier. Once the BL2 bootloader has finished execution, the Secure and Non-Secure Processing Environments will be configured by the single-threaded secure startup code. Then execution will be passed to the nonsecure application code within the NSPE.

Runtime partitions
Non-Secure Processing Environment

Once the device has booted and the system partitions have been configured, the application code will execute in the Non-Secure Processing Environment. This code can largely be developed as a standard application. Any lessons learned from a threat modeling exercise should feed into the design of this code along with a strict application of secure coding practices. The Non-Secure code can access secure services in the Secure Processing Environment through a local client, which provides a standardized API (Fig. 9.6).

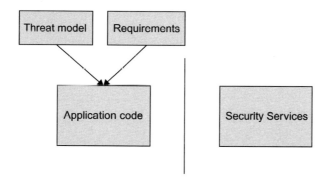

FIG. 9.6

The Non-Secure Processing Environment application code. The application code is developed using the project requirements and threat model recommendations.

No permission required.

Secure Processing Environment

All sensitive functions and data are located in the Secure Processing Environment in order to be isolated from the general application code. As discussed earlier, the SPE is used to provide security services to code in the NSPE. We could locate security libraries into the Secure Processing Environment and allow the Non-Secure code to make calls directly to the secure functions. However, this would create a large number of calls across the isolation boundary. Each of these would have to be policed for vulnerabilities that could be exploited by an attacker. This is akin to building the wall of a fortress, then creating dozens of gates and then having to defend each and every one.

We need a more sophisticated approach to accessing functions in the Secure Processing Environment. The PSA security model defines two regions within the SPE. These are called the PSA RoT and the Application RoT (Fig. 9.7). Here, code in the Partition Manager and PSA RoT are executing at the CPU privileged level, while code in the application RoT will execute at the unprivileged level.

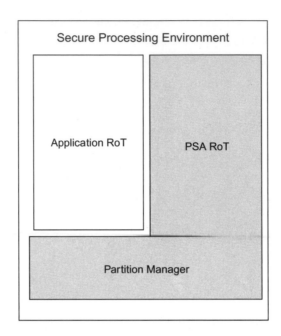

FIG. 9.7

The Secure Processing Environment components. The SPE is divided into a partition manager which controls access to services within an application and PSA RoT.

No permission required.

Both the PSA and Application RoT are further divided into execution partitions. These are somewhat similar to an RTOS thread in that they have their own code and RAM to create a dedicated execution subpartition within the SPE. Each execution subpartition is used to host a security service. The PSA RoT is used to host the mandatory security services while the Application RoT is used to host a protected storage service that is intended to provide general storage for application data. It is also possible to create additional user-defined custom services that are placed in the Application RoT.

Secure partition structure

In order to minimize the number of entry points into the SPE, the security service functions are not called directly from the NSPE. All calls to the different security services are routed through a Secure Partition Manager. This provides a single point of entry to the SPE. The Non-Secure code will make an API call that looks like a standard function call. The API call will actually invoke a Partition Manager Client located in the Non-Secure partition (Fig. 9.8).

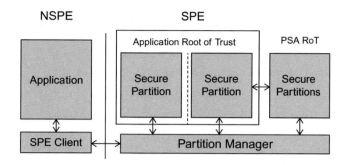

FIG. 9.8

SPE software architecture. The PSA Certified Security Model defines a software architecture to minimize entry points to the SPE.

No permission required.

The client generates a message to the Secure Partition Manager requesting a security service, and the Secure Partition Manager will, in turn, route this request to the relevant security service to be processed. Any resulting reply will be returned directly to the calling API function in the NSPE. The PSA security model also defines three levels of isolation for the SPE, as shown in Fig. 9.9.

Level 1 isolation
The minimum level of isolation required is to separate the Non-Secure Processing Environment code from the Secure Processing Environment.

Level 2 isolation
The next level creates an additional isolation barrier between the Application RoT and PSA RoT.

Level 3 isolation
To achieve the highest level of isolation each partition within both the Application and PSA RoT must be isolated from each other.

In practice, the TrustZone security peripheral is used to create the Secure and Non-Secure execution environments for level one isolation. The Cortex-M33 Memory Protection Unit is used to create additional isolation barriers within the secure environment.

This approach may look like complicated overkill and would require a lot of additional work to implement from scratch before you even get started on the application code. However, as we will see in the following chapters that much of the isolation requirements can be provided by the Armv8-M TrustZone security peripheral and the Memory Protection Unit. The secure partition and security services are provided

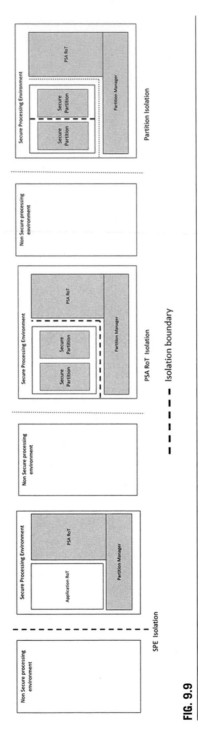

FIG. 9.9

Secure Processing Environment isolation levels. The PSA Certified Security Model defines three levels of isolation for the security services.

No permission required.

as an open-source reference platform called Trusted Firmware for Cortex-M. The TF-M software is also ported to specific microcontrollers as a ready-to-go platform, so you should not need to write any of the Secure Processing Environment code from scratch. Just know how to configure and use it correctly.

Secure Partition Manager (SPM)

The main task of the Secure Partition Manager is to provide an interprocess calling service between client functions and the partition security services. The client functions may be in the Non-Secure code or in other secure partitions within the SPE. For example, a Non-Secure function could request secure storage of a data item. The partition manager will receive this request and pass the command to the secure storage service. In turn, the secure storage service will request encryption and MAC functions from the cryptography service. In addition, the SPM is designed to manage interrupts from peripherals that have been routed to the SPE.

Secure services
PSA RoT services

The updatable Root of Trust provides a set of mandatory security services which are located in the PSA RoT and the Application RoT within the secure partition (Fig. 9.10).

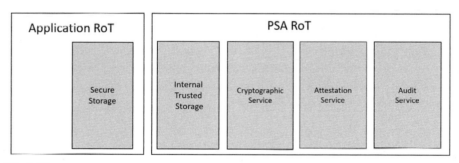

FIG. 9.10

SPE mandatory security services. The SPE must provide a minimum set of security services.

No permission required.

Each service will be introduced here, and then we will set them up and look at them in more detail in Chapter 13.

Secure storage service

The updatable RoT must provide a storage service to manage access to any sensitive data stored within the device, such as cryptographic keys, manufacturer, and user-generated secrets and user-generated private data. To protect this data, the storage service must provide integrity and privacy protection so unauthorized access cannot read or modify the stored data. Protection is further enforced by binding access control policies that ensure that only an owning service can access data stored and bound to that service. The storage service must also provide replay protection so that previously stored data or data acquired from another device cannot be reused on our device.

The secure storage service provides two types of storage volume: Internal Trusted Storage (ITS) and Protected Storage (PS) volumes.

The Internal Trusted Storage is generally a small storage volume that is designed to hold the most sensitive data, such as cryptographic keys. It is intended to be a simple block storage volume that makes use of isolated or shielded memory locations that are within the Secure Partition and are only accessible by the PSA RoT. In a standard microcontroller, this will typically mean that that the ITS is located in internal FLASH memory, which has been allocated to the Secure Processing Environment.

The Protected Storage provides a general storage volume for confidential application data. The Protected Storage Service, which is the service code, is located in the Application RoT, which isolates it from the ITS service. The actual PS volume can be located in either the Secure or Non-Secure partitions depending on your design requirement. It may be implemented as a simple block storage or a full file system.

Like the Internal Trusted Storage, the Protected Storage volume provides integrity, confidentiality, and antirollback. While integrity is always enabled, confidentiality and antirollback are optional and may be enabled or disabled on an item by item basis.

During operation, both the ITS and PS will make calls to the cryptographic service, and each service will have its own keys, which are bound to their respective security service. This concept of binding restricts the key usage to the given service. This associates stored data with a particular device instance, security partition, and lifecycle state.

Cryptographic service

In the earlier chapters covering the TLS cryptographic algorithms, we used the standard mbedTLS library. This library is a general-purpose library and can be used with any Cortex-M microcontroller. As we saw, it is designed to be accessed as a standard C library and makes no special allowance for securely storing cryptographic keys. The Arm Trusted Firmware provides a version of mbedTLS called mbedCrypto that is designed to execute as a cryptographic service within a PSA RoT partition. In addition to the cryptographic algorithms provided by mbedTLS, the mbedCrypto service provides extensive support for key management and storage.

Attestation service

The PSA RoT must also provide an Attestation Service. This service is used to generate tokens that provide proof of identity and integrity to an external attestation server. The attestation token presents the device measurements recorded during the boot process as a set of claims, which are signed by a device Initial Attestation Key (IAK). The device claims include the Implementation ID and information about the recorded boot state of each software component in the device, the current device lifecycle state, the boot seed, and an additional value called the instance ID.

The Initial Attestation Key is provisioned within the device immutable RoT during manufacture. It is the private key of an asymmetric key pair that must be unique to each device. The public half of the key is held in the attestation server, which is used to validate the attestation token and contains an unencrypted Instance ID. This is a public value that allows the attestation server to reconcile the token to the correct attestation public key. The instance ID is calculated as a hash of the public key value, and this can be stored in the device or calculated on the fly.

The device measurements include version numbers and signatures for each executable component, along with the device hardware revision. The boot seed is included each time an Initial Attestation Token is generated. This ensures that each token is unique and prevents impersonation and replay attacks.

Audit

The security services also provide an Audit service, which allows the secure partition to log messages and alerts. The audit messages may only be created by the security services. The audit log may be read and deleted by code in the nonsecure partition.

Application RoT services

By default, the Application RoT contains the Protected Storage service. It is possible to add additional custom services to the Secure Processing Environment. These will be placed in their own partition located in the Application RoT.

Trusted subsystem

In addition to custom services within the Application RoT, the PSA security model also has the concept of a "trusted subsystem." This could be a Secure Element or a Trusted Platform Module, which provides its own set of security services. Such a subsystem would need to be located within the boundary of the SPE but would have its own RoT that is created in a similar fashion to our main microcontroller RoT.

Secure Boot

As we have seen in the PSA security model, the initial microcontroller must provide a Secure Boot process that creates an immutable Root of Trust. Its key purpose is to validate the initial application boot code, which is the updatable Root of Trust and then hand it over to this code which will validate and boot the main application code.

If you are using a plain old microcontroller that does not provide a Secure Boot mechanism, you will need to provide a first-stage bootloader to perform this functionality. This bootloader must then be stored in the boot FLASH sector, which in turn must be locked from erase and write operations. Fortunately, an increasing number of Cortex-M33-based microcontrollers have been designed with PSA Certified Secure Boot ROM code. All compliant microcontrollers are listed on the PSA certification website. When you are selecting a device, this is the place to start!

PSA parameters

The PSA security model defines a set of stored parameters, which are summarized in Table 9.3.

Table 9.3 PSA parameters.

Parameter	Parameter	Initial parameter	PSA RoT parameters	Security class	Recommended provisioning
Implementation ID	Impl_ID	Yes	Yes	Public	Isolated location
Hardware Unique Key	HUK	Yes	No	Secret	Shielded/isolated location
Boot Validation Key	BVK	Yes	No	Public	Isolated location or Boot ROM
Boot Decryption Key	BDK	Yes	No	Secret	Derived from or stored in shielded/isolated location
Initial Attestation Key	IAK	Yes	Yes	Secret	Derived from or stored in shielded/isolated location
Instance ID	Ins_ID	Yes	Yes	Public	Isolated location

Lifecycle

Alongside the PSA RoT security services, the security model defines a device lifecycle. The device lifecycle is not a defined service but a set of states that the device may enter during its lifetime. A flow chart of the lifecycle states is shown in Fig. 9.11.

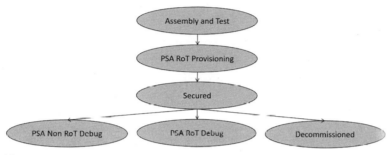

FIG. 9.11

Security model lifecycle. The security model defines a device lifecycle from manufacture through to decommissioning.

No permission required.

During the initial manufacture, the device will not be locked down in order to allow assembly and test. Once this phase is completed, the PSA RoT must be made fully operational before the device is shipped. This includes programming the SPE and NSPE firmware and provisioning of the PSA RoT parameters and secrets. In this state, the device debug port must also be locked down, and Secure Boot must be enabled.

Once the PSA RoT has been fully provisioned, it may be shipped into the retail chain, ready to be on-boarded into a customer system. At this point, the application code may require further secrets such as user and network credentials. Any application provisioning may only take place once the PSA RoT is operational and must use the PSA RoT services such as the Protected Storage. It is also important that the Application lifecycle is not placed in a state which conflicts with the PSA RoT lifecycle state, i.e., the application is active before the RoT has been fully provisioned.

Once fully provisioned and on boarded to a network the device will be in its operational secure state.

A device must also support debug and repair states. The security model specifies a range of lifecycle debug states as shown in Table 9.4.

Table 9.4 Lifecycle debug states.

Debug state	Security implications	Information
Nonrevealing diagnostics	Does not reveal any sensitive user data and secrets, application level secrets, or PSA RoT level secrets. Does not affect the trustworthy operation of any aspect of the device software.	Standard logging, basic diagnostics, and similar device management functions.
NS debug	Intrusive debug which compromises NS-level operation, including access to NS-level data and secrets. ARoT, PSA RoT, and boot remain intact and trustworthy. This level of debug must be attested.	Active debugging of nonsecure application software, which does not cross the ARoT isolation boundary.
ARoT debug	Intrusive debug which compromises ARoT operation, including access to ARoT level data and secrets. PSA RoT and boot remain intact and trustworthy.	Active debugging which crosses the ARoT isolation boundary, but does not cross the PSA RoT isolation boundary.
PSA RoT debug	Intrusive debug which compromises PSA RoT operation, or compromises Secure Boot.	Active debugging which crosses the PSA RoT isolation boundary. With this level of debug enabled the device is no longer attestable.

Mandatory debug states for the PSA Certified lifecycle.

The different debug states support a range of scenarios, such as nonrevealing logged messages that can be used by a service technician or a nonsecure debug state that allows an authorized technician to connect a debug adapter and view the state of the Non-Secure Application Code. In the case of a serious bug, it is necessary to fully enable the debug port to gain a view of the ARoT and PSA RoT. However, in this case, the device secrets will be compromised, and the device cannot be returned to service without being fully recommissioned.

Most (if not all) Armv7-M-based microcontrollers do not have a debug architecture that can support such finely grained access control. Typically, it is only possible to fully disable the debug port, and it can only be re-enabled by fully erasing the FLASH memory. However, as we will see in Chapter 10, the Cortex-M33 allows you to selectively restrict access to secure and nonsecure regions. It is then up to the Silicon Vendor to implement a hardware access scheme. As we will see in Chapter 11, a typical implementation could be a sophisticated certificate-based scheme that can be used to authorize different entities in combination with varying debug access levels.

This feature of the debug port can also be useful during development. The SPE of a device can be fully provisioned, and the debug view can be limited to the NSPE. This would allow third-party developers to write and debug application which accesses the SPE as a black box.

At the end of its life, a device must be placed in a decommissioned state where all of the PSA RoT parameters are put beyond use. Here, the term "beyond use" will generally mean erasing all sensitive information within the device. Some values may be permanently written into the device, such as OTP fuses, and may need extra care to destroy the stored value. Once a device has entered the decommissioned state, you have effectively killed it. An end-user or service engineer will not be able to return it to a functional state. If the hardware is still fully functional, it may be reclaimed by placing it back into the manufacturing process so that it can be reprogrammed with a fresh set of PSA RoT parameters and then be treated as a new device.

Device requirements

While we can implement the PSA on any Cortex-M-based microcontroller, having a device that provides supporting security features will make your life a lot easier. The features listed below should be considered when selecting a microcontroller.

Isolation architectures
Interrupt routing

Once the MCU's memory has been divided into Secure and Non-Secure Processing Environments, we must also route interrupt vectors to either partition. This allows us to place a peripheral into either partition. For example, we could connect an external interrupt line to an antitamper switch. We would then need to place its interrupt service routine within the secure partition to log any tamper events and take any necessary remedial action.

Secure Boot

The device should have a PSA Certified Secure Boot process. Unless you want to write this yourself this is really a must have.

Unique ID

Each microcontroller should have a unique ID, preprogrammed during its manufacture and accessible through internal registers.

Entropy

The device will contain a True Random Number Generator, which provides a source of high entropy data. This is another must have.

System clocks

The clock tree and other major system peripherals must be located in the Secure Processing Environment and only accessed by secure code.

Oscillator monitoring

The main system clock may be derived from an internal RC oscillator or an external crystal oscillator. Ideally, an internal oscillator should be used as this clock source is hard for an attacker to manipulate. If an external oscillator is used, the microcontroller should provide some form of clock monitoring hardware. In this case, the microcontroller should fall back to an internal oscillator and generate an interrupt or alarm if the external oscillator is halted.

Reset and power

The isolation architecture must be able to locate the registers for software reset and power control within the Secure Processing Environment.

Timers

The Trusted Firmware requires a hardware watchdog, hardware timer, and a real-time clock. Most microcontrollers have one or more hardware watchdog timers. Like the system clocks, the watchdogs must be enabled and maintained by functions running in the SPE. In addition to the watchdog timer, the Trusted Firmware requires a hardware timer and a real-time clock to be located within the SPE.

Monotonic counters

The microcontroller will provide a set of monotonic counters, which can be used for software versioning and antireplay protection.

Real time clock (RTC)

The RTC is used to maintain a calendar date and time for audit logging and to maintain an antirollback scheme for firmware updates. Like the main system clock, we need to ensure that an attacker has not reset, slowed down, or otherwise interfered with the RTC.

Debug

When a device is deployed, the coresight debug port is an obvious target for an attacker. As a minimum, the microcontroller must provide a means to fully disable unauthorized access by a debug agent. To effectively implement the PSA security model, it is desirable to have more configurable access to the debug port that permits different levels of access to the device depending on the user's credentials. For example, an end-user will not be permitted to connect to use the debug port. An authorized service technician may be allowed to connect but only view the nonsecure code, while the design team will be allowed to connect to the device with full debug access.

Shielded memory

It must be possible to place nonvolatile memory such as FLASH, on-chip EEPROM, and OTP fuses into the Secure Processing Environment. A Cortex-M33-based microcontroller may also provide a special section of FLASH memory that is intended to hold RoT data such as certificate and key hashes. Once this region is provisioned, it will be possible to permanently lock it against further updates. In an ideal system, there will also be a revocation system so that compromised secrets can be disabled. We will see a real-world example of this approach in Chapter 11.

Cryptographic accelerators

Ideally, the microcontroller will provide a hardware accelerator for commonly used cryptographic algorithms. Historically, cryptographic accelerators have been developed for symmetrical cryptographic algorithms. However, it is now becoming more common to find accelerators for asymmetrical algorithms.

Assistive architecture

Ideally, the microcontroller will provide additional security assistive hardware such as a key store. We will examine the support provided by a range of microcontrollers in Chapter 11.

Conclusion

In this chapter, we have examined the PSA security model and become familiar with its key requirements. However, these are deliberately abstract so that they can be applied to any type of IoT device. While it is possible to implement the full security model on an ARMv7-M-based microcontroller, you will be faced with a lot of extra work to make it a suitable platform. Such a "plain old microcontroller" has not been designed for the task and lacks many supporting hardware features that you will need to implement in software. Consequently, in the remainder of this book, we will examine how the PSA security model can be implemented on a Cortex-M33 processor using TrustZone and the additional "assistive security features" provided by a microcontroller which has been designed to form the basis of an secure IoT device.

Device partitioning with TrustZone

10

Introduction

In this chapter, we are going to look at the purpose of the TrustZone security extension and how it is implemented at the register level. Before we begin, it is necessary to define some terms that will be used throughout the chapter to avoid confusion. Like the earlier Armv7-M processors (Cortex-M3, -M4, and -M7), the Cortex-M33 has a set of operating modes that we need to review before looking at the new security states introduced by TrustZone.

Processor operating modes

Like the Armv7-M processors, the Cortex-M33 processor has two execution modes: Handler mode and Thread mode. The processor always enters the Handler mode when an interrupt or CPU exception is raised. The processor is in the Thread state when it is executing background (noninterrupt) code. In addition to the Thread and Handler operating modes, the processor can execute code at a privileged or unprivileged level. When executing privileged code, the processor has unrestricted access to all resources and CPU instructions. However, when executing unprivileged code, the processor is more restricted, as shown in Table 10.1.

Table 10.1 Processor execution rights.

Privileged	Unprivileged
The software can use all CPU instructions	Limited access to the MSR and MRS instructions, and cannot use the CPS instruction
The software can access all resources and processor registers	Cannot access the SysTick timer, NVIC, MPU, and general registers in the System Control Block

Execution rights for privileged and unprivileged code.

After reset, the CPU has full privileged access from either Thread or Handler state. It can execute any instruction and access any region of memory. By programming the System Control Block, Control Register, it is possible to restrict the capabilities of the processor to unprivileged access when it is operating in Thread mode.

Designing Secure IoT Devices with the Arm Platform Security Architecture and Cortex-M33
https://doi.org/10.1016/B978-0-12-821469-5.00011-9

In addition to restricting the Thread mode to unprivileged access, we can also enable a second stack pointer called the process stack. After reset, the CPU R13 register is used as the main stack pointer. However, R13 is a banked register, and it is possible to enable the Process Stack pointer, again via the CPU control register. When the processor has both the main and process stacks enabled, the main stack pointer will be used by privileged code when in handler mode, while the processor stack is used by unprivileged code running in the background Thread mode. These two features can be used to create a more advanced processor configuration that is intended to support the use of an RTOS. We can extend this model by using the Memory Protection Unit (MPU) to define memory regions with privileged and unprivileged access rights. The possible processor configurations are summarized in Fig. 10.1.

		Operations (privilege out of reset)	Stacks (Main out of reset)
Modes (Thread out of reset)	Handler **Processing of exceptions**	**Privileged execution Full control**	**Main Stack Used by OS and Exceptions**
	Thread **No exception is being processed Background code execution**	**Privileged or Unprivileged**	**Main or Process**

FIG. 10.1

Basic processor operating modes and stack configuration. Operating mode and stack configuration.

No permission required.

TrustZone security extension

The TrustZone security extension creates additional Secure (S) and Nonsecure (NS) execution states, as shown in Fig. 10.2. These operating states are also referred to as the Secure World and Nonsecure World to reflect the fact that they are two isolated execution environments. These worlds equate to the Secure Processing Environment and Nonsecure processing Environment defined by the security model in the previous chapter.

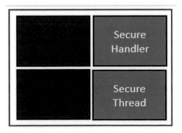

FIG. 10.2

Armv8-M operating states and security "worlds". Armv8-M processors have the same handler and thread modes of operation. TrustZone adds secure and nonsecure execution states.

No permission required.

The addition of TrustZone to the Cortex-M33 will impact the processor over a number of system peripherals, as shown in Fig. 10.3. Each of these system peripherals may hold different configurations for Secure and Nonsecure World operation. This allows the CPU to have different processing environments depending on which security world is currently active. When it switches worlds, it performs a context switch to the new state. Consequently, a number of the peripheral registers are mirrored or banked between the two execution states. At the register level, this banking may be register wide or bitwise within the register. There is one exception to this scheme. TrustZone introduces a new system peripheral called the Security Attribution Unit (SAU), which is used to partition the default Cortex-M33 memory map into the separate security worlds. The SAU registers may only be accessed when the processor is executing in its secure world state.

Non Secure World	Secure World
Implementation Control_NS	Implementation Control_S
SysTick_NS	SysTick_S
Nested Vector Interrupt Controller_NS	Nested Vector Interrupt Controller_S
System Control Block_NS	System Control Block_S
Memory Protection Unit_NS	Memory Protection Unit_S
Security Attribution Unit _NS	Security Attribution Unit _S
Software Interrupt Generation_NS	Software Interrupt Generation_S
Floating Point Extension_NS	Floating Point Extension_S
Cache Maintenance Operations_NS	Cache Maintenance Operations_S
	Implementation Control_NS_Alias
	SysTick_NS_Alias
	Nested Vector Iinterrupt Controller_NS_Alias
	System Control Block_NS_Alias
	Memory Protection Unit_NS_Alias
	Security Attribution Unit _NS_Alias
	Software Interrupt Generation_NS_Alias
	Floating Point Extension_NS_Alias
	Cache Maintenance Operations_NS_Alias

FIG. 10.3

CPU system peripheral register blocks and the TrustZone security worlds. Registers in the CPU peripherals and system control block may be banked between security worlds.

No permission required.

Each security partition is then fully defined by configuring its instance of the Memory Protection Unit, Nested Vector Interrupt Controller, and SysTick timer. The

System Control Block also contains additional TrustZone registers and new fields within some of the default registers, which we will look at later in this chapter. In addition to the banked registers, the Secure World code is able to configure the Nonsecure World peripherals through a set of alias registers mapped into the Secure world.

Programmers model

When the TrustZone security extension is fitted to the Cortex-M33 processor, the CPU programmers' model is also updated, as shown in Fig. 10.4. While we have the same register file of sixteen 32 bit wide registers, the R13 stack pointers are duplicated to create separate main and process stack pointers for both the Secure and Nonsecure operating modes. Within the Armv8-M architecture, each of the four stack pointers has an additional stack limit register, which is used to define the lower bound of each stack region. This limit register can be updated as the code executes to actively police the stack space and mitigate against stack smashing attacks.

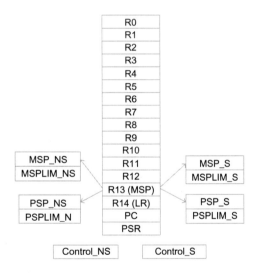

FIG. 10.4

Armv8-M programmers model. The CPU registers are extended to provide separate stack pointers and new stack limit registers for the secure and nonsecure processor operating modes.

No permission required.

TrustZone operation

Before we begin to look at TrustZone in detail, it is important to understand what TrustZone is for and how it should be used. TrustZone operates at the hardware level to partitioning the processor memory map into two separate execution environments or partitions. This allows us to execute our main application in the Nonsecure World and place sensitive data and functions in the Secure World. TrustZone itself does not provide any form of encryption or other security services and does not protect against physical attacks. The purpose of TrustZone is to defend against the kind of network and software attacks discussed in Chapter 8. To understand this a bit further, we need to consider how we could design a secure system with a plain old microcontroller. In the simplest case, we could use two devices. The nonsecure code would run the bulk of the application software and provide all the real-world interfaces. The second device would contain all the sensitive software and data, such as a cryptographic library and encryption keys. The two devices are interfaced together through shared memory or a local serial bus such as SPI or I2C. When the application software requires some data to be encrypted, it would place the data into the shared memory and signal the security processor. The security processor can then encrypt the data and hand it back to the application processor. In this system, the security services are fully isolated from the application processor. While the application processor can request any available security service, it has no way to see any sensitive data or the crypto library's internal workings. If an attacker successfully gains control of the application processor through a software attack, they have no means of reading any secure data or code as all this information is only visible to the security processor and cannot be accessed through the shared interface. The use of two processors with separated memory is an easy and well-defined way to achieve process isolation. However, it is an expensive solution, and for most applications, it is not an economic route unless you require a very high degree of security or are manufacturing in large volumes.

TrustZone is a means of achieving a similar level of process isolation at the hardware level within a single microcontroller. When the microcontroller starts, we can partition the device into two different operating modes: a Nonsecure execution mode and a Secure execution mode, as shown in Fig. 10.5.

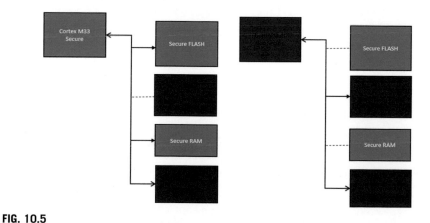

FIG. 10.5

TrustZone partitioning of microcontroller resources. TrustZone "marks" microcontroller resources as part of the secure or nonsecure world.

No permission required.

Once the SAU has been configured and enabled, the microcontroller has two distinct operating worlds that are mutually invisible to each other. In a real program, the microcontroller will startup in the secure mode and partition the device into Secure and Nonsecure Worlds. The main application code then runs in the Nonsecure partition while all sensitive code is located in the Secure partition. The two partitions can communicate by making function calls across the isolation boundary to a limited set of well-defined entry points, which are created by the addition of a new instruction to the Cortex-M33 instruction set. When a Nonsecure function calls a function located in the secure partition, as shown in Fig. 10.6, the processor will swap states. The first instruction executed in the Secure World must be a Secure Gateway (SG) instruction. If any other instruction is executed on entry to the secure world, a processor security exception is generated. Now we have two separate execution environments, and the secure code has a limited set of doorway entry points.

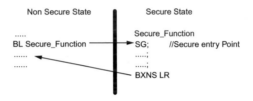

FIG. 10.6

Calling a secure function. A branch from the Nonsecure partition to the Secure partition must be to a Secure Gateway (SG) instruction. A return must use the Branch Exchange Nonsecure BXNS instruction.

No permission required.

When the code returns from a secure function, it must use a Secure Branch Exchange or Secure Branch Link Exchange (BXNS or BLXNS) instruction (Fig. 10.7). The use of any other branch instruction to cross back to the Nonsecure partition will again raise an exception.

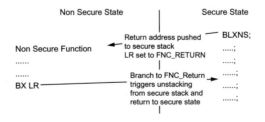

FIG. 10.7

Calling a Nonsecure Function. The Secure partition can call functions in the Nonsecure partition using a branch link exchange to Nonsecure instruction BLXNS. The Nonsecure function can return to the Secure partition using a BX instruction.

No permission required.

It is also possible for a function in the Secure World to call a Nonsecure function. In this case, the code will use a Branch to Nonsecure address (BLXNS or BXNS) instruction. When the stack frame is pushed, the return address to the secure code will be pushed to the secure stack, and a special code FNC_RETURN will be written to the link register. When the Nonsecure function reaches its return instruction, it will attempt to return by branching on the link register. However, the FNC_RETURN code will cause the true return address to be loaded from the secure stack along with a switch back to a secure state.

To create a fully secure execution environment, the secure world region needs to be slightly more complicated. The Secure Gateway (SG) instruction is used to provide entry points to the Secure World. However, like all instructions, the SG instruction is just a specific Boolean pattern. It would be possible for a program constant to have the same value as an SG instruction. If this happened, it would create a false entry point into the secure world, which could then be exploited by an attacker. To minimize this possibility, TrustZone does not allow a branch directly into the secure region but instead defines an intermediate region called "Secure NonSecure Callable" (NSC) (Fig. 10.8). This means the region is in the Secure World and is callable from the Nonsecure World. An attempt by the Nonsecure code to jump directly into the Secure World, bypassing the NSC region, will also cause a security exception.

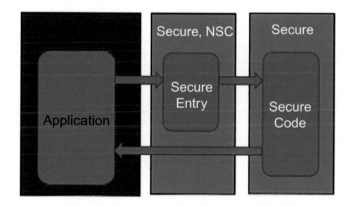

FIG. 10.8

Nonsecure Callable (NSC). The secure partition has an additional domain: Secure Nonsecure Callable. This region is intended to hold the Secure Gateway entry instructions.

No permission required.

All of the SG instructions must be located in the NSC region, which acts as a stepping stone to the main Secure region. Ideally, the NSC region should only contain the SG entry points and a jump table to the security functions located in the main secure world. This makes the NSC region quite small and easy to analyze for any false entry points in the shape of a constant that looks like an SG instruction. When we create code to reside in the secure region, we also need to create a lookup table called a veneer table that provides the SG entry point. The code following the SG instruction provides an onward jump to the associated function in the Secure region. Fortunately, this process is automated by the compiler and linker and does not require you to manually maintain a low-level lookup table.

The Cortex-M33 inherits the same interrupt model that is used in Armv7-M processors. Background code runs in thread mode, and an interrupt or processor exception will cause the processor to switch into Handler mode. When TrustZone is fitted, interrupt channels can be routed to the Secure or Nonsecure NVIC so that interrupt service routines can execute in the Secure or Nonsecure world depending on the needs of the application. We will look at managing interrupts later, but for now, it is important to understand that an interrupt service routine will always be served irrespective of the current security state of the processor (Fig. 10.9). The only limitation is an overhead of 12 cycles if the processor runs in the Secure World and a Nonsecure interrupt is triggered. In this one case, the process has to stack the entire processor register file and erase the CPU registers to prevent a possible information leak before serving the interrupt. In addition to stacking the CPU registers, a signature value will also be placed on the secure stack. This is intended to prevent an attacker from faking a return from a Nonsecure interrupt. When a valid Nonsecure interrupt ends and returns to the secure world the registers will be restored provided the signature is present. In the case of a faked interrupt return the signature will not be present and a security exception will be raised.

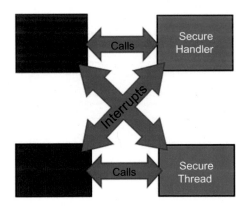

FIG. 10.9

TrustZone interrupt handling. TrustZone does not limit the execution of background or interrupt code.

No permission required.

SAU and IDAU

When the TrustZone security peripheral is added to the Cortex-M33 processor, the partitioning between the Secure and Nonsecure worlds is defined on two levels. When the device is designed, the silicon vendor will create a device level memory map that splits the resources into default Secure and Nonsecure regions that become active when TrustZone is enabled. The user can further modify this memory map by overlaying additional regions that mark the memory as Secure or Nonsecure.

This marking of the device resources is implemented by two system-level peripherals within the Cortex-M33 processor. The Security Attribution Unit (SAU) and the Implementation Defined Attribution Unit (IDAU) are used in combination to define the total security marking of the device resources (Fig. 10.10).

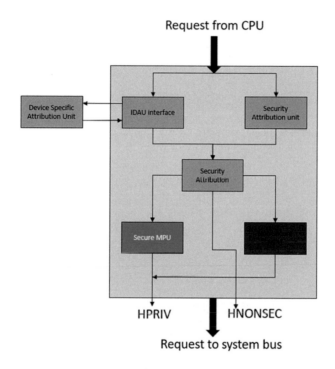

FIG. 10.10

Attribution unit. The IDAU defines a default secure/nonsecure memory map. This is combined with the user definitions in the SAU to create a global secure and nonsecure partition.

No permission required.

As its name implies, the Implementation Defined Attribution Unit is configured by the silicon designer when the chip is synthesized. The IDAU defines a default fixed partitioning of the Cortex-M33 address space that divides the default Cortex-M memory template into Secure and Nonsecure Regions.

A typical minimal implementation of the IDAU will divide the address space into pages of secure memory interleaved with Nonsecure memory pages. This approach is often used because it can be implemented by multiplexing bit 27–31 of the address bus to give a page size of 128 MB. This scheme creates default secure and Nonsecure Regions across FLASH memory, SRAM peripherals, and any memory-mapped external resources.

The Security Attribution Unit is then used to overlay the default IDAU memory map with additional user-defined regions. The number of regions supported by the SAU is fixed when the MCU is designed and can support two, four, or eight regions.

SAU registers

When we define the SAU regions, they will interact with the IDAU regions to create a final partitioned memory map. If either the SAU or IDAU defines a Secure region, it will take precedence over a Nonsecure or Nonsecure Callable region. Additionally, a Nonsecure Callable region will take precedence over a Nonsecure Region. These rules are summarized in Table 10.2.

Table 10.2 Attribution states.

SAU state	IDAU state	Resulting state
Secure	Secure	Secure
Nonsecure	Secure	Secure
Secure	Nonsecure	Secure
Nonsecure	Nonsecure	Nonsecure
Nonsecure Callable	Secure	Secure
Nonsecure Callable	Nonsecure	Nonsecure Callable

Memory marking between the IADU and SAU is combined to determine a final state.

The SAU is programmed through a set of memory-mapped registers, which are only accessible when the Cortex-M33 processor executes in its Secure State. Since the processor will initially start execution in Secure State, it is typical to configure the SAU and MPU at startup and then hand over to the main application running in the Nonsecure World (Table 10.3).

Table 10.3 Security attribution registers.

Security attribution unit register	Description
SAU_CTRL	SAU Control Register
SAU_TYPE	SAU Type Register
SAU_RNR	SAU Region Number
SAU_RBAR	SAU Region Base Address Register
SAU_RLAR	SAU Region Limit Address Register

The SAU is accessed by a set of memory mapped registers.

The SAU_Type register is a read-only register that returns the number of SAU regions implemented by the silicon vendor. You typically will not need to use this register if you are writing code for a standard MCU where the number of available regions is known in advance. However, it is useful if you are writing generic code to support a range of devices that have different numbers of SAU regions available.

By default, the SAU defines the entire address space as Secure. Each of the SAU regions are used to create Nonsecure or Nonsecure Callable areas. The SAU marking is then combined with the IDAU marking to derive a final TrustZone partitioning.

Each SAU region is configured through the Region Number Register (RNR), Region Base Address Register (RBAR), and Region Limit Address Register (RLAR). To configure a region, we first enter its number into the RNR register. The start of the region can then be entered into the RBAR. Bits 0–4 of the RBAR are reserved, so each SAU region can only be mapped to a 32-byte boundary.

The upper address of the SAU region is defined by the SAU RLAR. The upper limit address has a similar granularity to the base address register in that the first five bits of the limit address are fixed, but in the case of the RLAR, the reserved bits are set to logic one. The first two bits of the RLAR have some additional functionality. By setting bit one to logic one, the region is defined as Nonsecure Callable. Finally, the region is enabled by setting bit zero to logic one.

Although the regions are individually enabled as they are configured, they are not active until the SAU is fully enabled. When the required regions are configured and enabled, the SAU can be placed in its active state by setting bit zero in the SAU_CTRL register. The SAU_CTRL register contains one additional active bit which can be used to switch the SAU region from a default Secure marking to a default Nonsecure marking.

The example code below demonstrates creating a NSC region and a NS region.

```
//Configure SAU Region 0, Start Address 0x00200000, Limit
//Address 0x003FFFE0, Secure nonsecure callable

SAU->RNR = (0);
SAU->RBAR = (0x00200000U & SAU_RBAR_BADDR_Msk);
SAU->RLAR = (0x003FFFE0U & SAU_RLAR_LADDR_Msk)
            |((1U << SAU_RLAR_NSC_Pos)
            & SAU_RLAR_NSC_Msk)
            |1U;

// Select region 1 Start Address 0x20200000 Limit Address
// 0x203FFFE0 Non-Secure

SAU->RNR = (1);
SAU->RBAR = (0x20200000U & SAU_RBAR_BADDR_Msk);
SAU->RLAR = (0x203FFFE0U & SAU_RLAR_LADDR_Msk)
            |((0U << SAU_RLAR_NSC_Pos) & SAU_RLAR_NSC_Msk)
            1U;

// Enable SAU and set the default memory marking to Non Secure

SAU->CTRL = ((SAU_INIT_CTRL_ENABLE << SAU_CTRL_ENABLE_Pos)
            & SAU_CTRL_ENABLE_Msk)
            |((SAU_INIT_CTRL_ALLNS << SAU_CTRL_ALLNS_Pos)
            & SAU_CTRL_ALLNS_Msk);
```

TrustZone configuration

In this section, we will look at how a program image is created and how it executes within a microcontroller fitted with the TrustZone peripheral. There are many ways to construct a program to run using the TrustZone partitions. However, the recommended approach is to run the main application code in the Nonsecure world and treat the Secure partition as a secure enclave. This means we can place any sensitive data and functions in the secure world and make calls to them from the main application. This leads to the idea of "Security Services" provided as callable functions which are isolated from the main application along with their own Secure RAM and peripheral resources.

In the following description, we will cover the "One true way" to set up the TrustZone peripheral using a core simulator. Each silicon vendor is likely to deviate from this scheme to some extent, but once you understand the principles, you will be able to adapt to any differences. After reset, the processor will start execution in the Secure world, and we can extend the startup code (pre main()) to configure and enable the SAU. When we reach the main function in the secure code, the microcontroller resources will be partitioned between the Secure and Nonsecure worlds, as shown in Fig. 10.11.

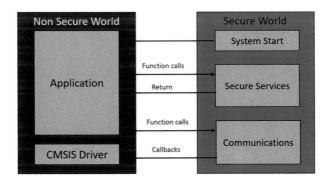

FIG. 10.11

Program structure with TrustZone partitions.

No permission required.

The code can then configure any secure peripherals and secure software components before leaving the Secure World and start executing code in the Nonsecure World. From this point onwards, the main user application will run in the Nonsecure World and make calls to the security services which execute in the Secure World and then return to the Nonsecure World.

The key to designing an application to execute between the Secure and Nonsecure partitions is to build two separate subprojects: one for the Secure partition and one for the Nonsecure partition. We can then provide the Nonsecure world with a table of entry points into the Secure services in the Secure partition. This allows the application code running in the Nonsecure partition to access functions in the Secure partition without having any to expose any code in the Secure project. In the next exercise, we will go through the steps required to set up both projects, but first, we will look at the overall application structure and its critical files.

CMSIS startup files

When we create a secure project, a new file will be added to the startup folder called *partition_<device.h>*. The partition header file contains a set of #defines, which are used by the *system_<device>.c* file to configure and enable the TrustZone SAU peripheral at startup (Fig. 10.12).

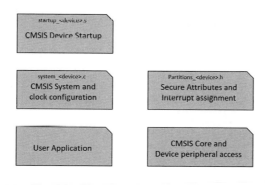

FIG. 10.12

CMSIS Core files. CMSIS Core project files.

No permission required.

A typical memory map will include a Secure region at the start of the FLASH memory, a Nonsecure-Callable region for the veneer table and a region of Nonsecure FLASH memory. The RAM and peripherals will also be divided into Secure and Nonsecure Regions. Once we enter the system_device.c file, the system configuration code will use some new CMSIS Core functions to configure the SAU using the *partition_<device>.h* header file values Table 10.4.

Table 10.4 CMSIS core SAU functions.

Function	Description
TZ_SAU_Setup()	Configure the SAU using the definitions in partitions.h
TZ_SAU_Enable()	Enable the SAU
TZ_SAU_Disable()	Disable the SAU

The CMSIS Core specification has been extended to provide support for TrustZone.

While the startup code is used to set up the SAU at run time, the linker scatter files for both the Secure and Nonsecure projects must also be configured to reflect this memory map (Fig. 10.13).

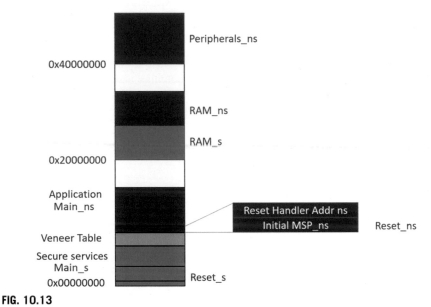

FIG. 10.13

TrustZone projects memory map.

This, in effect, creates two separate executable images within the one microcontroller. The Secure image is located at the base of the FLASH memory so that it can use the processor reset vector and secure interrupt vector table. The Nonsecure image is located to an arbitrary location in the FLASH memory but is built with a standard reset handler and vector table. The transition from the Secure code to the Nonsecure code is done by performing a "software reset" in the Secure code to start execution of the Nonsecure image. The software reset loads the initial Nonsecure main stack pointer value from the start of the Nonsecure image. It then loads the address of the Nonsecure reset handler into a function pointer and then uses the function pointer to leave the Secure code and enter the Nonsecure code via its reset handler. From this point onwards, the Nonsecure code will execute like a standard application. The CMSIS core specification has been extended to provide support functions that allow the Secure code to access the Nonsecure configuration registers. This allows the Secure code to configure the Nonsecure CPU resisters during the startup phase if required.

Secure veneer functions

Once we have entered the Nonsecure code, we will need to access functions in the Secure partition. To make a Secure function visible to the Nonsecure code, we need to create a veneer table in the Secure code. We also need to provide a linkable object to the Nonsecure project so that it can make calls to the secure functions. The veneer table provides a set of SG entry points for use by the Nonsecure. To create a veneer table, we can add an attribute to a "C" function that tells the compiler it is an entry point into the Secure World. When the Secure project is built, it also creates a "dummy" library file that exports the secure gateway entry points to the Nonsecure World. This library file must be added to the Nonsecure project to provide the entry point addresses for the linker.

Exercise: TrustZone configuration

This is a multiproject workspace that contains two projects. One project will run in the TrustZone Secure World, and one project will run in the Nonsecure World. At startup, the Secure project will configure the TrustZone SAU and then hand over to the Nonsecure code. The Nonsecure code will access functions in the Secure code. We will also trigger a security exception by making an illegal access to the secure world partition.

In the pack installer, select Exercise 10.1 and press the Copy button.

This project uses an Arm Cortex-M33 Fast Model simulation, which allows us to experiment with the standard CMSIS-Core files. There are slight variations in approach from each silicon vendor, but once you know the standard approach, these are easy to adapt to.

Highlight the CM33_s secure project right click and set it as the active project (Fig. 10.14).

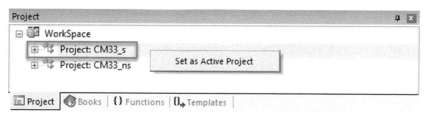

FIG. 10.14

TrustZone Workspace. The secure and nonsecure world projects are held in a multiproject workspace.

No permission required.

Open the RTE.
Select CMSIS::Core and Device::Startup (Fig. 10.15).

⚏ Manage Run-Time Environment

Software Component	Sel.	Variant
⬥ CMSIS		
⬥ CORE	☑	
⬥ DSP	☐	Library ⌄
⬥ NN Lib	☐	
⊞ ⬥ RTOS (API)		
⊞ ⬥ RTOS2 (API)		
⊞ ⬥ CMSIS Driver		
⊞ ⬥ CMSIS Driver Validation		API
⊞ ⬥ Compiler		ARM Compiler
⊞ ⬥ Components		
⊞ ⬥ Data Exchange		
⬥ Device		
⬥ Startup	☑	C Startup ⌄
⊞ ⬥ SDK Utilities		

FIG. 10.15

TrustZone RTE settings. The Run Time Environment Manager adds components to the project.

No permission required.

Then click OK.

The RTE device startup option will add the low-level startup code, including the reset handler and vector table, plus the system code. Two additional files are added *partition.h,* which holds the configuration options for the SAU and ARMCM33_ac6. sct, which is the linker scatter file (Fig. 10.16).

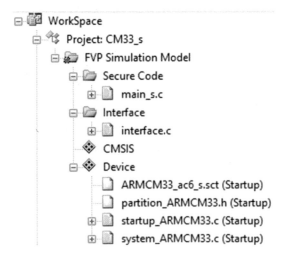

FIG. 10.16

TrustZone Secure world project. The secure world project with its linker script, startup code, and partition header file.

No permission required.

Open Partition.h.

This file is a templated file that contains configuration options to manually configure the TrustZone peripheral as shown in Fig. 10.17.

⊟ Initialize Security Attribution Unit (SAU) CTRL register	☑
Enable SAU	☑
When SAU is disabled	All Memory is Secure
⊟ Initialize Security Attribution Unit (SAU) Address Regions	
⊞ Initialize SAU Region 0	☑
⊞ Initialize SAU Region 1	☑
⊞ Initialize SAU Region 2	☑
⊞ Initialize SAU Region 3	☑
⊞ Initialize SAU Region 4	☐

FIG. 10.17

Partition header file. A configuration wizard in the partition.h header allows you to configure the SAU region settings.

No permission required.

The first section of the menu allows us to enable operation of the SAU and the default access model for the memory when the SAU is disabled.

Next we can configure each of the SAU regions by defining a start and end address along with the type access allowed.

The *partition.h* file is preconfigured with a default memory map so don't adjust any options for now.

Open ARMCM33_TZ_FPU_ac6_s.sct.

The second file is the default linker file for the Secure project, as shown in Fig. 10.18. This defines the resources allocated to the Secure world executable. This should match the secure regions allocated in the partition file.

⊟ Flash Configuration	
Flash Base Address	0x0000 0000
Flash Size (in Bytes)	0x0008 0000
⊟ RAM Configuration	
RAM Base Address	0x2000 0000
RAM Size (in Bytes)	0x0004 0000
⊟ Stack / Heap Configuration	
Stack Size (in Bytes)	0x0000 0200
Heap Size (in Bytes)	0x0000 0C00
⊟ CMSE Venner Configuration	
CMSE Venner Size (in Bytes)	0x0000 0200

FIG. 10.18

Linker script file wizard. Select the configuration wizard to visualize the linker memory layout.

No permission required.

This file is preconfigured so do not adjust any options.
Highlight the secure code folder, right click and select "Add new Item"
(Fig. 10.19).

FIG. 10.19

Add a new item to the project file project file. Select the project group and right click to add a new item.

No permission required.

Select Use Code Template and add the Core: main module support file
(Fig. 10.20).

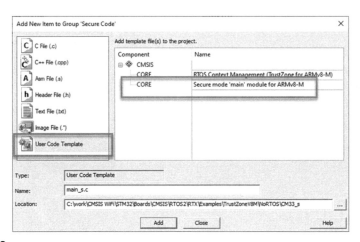

FIG. 10.20

The secure main template. A template file provides a minimal main() function.

No permission required.

On startup the secure project will configure the SAU and then reach *main( )*.

Once in *main( )* it will prepare the nonsecure project for execution by performing a software reset.

We first load the nonsecure main stack pointer with the first four bytes of the nonsecure image.

```
__TZ_set_MSP_NS(*((uint32_t *)(TZ_START_NS)));
```

The start of the nonsecure image is defined at the beginning of the *main_s.c* module.

```
#define TZ_START_NS (0x200000U)
```

Next we set a function pointer to the address of the nonsecure reset vector this is the image start address +4.

```
NonSecure_ResetHandler = (funcptr_void)(*((uint32_t *)
                                          ((TZ_START_NS) + 4U)));
```

Then we can exit the secure code and jump to the start of the nonsecure code.

```
NonSecure_ResetHandler();
```

Execution of the Secure *main()* function terminates at this point. From now on, the main thread of execution will be in the Nonsecure project. The CPU will only enter into the Secure code in response to function calls from the Nonsecure code.

We can declare a function in *main()*, which can be called by Nonsecure code by using an attribute *cmse_nonsecure_entry*.

The Secure code main_s.c has an additional function to perform a simple calculation. This function uses the attribute *cmse_nonsecure_entry* to inform the compiler and linker that it will be called from the Nonsecure code.

```
int func1(int x) __attribute__((cmse_nonsecure_entry)) {
  return x+3;
}
```

We now need to configure the compiler and linker to build our Secure project.

Highlight the project root right click and select Options for Target.
In the target menu, change the software model to Secure Mode and select the microlib library (Fig. 10.21).

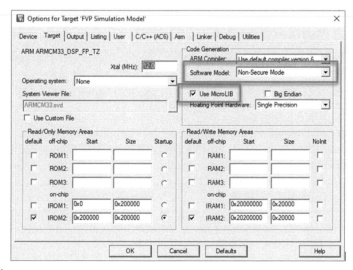

FIG. 10.21

Select secure software model. The project\target settings allows you to select the secure software model.

Microlib is an ANSI C library that is optimized for a small microcontroller and has no specific security features.

Next select the linker tab (Fig. 10.22).

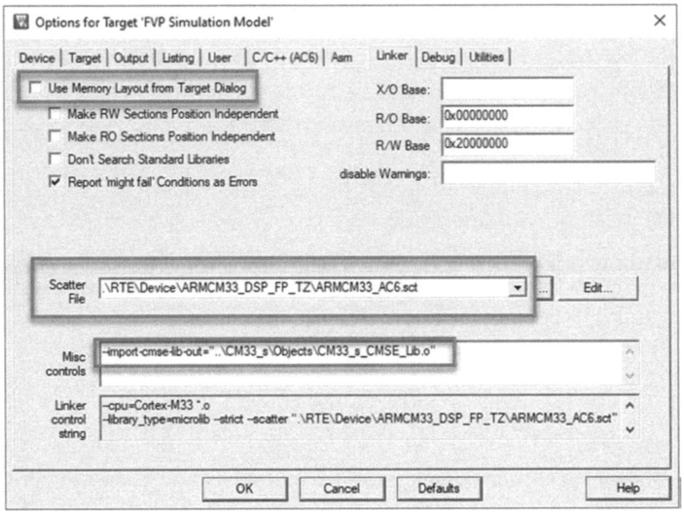

FIG. 10.22

Secure linker settings. The linker settings are provided by a script file, which matches the TrustZone marking.

No permission required.

Uncheck the Use memory layout from target.

This will disable the auto generated linker file and instead use a custom linker file called a scatter file.

Select the project scatter file which is in the RTE\device\ARMCM33_DSP_FP_TZ folder.

This will build the project to match the SAU settings.

We are providing functions in the Secure world which will be called from a different project running in the Nonsecure world. In order for the Nonsecure project to resolve the function symbols, we need to create a target import library that provides a symbol table and absolute address for each Secure Gateway instruction. This resolves Nonsecure function calls to functions located in the Secure partition. The target import library is created as a library object file by using the following linker directive:

`--import-cmse-lib-out=<filename>`

This will generate an object file that can be added to the Nonsecure code. This joins together the two separate projects to make a cohesive executable.

Add the following line to the linker misc. controls dialog box:

`--import-cmse-lib-out="..\CM33_s\Objects\CM33_s_CMSE_Lib.o"`

Build the project.
As the project is built the Target Import file will also be created.
Now set the Nonsecure project as the active project (Fig. 10.23).

WorkSpace
Project: CM33_s
Project: CM33_ns
Set as Active Project

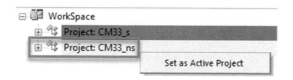

FIG. 10.23

Select the Nonsecure project. Highlight and right click on the project. Then set it as active.

No permission required.

In the RTE select the CMSIS::Core and Device::Startup options then press OK.
This will add the same startup files to the project including the linker scatter file.

Open ArmC33_ac6.sct.
Adjust the memory mapping to match the Nonsecure regions defined in partition.h of the secure project (Fig. 10.24).

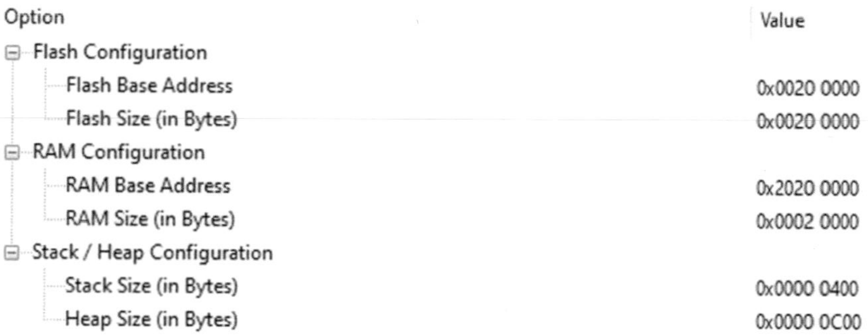

Option
Value
Flash Configuration
Flash Base Address
0x0020 0000
Flash Size (in Bytes)
0x0020 0000
RAM Configuration
RAM Base Address
0x2020 0000
RAM Size (in Bytes)
0x0002 0000
Stack / Heap Configuration
Stack Size (in Bytes)
0x0000 0400
Heap Size (in Bytes)
0x0000 0C00

FIG. 10.24

Nonsecure linker settings. A configuration wizard helps you to easily adjust the linker settings.

No permission required.

Highlight the Nonsecure code folder, right click, and select "Add an existing file".
Add main_ns.c.
Navigate to the Secure project directory and add the veneer object file CM33_s_CMSE_Lib.o (Fig. 10.25).

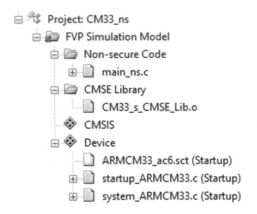

FIG. 10.25

Adding the Secure Veneer file. Add the veneer library to the Nonsecure project from its native directory.

No permission required.

The veneer file is in the cm33\objects directory and is called CM33_s_CMSE_Lib.o. Leave it in this location and add it to the nonsecure project in the Microvision IDE. If any memory map changes are made to the Secure project, this file will be updated in both projects.

We can now start to develop our application code. The Nonsecure *main()* will be the start of our application code. Here we can call Nonsecure and Secure functions. In this example code, we call a Secure function *func1()* to do a calculation then call another Secure function *func2()*. We pass a function pointer into *func2()*, which references a Nonsecure callback function. This will demonstrate calling a Nonsecure function from the Secure world. Finally, we set a function pointer to make an illegal call into the Secure area to demonstrate a security violation exception.

```
int main(void) {
funcptr_void illegalFunc = (funcptr_void)(((uint32_t *)
                                    ((ILLEGAL_SECURE_ENTRY))));

val1 = func1 (1);
val2 = func2 (func3, 2);
illegalFunc();
  while (1);
}
```

Open the Nonsecure project options for target.
The software model should be set to Nonsecure mode for this project and use of the MicroLIB library should be enabled (Fig. 10.26).

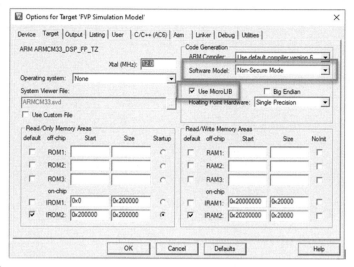

FIG. 10.26

Nonsecure project settings. The security model is now set to Nonsecure.

No permission required.

Switch to the compiler tab.

The Nonsecure project is accessing include files located in the Secure project.
Add a search path into the root of the secure project ..\CM33_s (Fig. 10.27).

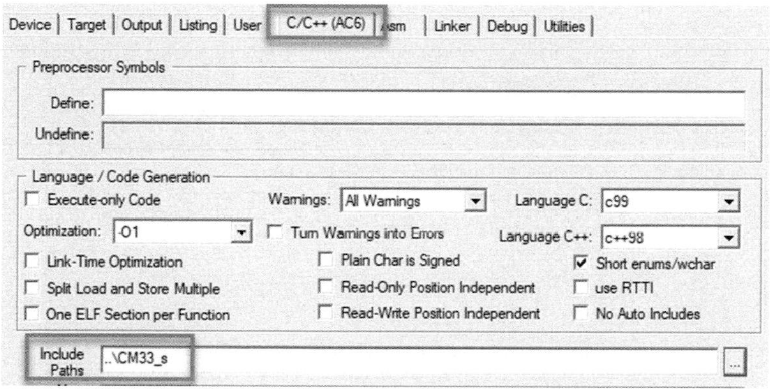

FIG. 10.27

Nonsecure compiler settings. The Nonsecure project must include a search path to the
Secure project to build the veneer file.

No permission required.

You can use the include path button to select the folder graphically.

Now go to the linker tab.

In the linker disable the "Use memory layout from Target tab."
Select the ARMCM33_ac6.sct scatter file in \RTE\Device\ARMCM33_
DSP_FP_TZ\ARMCM33_AC6.sct Fig. 10.28.

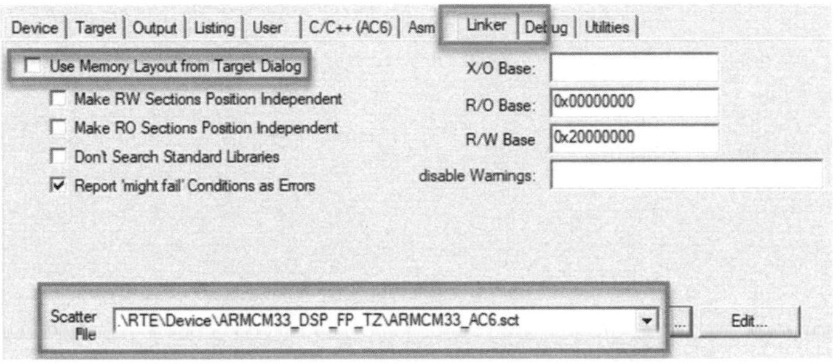

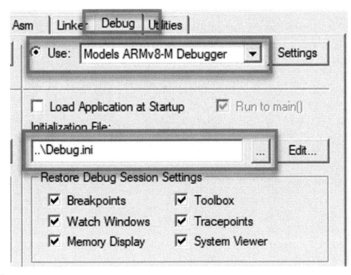

FIG. 10.28

Nonsecure linker configuration. The nonsecure project uses a matching linker script for the Nonsecure memory layout.

No permission required.

Now go to the Debug tab.
Uncheck the load application at startup (Fig. 10.29).

FIG. 10.29

Nonsecure debug settings. The debugger must use a script file to load both projects.

No permission required.

Normally, the debugger will program the FLASH memory and load the debug symbol set when the debugger starts. In this project, we will use a script file to load both the Secure and Nonsecure images. This is done by creating an initialization file that will automatically be executed once the debugger starts.

Press the Edit button to view the Debug.ini file.

```
LOAD "..\CM33_ns\Objects\CM33_ns.axf" incremental
LOAD "..\CM33_s\Objects\CM33_s.axf" incremental
RESET
g,\CM33_s\main_s\main
```

The script file downloads both the Secure and Nonsecure projects into the FLASH memory and loads both symbol sets into the debugger. The "incremental" keyword means add to the existing symbol set rather than replace existing symbols with a new set. The script then resets the processor and runs the code to the secure *main()*. Although we have two separate images, the debugger can switch seamlessly between both sets of symbols to maintain high level debug support across both projects.

The same debug.ini file can be added to the debugger initialization box in the Secure project.

Batch build both projects (Fig. 10.30).

FIG. 10.30

Batch building both projects. Use the batch build icon on the toolbar to build both projects.

No permission required.

The batch build option will build the Secure project first so that the import library is up to date we can then build the Nonsecure code.

Start the debugger.

Both projects will be loaded, and the code will run to *main()* in the Secure project. Here, the CPU is running in Secure mode, as we can see from the register window (Fig. 10.31).

FIG. 10.31

Register view. The debugger register view displays the current active security state and operating mode.

No permission required.

Open the peripherals\Core Peripherals\Security Attribution Unit (Fig. 10.32).

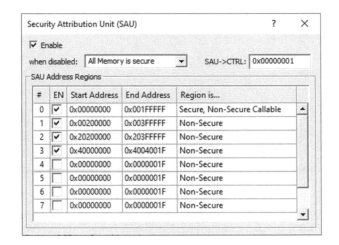

FIG. 10.32

Debug SAU peripheral view. The debugger peripheral/core peripheral view has a window for the SAU configuration.

No permission required.

Here, we can see the current configuration of the SAU and can check it matches the settings defined in our *partition.h* file.

The Nonsecure code has also been downloaded to the FLASH memory.

Open the view\memory window and set the address to 0x200000 (Fig. 10.33).

Memory 1

Address: 0x200000

```
0x00200000: 20220000 00200809 00200805 0020081D
0x0020002C: 00200805 00200805 00000000 00200805
```

FIG. 10.33

Nonsecure memory view. Use the memory window to view the address of the Nonsecure Reset handler.

No permission required.

Right click and set the display to unsigned int.

Here, we can see the first two words of the Nonsecure image. The first word is the initial main stack pointer value, and the second is the address of the reset handler.

The Secure code will load the Nonsecure MSP value into the Nonsecure R13 using a CMSIS core TrustZone function.

```
__TZ_set_MSP_NS(*((uint32_t *)(TZ_START_NS)));
```

Once this function has executed, you can see that the MSP_NS has been configured (Fig. 10.34).

FIG. 10.34

Nonsecure MSP. The resister window shows the initial value of the Nonsecure main stack pointer.

No permission required.

Then the code will jump to the Nonsecure reset handler by executing the function pointer.

```
NonSecure ResetHandler();
```

The function pointer is defined as a Nonsecure call.

```
typedef void (*funcptr_void) (void) __attribute__((cmse_nonsecure_call));
```

This will generate code that wipes the CPU registerbank and the FPU scalar registers.

Once this is done, the code will jump to the Nonsecure partition using a Nonsecure branch link exchange instruction.

```
0x00000A4C 4784 BLXNSr0
```

Once this is executed, we will reach the Nonsecure reset handler and the CPU will be in Nonsecure mode (Fig. 10.35).

FIG. 10.35

Entry to Nonsecure world. After the branch instruction the security state changes to Nonsecure.

No permission required.

The Nonsecure code will call *func1()* with a Branch link instruction.

```
0x00200804 BL func1 (0x00000A60)
```

This function is in the Secure partition, so rather than jumping directly to the entry point of the function, the code jumps to the veneer table using the address provided by the import library and reaches the Secure Gateway (SG) entry instruction; this is followed by a branch to the entry point of *func1()*.

```
0x00000A60 SG
0x00000A64 B func1 (0x000008F0)
```

On entry to the Secure partition the processor once again switches to Secure mode.

The function will execute a simple floating point calculation and then return to the Nonsecure code.

Before the return instruction, the compiler generates instructions to wipe the floating-point registers and then performs a Nonsecure branch exchange to return.

```
0x00000960 4774 BXNS 1r
```

TrustZone access violation

The Nonsecure code also configures a rogue function pointer to an illegal entry point within the Secure partition.

Execute the *illegalFunc()*; call.

This will create a Secure fault which will cause the processor to switch into Secure mode and vector to the secure fault exception vector.

Open the preipherals\Core Peripherals\NVIC (Fig. 10.36).

Nested Vectored Interrupt Controller (NVIC)

Idx	Source	Name	TZ	E	P	A	Priority
2	Non-maskable Interrupt	NMI	S	1	0		-2
3	Hard Fault	HARDFAULT	S	1			-1
4	Memory Management	MEMFAULT	S	0	0	0	0 = 0 s0
5	Bus Fault	BUSFAULT	S	0	0	0	0 = 0 s0
6	Usage Fault	USGFAULT	S	0		0	0 = 0 s0
7	Secure Fault	SECUREFAULT	S	1	0	1	0 = 0 s0
11	System Service Call	SVCALL	S	1	0	0	0 = 0 s0
12	Debug Monitor	MONITOR	S	0	0	0	0 = 0 s0
14	Pend System Service	PENDSV	S	1	0	0	0 = 0 s0
15	System Tick Timer (S)	SYSTICK (S)	S	0	0	0	0 = 0 s0
15	System Tick Timer (NS)	SYSTICK (NS)	NS	0	0	0	128 = 64 s0
16	ExtIRQ 0	ExtIRQ 0	S	0	0	0	0 = 0 s0

FIG. 10.36

The NVIC window in the debugger. The debugger NVIC window shows the current status of the CPU exceptions and interrupts.

No permission required.

TrustZone interrupt handling

Exception vector table

When TrustZone is added to the Cortex-M33 processor, both the Secure and Nonsecure worlds have their own NVIC and a dedicated vector table. The processor exceptions are routed between the Secure and Nonsecure vector tables in three ways. They may be solely accessible by the Secure state, or they may be routed to either the Secure or Nonsecure NVIC by setting a register flag. Alternatively, an exception may be banked so that it has both a Secure and Nonsecure service routine. For example this would allow a user fault exception in both the Secure and Nonsecure Worlds (Table 10.5). Peripheral interrupts use a separate set of routing registers to select their destination as either the Secure or Nonsecure NVIC.

Table 10.5 Secure world vector table.

Vector	Routing	Description
Nonmaskable Interrupt	Default: Secure State	May be routed to Nonsecure State
Hard Fault	Default: Secure State	May be routed to Nonsecure State
MemManager	Banked	Available in Secure and Nonsecure
Bus Fault	Default: Secure State	May be routed to Nonsecure State
Usage Fault	Banked	Available in Secure and Nonsecure
Secure Fault	Secure only	New Armv8-M TrustZone exception
SC Call	Banked	Available in Secure and Nonsecure
Debug Monitor	Implementation dependent	
Pend SV	Banked	Available in Secure and Nonsecure
SysTick	Banked	Available in Secure and Nonsecure
Peripheral Interrupts 0−xxx	Programmable	Routing defined by Interrupt Target Nonsecure state register

Two processor exceptions, Reset and Security Fault, are always routed to the secure NVIC. This guarantees that any reset will force the processor into a Secure State so that it can be fully configured before the main application code can start. If there is a security fault, the processor will again be forced into the secure state so that it can log the error and run the necessary mitigation code.

The Memory Manager exception is banked so that we can provide separate service routines for the Secure and Nonsecure memory protection units.

The Supervisor Call (SVC) PEND and SYSTICK exceptions are primarily used to support an RTOS. When TrustZone is present, these exceptions are banked to allow an RTOS kernel to run in either a Secure State or Nonsecure State. We will discuss this further later in this chapter. The SYSTICK exception is slightly more complicated. If the processor is fitted with both a Secure and Nonsecure SYSTICK timer, the exception is banked. However, it is possible to have a single SYSTICK timer. In this case, the exception can be routed to either the Secure or Nonsecure processor state.

The USAGE FAULT exception is also banked. Since this exception is used to catch programming errors like divide by zero, we can usefully provide exception service routines for both Secure and Nonsecure execution errors.

The remaining processor exceptions can be routed to either the Secure or Nonsecure state. You can select their security state through the Application Interrupt and Reset Control Register (AIRC) in the Secure system control block. When the processor is fitted with TrustZone, the AIRC register has a number of additional fields, as shown in Table 10.6.

Table 10.6 Application interrupt and reset control (AIRC) register.

Bits	Field	Description
1	VECTCLRACTIVE	Clear active state (for use by a debugger)
2	SYSRESETREQ	System reset request. Access depends on SYSRESETREQS
3	SYSRESETREQS	System reset state 1 = from secure state only 0 = from secure and nonsecure states.
8–10	PRIGROUP	Banked between security states. Sets interrupt priority grouping
13	BFHFNMINS	Bus Fault, Hard Fault and NMI routing 1 = Nonsecure	0 = Secure
14	PRIS	1 = Secure exceptions have priority	0 = priority ranges between Secure and Nonsecure are equal
15	ENDIANNESS	Returns the Endianness of the system 0 = Little Endian	1 = Big Endian
16–31 Read	VECTKEYSTAT	You must write 0x05FA to this field when updating any other field in this register.
16–31 Write	VECTKEY	On a read this field return the bit wide inverse of the VETKEY write value (0x0A05)

By default, the selectable processor exceptions (Hard Fault, Bus Fault, and NMI) are routed to the Secure state NVIC. However, they can be routed to the Nonsecure NVIC by setting the BFHFNMINS bit to logic one. The processor Secure state has read\write access to the BFHFNMINS bit while Nonsecure state has read-only access.

The AIRC register also contains the SYSRESETREQ bit. When set to logic one, this bit forces a processor reset. When the processor is fitted with TrustZone, an additional bit SYSRESETREQS is used to qualify which security state can write to SYSRESETREQ and reset the processor. When SYSRESETREQS is set to logic zero (default), both security states can reset the processor via SYSRESETREQ. If the SYSRESETREQS is set to logic one, the processor SYSRESETREQ can only be written to when the processor is in the Secure State.

The PRIGROUP field is used to define interrupt preemption and priority levels, but when TrustZone is present, this field is banked to allow different PRIGROUP settings in Secure and Nonsecure Worlds.

It is likely that in a real-world application, the processor will have to deal with both Secure and Nonsecure processor exceptions. At reset, the PRIS bit is set to zero, which gives equal priority to Secure and Nonsecure exceptions. If this bit is set to logic one, the Secure exceptions will be given priority over Nonsecure exceptions.

The security fault exception will also place the processor into the Secure World. The fault exceptions, hard fault and bus fault can be routed to service routines in either the Secure or Nonsecure worlds while the Usage and Memory Manager faults have banked registers that will jump to service routines in both security worlds.

Once the Secure and Nonsecure MPU's are configured and enabled, they will generate an exception if the processor causes an access violation to an MPU region.

Finally, when writing to the AIRC register the VECTKEY field must have a write value of 0x0AF5 for the register to be updated.

Locating the nonsecure vector table

The Nonsecure code needs to perform one additional configuration before it reaches *main()*. The Nonsecure software vector table is programmed into the FLASH memory at the start of the Nonsecure region, but the processor Nonsecure hardware vector table is located at the beginning of FLASH memory. In order to service the Nonsecure interrupts, we need to align the Nonsecure hardware and software vector tables as shown in Fig. 10.37. This is done by programming the start address of the Nonsecure image into the Nonsecure Vector Table Offset register VTOR_NS. This is done in the Nonsecure *system_init()* function located in *system_<device>.c* code.

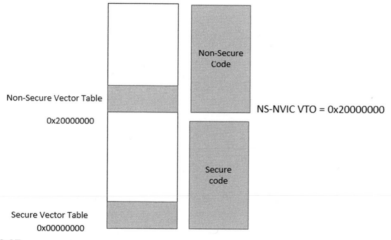

FIG. 10.37

Memory and vector table layout. The Secure and Nonsecure hardware vector tables must be adjusted to match the project memory map.

Secure/nonsecure peripheral interrupt routing

The peripheral interrupt vectors grow upwards in memory from the end of the processor exception table. The Cortex-M33 can support up to 512 peripheral interrupt sources, which should keep us going for a bit. Each of these interrupt sources may be routed to either the Secure or Nonsecure NVIC. This routing is done through the NVIC "Interrupt Target Nonsecure" Registers ITENS0–15. Each peripheral interrupt channel has a dedicated bit within the ITENSxx registers, allowing each interrupt to be routed to either the Secure or Nonsecure vector table. When this bit is set to logic zero, the interrupt will be routed to the Secure NVIC. When the bit is set to logic one, the bit will be routed to the Nonsecure interrupt channel. After a processor reset, the ITENSxx registers are set to zero, routing all peripheral interrupt channels to the Secure NVIC.

Exercise: TrustZone interrupt routing

Now that we have enabled the TrustZone peripheral and partitioned the memory map using the SAU, we will also need to route the interrupt channels between the Secure and Nonsecure NVIC's. This is done by the Secure startup code using settings for the ITNSxx registers defined in the partition.h header.

In the pack installer, select exercise 10.2 and press the copy button.
Open partition.h in the Secure project.
Expand the setup Interrupt Target branch and then the Initialise ITNS 0 branch.
Change the setting of Interrupt 1 from Secure to Nonsecure state.
Open *main_s.c.*
Uncomment the following lines of code:

```
NVIC_EnableIRQ(0);
NVIC_EnableIRQ(1);
```

This will enable the first two interrupt channels.

The Secure and Nonsecure interrupt vector tables are defined in their respective startup files.

In the Secure code, the vector table in startup_s.c declares a vector for channel zero:

```
void Interrupt0_Handler (void) __attribute__ ((weak, alias("Default_
                                                        Handler")));
```

and an ISR function in *main_s.c*

```
void Interrupt0_Handler (void)
```

This is mirrored in the Nonsecure code for Interrupt channel 1. The interrupt vector is defined in startup.

```
void Interrupt1_Handler (void) __attribute__(weak, alias("Default_
                                                        Handler")));
```

And the ISR is created in main_ns.c.

```
void Interrupt1_Handler (void)
```

Batch build the code and restart the debugger.
Open the peripherals/core peripherals/nested vector Interrupt controller.
Run the code so it enters the Nonsecure project.
Open *main_ns.c.*
Set a breakpoint on the entry to void *Interrupt1_Handler (void) line 52.*
In the NVIC window select ExtIRQ 1.
Set the Pending bit in the "Select Interrupt" panel Fig. 10.38.

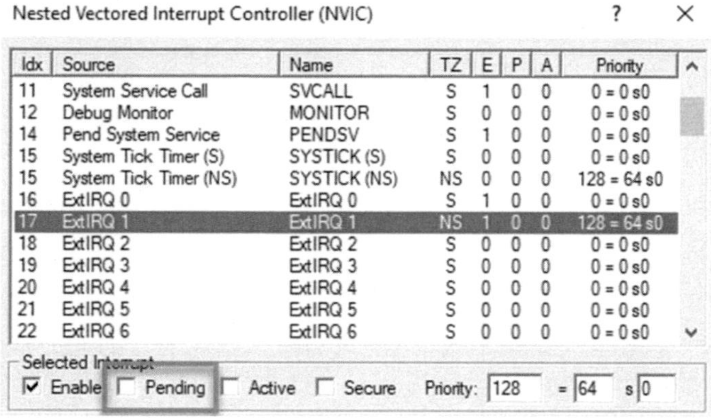

FIG. 10.38

NVIC interrupt routing. The debugger NVIC window shows the interrupt current state. We can also simulate a pending interrupt.

No permission required.

Run the code.

This will simulate an interrupt on NVIC channel 1 which will be routed to the ISR handler in the Nonsecure code.

Now set a breakpoint on the secure ISR in main_s.c.
Run the code and trigger an interrupt by setting the NVIC pending bit for ExtIRQ0.

The channel 0 interrupt will be routed to the ISR handler in the Secure code.

TrustZone system control block

The system control block registers are also modified when TrustZone is fitted with the Cortex-M33 processor. TrustZone adds some new registers and additional bit fields in existing registers. The SCB registers are selectively banked between the Secure and Nonsecure state. In addition, there is an alias region for the Nonsecure SCB, which allows the Secure world to configure the Nonsecure world SCB registers. A summary is shown in Table 10.7.

A full description of the SCB registers is provided in the Armv8-M architectural manual. However, it is worth noting that the BHFHFNMINS bit in the AIRCR is set to logic one, then the visibility of some bits will be limited to the Secure world.

Table 10.7 TrustZone system control block.

Register	Banked between states?	Contains TrustZone fields	Notes
Interrupt Control and State Register	Bitwise	✓	NS World access to some exception bits is controlled by the AIRCR.BFHFNMINS bit
Vector Table Offset Register	✓	✗	Write Access is implementation defined
Application Interrupt and Reset Control Register	Bitwise	✓	May elevate priority of Secure interrupts over Nonsecure interrupts. Defines if a software reset may be executed from Secure world only. Hard fault, bus fault and NMI may be Secure world only (BFHFNMINS=0)
System Control Register	Bitwise	✓	Configures SLEEPDEEP and SEVONPEND options for a given security state
Configuration and Control Register	✓	✓	The configuration flags a banked between security states
System Handler Priority Register 1–3	Bitwise	✓	Processor exception priority fields. These will be banked to match the routing of the CPU exceptions as discussed in section.
System Handler Control and State Register	Bitwise	✓	CPU exception status flags. These will be banked to match the routing of the CPU exceptions as discussed in section.
Configurable Fault Status Register	Bitwise	✓	
MemManage Fault Status Register	✓	✗	
BusFault Status Register	✗	✗	Provides Bus Fault error flags
UsageFault Status Register	✓	✗	Provides Usage Fault error flags
HardFault Status Register	✗	✗	Provides hard Fault error flags
MemManage Fault Address Register	✓	✗	Provides Memory manager fault address
BusFault Address Register	✗	✗	Provides Bus Fault address
Auxiliary Fault Status Register	✗	**Implementation Defined**	May contain nonstandard vendor specific flags
Co Processor Access Control	✓	✗	Defines privileged/unprivileged access rights for Co Processors 0–07, Defines access rights for the floating point unit as Co Processor 10–11
Nonsecure Access Control	✗	✓	Defines Nonsecure access permission for co processor 0–7 and Floating point Unit as Co Processor 10–11

Additional TrustZone fields are added to the SCB registers which may also be banked between security worlds.

SysTick

When TrustZone is fitted to the Cortex-M33 processor, the silicon designer has a number of choices on how to implement the SysTick timer. It is possible to have zero, one or two SysTick timers. In the case of dual timers, each security mode has an independent SysTick timer, and the SysTick exception is banked, providing a dedicated interrupt for each security mode. If a single SysTick timer is present, it may be owned by either security state depending on the state of the STTNS (SysTick Targets Nonsecure) bit in the Interrupt Control and State ICS register.

The CMSIS core specification provides a standard function to enable the SysTick exception and configure its countdown period. This function can be used in either security mode to configure the local timer. An additional function is also provided, which allows the Secure mode to configure the Nonsecure SysTick timer, as shown in Table 10.8.

Table 10.8 SysTick timer functions.

Function	Security state	Description
uint32_t SysTick_Config (uint32_t ticks)	Secure or Nonsecure	Configures the SysTick timer for the active security state
uint32_t TZ_SysTick_Config_NS(uint32_t ticks)	Secure	Configures the Nonsecure SyTick timer from the Secure state

The CMSIS SysTick timer functions are extended to include access to the secure alias registers.

Exercise: TrustZone SysTick support

The simulation model implements both the Secure and Nonsecure SysTick timers. This allows us to extend our example to enable both timers and generate interrupts in both the Secure and Nonsecure Worlds.

In the pack installer select and copy exercise 10.3.
Open main_s.c.
Uncomment the following lines:

```
SysTick_Config(1000);
TZ_SysTick_Config_NS (10000);
```

This will enable both the Secure and Nonsecure SysTick timers.
Batch build the code and start the debugger.

When each SysTick reaches count zero an exception is generated and will be routed to a handler in the matching security mode.

In main_s.c locate the ISR handler SysTick_Handler() and set a breakpoint at the start of the function.

> **Open main_ns.c and set a breakpoint on the nonsecure SysTick_Handler()**
> **function.**
> **Run the code.**

As each timer generates an exception the debugger will halt at the matching ISR
routine.

Using an RTOS with TrustZone

When we are using an RTOS with a Cortex-M33 fitted with TrustZone, we have to
decide if the RTOS kernel will be located in the Secure world or the Nonsecure world.
While it is possible to locate the RTOS kernel in either partition, the recommended
option is to place the kernel in the Nonsecure partition (Fig. 10.39). The RTOS does
not contain any sensitive code, so it does not really need to be placed in the secure
partition. We also want to keep the complexity and size of the secure code as low
as possible. Furthermore, we do not want to do a field update of the secure partition
unless absolutely necessary and placing the RTOS kernel in the Nonsecure world
allows us to update the RTOS at will. Keeping the RTOS kernel in the Nonsecure
partition also allows existing Cortex-M RTOS implementations to port easily to the
Armv8-M architecture. Therefore, the RTOS kernel is best located in the Nonsecure
partition, but there are still some issues that we need to address.

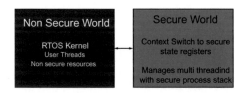

FIG. 10.39

TrustZone RTOS integration. While either security world will support an RTOS kernel we will
generally place the kernel in the Nonsecure world.

No permission required.

Multi-threaded access to secure functions

When we use an RTOS, the Nonsecure code will be running as RTOS threads.
Several different threads may need to make calls to functions in the Secure world.
This leads to the problem that one thread could call a Secure function and before the
Secure function returns, there is a task switch, and the Secure function is called again
by the newly active thread. Since the Secure partition does not access the Nonsecure
RAM, the Secure function cannot use the active thread stack memory. Effectively,
the Secure world functions are single-threaded and use a common region of RAM. If

we have multiple calls to the Secure function, this Secure RAM will be corrupted. To solve this problem, we need to provide some additional functions within the Secure partition that provide dedicated memory for each call to the Secure function. It is also important to standardize this context management, so any firmware designed to run in the Secure partition can be used with any RTOS.

CMSIS core TrustZone functions

The CMSIS core specification has been extended to provide a set of context management functions that can be used by any RTOS, as shown in Table 10.9. These functions are used to divide the Secure process stack into a number of slots. When a thread calls a Secure function, it is allocated a process stack slot which will be used as working memory by the secure function.

Table 10.9 CMSIS context management functions.

Function	Description
uint32_t TZ_InitContextSystem_S (void)	Initialize stack memory and context management
TZ_MemoryId_t TZ_AllocModuleContext_S (TZ_ModuleId_t module)	Allocate secure memory for a given thread
uint32_t TZ_FreeModuleContext_S(TZ_MemoryId_t id)	Free the context memory
uint32_t TZ_LoadContext_S (TZ_MemoryId_t id)	Load the new thread context during a task switch
uint32_t TZ_StoreContext_S(TZ_MemoryId_t id)	Store the current context during a task switch

The CMSIS core specification now include support for TruztZone context management.

When the RTOS starts, it will call the *TZ_InitContextSystem_S ()*, which will initialize the context management and secure stack. The context functions divide the process stack space into blocks of memory termed slots. As we create threads in the Nonsecure World, their run-time parameters are defined by a thread attribute structure. This structure includes a TrustZone Module identifier. This identifier should be set to logic one for any thread that will access Secure functions and logic zero if the thread will only be used for Nonsecure code. As the thread is created, it will call the *TZ_AllocModuleContext_S()* function, which will define the Secure runtime stack slot for that thread. During runtime, the Secure stack slots are managed by two functions which are used to load and store the current context. When a task switch occurs, the current thread context will be stored into the stack slot using *TZ_StoreContext()*, and the new thread context will be loaded using the *TZ_LoadContext()* function to assign a new stack slot and thread memory ID (Fig. 10.40).

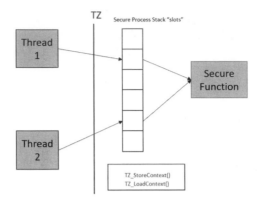

FIG. 10.40

Secure world process stack. The secure world process stack is segmented into context slots to support multithreaded execution.

No permission required.

Each of these functions are only a few lines of code, so do not impose any real overhead on the processor. We can see this in action in the next example.

Exercise: Using an RTOS with TrustZone

In this exercise, we will add an RTOS and secure function context management to the last project. The application code has been modified to start the RTOS and call the Secure functions via multiple threads.

In the pack installer select Exercise 10.4 and press the Copy button.
Set the secure project as the active project (Fig. 10.41).

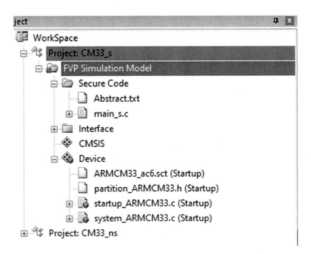

FIG. 10.41

RTOS project workspace. Open the workspace and set the secure project as the active project.

No permission required.

Highlight the interface folder right click and select "Add new Item."
Select the user code template.
Add the CMSIS core RTOS context management tz_context.c (Fig. 10.42).

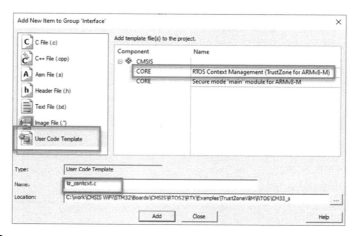

FIG. 10.42

Secure context template. Add the secure context template to the secure project.

No permission required.

Set the Nonsecure project as the active project.
Open the RTE and select the CMSIS::RTOS2:Keil RTX5.
Ensure the variant is set to Source_NS or Library_NS (Fig. 10.43).

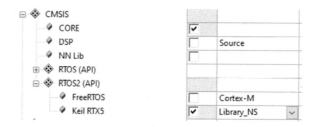

FIG. 10.43

Selecting RTOS security model. Use the RTE to add the Nonsecure version of the RTX RTOS.

No permission required.

Then click OK to close the RTE.
Open main_ns.c in the Nonsecure project.

When the *main()* function initializes the RTOS, the kernel will call the secure *TZ_InitContextSystem_S()* function. This function initializes the Secure process stack pointer and subdivides the stack space into a set of slots. The number of available slots is defined at the top of the module, along with the size of each slot in bytes.

```
#define TZ_PROCESS_STACK_SLOTS 8U
#define TZ_PROCESS_STACK_SIZE 256U
```

The slot details are held in an array of structures called processStackInfo. This contains the PSP value for the start of the stack, the top of the stack, and a value for the stack limit register (Fig. 10.44).

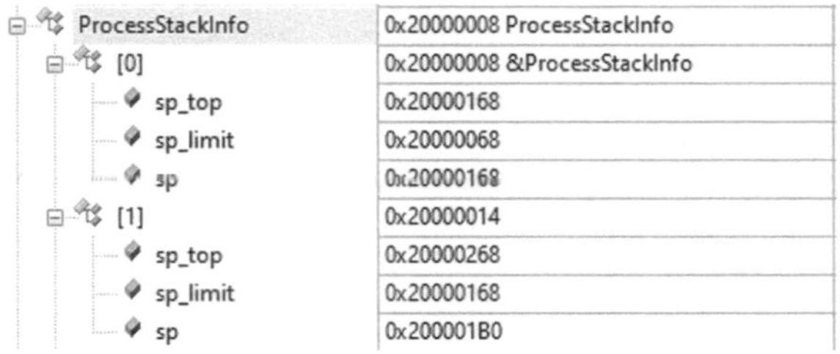

ProcessStackInfo	0x20000008 ProcessStackInfo
[0]	0x20000008 &ProcessStackInfo
sp_top	0x20000168
sp_limit	0x20000068
sp	0x20000168
[1]	0x20000014
sp_top	0x20000268
sp_limit	0x20000168
sp	0x200001B0

FIG. 10.44

Secure process stack context slots. The secure process stack is divided into eight context slots.

No permission required.

The main function can now create some threads. The first two threads, *ThreadA()* and *ThreadB()*, contain code that will access the secure functions. Both threads are created with a thread attribute as shown below:

```
static const osThreadAttr_t ThreadAttr = {
.tz_module = 1U, // indicate calls to secure mode
};
ThreadA_Id = osThreadNew(ThreadA, NULL, &ThreadAttr);
ThreadB_Id = osThreadNew(ThreadB, NULL, &ThreadAttr);
ThreadC_Id = osThreadNew(ThreadC, NULL, NULL);
```

The thread attribute sets the TrustZone module identifier to logic one, which will force the RTOS kernel to call the secure *TZ_AllocModuleContext()* function. This will allocate a stack slot and memory ID to this function. The final thread is created with a default thread attribute structure. Here, the TrustZone module identifier is set to zero, meaning that this thread does not access any secure functions.

Once the RTOS has started, each of the threads will task switch. During each task switch, the kernel will call the *TZ_StoreContext_S()* function. This function performs limit checks to ensure the current value of the stack pointer is within the active slot. If everything is OK, it stores the current value of the stack pointer in the *processStackInfo* array.

```
ProcessStackInfo[slot].sp = sp;
```

We then load in the new thread context with *TZ_LoadContext_S()*. On entry, this function checks for a valid slot number before restoring the secure process stack value and setting the stack limit register for the current slot.

```
__set_PSPLIM(ProcessStackInfo[slot].sp_limit);
__set_PSP(ProcessStackInfo[slot].sp);
```

Use batch build to build both projects.
Start the debugger.
Breakpoints are set on each of the TrustZone context functions and also on the nonsecure thread functions.
Open the register window so you can see the secure stack pointers.

The watch window contains the ProcessStackInfo array.
Run the code between the breakpoints to see the TrustZone context functions manage the secure memory allocation between the Nonsecure threads.

Memory protection unit (MPU)

The Memory Protection Unit (MPU) is an optional system level peripheral that may be added to the processor when the silicon vendor designs their microcontroller. Strictly speaking, the MPU is not part of TrustZone and may be fitted in isolation. However, it is likely that if TrustZone is fitted, the MPU will also be present. The purpose of the MPU is to mark the Cortex-M33 memory map into different memory regions, which are each granted different access permissions. So, for example, we can define a region over the FLASH memory, which has execute only access, privileged access, nonprivileged. Another region can be defined over the SRAM, which has Read/Write access and no execute access. While this sounds similar to TrustZone and the SAU, the MPU is a means of further policing memory access. Another important difference is that the TrustZone Secure and Nonsecure regions are defined at startup and never changed during normal execution. Whereas the MPU regions can be changed on the fly as different code executes. In an ideal system, we can use TrustZone to partition the device memory and the MPU to sandbox the resources of each RTOS thread to achieve a high level of memory protection.

The Armv8-M architecture has a new generation of MPU, which supports 4, 8, 12, or 16 protection regions. Each region is defined by a start address and an end address and can overlay any memory area and can be any size from 32 bytes up to 4 GB. This gives us a lot more flexibility compared to the original Armv7-M MPU, which could only allocate region sizes from a range of fixed block sizes. With the Armv8-M MPU, the only limitation is that the start and end address must be aligned to a 32-byte boundary. Access to each memory region is then controlled by a set of attributes that define the access type, operating mode and TrustZone state. Once active, they will monitor each region, and any infraction of the region attributes will cause an MPU exception.

When the MPU is present in a microcontroller that has TrustZone, there are effectively two MPUs: one which is used to configure regions in the Nonsecure partition and the other which is used to define regions in the Secure partition. Both MPUs are programmed in exactly the same way through mirrored sets of registers. The MPU registers are banked, with one set appearing in the Secure partition and one set appearing in the Nonsecure partition. An application can only access the Nonsecure MPU when it is executing in the Nonsecure mode. However, code running in the Secure partition can access the Secure MPU through the standard registers and also access the Nonsecure MPU through a set of alias registers. To complicate things a little bit more, it is only possible to program either the Nonsecure or Secure MPU when the processor is running in privileged mode.

The Armv8-M MPU is designed to work with all Arm Cortex-A/ -R/ -M processors, not just Cortex-M. Consequently, it supports some hardware features that are not available within the Cortex-M family. This can make reading the datasheet confusing, particularly when it defines supported memory types. I will give a brief overview of the MPU memory options here, and then we will look at how to configure the MPU for a practical Cortex-M33 application.

MPU memory types

The MPU allows you to define two different types of memory region that describe how the processor can interact with the MCU memory. The two types of region are termed Normal and Device.

Normal memory

Normal memory allows more advanced Cortex-A processors to optimize code execution by reordering and merging memory accesses. In addition, normal memory can be made to work with any caches that are present in the MCU and the cache policy for each region is configured as part of the MPU region attributes Table 10.10. For future use, the Cortex-M33 is designed to work with multiple cache units for both internal and external memory, but at the time of writing, there are no Cortex-M33 MCU's available with a cache.

Table 10.10 Normal memory attributes.

Attribute	Description
Cacheability	Define the Cache policy
Shareability	Define if the memory region can be shared with other bus masters
eXecute never	The memory region may be executable or Never Execute

The MPU can define the normal memory attributes.

The cacheability field has several subfields as shown in table that allow the MPU to define the full cache policy (Table 10.11).

Table 10.11 Cache options.

Attribute	Description
Cache Policy	Write Through or Write Back
Allocation	Cache line allocation hints
Transient Hint	Hint to the cache that the data is only needed temporarily

The MPU can control the cache policy of an internal cache.

Shareability

In a system with multiple bus masters, which may be in the form of DMA units or other processors, we can define a memory region as shareable between these different bus masters. It is also possible to create a number of separate sharable regions that are shared by different groups of bus masters. The shareability is further divided into inner and outer sharable groups.

Nonshareable. The region is only accessed by the CPU and is not accessed by any other bus masters.

Inner shareable. The inner shareable regions are associated with caches integrated within the microcontroller. In a complex memory system, the inner cache signals may be exposed to the external memory system. Multiple inner sharable regions can be defined and associated with groups of bus masters.

Outer shareable. The outer sharable regions are associated with the external memory system and allows for the implementation of an external hardware cache, which may also be shared with other system agents. The outer sharable regions can also group together inner regions so that an operation on the outer region effects all the associated inner regions.

Device memory

Device memory is used for regions that contain peripheral registers. This replaces the "Strongly Ordered" memory definition used in the earlier Armv7. MPU device memory can be used to control the type of memory access optimizations used over the MPU region (Table 10.12). With device memory, you can control if the processor can gather a number of memory accesses into a single memory transaction and whether it can reorder accesses to optimize the use of CPU registers.

Table 10.12 Device memory attributes.

Attributes	Operand	Description
Gathering	G or nG	Writes to a memory region; may be merged into a single access unless they are interleaved with a memory barrier instruction
Reordering	R or nR	Writes to a memory region; may be reordered
Early Write Acknowledge	E or nE	Writes to a memory region; will use a write buffer to provide an early write acknowledge

The device memory attributes may be combined to support four different types of memory access (Table 10.13).

Table 10.13 Device memory access.

Access type	Description
nGnRnE	Strongly ordered memory that must be accessed as the code is written
nGnRE	Peripheral registers that may be written to without race conditions
nGRE	Writing to a buffer where order doesn't matter but there is a limited access size
GRE	Writing to a peripheral buffer where order and access size do not matter

MPU configuration

The MPU is configured through a set of registers that are similar in format to the SAU (Table 10.14).

Table 10.14 MPU registers.

Register	Description
MPU_TYPE	Number of available MPU regions
MPU_CTRL	Activate the MPU regions
MPU_RNR	Region Number
MPU_RBAR	Region Base Address
MPU_RLAR	Region Limit Address
MPU_RBAR_A1—MPU_RBAR_A3	Region Base Address Alias Registers 1–3
MPU_RLAR_A1—MPU_RLAR_A3	Region Limit Address Registers 1–3
MPU_MAIR0—MPU_MAIR1	Attribute Indirection Registers 0–1

The MPU_Type register contains a field called DREGION that returns the total number of MPU regions available for the current security state. If you are writing code for a specific microcontroller, you will know this from the datasheet.

The MPU_CTRL contains three bits as shown in Table 10.15.

Table 10.15 MPU CTRL register.

MPU CTRL bit	Name	Description
0	ENABLE	Enable/Disable the MPU
1	HFNMIENA	Enable for hard fault and NMI exceptions
2	PRIVDEFENA	Set privileged access for the entire memory map

Once we have configured the required MPU regions, they will become active when the CTRL enable bit is set to logic 1. If we want to reconfigure a region, it is first necessary to disable the MPU, adjust the region then re-enable the MPU. The PRIVDEFENA bit is used to define the default global memory map. If it is set to logic 1, then the default is privileged access across the entire 4GB address space, whatever the current security state. The MPU regions are then used to create unprivileged regions for the background code. If PRIVDEFENA is set to logic zero, the processor can only access regions defined in the MPU, and a fault will be raised if the code tries to access memory outside of the defined MPU regions.

Region number register

The MPU has a small number of registers that are used to program any of the available MPU regions. When we need to configure a specific region, it is first selected by entering the desired region number into the region number register (Table 10.16). The remaining MPU region registers can then be used to configure the selected region.

Table 10.16 Region number.

Bit field	Description
0–7	Region number

Base address register

Once the region has been selected, we define its base address by programming bits 31–5 in the base address register (Table 10.17). The lower five bits of the region base address are always set to zero. However, in the actual Base Address Register, the lower five bits have a secondary function that allows us to configure the access permissions for the region. If bit zero is set to logic 1, this region will not allow code execution.

Table 10.17 Base address register.

Bit field	Name	Description
0	XN	Execute Never
1–2	AP	Access Permissions
3–4	SH	Shareable
5–31	BASE	Base Address of the region (zero extended over bits 0–4)

Read-write access permissions can be defined with bits 2–1, as shown in Table 10.18. Here, we can allow read/write or read-only access. This can be further qualified by the operating mode of the processor (privileged or unprivileged).

Table 10.18 Access permissions.

Bit field	Description
00	Read/Write by privileged code only
01	Read/Write by privileged and unprivileged code
10	Read only by privileged code
11	Read only by privileged and unprivileged code

We can also define how the memory region is shared between the processor and other bus masters such as DMA units and other processors (Table 10.19). Memory used solely by the Cortex-M33 processor should be declared as nonshareable. Then, depending on how the silicon vendor has designed the MCU, there may be regions of memory shared between bus masters. These can be grouped into inner regions and outer regions. Each inner region is independently defined, but inner regions may be grouped within an outer region. Then operations on an outer region will affect all the associated inner regions.

Table 10.19 Share permissions.

Bit field	Description
00	Nonshareable
01	Outer shareable
10	Inner shareable

Memory attribute indirection registers

The Memory Attribute Indirection Registers allow you to define a further "table" of memory attributes that can be used as a fast method of setting up and changing MPU regions on the fly. The two indirection registers are each divided into four attribute fields (Fig. 10.45). Each attribute field is eight bits wide and is used to hold a set of user-defined memory attributes that may be assigned to multiple MPU regions.

Attr3	Attr2	Attr1	Attr0

FIG. 10.45

Attribute registers. Memory attribute fields.

No permission required.

Each attribute field can be configured to support Normal or Device memory. To configure an attribute field for device memory, all bits in the field should be set to zero except bits 3–2, the device field (Fig. 10.46).

FIG. 10.46

Device attribute field. The attribute field can support device memory.

No permission required.

In the device field, we can define the type of access permitted to the memory region in terms of gathering, reordering, and write acknowledgement (Table 10.20).

Table 10.20 Device attributes.

Bit field	Type	Description
00	Device—nGnRnE	Nongathering, nonreordering, nonearly write acknowledge
01	Device—nGnRE	Nongathering, nonreordering, early write acknowledge
10	Device—nGRE	Nongathering, reordering, early write acknowledge
11	Device—GRE	Gathering, reordering, early write acknowledge

Generally, when defining an MPU region that will cover the MCU peripheral registers, you should declare the region as "Nongathering, Nonreordering with early write acknowledge" nGnRE.

An attribute field can be programmed to configure normal memory. In this case, the field is split into two nibbles, which are used to configure the inner and outer caches (Fig. 10.47).

FIG. 10.47

Normal memory attributes. The same attribute field can also support normal memory cache policy.

No permission required.

The upper nibble is then used to configure the outer cache policy while the lower nibble is used to configure the inner cache policy.

Region Limit Register.

The region limit register defines the end address of the MPU region. The upper limit address is defined in bits 31–5, and the lower 5 bits are extended using the value 0x1F.

The lower five bits within the Region Limit Register can be programmed by a user to configure the MPU region attributes. Bits 3–1 act as a pointer to the eight attribute fields defined in the memory attribute indirection registers (Fig. 10.48). This allows us to select from a group of predefined attributes.

FIG. 10.48

MPU limit register. The limit register defines the region upper address. The attribute pointer select one of eight attribute definitions

No permission required.

Finally, we can enable a region by setting bit zero. The MPU regions will not become active until the global enable bit is set in the MPU CTRL register.

Region Base Address Alias 1–3 and Region Limit Address Alias 1–3.

The Region Base and Limit Alias Registers provide a fast method of configuring MPU up to three additional regions without having to individually configure the Region Number Register Address and Limit Registers. Each pair of Region Alias Registers contain the same fields as the Region Base and Region Limit Address Registers. This allows us to pre-program each pair of alias registers with the configuration values for an MPU region. When the Region Number Register is updated, the alias regions will be programmed in addition to the Region Base Address and Limit Registers. The regions accessible by the alias registers is defined by bits [7:2] of the Region Number Register using the formula $(RNR[7:2] << 2 + n)$, where n is the number of the alias register pair (Fig. 10.49).

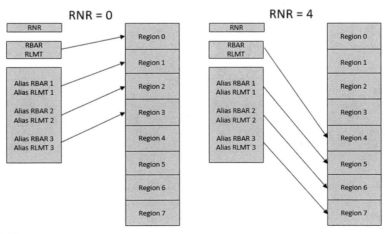

FIG. 10.49

MPU Alias registers. The alias region registers allow you to define an additional three region configurations. The MPU can then configure a block of four regions relative to the RNR.

No permission required.

Exercise: Memory protection unit

This example demonstrates configuration and reconfiguration of the Secure and Nonsecure MPU during code execution.

> **In the pack installer select and copy exercise 10.5.**
> **Set the Secure project as the active project.**
> **In the project window select the Secure Code Group.**
> **Right click and select Add existing files.**
> **Add the file MPU.c.**
> **Open MPU.c.**

This file uses the CMSIS Core MPU functions to define protection regions for the Secure and Nonsecure MPU's.

We first need to define settings for the attribute registers, this can be done directly by a CMSIS core function (Table 10.21).

Table 10.21 CMSIS-Core MPU attribute functions.

Function	Description
void ARM_MPU_SetMemAttr(uint8_t idx,uint8_t attr)	idx The attribute index to be set [0–7] attr The attribute value to be set.
ARM_SetMemAttr_NS(uint8_t idx,uint8_t attr)	idx The attribute index to be set [0–7] attr The attribute value to be set.
void ARM_MPU_SetMemAttrEx(MPU_Type * mpu,uint8_t idx,uint8_t attr)	MPU pointer to the required MPU idx The attribute index to be set [0–7] attr The attribute value to be set.

Some additional macros are provided to define the attribute bit field (Table 10.22).

Table 10.22 Attribute macros.

Function	Description
ARM_MPU_ATTR(O,I)	Defines attributes as Normal or device memory
ARM_MPU_ATTR_MEMORY_(NT, WB, RA, WA)	Normal Memory attributes NT Nontransient: WB Write-Back RA Read Allocation WA Write Allocation
ARM_MPU_ATTR_DEVICE (0 U)	Device memory
ARM_MPU_ATTR_DEVICE_nGnRE	Nongathering, Nonreordering, No Early Write Acknowledge
ARM_MPU_ATTR_DEVICE_nGnRnE	Nongathering, Nonreordering, No Early Write Acknowledge
ARM_MPU_ATTR_DEVICE_nGRE	Nongathering, Reordering, Early Write Acknowledge

We can use the CMSIS functions and macros to define attributes for a FLASH and RAM region.

```
/* Normal memory */
ARM_MPU_SetMemAttr(0UL, ARM_MPU_ATTR(

/*Outer Write-Backtransient with read and write allocate*/
ARM_MPU_ATTR_MEMORY_(0UL, 1UL, 1UL, 1UL),
```

```
/*Inner Write-Throughtransient with read and write allocate*/
ARM_MPU_ATTR_MEMORY_(OUL, OUL, 1UL, 1UL) );
```

Now when we define an MPU region the attributes will be referenced to define the access rights (Table 10.23).

Table 10.23 MPU region functions.

Function	
void ARM_MPU_SetRegion(uint32_t rnr,uint32_t rbar,uint32_t rlar)	rnrRegion number to be configured.rbarValue for RBAR register.rlarValue for RLAR register.
void ARM_MPU_SetRegion_NS(uint32_t rnr,uint32_t rbar,uint32_t rlar)	rnrRegion number to be configured.rbarValue for RBAR register.rlarValue for RLAR register.
ARM_MPU_RBAR(BASE, SH, RO, NP, XN)	BASE The base address bits SH Shareability RORead-Only: Set to 1 for a read-only memory region. NP nonprivileged: (unprivileged) Set to 1 for a nonprivileged memory region. XN eXecute Never: Set to 1 for a nonexecutable memory region.
ARM_MPU_RLAR(LIMIT, IDX)	LIMIT The limit address bits IDX The attribute index to be associated with this memory region.

Open the MPU window in the peripherals\core peripherals Memory Protection Unit (Fig. 10.50).

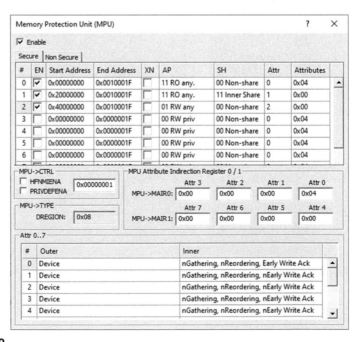

FIG. 10.50

MPU debug view. The debugger can display the current MPU settings in a peripheral window.

No permission required.

Step through the example code and observe the MPU configuration and code execution.

CMSIS-zone

So far, we have looked at configuring the TrustZone SAU and the MPU through handwritten source code. While this is OK in a simple system, in a real project, the complexity can rise very quickly, particularly if our hardware contains multiple processors. In a real system, this makes it difficult to create and maintain an accurate set of configuration files across multiple projects. To make this process, easier CMSIS-Zone is a new standard that specifies a markup language to describe the full project memory map and how it subdivides between subprojects and execution regions within those projects. CMSIS-Zone is based on an open-source markup language called FreeMarker (Fig. 10.51).

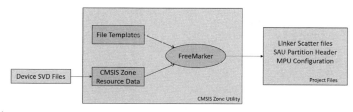

FIG. 10.51

CMSIS-zone utility markup language. CMSIS-Zone uses the FreeMarker language to create configuration templates.

No permission required.

CMSIS-zone utility

CMSIS-Zone provides a plugin utility for the Eclipse IDE, which can be used to graphically define the full project resources and then subdivide and allocate them to the application projects and their execution regions. The CMSIS-Zone utility will then generate a set of C source files that configure the SAU and the MPU, plus a set of matching linker script files.

Exercise: Using the CMSIS-zone utility

In this exercise, we will use the CMSIS-Zone utility to configure Zones (projects) for the Secure and Nonsecure TrustZone partitions. The utility will then generate the necessary source, header, and project files, which can be added to our Microvision projects.

In the pack installer select and copy exercise 10.6.

The CMSIS-Zone project can use the CMSIS pack files to define the microcontroller resources or we can use an existing Resource Zone file (rzone). The example project contains a resource file and template files to generate the final zone support files

Typically, a resources file will be provided by the silicon vendor, if one is not available you can use the pack system.

To avoid having to reinstall the packs, we can use the existing microVision pack repository.

Download an install the CMSIS-Zone utility from the link below.
https://arm-software.github.io/CMSIS_5/Zone/html/zTInstall.html
StartEclipse.
Import the example Zone project using File\Import\General\Projects from Folder or Archive
In the top right hand corner select the pack installer icon (Fig. 10.52).

FIG. 10.52

Eclipse pack installer. Open the pack installer in the CMSIS-Zone Eclipse IDE.

No permission required.

This will open the pack perspective.

Rather than reinstall the Device Family Packs we can set the CMSIS-Zone utility tool to access the packs installed in the MDK-Arm repository.

Press the "Manage Local Repositories" icon on the packs toolbar.
Select the CMSIS Packs tab.
Enter the path to the MDK-Arm pack folder C:\Keil\arm\pack (Fig. 10.53).

FIG. 10.53

CMSIS pack path. Set the CMSIS-Zone pack path to import the existing Arm-MDK repository.

No permission required.

Close the menu and switch back switch back to the project perspective (Fig. 10.54).

FIG. 10.54

Eclipse project perspective. Open the Eclipse project perspective.

Select new\project\CMSIS\CMSIS-Zone Project (Fig. 10.55).

FIG. 10.55

Eclipse zone project. Create a CMSIS-zone project.

Click the Next button and we have a choice to use a resource file or the pack system (Fig. 10.56). Select the LPC55S69.rzone resource file in the example project.

The silicon vendor may provide a resource file that defines the FLASH, RAM, and peripherals within on their device. If this is not available, you can select the device pack, and the CMSIS-Zone utility will create a resource file from the pack description files. This route may require you to add and check definitions, so a resource file is the best route.

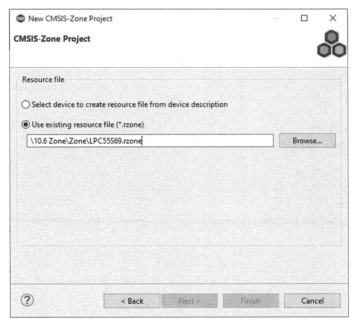

FIG. 10.56

Resource file selection. Import the resource file to define the microcontroller memory map.

No permission required.

Select the Resources tab to display the microcontroller memory and peripheral resources (Fig. 10.57).

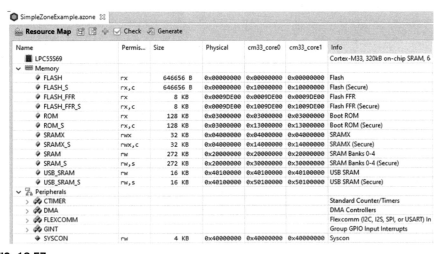

FIG. 10.57

Zone memory map. Once the project has been created the microcontroller memory map is displayed.

No permission required.

Creating a zone project is a two-step process. First, we must define which re-sources belong to the Secure and Nonsecure world. This means subdividing the physical memory into subregions within the Secure and Nonsecure alias regions.

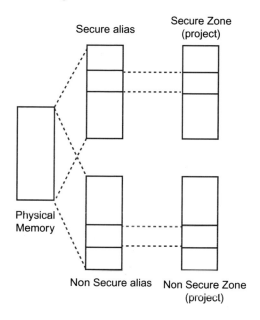

FIG. 10.58

Zone memory mapping. The physical memory is subdivided into Secure and Nonsecure regions and then allocated to project zones.

No permission required.

The second stage is to allocate the memory subregions as resources to separate zones where a zone corresponds to a Microvision project (Fig. 10.58).

First we need to create memory regions for the Secure and Nonsecure projects by defining subregions within each block of memory.

Select the secure flash (FLASH_S) right click and select add memory region (Fig. 10.59).

Name	Permis...	Size		Physical	cm33_core
■ LPC55S69					
∨ ▦ Memory					
⦿ FLASH	rx	646656 B		0x00000000	0x0000000(
⦿ FLASH_S	rx,c	646656 R		0x00000000	0x1000000(
⦿ FLASH_FFR	rx	8 KI	Expand all Selected		
⦿ FLASH_FFR_S	rx,c	8 KI	Expand All		
⦿ ROM	rx	128 KI	Collapse All		
⦿ ROM_S	rx,c	128 KI			
⦿ SRAMX	rwx	32 KI	Add memory region		
⦿ SRAMX_S	rwx,c	32 KI			
⦿ SRAM	rw	272 KI	Properties		

FIG. 10.59

Allocate resources to project zones. The default memory map can be subdivided into memory regions, which can be allocated to zone projects.

No permission required.

Name the region as Startup, set the size to 10 K and select its security type
as Secure (Fig. 10.60).

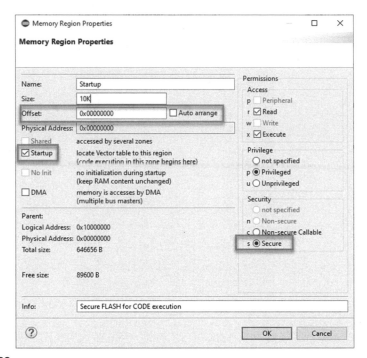

FIG. 10.60

Memory region configuration options. We can configure the memory region options in its
local dialogue.

No permission required.

The memory region dialogue allows us to configure the size location and access
properties for our new segment.

Define the following memory regions (Table 10.24).

By default the each of the microcontroller peripherals interrupt lines will be
routed to the secure NVIC.

We can change this by explicitly defining a peripheral as Nonsecure.

Table 10.24 Zone utility regions.

Parent region	Sub region name	Size	Offset	Security	Additional
FLASH_S	TF_M Startup	10K	0×00000000	Secure	Startup
FLASH_S	VENEER	4K		Nonsecure callable	
FLASH_S	TF-M	128K	Auto	Secure	
FLASH	Application_NS	128K	0×30000	Nonsecure	
SRAM_S	Secure_RAM	128K	Auto	Default Secure	
SRAM	Application_RAM_NS	128K	Auto	Nonsecure	DMA

Project zone memory regions.

Select CTIMER0.
Right click and select Properties (Fig. 10.61).

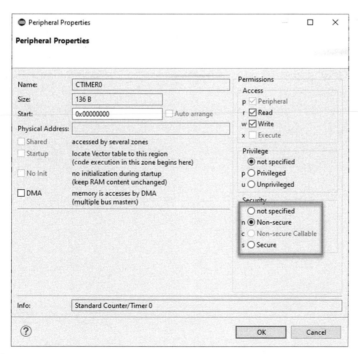

FIG. 10.61

Peripheral configuration options. Each peripheral can be marked for either security world.

No permission required.

Within the Properties menu set the security type to Nonsecure.

This creates the memory map regions that we are going to need for our projects. The next step is to create the project Zones and allocate resources to each project.

Select the Zones tab (Fig. 10.62).

FIG. 10.62

Zone selection tab. Select the zone tab at the bottom of the screen.

No permission required.

On the zone map tool bar press the green cross (light gray in print version) to create a new zone (Fig. 10.63).

FIG. 10.63

CMSIS zone utility toolbar. Now create a new Zone (project) using the green cross icon (light gray in print version) on the toolbar.

No permission required.

Call this zone secure_world and set the security type to Secure (Fig. 10.64).

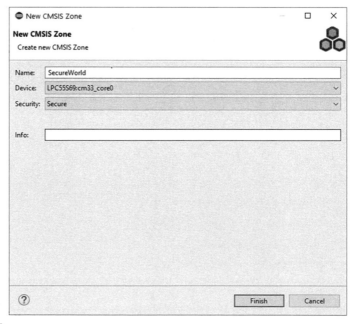

FIG. 10.64

New CMSIS zone dialogue. As a new CMSIS zone is created, we can define its name and security world.

No permission required.

Create a second zone called non_secure_world and set its security type to Nonsecure. This now creates an additional selection column for each zone (Fig. 10.65).

Name	Permis...	Size	Start	End	SecureWorld	NonSecure...	Info
▪ LPC55569							Cortex-M33, 320kB on-chip SRAM, 6
✓ ▦ Memory							
∨ ❂ FLASH	rx	646656 B	0x00000000	0x0009DDFF	☐	☐	Flash
❂ Application_NS	rx,n	128 B	0x00030000	0x0003007F	☐	☑	
∨ ❂ FLASH_S	rx,c	646656 B	0x10000000	0x1009DFFF	☐		Flash (Secure)
❂ TF-M-Startup	rx,s	4 KB	0x10000000	0x10000FFF	☑		
❂ Veneer	rx,c	4 KB	0x10021000	0x10021FFF	☑		
❂ TF-M	rx,s	128 KB	0x10001000	0x10020FFF	☑		
❂ FLASH_FFR	rx	8 KB	0x0009DE00	0x0009FDFF	☐	☐	Flash FFR
❂ FLASH_FFR_S	rx,c	8 KB	0x1009DE00	0x1009FDFF	☐		Flash FFR (Secure)
❂ ROM	rx	128 KB	0x03000000	0x0301FFFF	☐	☐	Boot ROM
❂ ROM_S	rx,c	128 KB	0x13000000	0x1301FFFF	☐		Boot ROM (Secure)
❂ SRAMX	rwx	32 KB	0x04000000	0x04007FFF	☐	☐	SRAMX
❂ SRAMX_S	rwx,c	32 KB	0x14000000	0x14007FFF	☐		SRAMX (Secure)
∨ ❂ SRAM	rw	272 KB	0x20000000	0x20043FFF	☐	☐	SRAM Banks 0-4
❂ Application_SRAM_NS	rw,n	128 KB	0x20000000	0x2001FFFF	☐	☑	
∨ ❂ SRAM_S	rw,s	272 KB	0x30000000	0x30043FFF	☐		SRAM Banks 0-4 (Secure)
❂ Secure_RAM	rw,s	128 KB	0x30020000	0x3003FFFF	☑		
❂ USB_SRAM	rw	16 KB	0x40100000	0x40103FFF	☐	☐	USB SRAM
❂ USB_SRAM_S	rw,s	16 KB	0x50100000	0x50103FFF	☐		USB SRAM (Secure)
✓ ▦ Peripherals							
∨ ◈ CTIMER							Standard Counter/Timers
◆ CTIMER0	rw	136 B	0x40008000	0x40008087	☐	☑	Standard Counter/Timer 0
◆ CTIMER1	rw	136 B	0x40009000	0x40009087	☐	☐	Standard Counter/Timer 1
◆ CTIMER2	rw	136 B	0x40028000	0x40028087	☐	☐	Standard Counter/Timer 2

Resources | Zones | Setup

FIG. 10.65

CMSIS-zone utility with project zones. The new zones are added to the zones view.

No permission required.

Each column will contain selection boxes for memory regions associated with its security type.

We can now allocate resources to the Secure and Nonsecure zones. This will allow CMSIS Zone to generate the support files from a set of generic template files which must be located in the projects FTL directory

Before we can generate the zone support files you must copy the contents of the example FTL directory to your projects FTL directory.

Once you have allocated the memory resources press the generate button on the toolbar.

This will create the memory map header file, SAU and MPU configuration code and the matching linker scatter files.

Code is also produced for some additional device-specific bus filters called the Memory Protection Controller and Peripheral Protection Controller, which we will see in the next chapter.

Once the files are generated open the zone project directory and copy the files to the example project directory.

Start microVision and build the example project using the CMSIS-Zone files.

You should now be able to start the debugger and use the peripheral\core peripheral windows to examine how the processor TrustZone and MPU registers are configured.

Conclusion

As well as providing code to configure the Cortex-M33 TrustZone regions, some additional functions configure additional security peripherals called the Memory Protection Controller (MPC) and Peripheral Protection Controller (PPC). These are additional bus filtering gateways that are used to extend the memory partition definitions to a wider system that contains further bus Masters (additional processors, DMA units). The MPC and PPC are used to fully enforce the security memory map to create a Trusted Execution Environment. In the next chapter, we will see how TrustZone is integrated into a standard microcontroller.

The NXP LPC55S69 a reference IoT microcontroller

Introduction

In this chapter, we will look at a real-world microcontroller and the ideal hardware feature set required to support the PSA security model. For the purposes of this chapter, we will use the NXP LPC55S69 as a reference Cortex-M33 microcontroller. The LPC55S69 has a security structure on three levels, compute environment, device security, and assistive security peripherals (Fig. 11.1).

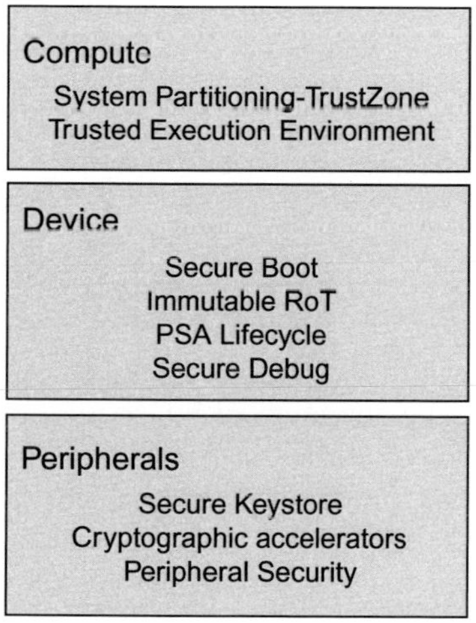

FIG. 11.1

LPC55S69 security structure. The LPC55S69 has a three level security structure.

No permission required.

The first requirement for our microcontroller is the ability to create a secure compute environment. This means that we need to extend the TrustZone partitioning to all the other bus masters within the system. Here, bus master means any unit within the microcontroller that can initiate a memory transfer. This will typically be DMA units and additional secondary processors. In order to achieve this, the microcontroller must provide additional bus filters that lock down all the bus masters to create a Trusted Execution Environment.

Designing Secure IoT Devices with the Arm Platform Security Architecture and Cortex-M33
https://doi.org/10.1016/B978-0-12-821469-5.00005-3

In addition, the microcontroller must also implement a secure boot process that validates the executable images and establishes a Root of Trust. We also need a way to store security credentials in immutable memory and ideally a method of concealing secrets within the device so they cannot be retrieved by an attacker. The microcontroller must also provide support for the Platform Security Architecture lifecycle, including the ability to define several levels of debug access. The PSA security model also requires a set of counters for firmware version numbers. These counters should be monotonic in that they can be incremented but not decremented. This is intended to prevent an attacker from installing an old firmware version with known vulnerabilities.

A microcontroller designed to form the basis of an IoT device is also likely to provide hardware acceleration for cryptographic primitives. To date, accelerators have mainly been for symmetrical encryption algorithms such as ciphers like AES, DES, and hashing algorithms SHA1 and SHA2. More recent devices now provide support for asymmetrical algorithms like RSA and also elliptic curve algorithms, which is a big step forward in both performance and energy consumption. The LPC55S69 is also able to store execution images in an encrypted format. During run-time, blocks of instructions are decrypted on the fly by a dedicated hardware accelerator called PRINCE before execution with no loss of processor performance. Finally, when looking at a device, it is important to check that peripherals like GPIO and DMA have appropriate security features that prevent sensitive information from being exposed to an attacker. So with these requirements in mind, let us look at the LPC55S69 security architecture.

Trusted execution environment (TEE)

In the last chapter, we saw how the TrustZone security peripheral may be configured to create a secure processing environment by creating secure and nonsecure partitions. However, a typical Cortex-M33 microcontroller will have multiple additional bus masters that are separate from the CPU and will not have their memory access restricted by the TrustZone peripheral. For example, to an adversary, a DMA unit looks like a Trojan horse that can be used to tunnel into a secure region; a secondary processor can be used to snoop on user data. In order to create a fully Trusted Execution Environment, we need additional hardware support to extend the partitions created within the Cortex-M33 processor so that it applies to all the bus masters within the microcontroller. In the case of the LPC55S69, this includes a second Cortex-M33 processor, multiple general-purpose DMA units, and multiple peripherals with dedicated DMA.

Secure bus matrix

Like the earlier Cortex-M processors, the Cortex-M33 has an internal bus structure that consists of an advanced high-performance AHB bus matrix. This provides an array of parallel high-speed busses that connect each bus master to memory resources and groups of peripherals located on separate advanced peripheral busses (APB).

This bus structure provides a dedicated path for each bus master to a resource, be it memory or a group of peripherals, to improve performance by minimizing bus arbitration (Fig. 11.2).

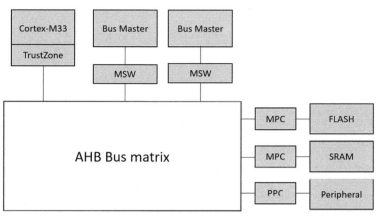

FIG. 11.2

Trusted execution environment. The LPC55S69 uses additional security filters to create a Trusted Security Environment.

No permission required.

With the introduction of TrustZone, the bus matrix has an additional pair of sideband signals, which are generated by a Master Security Wrapper (MSW) associated with each bus master. These signals are used to relay the security state of the bus master to the different AHB slave ports. Each slave port has a protection checker, which is configured with access rights based on the state of the security sideband signals. The TrustZone IP provides two different types of protection checker: a Peripheral Protection Checker (PPC) and a Memory Protection Checker (MPC). Together the PPC and MPC are used to enforce the TrustZone security partitions across all bus masters within the microcontroller. Each additional bus master within the microcontroller will generate the same pair of security sideband signals. The state of the bus master security signals are defined by programming the bus masters access rights into the dedicated MSW when the microcontroller is configured. This layer of additional filtering creates a rules-based Trusted Execution Environment.

Security sideband signals

Two security sideband signals are added to the bus matrix. These are HPRIV, which determines the privilege access level (privileged or unprivileged), and HNONSEC, which determines the TrustZone security access level (secure or nonsecure). These signals will be asserted for a processor Cortex-M33 fitted with TrustZone but must be defined for any other bus master on the system.

Trusted execution environment configuration

How MPC and PPC registers are exposed (register naming) within a given microcontroller will vary between manufacturers, but this section will give you an introduction to how the TEE access levels are configured.

In the LPC55S69, the TEE is configured through a set of Security Control registers. The overall device access rules are defined in a two-step process. First, we must define access rights for each of the bus masters. We then need to set the access levels for each region of memory and peripheral bus (Fig. 11.3).

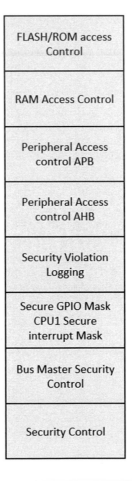

FIG. 11.3

Trusted execution environment configuration. The TEE is configured through a page of memory mapped registers.

No permission required.

Master security wrapper

The security rights for each additional bus master are managed by a local Master Security Wrapper (MSW). Each bus master other than core 0 is allocated two bits within this register. These bits are used to define four access levels, as shown in Table 11.1.

Table 11.1 Master security level register.

Master security level bit pattern	Master security level anti pole	Access level
0x03	0	Secure privileged
0x02	1	Secure unprivileged
0x01	2	Nonsecure privileged
0x00	3	Nonsecure unprivileged

The Master Security Level Register is mirrored by a master security antipole register. This register must be written with the inverse bit pattern to complete configuration of the MSW.

Once the access levels have been set, the MSW is locked by writing to a pair of lock bits located at the top of Master Security Level Register.

Memory protection checker

Access to each page of memory is managed by a local Memory Protection Checker (MPC). The MPC divides each memory region into a number of subregions so that different levels of access rights may be defined for each region and subregion. The FLASH memory within the LPC55S69 is divided into 32K regions, while the SRAM is divided into 4K pages. Configuration of the MPC checkers are controller through registers in the Advanced Highspeed Bus (AHB) controller. The AHB controller contains a set of rules registers. Within these registers, each memory region is assigned two bits, which are used to define the access level for the region.

Peripheral protection checker

The Peripheral Protection Checkers (PPC) work in a similar fashion. A set of rules registers located in the AHB and APB bus controllers allow you to define the access level for each peripheral within the microcontroller.

If a security violation occurs, a security exception is generated, which will cause the processor to enter the secure world and vector to the secure fault handler. The secure fault is logged in a set of registers within the Security Control peripheral. The access address violation is logged along with details of the bus master peripheral.

Example: Trusted execution environment

In this example, we will examine the Trusted Execution Environment (TEE) Configuration for the LPC55S69, which has been generated by a CMSIS Zone project.

In addition to configuring the Trust Zone peripheral, the code will set the DMA0 MSW so that it can only access nonsecure memory. The nonsecure code will configure DMA0 to copy data in the secure world ram to generate a memory violation.

In the pack installer, select Example 11.1.

This is our original TrustZone project that has been configured using the CMSIS-Zone Utility tool. As discussed in the last chapter, the CMSIS-Zone Utility generates configuration files for the Cortex-M33 processor and the TrustZone peripheral. In addition, it will also generate configuration functions that match the TrustZone configuration for a specific microcontroller.

Open TZN_MPC_PPC.c.

The peripheral access rights are defined in TZ_Config_PPC().

```
void TZM_Config_PPC(void)
{
/* Setup Peripheral Protection Controller (PPC) */
AHB_SECURE_CTRL->SEC_CTRL_AHB0_0_SLAVE_RULE
= 0x02000000U;
AHB_SECURE_CTRL->SEC_CTRL_APB_BRIDGE[0]
.SEC_CTRL_APB_BRIDGE0_MEM_CTRL0
 = 0x00000022U;
}
```

The memory access rights are defined in TZ_Config_MPC().

Here, we can program the access rights for the internal FLASH pages in 32 K blocks:

```
AHB_SECURE_CTRL->SEC_CTRL_FLASH_ROM[0].SEC_CTRL_FLASH_MEM_RULE[0]=
0x00000002U |/* memory:CODE_S */
0x00000020U |/* memory:CODE_S */
0x00200000U |/* memory:CODE_S, memory:VENEERS */
0x00000000U |/* memory:CODE_NS */
0x00000000U;/* memory:CODE_NS */
```

and also the internal SRAM pages in 4 K blocks:

```
AHB_SECURE_CTRL->SEC_CTRL_RAMX[0].MEM_RULE[0]=0x00000000U | /*
memory:SRAMX */|0x00000000U ; /* memory:SRAMX */
/* SRAM Bank 0 */
 AHB_SECURE_CTRL->SEC_CTRL_RAM0[0].MEM_RULE[0]=0x00000002U | /*
memory:DATA_S */|0x00000020U ; /* memory:DATA_S */
```

We can now configure the Master_Sec_Level and antipole register to define the access rights for a given bus master. In this case, we are assigning DMA0 with nonsecure privileged access rights. The top two bits are used to lock the MSW.

```
AHB_SECURE_CTRL->MASTER_SEC_LEVEL = 0xC0000400; // SDMA0 non
secure priv and lock MSW
```

and then program the master security antipole register.

```
AHB_SECURE_CTRL->MASTER_SEC_ANTI_POL_REG = ~(0xC0000400);
```

Now, as part of the system configuration, we must initialize the full TEE by configuring the Core0 TrustZone SAU along with the MPC, PPC, and the Master Security Wrapper.

```
TZM_Config_SAU();
TZM_Config_MPC();
TZM_Config_PPC();
TZM_Config_MSW();
```

Once the TEE is configured, the code will jump to the nonsecure code. Which will configure a DMA0 transfer into the secure memory to cause a security violation.

Run the code and observe the messages in the Tera Term console window.

Security architecture
Overview

In addition to creating a TEE, the LPC55S69 provides extensive support for the PSA Security Model. This includes a PSA compliant secure boot ROM that is used to create a Root of Trust along with secure key storage and lifecycle management. Although these features are unique to the NXP microcontrollers, the remainder of this chapter will examine them to get an overview of how a microcontroller can provide hardware features that support the PSA security model.

Protected flash

To begin to understand the LPC55S69 device security, we will first look at a special region of the FLASH memory, which contains many of the overall device security configuration options. This region is called the Protected FLASH and is divided into four subregions as shown in Fig. 11.4.

FIG. 11.4

Protected FLASH. The security configuration values are stored in Protected FLASH, which is subdivided into four pages.

When the device is manufactured, the Customer Manufacturing Programmable Area (CMPA) must be provisioned with the default security options. Once provisioned, the CMPA is permanently locked to become an immutable RoT. During the device's lifetime, any updates to the default options can be stored or modified through the Customer Field Programmable Area (CFPA). The protected FLASH region also provides a Keystore that holds keycodes that are used to reproduce encryption keys. As we will see, the actual encryption keys are never physically stored within the device but can be reconstructed at run time through a key store peripheral called the Physically Unclonable Function (PUF). Finally, the NXP region is used to store vendor data, which includes a Unique Device ID. Access to the protected FLASH region is managed by the secure boot ROM and will depend on the current lifecycle state of the device. We will look at this later, but for now, during development, the protected flash will be in a programmable state. Once the device is in active service, the lifecycle state will be changed to OEM_Closed. This will secure the CMPA against writes while the CFPA can be updated using an API provided by the boot ROM. The values of each page must also be used to create an SHA2 hash, which is stored in the last 32 bytes of the protected FLASH memory. This is checked by the boot ROM after reset to ensure the protected FLASH configuration has not been tampered with.

Customer manufacturing programmable area (CMPA)

The CPMA holds many of the default device security options. These can be divided into four regions as shown in Fig. 11.5.

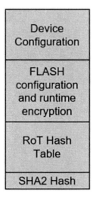

FIG. 11.5

Protected FLASH CMPA Page. The security configuration is locked in the CMPA page when the device is manufactured.

No permission required.

The device configuration region is used to define the boot configuration and enable the secure boot process within the boot ROM.

The LPC55S69 is also able to store executable code and constant data as an encrypted image within the user FLASH memory. As the code executes each instruction, it is then decrypted on the fly as the code executes using a custom symmetrical cipher called PRINCE. Up to three separate FLASH regions are supported, and each region has its own encryption key. As we will see later, these keys are provisioned when the device is manufactured by storing access keycodes in the CMPA FLASH configuration region.

The CMPA also defines security policies for debug access. Depending on a debuggers credentials, the on-chip debug will allow varying debug access levels from full debug access to all memory regions or restrict debug access to the nonsecure code.

When the secure boot process is enabled, the executable image in the FLASH must be signed by a dedicated RoT private key. The RoT public key is stored as part of the image, and it is anchored to the device by storing its hash in the protected FLASH CMPA RoT hash table (Fig. 11.6).

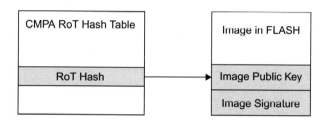

FIG. 11.6

Root of trust anchor. A public key hash is locked in the CMPA as an immutable RoT.

This is a vitally important hardware-based mechanism to establish an immutable RoT and is an intrinsic function of the microcontroller. We will have a closer look at how this works a bit later in this chapter. Finally, this region also contains fields to remap a (shadow) region of FLASH memory over the device reset vector.

Customer field programmable area (CFPA)

The CFPA is intended to update the CPMA settings as required during the device lifetime. In order to minimize the chance of the data being corrupted as it is modified, the CFPA data are duplicated on two pages (ping and pong) plus an additional scratch page. Each page has a version field, and when the device boots, the ROM code will use the values from the page with the highest version number. When the application needs to update the CFPA data, the new values are first written to the scratch page, and a higher version number is assigned. When the device boots, the buffered version will be written to the CFPA page with the lowest version number so that it becomes the active page (Fig. 11.7).

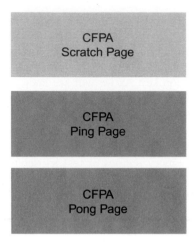

FIG. 11.7

Protected FLASH CFPA. Updatable security values can be written to the CFPA during the devices lifetime.

No permission required.

The CFPA has three counters, which are used to store image version numbers. These counters are monotonic (increment only) to prevent an attacker from attempting to roll back an execution image by using an old firmware update. When an update is presented, it is first validated, and then the version number is checked against the version counter. The new firmware must have a version equal to or later than the counter version in order for it to be installed. When a new version with a higher version number is installed, the counter is incremented to be equal to the latest version. This prevents an attempt to downgrade the firmware to an earlier version that may have known vulnerabilities.

The CFPA contains a second key hash table, which is used as a revocation table for currently installed keys. This functions in the same way as the RoT hash table in the CMPA but is used to hold the hash of a key that is to no longer be used. The final entry in the CFPA is a set of initialization vectors for the PRINCE run-time image encryption/decryption algorithm.

NXP programmed area

The factory programmed area contains a Universally Unique Identifier (UUID). This is a 128-bit number. There is an additional security peripheral called the Device Identifier Composite Engine (DICE), which can be used to combine the UUID with a further key to produce an identity string defined by the Trusted Computing Group. However, at the time of writing, the DICE peripheral is not supported by NXP for broad market adoption.

Key storage

One of the major difficulties in using a "plain old microcontroller" as an IoT device is being able to store secrets such as encryption keys within the device securely. These secrets have to be held in nonvolatile memory, which will be general-purpose FLASH or EEPROM. Hence, they are at risk of being exposed through a software attack or device tampering. With the new generation of Cortex-M33 microcontrollers, silicon vendors have addressed this issue by adding Keystore peripherals to provide secure storage for encryption keys. The LPC55S69 Keystore does not hold encryption keys directly. Instead, it uses keycodes that are used to regenerate a specific encryption key using a peripheral called the Physically Unclonable Function (PUF). While it is possible to regenerate user keys by supplying a keycode to the PUF directly, the Keystore storage slots are designed to hold keycodes that are used for specific security functions. There are specific slots for the secure boot ROM, a user Key of Keys (KEK), a Unique Device Secret (UDS), and slots for each PRINCE encryption region, as shown in Fig. 11.8.

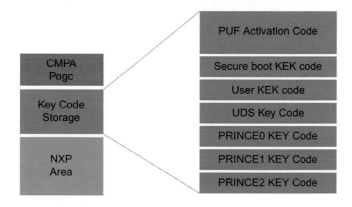

FIG. 11.8

Key storage. The key code storage provides dedicated slots for specific security functions (i.e., secure boot).

No permission required.

Physically unclonable function

Developed by Intrinsic ID, the Physically Unclonable Function (PUF) removes the need to store any secret keys within the device. The PUF works by combining a digital fingerprint, which is unique to the device, with a keycode to derive a unique encryption key. This key may then be regenerated after a reboot by using the same key code and the device digital fingerprint. The digital fingerprint is derived from the values held in an uninitialized SRAM. These values are random on a given device, but they are deterministic in that the SRAM will always have the same values after reset. For the purposes of this chapter, we can call this a Deterministic Uninitialized SRAM (DU SRAM). Once the power is removed, the DU SRAM data disappears, so no secret values are permanently stored on the device. This prevents retrieval of stored secrets through tampering attacks such as microprobing.

To use the PUF, we first must perform an enrolment process to generate a unique device fingerprint. Each time the enrolment process is started, it will create a new and different digital fingerprint. During the enrolment process, an activation code (AC) is output from the PUF. The device needs to be enrolled once to generate the AC, which is then used to initialize the PUF in all future sessions. During initialization, the AC is combined with the values in the DU SRAM to recreate the digital fingerprint. Second, it provides error correction codes to manage any degradation in the DU SRAM over time. When the secure boot is enabled, an AC must be stored at the start of the protected FLASH key store along with a secure boot key code. Once the PUF has been enrolled and initialized, we can create encryption keys. A new key is created within the PUF through a random process, and a unique key code will be output from the PUF. This key code acts as a handle that can then be used to regenerate the same key after the PUF has been reset. A get key function can then use the key code to read the stored key from the PUF. If we have an existing key, it can be registered with the PUF and its keycode generated. Then, the key can be regenerated using its keycode in the same fashion as PUF generated keys.

While we can use the keycodes to read out a key registered with the PUF, the LPC55S69 also contains a hardware accelerator for the AES and SHA algorithms called HashCrypt. It is possible to supply a key to this unit directly from the PUF using a local bus that is not visible to the CPU, as shown in Fig. 11.9. This creates an encryption subsystem where a secure function such as the secure boot can access a key code stored in the CMPA to reconstruct a key registered in the PUF and send the key directly to the HashCrypt encryption unit.

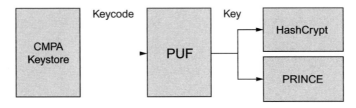

FIG. 11.9

Key storage sub system. The LPC55S69 provides an isolated sub system for security function keys that is not visible to either Cortex-M33 processor.

No permission required.

The PUF is controlled through a set of memory mapped registers; a subset of the critical registers is shown in Table 11.2.

Table 11.2 PUF registers.

Register	Description
CTRL	Control register
KEYINDEX	Key index register
KEYSIZE	Key size register
KEYINPUT	User key input register
CODEINPUT	Code input register
CODEOUTPUT	Code output register
KEYOUTINDEX	Output index register
KEYOUTPUT	Key output register

The keycode format is shown in Fig. 11.10. The key code contains fields for the registered keys size and storage index (0–15). All the index slots work the same way, except any key that is stored with index zero will be sent to either the HashCrypt or PRINCE hardware encryption units through a dedicated hardware bus that is not visible to the processor.

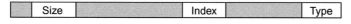

| | Size | | Index | | Type |

FIG. 11.10

Key code. A PUF keycode consists of a key size field, storage index, and a type that indicates if it is a user key or randomly generated key.

No permission required.

The type field is set to "0" for a randomly generated key and "1" for a stored user key.

Each PUF operation is controlled by writing a command code to the control register. Data transfers are managed through the CODEINPUT and CODEOUTPUT registers. The LPC55S69 provides a support library for the PUF, which includes the functions shown in Table 11.3.

Table 11.3 PUF Functions.

Command	Parameters	Description
PUF_Init()	PUF Base Address	Enables the PUF and waits until the block initializes
PUF_Enroll()	Base Address, [out]activation code	Performs an Enroll operation and returns an activation code
PUF_Start()	Base Address, activation code, activation code size	Starts the PUF with the generated activation code
PUF_SetIntrinsicKey()	Base Address, key index, key size, [out] key code, [out] key code size	Generates a random key and returns a key code to reconstruct the key
PUF_SetUserKey()	Base Address, key index, user key, user key size,[out] key code,[out] key code size	Accepts a user key and returns a key code to reconstruct the key
PUF_GetKey()	Base Address, key code, key code size, [out] key, [out] key size	Reconstruct a key from a key code and returns it to the user
PUF_GetHwKey()	Base Address, key code, key code size, key slot, key mask	Reconstruct a key from a key code and send to Hash Crypt via local bus
PUF_Zeroize()	Base Address	Clear all internal logic and enter error state
PUF_IsGetKeyAllowed()	Base Address	Checks if the get key operation is allowed
PUF_PowerCycle()	Base Address	Power cycles the PUF

Before we can start using the PUF, we first need to perform an enroll process to generate an activation code by writing the PUF_ENROLL command to the CODEINPUT register (Fig. 11.11).

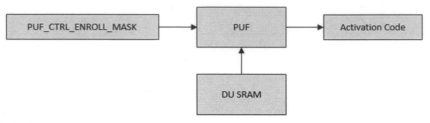

FIG. 11.11

PUF Enroll. The PUF enroll will generate a unique activation code, which can be used to recreate the digital fingerprint for each session.

No permission required.

When the enroll is completed, the activation code can be read from the PUF CODEOUTPUT register. The activation code is 1192 bytes in size, and it can be stored in any nonvolatile location. The CMPA protected flash page provides a storage location for the activation code so that it can be used by the secure boot ROM at startup. Ideally, it will only be necessary to perform an enroll process once per device. Once the activation code has been generated, it is possible to disable further enroll commands by setting on OTP fuse (Fig. 11.12).

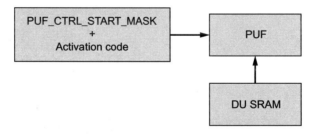

FIG. 11.12

Starting the PUF. A the start of the session the activation code is used to recreate the device unique fingerprint.

No permission required.

When the activation code has been generated, we can place the PUF into its operational mode by issuing a START command. During this operation, the activation code is written to the CODEINPUT register in 32-bit chunks. Once the start command has been successfully executed, we can configure the PUF to hold our encryption keys.

Once the PUF has been started with a valid activation code, there are two methods of registering a key. You can either use the PUF to create a random key by using the GENERATEKEY command or register an existing user key with the SETKEY command (Fig. 11.13).

In either case, the PUF will return a keycode that in combination with a PUF_CTRL_GETKEY_MASK command to retrieve the key. In the case of a key that has been stored with index zero, the key will be sent via the hardware bus to the PRINCE and HashCrypt units (Fig. 11.14).

FIG. 11.13

Key Storage and Creation. A user key can be "stored" in the PUF or a random key may be generated in each case.

No permission required.

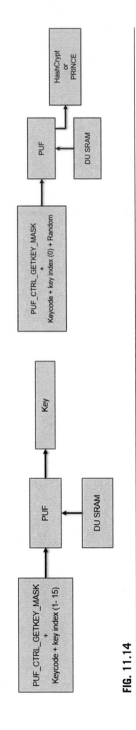

FIG. 11.14

Accessing The Key. The keycode can be used to access a key or in the case of index 0 it will be written over a local bus to an encryption unit.

When we use a key with index zero, an additional block of random data must be passed to the PUF. This is used as "blinding" data, which masks the encryption key as it is transferred to the encryption engine. This is intended to mitigate against side-channel attacks.

Exercise: Key storage using the PUF

This exercise demonstrates how to use the PUF to "store" and generate a pair of keys. Both keys are retrieved from the PUF, and the "stored" key is tested against the original.

In the pack installer, select Example 11.1 and press the Copy button.
Build the project and start the debugger.
Step through the enroll and start functions.

This will create and use the activation code.

Now step through the key set and generate key functions.

This will "store" the user key and create a new random key and return keycodes for future access.

The key codes and activation codes are public information. They cannot be used to reconstruct the "stored" keys without access to the deterministic uninitialized SRAM values, which are both hidden and unique to each device.

Now run the getkey function and key compare functions.

This will retrieve the "stored" key and check that it matches the original values.

Secure boot

After a reset, the LPC55S69 will execute code in the boot ROM before passing execution to the application image in the FLASH memory. The boot ROM can be configured to perform a secure boot process that validates the device images to provide an immutable RoT. The LPC55S69 secure boot is certified as a PSA Level 1 and Level 2 device. The secure boot process is a critical part of the Arm Platform Security Architecture that is used to establish an initial RoT that all future device security is based on.

The LPC55S69 is designed to support a standard plain boot which will automatically execute any image that is programmed into the internal FLASH memory. This is used during development when it is necessary to update the execution image frequently. The LPC55S69 also supports a boot process that validates the execution image using a CRC32 checksum. While this is a useful self-test measurement, it only provides a weak (in cryptographic terms) measure of image integrity and does nothing to authenticate the image. This would leave our device wide open to rogue images and potential malware. We need something stronger.

For our uses, the LPC55S69 has both hardware support and ROMed system code for a sophisticated secure boot process. While this is specific to this family of devices, understanding how it works provides a useful introduction to the implementation of the of the PSA secure boot requirements.

The LPC55S69 secure boot performs the following functions:

- Validation of the FLASH memory images before starting execution.
- Configure and enable the TrustZone SAU.
- Perform an In System Programming (ISP) software update over a range of serial interfaces, such as USART SPI or USB.

The ROM also provides an API to the application code so we can access its functions to perform In-Application Programming (IAP) via a second-stage bootloader.

When the secure boot is enabled, the FLASH image must be formatted is shown in Fig. 11.15.

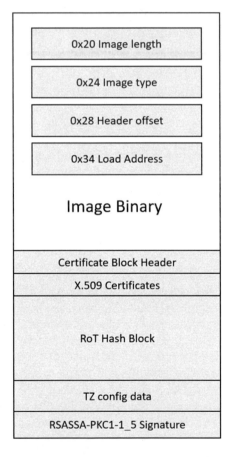

FIG. 11.15

Image Security Format. The secure boot image must be formatted with a header. It may also be encrypted prior to download.

No permission required.

In addition to the binary application code, the image contains a block of security credentials. These consist of an X.509 certificate block and a set of RoT key hashes followed by TrustZone configuration information. The code image and security block are signed by the private half of an RSA (2048) key pair. This is called the Image-Signing Key (IPK). Typically, the security credentials will be appended to the end of the code image but can be located anywhere within the signed region. The address of the security header block is stored in the exception vector table and occupies the reserved (unused) vector at 0x00000024. This allows the secure bootloader to locate the security credentials and validate the FLASH image.

The security credentials start with a block of X.509 certificates. While this block is capable of holding a chain of up to sixteen certificates, the most common configuration uses two certificates. The first certificate is a self-signed root certificate that contains a Root Public Key (RPK), which is used as a Certificate Authority (CA). The second certificate contains the Image Signing Public Key (IPK) and is signed by the private half of the RPK. In order to anchor the certificates to the LPC55S69, a Hash of the RPK is stored in the CPMA page of the protected FLASH. Once the CPMA page has been programmed, it can be sealed, which makes its contents immutable. This gives us an immutable RoT hash value, which is used by the secure boot loader to validate the public key stored in the root certificate. The root certificate is then used to extend the chain of trust by validating the image signing certificate IPK. If this is successful, the IPK public key can be used to validate the full image signature. The full Chain of Trust is shown in Fig. 11.16.

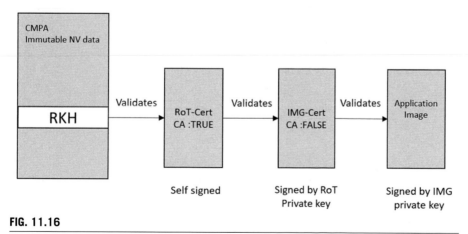

FIG. 11.16

Chain of Trust. The RoT establishes a chain of trust to validate each system image.

No permission required.

So why use two certificates? It is possible to use a single certificate and use its key to validate the image. However, this certificate is bound to the device through the Immutable Root Key Hash Table. If its matching private key is compromised, we have no way of updating the public certificate and hash value. By using two certificates, we are creating an additional "bastion" layer of security that future-proofs our devices against such a compromise. In this approach, the root certificate private key will be used as little as possible and stored away very securely. Typically, the RPK private key is used just once to sign the Image Signing Certificate (IPK). Now all update images will be signed by the IPK private key. This means we make regular use of the IPK private key, potentially making it more liable to be compromised to an unauthorized third party. If this does happen, we can create a new IPK signing key pair and a fresh X.509 image certificate, which will again be signed by the RPK private key since this is still valid.

All new images will be signed with the fresh Image Signing Key (IPK private), and the image will be encapsulated with the original RPK and the new IPK certificates. This allows us to recover from the compromise without having to modify the RoT hash in our devices. As mentioned earlier, a hash of the RKP public key is stored in the CMPA block protected flash area. Since this is immutable once programmed, it would be a big problem if the RKP private key was compromised. We would have no easy way to make our devices trust a different key. In order to minimize this threat, the CMPA block has a RoT hash table that can store up to four RPK public key hashes (Fig. 11.17).

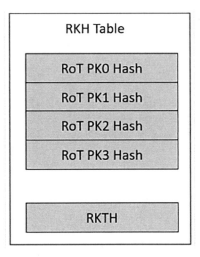

FIG. 11.17

RoT Hash Block. Up to four RoT hashes may be stored in the hash table. The table is further protected by a hash of the hashes (RKTH).

No permission required.

This allows us to pre-generate up to four RPK key pairs and store their hashes in our devices when they are manufactured. The first key in the table will automatically be the active key, and the remainder are stored for possible future use. If we need to switch to a new Root Key, the Protected Flash CFPA block provides a mechanism to revoke the existing RoT key hash and activate the next entry in the table. This can be done up to four times (to lose one private key…). The hash table is further protected by a root key table hash (RKTH), which is a hash of the hash table.

Monotonic counters

To prevent an attacker from installing an unauthorized or older version of the device firmware, the Protected flash CFPA page contains three monotonic counters (they can be incremented but not decremented). These counters are used for firmware version control and revocation of the secure boot certificate keys.

If the IPK private key has been compromised, it would be possible for an attacker to create their own image and sign it with the compromised IPK. The CFPA provides a counter that is used to store the serial number of the Image Signing Certificate. For the image update to be accepted, the serial number must either match or be one count higher than the current counter value. The counter is restricted to a range of seventeen set values, which effectively restrict the range of the IPK certificate serial number.

The first two counters are used to store the current Secure firmware version and the current nonsecure firmware version. When a new image is installed the version, numbers stored in the update image must be the same or later than the value stored in the hardware counters. If this is not the case, the firmware will be rejected. This is intended to prevent an attacker from rolling back the firmware to an earlier version with known vulnerabilities.

Once enabled, the secure boot ROM within the LPC55S69 is always the first code to execute after reset. The secure boot ROM will validate an initial image located within the FLASH memory. In terms of our security model, this will be the updatable Root of Trust, which is the second stage bootloader BL2. If this image is successfully validated, the boot ROM will pass execution to the BL2 image. The BL2 bootloader will, in turn, validate the remaining secure code image and the nonsecure image before passing execution to the secure application code. We will have a look at the BL2 bootloader in Chapter 14.

Exercise: Secure boot

NXP has made the process of creating the necessary credentials and secure boot image very straight forward, with an easy to use an application called "MCU Expresso Secure provisioning." This tool can be downloaded from their website to provide a self-contained environment that automates the entire provisioning process.

> **However, before we look at this tool, it is important to note that it will fully enable the secure boot support, which cannot be reversed. This tool should only be used to program a device where you want the boot security permanently enabled.**

You can download the secure provisioning tool from the following URL:

https://www.nxp.com/design/software/development-software/mcuxpresso-software-and-tools-/mcuxpresso-secure-provisioning-tool:MCUXPRESSO-SECURE-PROVISIONING

Start the tool and select the LPC55Sxx as the target device.
First select the Key management tab.
Press the Generate Key tab (Fig. 11.18).

FIG. 11.18

Secure provisioning utility. The secure provisioning utility will generate the keys and certificates.

No permission required.

This will generate four sets of RoT certificates and associated image signing certificates along with their private keys. It will also generate a symmetrical Secure Binary Encryption Key SBKEK, which is used to encrypt the binary update image. During provisioning, the SBKEK key is stored in the CMFA.

Next, select the build image tab. Here we need to provide the raw binary file and a name for the output secure boot image. The start address for the image is zero. In this example, we are not going to use the secure boot ROM to configure TrustZone, so this is disabled. Finally, we can select the Root of Trust Hash that will be used to anchor the certificate chain. Once these options are set, press the build image button, and the tools will generate the bootable image and the provisioning credentials for the protected FLASH CMPA page (Fig. 11.19).

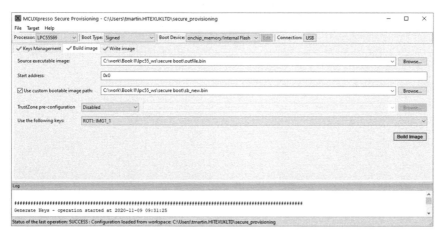

FIG. 11.19

Build the secure image. Once the credentials have been generated we can build the secure image.

No permission required.

Once the image has been generated, we can use the provisioning tool to download it into the device.

This is the bit you should not do unless you want to permanently enable the secure boot! (Fig. 11.20).

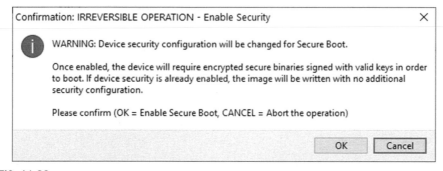

FIG. 11.20

Secure Boot Warning. Do not proceed beyond this screen unless you want to permanently enable secure boot!

No permission required.

Connect a USB cable to the Xpresso P9 USB port.
Place the board into its bootloader mode by holding down the ISP button and pressing Reset.

Now press the Write Image button.

This will download the secure boot image into the internal flash and program the CMPA page. It will also seal the device by setting the CMPA Hash value (Fig. 11.21).

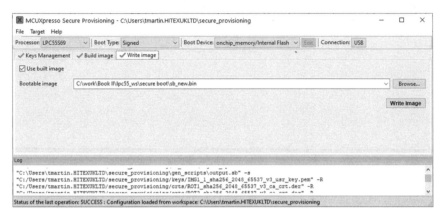

FIG. 11.21

Programming the Device. The final stage is to download an image and seal the device.

No permission required.

Once the board is reset, the secure boot process will be active. Any updated application image must be correctly encapsulated and signed before it will be accepted by the microcontroller.

Debug authentication

The LPC55S69 extends the Cortex-M33 processor debug authentication to enable tiered debug access in a final product. The debug architecture provides debug access points for each Cortex-M33 core plus a debug mailbox, which is used by the debugger to negotiate a secure debug session (Fig. 11.22).

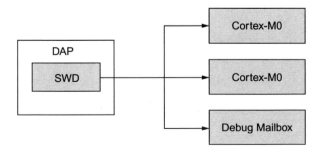

FIG. 11.22

CoreSight Debug. The CoreSight debug architecture supports multicore debug and includes a "mailbox" to negotiate a secure access rights.

No permission required.

When the debug security is configured, the debug mailbox remains enabled, while both of the core debug access points are disabled. When a debugger wants to connect, it must go through a challenge-response messaging protocol using the debug mailbox.

To configure the LPC55S69 debug authentication, an asymmetric key pair must be generated to act as the Root of Trust. The public key is then stored in the device along with a set of credentials that define different types of debug access. Different users are granted access through a debug credential certificate. To create this certificate, the user must generate a second public key pair. The public key is given to the OEM vendor, and this is placed into the certificate along with the credential constraints appropriate to the access he requires. The certificate may also include a UUID field which, limits the certificate to activate a specific device. This binds together the end user's identity and access rights (Fig. 11.23).

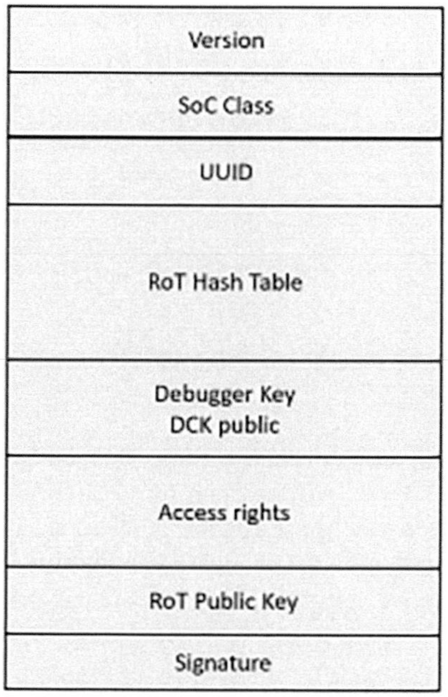

Version
SoC Class
UUID
RoT Hash Table
Debugger Key DCK public
Access rights
RoT Public Key
Signature

FIG. 11.23

Debug Certificate. The debug certificate defines the range of devices a technician can access and the level of debug access.

No permission required.

To start a debug session, the technician connects to the debug mailbox, and the device will send a debug authentication challenge. This contains the stored credential constraints and some random data. The debugger must now have a matching debug credential that will allow it to negotiate its authorized level of debug access. In order to reply, the debugger then generates a response packet which includes its debug credential certificate and the random data. The random data act as a nonce to prevent replay attacks. If the authentication is successful, the device will enable the debug ports, and grant access appropriate to the certificate credentials (Fig. 11.24).

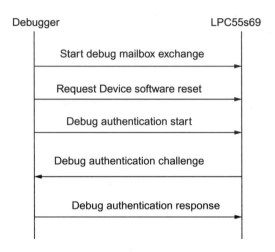

FIG. 11.24

Secure debug. The debug mailbox is used to establish a secure debug session and negotiate access rights.

No permission required.

Lifecycle

This system allows us to implement the PSA lifecycle model for debug access. During manufacture, the device will be open for assembly and test. When it is programmed with the application firmware, the device can also be provisioned with secrets, including the debug private key and the credential constraints. At this point, the device can enter its active state with secure boot enabled, and the debug port will be locked down.

As part of the service contract, the vendor can create a range of the third-party debug credential certificates that allow debug access to the nonsecure code and OEM debug credential certificates to allow full access for vendor technicians.

Hardware accelerators

The LPC55S69 has three cryptographic hardware accelerators: HashCrypt, which provides symmetric encryption and hash algorithms, CASPER, which supports rapid calculation of asymmetric algorithms and PRINCE, which is able to support execution of encrypted images with a zero cycle overhead (Table 11.4).

Table 11.4 Hardware accelerators.

Function	Algorithms	Accelerator
Symmetric Cipher	AES (ECB, CBC,CTR) PRINCE (CTR)	Hash Crypt 128,192 & 256 bit keys
Asymmetric Cipher	RSA, ECC	CASPER
Hash	SHA-1, SHA-256	HASH Crypt
MAC	HMAC, CMAC	HashCrypt + Software
Signature	RSA, ECDSA	HashCrypt and CASPER

Asymmetric encryption

The CASPER hardware unit supports hardware calculation of the RSA asymmetric encryption algorithm, the Diffe Hellman Key Agreement algorithm, and Elliptic Curve Cryptography, including the Elliptic Curve Digital Signature Algorithm. In order to reach a high level of security, each of these algorithms uses very large numbers. While arithmetic with these numbers can be done in software using the mbedTLS Bignum library, it is both computationally intensive and energy-hungry. Being able to offload these calculations into a hardware co-processor has clear advantages.

The CASPER unit is a general-purpose computational engine. The acronym stands for **C**ryptographic **A**ccelerator and **S**ignaling **P**rocessing **E**ngine with **R**AM sharing. While it is primarily intended for cryptographic use, the CASPER coprocessor can be programmed to perform a wide range of mathematical algorithms such as DSP algorithms, matrix math, and even graphics acceleration such as shading.

The CASPER coprocessor takes its input from four RAM banks that can be accessed simultaneously, allowing the CASPER coprocessor to load 128 bits of data in a single cycle. The coprocessor has several layers of computational blocks. The first layer provides two 32 bit multipliers that can multiply various combinations of the input words to give a 64- or 32-bit intermediate result. These results may either be carried through to the final output layer, or a half word from each intermediate result may be combined in an adder unit. In this case, the lower half word from one intermediate result and the upper half word from the second intermediate result are used. The final output layer consists of four results blocks that can load the intermediate results via a multiplexer (Fig. 11.25).

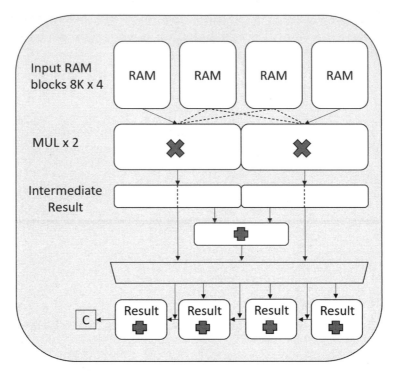

FIG. 11.25

CASPER Block Diagram. CASPER provides a set of general purpose MAC and addition units.

Each of the results blocks contains an adder unit and results register which operate in parallel. There are several different data paths for each results block that can be individually configured. This array of hardware arithmetic units and multiplexers allows us to perform complex calculations, store constants, and use data from the previous calculation.

The CASPER coprocessor is programmed as a state machine with each calculation step programmed by a mode command. Fortunately, a number of low-level cryptographic primitives are provided for the CASPER coprocessor, so unless you need to implement a custom algorithm, it is unlikely you will need to program it directly.

Exercise: Casper primitives

In the pack installer, select Example 11.2 and press the Copy button. Build the project and download to the debugger.

The code will use the CASPER unit to perform modular exponentiation. The code is annotated with debugger event recorder macros, which are used to display the execution time:

```
CASPER_ModExp(CASPER,
  (void *)signature0,
  (void *)pubkey0,
  sizeof(plaintext0) / sizeof(uint32_t),
  pub_e, plaintext);
```

Set a breakpoint after the casper_modEXP function.

Run the code and note the execution time in the view\event statistics window.

The code will next perform elliptic curve scalar multiplication, which has also been annotated with event recorder macros.

Set a further breakpoint at the end of the code and note the timing measurements in the event statistics window.

The mbedTLS library has been ported to use the CASPER coprocessor for the asymmetric algorithms. The table below shows the performance boost for each of the supported algorithms (Table 11.5).

Table 11.5 CASPER performance.

Algorithm	Operation	SW execution time (mS)	CASPER execution time (mS)	Improvement %
Signing	ECDSA—secp256r1	333.33	142.86	233
Verification	ECDSA—secp256r1	598.80	149.93	399
Key Exchange	ECDSA—secp256r1	300.30	130.38	230
Signing	RSA—1024	250.00	272.48	−9
Verification	RSA—1024	8.9	1.81	493
Signing	RSA—2048	1000.00	1000.00	0
Verification	RSA—2048	31.92	5.03	635

Symmetric cryptography

The LPC55S69 provides a second dedicated cryptography processor for the key symmetric cryptography algorithms. The HashCrypt processor provides hardware acceleration for the AES cipher and the SHA message digest algorithms. A hash or cipher based MAC can be implemented with additional software, as discussed in Chapter 4.

The HashCrypt processor provides a fixed implementation of the AES algorithm and supports encryption key sizes of 128, 192, 256 bits. The user software may provide the encryption keys in the case of session keys, or as we saw earlier, a key may be provided from the PUF key store. In this case, the key will be sent to the HashCrypt unit via a local bus which is not observed by the CPU. While the AES supports ECB mode, it also supports various streaming modes, including CBC and CTR modes. The HashCrypt processor provides an additional streaming mode called IBC, which is designed to prevent side-channel analysis and is intended to protect data at rest rather than communications data. Once configured encryption/decryption operations will take $32 + 2$ cycles per AES block.

As its name implies, the HashCrypt processor also provides a hashing or message digest function using the SHA-1 and SHA-2 algorithms. The HASHING function will process blocks of 512 bytes at a time for the SHA-1 algorithm. This will take 80 cycles while the SHA-2 takes only 64 cycles, which is much faster than a software implementation. To further speed things up, the data blocks can be provided by internal DMA transfers from memory or peripheral buffers.

Exercise: HashCrypt

In this exercise, we will use the HashCrypt peripheral to encrypt and decrypt data using the AES cipher and its chaining modes. The code uses both a user-supplied key and a key that is securely stored in the PUF unit. The project then uses the HashCrypt peripheral to generate SHA1 and SHA256 hashes.

> **In the pack installer, select Example 11.3 and press the Copy button.**
> **Examine the code in the HashCrypt.c file.**

The first section of the code provides functions that test the AES engine in Electronic Code Book format and chained modes CBC and CTR with a user-supplied key.

The second section uses an encryption key stored in the PUF using index zero, so it is delivered through the dedicated hardware bus. This ensures that no secret key is held on the device, and during operation, the reconstructed key is never visible to the CPU.

The final section is used to generate SHA1 and SHA256 hashes.

> **Build the project and Start the debugger.**
> **Run the code and check the output messages in the console window.**

Executable image encryption

The final cryptographic co-processor is used to encrypt and decrypt the firmware image using a lightweight symmetrical block cipher called PRINCE. However, while the PRINCE algorithm is a proprietary algorithm it has been subjected to extensive cryptoanalysis and was selected through a challenge competition. The cipher itself is used to encrypt/decrypt 64-bit blocks of data using a 128-bit key. Interestingly, the program images do not need to be encrypted before being downloaded into the microcontroller. Once image encryption is enabled, the PRINCE cipher will automatically encrypt image data as it is programmed into the FLASH memory. Then during normal execution, each instruction will be decrypted on the fly with zero overhead beyond the standard FLASH access time.

The program FLASH memory is divided into three sections, two of 256 K and a final section of 128 K. Each section has a separate encryption key, which are each stored in the PUF. The CMPA has dedicated storage slots for the resulting PUF keycodes, which are accessed by the PRINCE unit when image encryption is enabled.

Exercise: Image encryption

In this exercise, we will first provision the CMPA with keys for the three PRINCE regions and then download an image using the ISP programming support. This will allow the PRINCE engine to encrypt the image as it is downloaded. We can then check that the image executes successfully and view the encrypted code using the debugger assembler view.

> **Warning: Like the secure boot example, this exercise is for information only. Once you have set the encryption options, your device will automatically encrypt the code that is downloaded via the bootloader.**
> **Install the J10 jumper to allow the ISP mode after the reset.**
> **Connect a micro USB cable between the PC host and the CMSIS DAP USB port (P6) on the board.**
> **Open the Command Prompt, move to the folder with the blhost.exe and apply the following commands:**

```
blhost -p comX -- key-provisioning enroll
blhost -p comX -- key-provisioning set_key 7 16
blhost -p comX -- key-provisioning set_key 8 16
blhost -p comX -- key-provisioning set_key 9 16
blhost -p comX -- key-provisioning write_key_nonvolatile 0
```

> **Remove the J10 jumper and reset the board.**
> **Open a serial terminal with the following settings 15200 8N1.**
> **Download the program to the target board.**
> **Either press the reset button on your board.**
> **Once you have seen the code execute correctly start the debugger.**
> **Open the view\assembly window.**
> **Run the code to main().**
> **Examine the code in the assembly window.**

Security peripherals

Entropy source

As we saw in the cryptography chapters, the generation of secret keys should be done through a random process. Random numbers are also used during the TLS handshake. This makes a cryptographically strong RNG as important to our overall security as the secrecy of our encryption keys. Like most microcontrollers designed for IoT use, the LPC55S69 has a True Random Number Generator (TRNG) with 256 bits of entropy (uncertainty). The TRNG is certified to meet and exceed current standards such as FIPS140–2, AIS31, and P2/PTG.3.

Secure user peripherals

The security control block contains a number of additional registers to manage other security concerns within the LPC55S69. While controlling memory access is a driving concern, other signals such as interrupt channels also cross the boundary between secure and nonsecure code. We need to ensure that useful information does not leak from the Secure world. Within the Security Control Block, we can also lock some important processor configuration options so that an attacker cannot modify them while the device is running.

Secure interrupt masking

The LPC55S69 contains two Cortex-M33 CPU's but only CPU-0 is fitted with TrustZone. The memory and peripheral access rights for CPU-1 are defined by a Master Security Wrapper in the same fashion as the other bus masters. However, all of the peripheral interrupts are also routed to the NVIC in CPU-1. If CPU-1 is being used to execute nonsecure code, it is still able to see interrupt activity from the secure peripherals. To close this loophole, the Security Control Module provides a set of masking registers that can be used to disable the connection of selected peripheral interrupts to the NVIC in CPU-1.

Secure DMA unit

The LPC55S69 has two general-purpose DMA units with multiple independent channels. After reset, either DMA unit may be accessed by each of the Cortex-M33 processors. To prevent this from becoming a security risk, one unit can be assigned to the nonsecure code, while the second is used by the secure code by defining its access rights using its Master Security Wrapper. However, all of the peripheral interrupt signals are routed to both DMA units so they can act as flow controllers. This could potentially expose some secure information to the nonsecure DMA unit. To prevent this from becoming a problem once a DMA unit is assigned to the secure code, a set of masking registers can be used to prevent DMA requests from secure peripherals from being routed to the nonsecure DMA unit.

GPIO masking

On LPC55S69, all digital pins states are readable through GPIO controller registers, which means that information can leak through pins connected to peripherals configured as a secure peripheral.

On the LPC55S69, any digital I/O that is sensitive to information leakage can be masked using SEC_GPIO_MASK0/1/2/3 registers to ensure that the nonsecure code cannot snoop on the activity of secure peripherals.

Secure GPIO

The LPC55S69 provides a secondary set of GPIO registers for GPIO port 0.

The security control block provides a pair of registers than are used to lock access to processor configuration options within CPU-0 and CPU-1.

The CPU-0 and CPU-1 lock registers contain bit fields that, when set, prohibit further configuration of each processor. Each lock register also contains a bit that, when set, locks the register itself from further updates until a device reset is performed.

Conclusion

In this chapter, we have seen how a Cortex-M33 based microcontroller can build on the TrustZone security extension to create a run time trusted execution environment. Typical microcontrollers designed to be the basis of an IoT device will also provide a PSA-certified secure boot process that is held in immutable ROM. The silicon vendor should also provide a region of memory that can be programmed with key device information when the device is manufactured. The device must also have a strong source of entropy in the form of a true random number generator. Ideally, the microcontroller will also have a set of monotonic counters for image versioning. Beyond these base features, the device is likely to provide a range of security assistive peripherals such as a secure key store and cryptographic accelerators. Once you have a device that meets all these requirements, you can start thinking about the application.

Trusted firmware

12

Introduction

The Trusted Firmware for Cortex-M TF-M is an open-source reference platform for the Secure Processing Environment (SPE). The structure and design of the TF-M platform assumes that an attacker has control of the Nonsecure Processing Environment (NSPE) and can launch software attacks against the SPE. In addition to the security provided by the TrustZone isolation boundary, the TF-M platform is designed using the secure coding principles outlined in Chapter 8, including Fault Injection Hardening (FIH). In this chapter, we will take a closer look at the structure of the TF-M platform to gain a basic understanding of how it works and what you need to do to configure it correctly. The TF-M platform consists of the elements shown in Fig. 12.1.

Security services

The TF-M platform provides the mandatory security services that run in the PSA RoT and Application RoT.

Secure partition manager

The TF-M also includes the Security Partition Manager (SPM) that provides message routing and RTOS-type signals to the security service partitions. The signals and messages can be generated by API calls from the Nonsecure Client, secure interrupts, or between security services.

Secure partition manager hardware abstraction layer

The TF-M is integrated into the microcontroller through a Hardware Abstraction Layer (HAL), which must be adapted for a specific device. The SPM HAL is also used to manage interrupt requests that are routed to the SPE.

Nonsecure client

The application in the NSPE is provided with a set of API calls to the security services in the SPE. These are made through a dedicated client, which provides two different communication methods. At design time, the developer can select between either an Interprocess Communication (IPC) model or a Secure Function (SFN) model. The choice of communications model will also affect how the secure interrupts are managed.

BL2 bootloader

During the boot stage, after the microcontroller secure boot has ended, execution is passed to the second stage bootloader BL2, which validates the NSPE and SPE images. We will see the operation of the BL2 bootloader in Chapter 14. Once BL2

Designing Secure IoT Devices with the Arm Platform Security Architecture and Cortex-M33.
https://doi.org/10.1016/B978-0-12-821469-5.00001-6

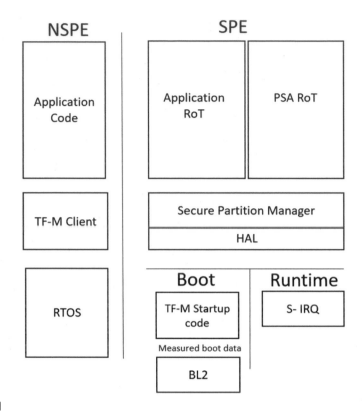

FIG. 12.1

Trusted firmware structure. The trusted firmware provides a full reference implementation for the SPE.

No permission required.

has finished execution, it will pass control and a boot record of image measurements to the TF-M startup code.

TF-M secure startup code

The TF-M startup code sets up the TrustZone partitions, configures the Trusted Firmware, and starts the Nonsecure code executing.

Installation

The TF-M reference platform is provided as two software packs. The first is a core library that provides the SPM and mandatory security services. A second pack provides the platform files for a specific microcontroller family and default (dummy) secrets, which are used for initial configuration and testing. Make sure that you have the following packs installed (Table 12.1).

Table 12.1 Trusted firmware software packs.

Pack	Description
ARM::TFM	Trusted Firmware core library
Keil::LPC55S6x_TFM-PF	Platform files for the LPC55S69
ARM::TFM-Test	Test Framework for the TF-M Firmware

Important

At the time of writing, the TF-M was still in development. Consequently, some of the details may change. Any updates to the exercise instruction will be provided as a pdf within the project folder.

Exercise: TF-M setup and testing

A set of installation test harnesses are provided alongside the reference platform. These are a good place to start when bringing up the TF-M platform for the first time. In this exercise, we will examine a TF-M template project and use a test framework to validate the secure partition configuration.

In the pack installer, select Exercise 12.1 and press the Copy button.

The exercise consists of a secure partition project that has been configured to contain the Trusted Firmware and a Nonsecure partition that contains the Trusted Firmware client. We will look at how the platform is configured and use the TF-M secure partition test framework to validate its installation.

Please check the actual project for any updated instructions.

The project memory layout is configured as a CMSIS-Zone project, which is located in a Zone directory as part of the main project layout (Fig. 12.2).

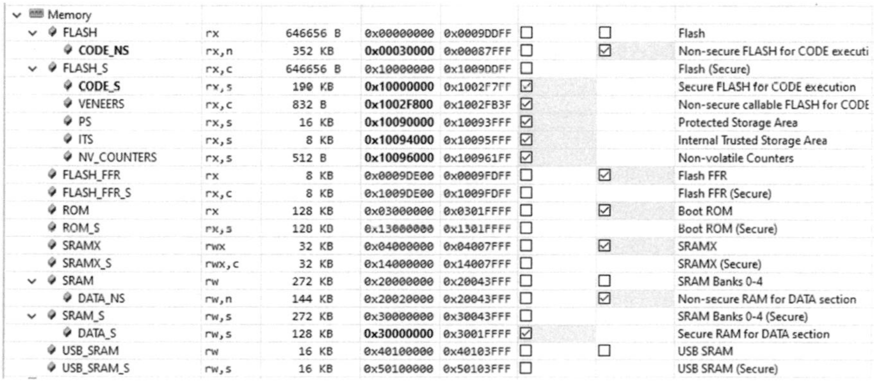

Memory							
FLASH	rx	646656 B	0x00000000	0x0009DDFF	☐	☐	Flash
CODE_NS	rx,n	352 KB	0x00030000	0x00087FFF	☐	☑	Non-secure FLASH for CODE executi
FLASH_S	rx,c	646656 B	0x10000000	0x1009DDFF	☐		Flash (Secure)
CODE_S	rx,s	190 KB	0x10000000	0x1002F7FF	☑		Secure FLASH for CODE execution
VENEERS	rx,c	832 B	0x1002F800	0x1002FB3F	☑		Non-secure callable FLASH for CODE
PS	rx,s	16 KB	0x10090000	0x10093FFF	☑		Protected Storage Area
ITS	rx,s	8 KB	0x10094000	0x10095FFF	☑		Internal Trusted Storage Area
NV_COUNTERS	rx,s	512 B	0x10096000	0x100961FF	☑		Non-volatile Counters
FLASH_FFR	rx	8 KB	0x0009DE00	0x0009FDFF	☐	☑	Flash FFR
FLASH_FFR_S	rx,c	8 KB	0x1009DE00	0x1009FDFF	☐		Flash FFR (Secure)
ROM	rx	128 KB	0x03000000	0x0301FFFF	☐	☑	Boot ROM
ROM_S	rx,s	128 KB	0x13000000	0x1301FFFF	☐		Boot ROM (Secure)
SRAMX	rwx	32 KB	0x04000000	0x04007FFF	☐	☑	SRAMX
SRAMX_S	rwx,c	32 KB	0x14000000	0x14007FFF	☐		SRAMX (Secure)
SRAM	rw	272 KB	0x20000000	0x20043FFF	☐	☐	SRAM Banks 0-4
DATA_NS	rw,n	144 KB	0x20020000	0x20043FFF	☐	☑	Non-secure RAM for DATA section
SRAM_S	rw,s	272 KB	0x30000000	0x30043FFF	☐		SRAM Banks 0-4 (Secure)
DATA_S	rw,s	128 KB	0x30000000	0x3001FFFF	☑		Secure RAM for DATA section
USB_SRAM	rw	16 KB	0x40100000	0x40103FFF	☐	☐	USB SRAM
USB_SRAM_S	rw,s	16 KB	0x50100000	0x50103FFF	☐		USB SRAM (Secure)

FIG. 12.2

Zone project for the Trusted Firmware platform. A CMSIS-Zone project defines the full memory layout for the TF-M platform.

No permission required.

In addition to allocating a FLASH region to the secure code, FLASH regions are also created for the protected storage, internal trusted storage and nonvolatile counters (Fig. 12.3).

USBHSH	rw	84 B	0x400A3000	0x400A3053	☐	☑	USB1 High-speed Host Controller
HASH-AES	rw,s	160 B	0x500A4000	0x500A409F	☑		HASH-AES
CASPER	rw,s	4 KB	0x500A5000	0x500A5FFF	☑		Cryptographic Accelerator
SGPIO	rw,s	9360 B	0x500A8000	0x500AA48F	☑		Secure General Purpose I/O
AHB_SECURE_CTRL	rw,s	4 KB	0x500AC000	0x500ACFFF	☑		AHB Secure Controller
POWERQUAD	rw	608 B	0x40150000	0x4015025F	☐	☑	PowerQuad DSP Coprocessor and Ac

FIG. 12.3

FLASH storage regions. The zone project also creates FLASH regions for storage and monotonic counters.

No permission required.

The Assistive Security Structure that we saw in Chapter 11 has been configured to be accessed from the secure code.

When generated, the linker and project files provide a full description of the memory map. This memory map uses a standard set of defines, which are in turn used by the TF-M code.

In the RTE open the TFM branch (Fig. 12.4).

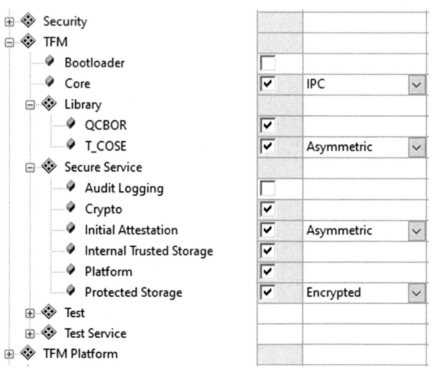

FIG. 12.4

TF-M software components. The RTE allows you to add the TF-M core and selected software components.

No permission required.

The Trusted Firmware is added to the project as a set of core services and libraries. While the HAL and device-specific files are added as a set of platform files (Fig. 12.5).

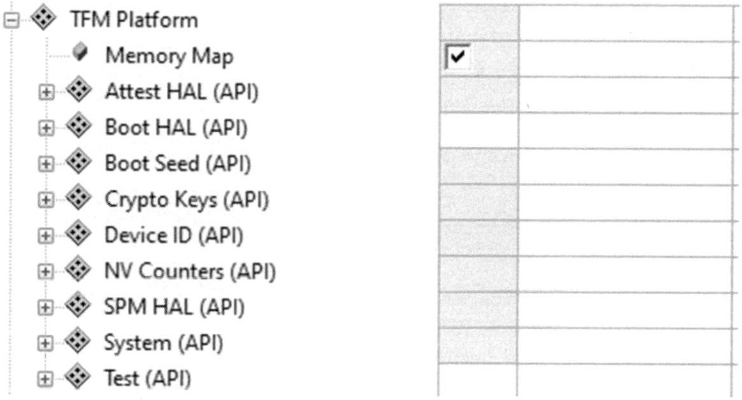

FIG. 12.5

Trusted firmware platform. The platform files adapt the TF-M core to the specific microcontroller.

No permission required.

The initial platform files contain minimal dummy functions, which must be tailored to a given microcontroller using the supporting hardware discussed in Chapter 11. Ideally, this should be done by the Silicon Vendor and be provided as an already configured platform.

Open TF-M::TFM_config.h and enable the config wizard (Fig. 12.6).

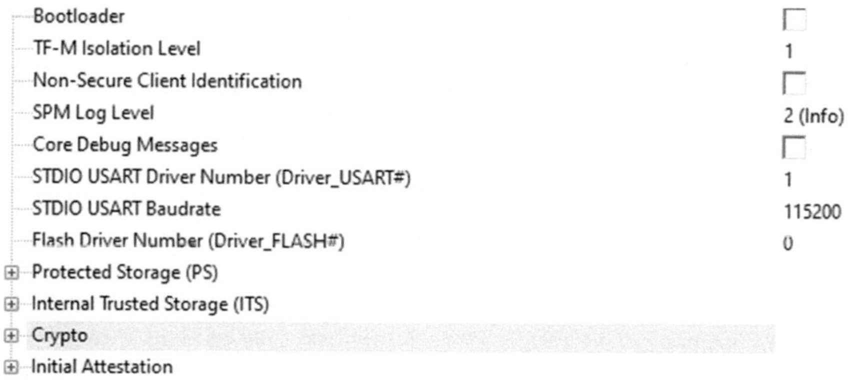

FIG. 12.6

TF-M Platform. The platform files provide the device-specific adaptation functions.

No permission required.

This file contains the main project-wide configuration options for the secure partition. The Trusted firmware is designed to integrate with the BL2 bootloader, which will be introduced in Chapter 14. To configure the secure partition, we first need to select the isolation level and also select the CMSIS USART and Flash driver numbers. Now we can configure each of the mandatory services, and we will look at each of these in the next chapter.

Open the RTE and add the TFM test framework and all the partition tests except the Audit service. Also add the Test service by selecting all of its options (Fig. 12.7).

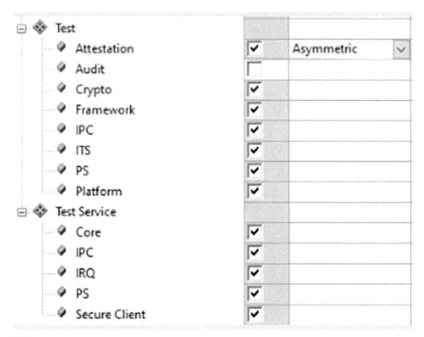

FIG. 12.7

Secure test framework. The RTE.

Also add the TFM Platform::Test:platform option.
Build the project.

Select the nonsecure project and make it the active project.
Open the RTE.

In the TFM branch, the core is set to use the IPC communications model. The platform client has been added along with the API support for each of the services except the Audit service (Fig. 12.8).

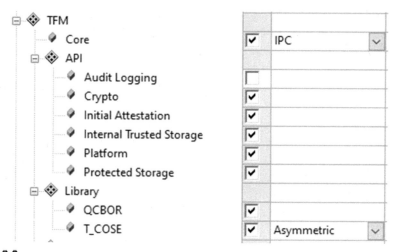

FIG. 12.8

Nonsecure client. The RTE is used to add a Nonsecure client to the application.

No permission required.

Now open the TFM::Test branch and add all of the test components except Audit (Fig. 12.9).

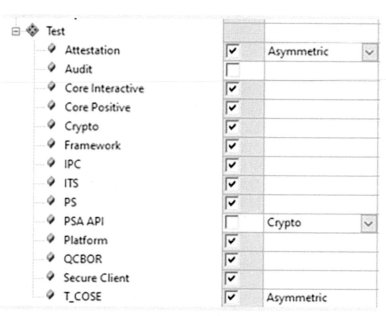

FIG. 12.9

TF-M Nonsecure test framework. A test framework is provided for the nonsecure partition.

No permission required.

Build the project.

Start the debugger and connect a serial terminal emulator, such as Tera Term to the debug serial port at 115200 Baud.

Run the code.

The test framework will execute and the test results will be written to the terminal window (Fig. 12.10).

```
Non-Secure system starting...

#### Execute test suites for the Secure area ####
Running Test Suite PSA protected storage S interface tests (TFM_PS_TEST_2XXX)...
> Executing 'TFM_PS_TEST_2001'
  Description: 'Set interface'
  TEST PASSED!
> Executing 'TFM_PS_TEST_2002'
  Description: 'Set interface with create flags'
Note: The UID in this test has already been created with
the PSA_STORAGE_FLAG_WRITE_ONCE flag in a previous test
run. Wipe the storage area to run the full test.
  TEST PASSED!
> Executing 'TFM_PS_TEST_2003'
  Description: 'Set interface with NULL data pointer'
  TEST PASSED!
> Executing 'TFM_PS_TEST_2004'
  Description: 'Set interface with invalid data length'
  TEST PASSED!
```

FIG. 12.10

TF-M test results. The TF-M test results will be printed to the Tera Term.

No permission required.

This now gives us a validated platform from which to start building our application code.

TF-M software design

As we discussed in Chapter 9, the secure partition is used to host a set of security services that are controlled by a Secure Partition Manager. The Partition Manager provides a secure entry point for function calls from the application code located in the Nonsecure partition. This entry point provides an RTOS-like message queue for a client interface in the Nonsecure code. This allows the Nonsecure application code to make requests to access the secure services through an API of standardized function calls. The Nonsecure client then turns the function call and passed data into a formatted message, which is passed through the TrustZone isolation boundary to the partition manager. The partition manager then routes the message to the requested secure partition and the requested secure service (Fig. 12.11).

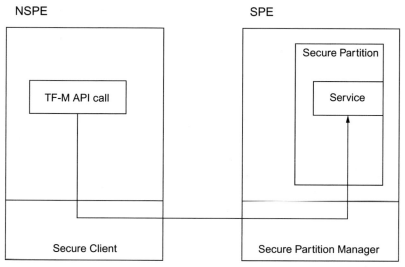

FIG. 12.11

Trusted firmware communication model. The trusted firmware provides a messaging service between the Nonsecure code and the secure services.

No permission required.

The message routing information is defined at design time and must remain fixed over the lifetime of the implementation. The routing metadata identifies the endpoint service partition with a unique Partition ID number (PID) and a partition name as a text string. Within the partition, a further Service ID number (SID) identifies the requested service function (Fig. 12.12).

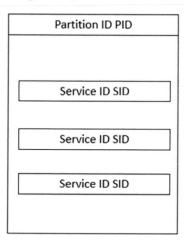

FIG. 12.12

Secure partition. Each service partition has a partition ID and each secure function has a service ID.

No permission required.

Client data

The Trusted Firmware provides two message-passing models, Interprocess Communication (IPC) model and the Secure Function (SFN) model. In both cases, the client data is transferred through a message structure as defined below.

```
typedef struct psa_msg_t {

    int32_t type;

    psa_handle_t handle;

    /* Partition ID of the sender of the message*/
int32_t client_id;

    void *rhandle;

/* Provide the size of each client input vector in bytes. */
    size_t in_size[PSA_MAX_IOVEC];

/* Provide the size of each client output vector in bytes. */
    size_t out_size[PSA_MAX_IOVEC];
    } psa_msg_t;
```

In the IPC model, the type element is used to manage the message transaction and carries values for each stage of the message transaction. During the initial connection, the SPE service will return a handle that is used for further transactions. A client ID and reverse handle may also be defined, which allows an NSPE client to be bound to the SPE service. Once a connection has been established, IO data buffers are defined in the form of Input and output IO vectors.

```
typedef struct psa_invec {

/* the start address of the memory buffer */
const void *base;

/* the size in bytes */
size_t len;
} psa_invec;
```

Each IO vector is defined as a pointer to the buffer base address and the size of the buffer in bytes. The NSPE client can support multiple input and output vectors up to a maximum defined by PSA_MAX_IOVEC. The default is for a maximum of four vectors. The IO vectors are passed through a region of the memory located at the top of the secure process stack.

The IOVEC region is isolated from the other contents on the process stack by a pair of "stack seal numbers." These numbers are checked during an API call to ensure the integrity of the IO vector space. This prevents stack attacks which can be created if an attacker has control of the NSPE.

SPE structure

As we have seen in the PSA Security Model, the SPE consists of three main regions: the Secure Partition Manager, the PSA RoT and the Application RoT. To help provide higher levels of isolation within the SPE, the PSA RoT and the Secure partition manager are accessed by the CPU when it is running in Privileged Mode, while the Application RoT is accessed with the CPU running in Unprivileged Mode (Fig. 12.13).

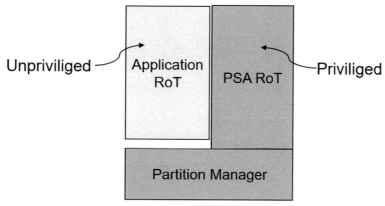

FIG. 12.13

SPE regions and operating mode. To aid isolation, the SPE regions are further accessed as privileged or unprivileged code.

No permission required.

The Trusted Firmware provides three levels of Isolation, which are implemented as follows:

Level one.

Separation between the NSPE and the SPE using TrustZone.

Level two.

Additional isolation between the PSA RoT and the Application RoT using MPU regions based on Privileged and Unprivileged access.

Level three.

Further isolation between each of the security service partitions using further MPU regions.

Interprocess communication (IPC) model

On the client-side, the application code will access a secure service by making an API call to security service client functions. Inside the NS client function, the secure service request is packaged into a message and dispatched to the SPM. The dispatcher will also use a supervisor call to place the CPU in privileged execution mode prior to entering the SPM.

In the IPC model, the interface between the Secure Partition Manager and the Secure Partition consists of a set of RTOS-like signal flags and a message queue. The Secure Partition Manager will also deliver interrupt signals from secure peripherals as well as signal and messages between different secure services within the Secure Processing Environment. This allows the Trusted Firmware to support complex transactions, which involve multiple security services, hardware accelerators, and peripherals (Fig. 12.14).

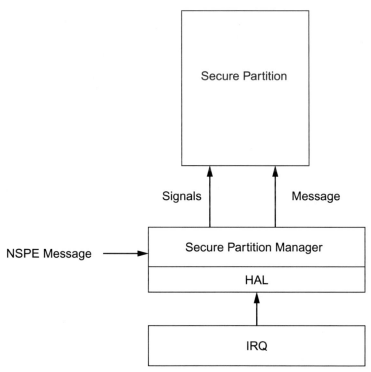

FIG. 12.14

SPM Communication Model. The SPM manages communication between NSPE client, secure interrupts, and between secure partitions.

No permission required.

In the IPC model, the security service executes as a loop, much like an RTOS thread. Each security service has a defined entry point that acts as the start of the service thread (Fig. 12.15).

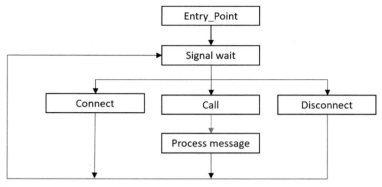

FIG. 12.15

Secure Partition Execution. In the IPC model, the secure partition executes like an RTOS thread using signals to control its transactions.

No permission required.

Once it has performed any initialization code, it will enter the main service loop where a connection-based service is transacted using the interface signals and message queue. Once the main service loop is entered, it will immediately block using a signal function psa_wait(). The SPM will deliver one of three signals (Table 12.2).

Table 12.2 Secure partition signal types.

Action	Description
Message	A message from the NSPE is pending
Interrupt	A secure peripheral interrupt is pending
Doorbell	A message from another secure service is pending

Once the service has been signaled by the SPM, it will establish a connection to the message queue and provide a handle to the calling service (NSPE or SPE). Once the connection has been established further signal/message transactions are processed until the calling service disconnects. The messages are processed using the following functions (Table 12.3).

Table 12.3 IPC communication functions.

Function	Description
psa_wait()	Returns the Secure Partition interrupt signals that have been asserted
psa_connect()	The RoT Service completes the connection request
psa_get()	Retrieves the message which corresponds to a given RoT Service signal
psa_set_rhandle()	Associates a RoT Service return handle with a client connection
psa_call()	The RoT Service completes the request
psa_reply()	Completes handling of a specific message and unblocks the client

(Continued)

Table 12.3 IPC communication functions—cont'd

Function	Description
psa_close()	The RoT Service completes the disconnection request
psa_read()	Reads a message parameter or part of a message parameter from a client input vector
psa_write()	Writes a message response to a client output vector
psa_skip()	Skips over part of a client input vector
psa_eoi()	Informs the SPM that an interrupt has been handled
psa_notify()	Sends a PSA_DOORBELL signal to a specific Secure Partition
psa_panic()	Terminate execution within the calling Secure Partition and will not return

This allows a typical service to be constructed in a similar fashion to an RTOS thread. This means that the service is constructed as a loop with an initial blocking point that waits for a signal from the SPM.

```
void psa_<service>_main(void) {
uint32_t signals; psa_msg_t msg; int r;
for (;;) {
signals = psa_wait(PSA_WAIT_ANY, PSA_BLOCK);
psa_get(PSA_service_SIGNAL, &msg);
.......................
}}
```

The first signal received must establish a connection to the service. We can also check if the service is currently active, and if this is the case, we can refuse additional connections. If the connection is established, we can then run any initializing code for the requested function and reply back to the calling agent to acknowledge the connection.

```
if (msg.type == PSA_IPC_CONNECT) {
  if (inuse) {
  r = PSA_ERROR_CONNECTION_BUSY;
  }else{
  r = PSA_SUCCESS;
  inuse = 1;

// here we setup the requested security function.
<service >_init();

}
psa_reply(msg.handle, r);
}
```

After the client has connected, the service will receive a psa_call() signal and a message that contains the calling parameters of the original API function stored in the IOVEC buffers. We can then process the message data in the requested function and reply back to the client.

```
if (signals & PSA_<service>_SIGNAL) {
    if (psa_get(PSA_<service>_SIGNAL, &msg) != PSA_SUCCESS){
        continue;
        }
    if (msg.type >= 0) {
    psa_reply(msg.handle, <service>_process(&msg));
}
```

Once the call has been processed the last transaction will be a signal to disconnect from the service:

```
if (msg.type == PSA_IPC_DISCONNECT) {
 inuse = 0;
 psa_reply(msg.handle, PSA_SUCCESS);
 }
```

Exercise: Inter Process Calling

In this exercise we will examine the Inter Process Calling functions between the nonsecure code and secure services. As a simplified example, we will use the basic test service to see how the system works. The description below presents the relevant function calls. You can then experiment with the debugger to see them in action.

In the pack installer select exercise 12.2 and press the copy button.

This is a stripped down version of the test framework with only the basic test service installed.

Batch build projects and download them into the evaluation board.

Open the file tfm_ipc_service_test.c in the secure project.

This file contains a minimal test service within the ipc_service_basic() function. The service is based around a switch statement that provides PSA_IPC_CONNECT, PSA_IPC_CALL and PSA_IPC_DISCONNECT cases.

Open ipc_ns_interface_testsuite.c in the nonsecure project.

Locate the tfm_ipc_test_1005() function.

This contains IPC calls to the basic service in the secure code.

The test case uses the raw psa functions to connect to the service. As we will see in the next chapter. These calls are placed within a wrapper function to provide an easy to use API for each service.

```
handle = psa_connect(IPC_CLIENT_TEST_BASIC_SID,
                     IPC_CLIENT_TEST_BASIC_VERSION);
```

Once connected, we can call a service function and pass the outvec structure to receive a reply from the service.

```
status = psa_call(handle, PSA_IPC_CALL, NULL, 0, outvecs, 1);
```

and then finally close the connection

```
psa_close(handle);
```

Open tfm_psa_ns_api.c

This file contains the low level dispatcher functions which are used to create and send the Non Secure requests to the partition manager, which will, in turn, route them to the required service

Set a breakpoint on the nonsecure client connect function (ipc_ns_interface_testsuite.c line 179) and follow the calling process to the secure service.

Once the nonsecure client has connected to the secure service it will be able to call functions within the service before disconnecting. Although this approach may seem overly complex, it does allow the secure services to support multiple transactions from the nonsecure client.

Secure function communications model

The Secure Function calling model uses a much lighter framework than the IPC model. When the security service is built using the Secure Function model, each security service function is accessed as a callback function by the partition manager. In this model, the secure partition does not use signals or the IPC message processing methods. On receipt of a message, the message object is forwarded to the called secure function based on the associated SID number Fig. 12.16. While this is a lower code overhead compared to the IPC model, it has the limitation that it is inherently single-threaded as only one function can be active. The SFN model still specifies an entry point function which is used as an initializing function for the partition security service.

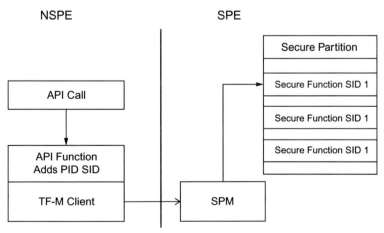

FIG. 12.16

Secure function model. The secure function model provides a single context transaction model.

No permission required.

Memory mapped IO

The secure function model also supports the use of memory mapper IO vectors. This allows the secure code to directly access and work on IOVEC buffers located in the Nonsecure client memory (Fig. 12.17). This has the advantage that data in the Nonsecure world does not need to be transferred into the secure processing environment. The data is also available to be worked on by security services in multiple partitions without the need to be moved or copied. While this approach has considerable advantages in terms of performance, it is vulnerable to the sorts of coding issues discussed in Chapter 8. In addition, the use of the MMIO buffers also reduces the isolation between different security partitions.

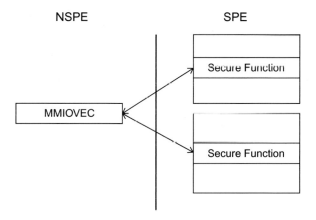

FIG. 12.17

Memory Mapped IO. The SFN model supports access to memory Mapped IO buffers located in the NSPE.

No permission required.

While signals are not used for service API calls between the NSPE and the SPE they are used for interrupt signaling and calls between partitions in the SPE.

Exercise: Secure function call

In this exercise, the secure and nonsecure projects are built to use the secure function calling method.

In the pack installer select Exercise 12.3 and press the copy button.
Build and download the code.
Run to the nonsecure main.

In main() we are making our first call to a secure service using the PSA API functions.

```
res = psa_its_set( ITS_Block,
    ITS_BlockSize,
    ITS_Blockdata,
    ITS_CreateFlags);
```

Run to this function, then use F11 to step into the function.

The PSA wrapper function calls the PSA dispatcher, as we saw in the last example.

```
status = fm_ns_interface_dispatch((veneer_fn)tfm_tfm_its_set_req_veneer,
                                  (uint32_t)in_vec,
                                  IOVEC_LEN(in_vec),
                                  (uint32_t)NULL, 0);
```

However, in the SFN model, the dispatcher references the secure service function directly using a function pointer. Data is sent and received using the IOVEC structures.

Once the message is passed to the Secure partition manager it will call the psa_its_set() function directly using the parameters stored in in_vec structure.

```
psa_status_t tfm_its_set(int32_t client_id,
                                  psa_storage_uid_t uid,
                                  size_t data_length,
                                  psa_storage_create_flags_t
                                  create_flags)
```

In the secure project open tfm_internal_trusted_storage.c and locate the tfm_its_set function() (line 128)

Set a breakpoint at the start of the function.

Step the code in the nonsecure project and observe the switch to the secure code and entry to the secure service function.

Here the function is invoked as a callback directly from the partition manager. This is a much lighter approach than the IPC method but only supports single threaded calls from the nonsecure code.

Secure partition manager

The secure partition manager discovers each of the partition services through a partition database. This is a global array of structures that describe each of the available services.

The full database record defines additional structures that hold static initialized data and updated runtime data.

```
struct tfm_spm_service_t {

/* Service database pointer */
const struct tfm_spm_service_db_t *service_db;

/* Pointer to secure part */
struct partition_t *partition;

/* Service handle list*/
struct tfm_list_node_t handle_list;
```

```
/* For list operation */
struct tfm_list_node_t list;
};
```

This file is autogenerated from a manifest written as a YAML document. A partial manifest template is shown below.

The header defines the service name and location along with the partitions priority, memory requirements, and the entry function.

```
{
    "psa_framework_version": 1.0,
    "name": "TFM_SP_IIS",
    "type": "PSA-ROT",
    "priority": "NORMAL",
    "entry_point": "tfm_its_req_mngr_init",
    "stack_size": "0x680",
    "heap_size": "0x800"
```

It then lists each of the security functions for the SFN model and the IPC model.

```
    "secure_functions": [
    {
    "sfid": "TFM_ITS_SET",
    "signal": "TFM_ITS_SET_REQ",
    "non_secure_clients": true,
    "version": 1,
    "version_policy": "STRICT"
    }
............. additional functions
    ],
    "services" : [{
    "name": "TFM_ITS_SET",
    "sid": "0x00000070",
    "non_secure_clients": true,
    "version": 1,
    "version_policy": "STRICT"
    },
.........additional services
]}
```

The manifests are added to a python script tfm_parse_manifest_list.py' which generates the database description for each secure partition. These are held in tfm_spm_db.inc and /psa_manifest/pid.h, which is used to provide a list of available partitions. A dedicated service header file is also created to provide the signal names to the service code. When the device boots the secure startup code loads this data into the SPM database.

Exercise: Secure partition manifest

The Trusted Firmware uses a build system based on python scripts that read a set of manifest files. The scripts then autogenerate header files and an SPM database file that are used to configure the partition manager and install the required secure services.

In this exercise, we will examine how the manifest build system is constructed and then take a tour of the files that it generates.

The build system is installed as part of the pack system, and the script files are stored in a tools directory within the pack file structure

Go to the C:\Keil_v5\ARM\PACK\ARM\TFM\2.1.0\tools directory.

This includes a python script file that is used to process the PSA service manifests.

Install the support packages using the requirements file using the following command

```
pip install -r requirements.txt
```

The trusted firmware test code is located in a separate file structure. We need to create a windows environment variable to point to this code.

In windows, Environment Variables add the following Environment Variable

Environment Variable	Path
TFM_TEST_PATH	C:\Keil_v5\ARM\PACK\ARM\TFM-Test\1.0.0\test

Both the TF-M test files and the TF-M files are stored as read only files. To re-generate these files we need to make both files read/write using windows explorer.

Now run the following command.

```
tfm_parse_manifest_list.py -m tfm_manifest_list.yaml -f tfm_generated_
file_list.yaml
```

This will create the secure service header files and the SPM database file.

Go back to project 12.2

Set the secure code as the active project.

Open TFM :: tfm_ipc_service_test.c

Locate and open the header file tfm_ipc_service_test.h

This is an autogenerated file that provides the IPC and SFN service information. It is installed into the SPM database by adding it to the list of services.

Open TFM::spm_ipc.c

In this file, locate and open the header tfm_service_list.inc

The service list compilers the partition manager database, which is used to route the SFN or IPC messages.

The service manifests are also used to create supporting files for the nonsecure code.

Switch to the nonsecure project.

Make sure the nonsecure project is set to use the SFN model in the RTE.

Open tfm_crypto_func_api.c.

This file provides the client dispatcher functions that allow the nonsecure API to access the secure services using the SFN model.

At the top of this file locate and Tfm_veneers.h

This is an autogenerated file which defines the calling veneers for each of the security service functions which are used by the SFN model.

Two additional header files are generated,Pid.h and Sid.h. Here Pid.h contains the ID numbers for each secure service.While SID.h contains the ID values for each of the secure services

Although you will not normally need to create of manage the TF-M manifest files it is useful to understand how the system works. Once you understand the system it is also then possible to create your own custom secure service in the application RoT.

SPE interrupt handling

Interrupts will be routed to the secure partition using the TrustZone ITNS registers and declared in the SPM database. The Trusted firmware provides two different methods of interrupt handling. An IRQ can be managed with either a First Level Interrupt Handler FLIH or a Second Level Interrupt Handler SLIH. It is important to note here that the SNF model supports both FLIH and SLIH, while the IPC model only supports SLIH.

In the SLIH model, the SPM will provide the low-level interrupt handling and then signal the relevant security service. This means that SLIH interrupt handling is dcfcrrcd until thc signal is acknowlcdgcd by a PSA_wait() function in thc scrvicc. So, if the service is busy with an NSP client, call processing of the interrupt will be delayed until the NSP call has ended and the main service loop reaches a psa_wait() function. Once an outstanding interrupt request has been serviced, it must be acknowledged to the SPM by calling psa_eoi().

Interrupt handling FLIH

In the first level interrupt handling model, a dedicated FLIH function is provided for each IRQ so that an interrupt signal from the SPM can be immediately processed with minimal latency.

The interrupt source must first be defined in the manifest with a source signal name and priority.

```
"irqs": [
  {
  "source": "TFM_TIMER0_IRQ",
  "signal": "SPM_CORE_IRQ_SIGNAL_TIMER_0_IRQ",
  "tfm_irq_priority": 64,
  }
  ],
```

To allow access we must also define the peripheral registers as an allowable memory mapped IO region and grant an access permission.

```
"mmio_regions": [
  {
  "name": "TFM_PERIPHERAL_TIMER0",
  "permission": "READ-WRITE"
  }
],
```

When the manifest is executed an autogenerated definition file tfm_peripharals_ def.h will be generated, which defines a pointer to the physical timer definition.

```
#define TFM_PERIPHERAL_TIMER0(&tfm_peripheral_timer0)
```

The physical peripheral definition is declared in Target_cfg.c, which provides the timer address range and settings for the Trusted Execution Environment.

```
struct tfm_spm_partition_platform_data_t
  tfm_peripheral_timer0 = {
  CTIMER0_BASE,
    CTIMER0_BASE + 0xFFF,
      &(AHB_SECURE_CTRL->SEC_CTRL_APB_BRIDGE[0]
.SEC_CTRL_APB_BRIDGE1_MEM_CTRL1),
      AHB_SECURE_CTRL_SEC_CTRL_APB_BRIDGE1_MEM_CTRL1_CTIMER2_RULE_
      SHIFT
};
```

During run time an interrupt raised by the peripheral will trigger the default interrupt service routine.

```
void TFM_TIMER0_IRQ_Handler(void)
{
//Partition ID
priv_irq_handler_main(TFM_IRQ_0,
//Handler function
(uint32_t)SPM_CORE_IRQ_1_SIGNAL_TIMER_0_IRQ_isr,
//IRQ Signal
SPM_CORE_IRQ_1_SIGNAL_TIMER_0_IRQ,
//IRQ Line
TFM_TIMER0_IRQ);
}
```

Where void priv_irq_handler_main() provides the necessary code to prevent any information leak by saving the CPU registers and deprioratising the interrupt from handler mode to thread mode before calling the function *SPM_CORE_IRQ_ SIGNAL_TIMER_0_IRQ*, which is our actual secure service routine.

```
void SPM_CORE_IRQ_SIGNAL_TIMER_0_IRQ_isr(void)
{
timer_ISR_Code();
}
```

The FLIH interrupt model allows us to service peripheral interrupts in much the same fashion as a standard application with the minimal overhead necessary to ensure the isolation barrier is maintained.

Interrupt handling SLIH

The second level interrupt handling model initially uses the same manifest structure as the FLIH model, but in place of a dedicated ISR function the SPM will raise a signal which must be managed by the secure partition.

The code first creates an alias for the specific timer:

```
#define CTIMER_IRQ_HANDLER CTIMER0_IRQHandler
```

This becomes the initial IRQ handler which will pass the manifest partition and signal ID as well as the IRQ interrupt line to the second level interrupt handler.

```
void TFM_TIMER0_IRQ_Handler(void) {
__disable_irq();
tfm_slih(TFM_IRQ_0, //Partition ID
SPM_CORE_IRQ_SIGNAL_TIMER_0_IRQ, // Signal
TFM_TIMER0_IRQ); // IRQ Line
__enable_irq();
}
```

Now we can de assert the IRQ line and notify the partition that an IRQ is pending:

```
void tfm_slih(uint32_t partition_id, psa_signal_t signal, uint32_t
  irq_line)
{
__disable_irq();
tfm_spm_hal_disable_irq(irq_line);
notify_with_signal(partition_id, signal);
__enable_irq();
}
```

Once the service wakes from a psa_wait() function it will process the IRQ and acknowledge the interrupt with psa_eoi().

Exercise: Secure IRQ

Some secure services may require the support of a hardware peripheral. To maintain an adequate level of real time performance the Secure services will need to enable and respond to interrupts raised by the peripheral. In this exercise we will see how a peripheral interrupt is managed by the secure services and partition manager. The test service provides an example of how to integrate a timer interrupt. This may be difficult to follow in the debugger but it is worth following through in the microvision editor to gain an overview of how secure interrupts are managed.

In the pack installer select Exercise 12.5 and press the Copy button.

In the directory

\Keil\ARM\PACK\ARM\TFMTest\1.0.0\test\test_services\ tfm_irq_test_service_1

Open the manifest file tfm_irq_test_service_1.yaml

Here the service manifest has been extended to include a test service which includes a secure peripheral interrupt. The manifest defines the service IRQ function, signal and interrupt priority.

```
"irqs": [
  {
    "source": "TFM_TIMER0_IRQ",
    "signal": "SPM_CORE_IRQ_TEST_1_SIGNAL_TIMER_0_IRQ",
    "tfm_irq_priority": 64,
  }
```

The manifest is also used to define the peripheral as a memory mapped IO region.

```
"mmio_regions": [
  {
    "name": "TFM_PERIPHERAL_TIMER0",
    "permission": "READ-WRITE"
  }
],
```

SPM database

When the TF-M is configured, the manifest will be used to create local headers and an entry into the SPM signal database.

```
Tfm_secure_irq_handlers_ipc.inc
const struct tfm_core_irq_signal_data_t tfm_core_irq_signals[] = {
#ifdef TFM_ENABLE_IRQ_TEST
  { TFM_IRQ_TEST_1, SPM_CORE_IRQ_TEST_1_SIGNAL_TIMER_0_IRQ, TFM_
  TIMER0_IRQ, 64 },
#endif /* TFM_ENABLE_IRQ_TEST */
  {0, 0, (IRQn_Type) 0, 0}
};
```

MCU interrupt

Once the IRQ has been defined within a service it can be mapped to a suitable hardware IRQ

In this case we are using one of the microcontroller hardware timers to generate a periodic interrupt

```
Tfm_peripherals_def.h
#define CTIMER_IRQ_HANDLER  CTIMER2_IRQHandler
#define TFM_TIMER0_IRQ  CTIMER2_IRQn
```

ISR routing

On entry to the secure main() function all TF-M firmware defaults to routing all the MCU interrupts to the nonsecure NVIC. A second function call is used to map any secure interrupts to the secure NVIC.

```
irq_target_state = tfm_spm_hal_set_irq_target_state()
```

The default IRQ service routine defined in the startup vector table is then used to trigger the secure service IRQ handler function.

IPC ISR service

The IPC model sends the IRQ signal (*TPM_CORE_IRQ_TEST_1_SIGNAL_TIMER_0_IRQ*) to the service partition (*TFM_IRQ_TEST_1*) *along with the IRQ line number (TFM_TIMER0_IRQ)*

```
Tfm_secure_irq_handlers.inc
TFM_TIMFR0_IRQ_Handler()
{
__disable_irq();
tfm_irq_handler(TFM_IRQ_TEST_1,
                TPM_CORE_IRQ_TEST_1_SIGNAL_TIMER_0_IRQ,
                TFM_TIMERO_IRQ);
__enable_irq();
}
```

SFN ISR service

In the SFN model the secure service function (*SPM_CORE_IRQ_TEST_1_SIGNAL_TIMER_0_IRQ_isr*) is called directly from the IRQ handler along with the ISR signal and interrupt channel number.

Use the RTE to switch the secure project to the SFN model.

```
Tfm_secure_irq_handlers.inc
void TFM_TIMERO_IRQ_Handler(void)
{
        priv_irq_handler_main(TFM_IRQ_TEST_1,
                  (uint32_t)SPM_CORE_IRQ_TEST_1_SIGNAL_
                  TIMER_0_IRQ_isr,
                  SPM_CORE_IRQ_TEST_1_SIGNAL_TIMER_0_IRQ,
                  TFM_TIMERO_IRQ);
}
```

Terminating the interrupt

In either the IPC or SFN model the final function must clear the signal by calling the end of interrupt function psa_eoi();

Open the file Tfm_irq_test_service_1.c in the secure project.

The Timer IPC service routine uses the psa_eoi() function to signal the end of the interrupt processing for each test case.

```
void SPM_CORE_IRQ_TEST_1_SIGNAL_TIMER_0_IRQ_isr(void) {
    ............................. .
    switch (current_scenario) {
    case IRQ_TEST_SCENARIO_NONE:
      psa_eoi(SPM_CORE_IRQ_TEST_1_SIGNAL_TIMER_0_IRQ);
      break;
    ................... .
}
```

As we saw in the manifest example it is possible to add you own custom secure service and if necessary, it can be configured to manage peripheral interrupts within the Secure partition.

Selecting the communication model

The Trusted Firmware is designed so that we can easily swap between communication modes with a recompile, so it is possible to test out both methods during the early stages of a project. The secure function model provides the fastest method of interrupt handling and the lowest overhead when making calls from the Nonsecure partition so it is likely to be the best choice for most applications. The main disadvantage of the Secure Function method is that it is inherently single-threaded. In contrast, the Interprocess communications model can support multiple transactions between partitions and from the Nonsecure code. If you need the highest level of security, then you should consider using the IPC model.

Secure partition runtime library

The TF-M uses the compiler toolchain run-time library to generate its final image. This is not ideal since the compiler library is unlikely to have been developed using secure coding techniques and the implementation of the library is out of our control. While a standard library will work with isolation level one, it will fail at higher isolation levels which create boundaries within the SPE. For these reasons, the Secure partition uses a dedicated "security first" library called the Secure Partition Runtime Library (SPRL) for critical library functions, which overcomes the technical limitations of a standard C library. The library is designed using a "code only" approach where no additional read-write data is introduced, is thread-safe and the library functions only access the caller stack and caller provided memory. This allows the library to operate within an MPU region that has been set to executable and read-only to support high partition isolation levels. The library is also under the control of the TF-M project and which also makes it toolchain independent. As a minimum, the SPRL provides the following functions (Table 12.4).

Table 12.4 SPRL Functions.

Function	Description
memcmp()/memcpy()/memmove()/memset()	Mandatory
Division and modulo aritmetic	Recommended
malloc()/free()/realloc()	Optional
assert()/printf()	Optional

TF-M profiles

The TF-M platform can be configured to support devices with different ranges of capabilities through three profiles. To a certain extent, it is possible to pick and mix between the two profiles at compiler time to meet your project's needs. Each of the profiles is aligned with the PSA certification levels.

The Large model provides the most security features for less resource constrained devices in order to meet complex use cases (Table 12.5).

Table 12.5 Large profile.

Feature	Description
Firmware framework	Interprocess Communication (IPC) model Isolation level 3 Software countermeasures against physical attacks (Fault Injection Hardening)
Cryptography	Support both symmetric ciphers, asymmetric ciphers and key exchange Asymmetric signing and verification AES AEAD Hash MAC
Internal trusted storage	Confidentiality Integrity Antiroll back
Protected storage	Data confidentiality Data integrity Rollback protection
Attestation	Asymmetric key algorithm based Initial Attestation
PSA bootloader	Antirollback protection Multiple image boot

The Medium profile aims to provide a secure device with a wide range of capabilities that allow it to work with most cloud platforms (Table 12.6).

Table 12.6 Medium TF-M profile.

Feature	Description
Firmware framework	Interprocess Communication (IPC) model Isolation level 2
Cryptography	symmetric ciphers and asymmetric ciphers AEAD AES HASH MAC
Internal trusted storage	Confidentiality Integrity Antiroll back
Protected storage	Confidentiality Integrity Antiroll back
Attestation	Asymmetric
PSA bootloader	Multi Image support Antirollback

For more constrained microcontrollers, which are likely to communicate with a local edge router, the following configuration is recommended (Table 12.7).

Table 12.7 Small TF-M profile.

Feature	Description
Firmware framework	Isolation level 1 Secure Function model Buffer sharing allowed Single secure context
Cryptography	Symmetrical Ciphers only Support for TLS preshared key AES HASH SHA256 only MAC as a HMAC
Internal trusted storage	No Encryption No Antiroll back Decrease Internal Transient buffer
Protected storage	Disabled by default
Attestation	Based on symmetric key algorithms
PSA bootloader	Single Image support Antirollback
Audit logging	Disabled by default

Configuration files for mbedCrypto are located in the following directory within the TF-M pack.

C:\Keil_v5\ARM\PACK\ARM\TFM\ < version >\lib\ext.\mbedcrypto\ mbedcrypto_config\.

TF-M platform

The Trusted Firmware is divided into a core library that provides the security service algorithm code and a separate set of platform files that define the memory layout, a Hardware Abstraction Layer (HAL), and a set of low-level device interface files that must be ported to a specific device.

CMSIS drivers

The TF-M uses the CMSIS Driver interface where possible. In practice, this means that the CMSIS-Flash driver is used to manage the microcontroller FLASH for the Protected Storage and Internal Trusted Storage volumes and also the non-volatile counters. During development, it is possible to enable a diagnostic USART, which is configured to use the CMSIS USART driver.

Memory layout

In addition to the TrustZone partitioning and linker files, CMSIS-Zone utility also generates a header file mem_layout.h.

As its name implies the memory layout.h file contains a set of standard defines that provides the start address and size for each of the TF-M memory regions. The mem_layout.h file is used by two additional header files flash_layout.h and region_defs.h to fully describe the memory configuration.

Isolation configuration

The TrustZone configuration files generated by the CMSIS-Zone utility (tz_config.c,tz_mpc_ppc, and tz_sau_nvic.c) are used by the initial secure partition startup code to configure the Trusted Execution Environment. TrustZone and MPU

config. The setup functions are called by the TF-M main() function via tfm_hal_
isolation.c. In addition to the CMSIS TrustZone function, a low-level driver for the
MPU is provided by Mpu_armv8m_drv.c.

Trusted firmware platform

The platform layer provides the TF-M HAL functions that have been adapted for
a specific device plus a set of files that contain dummy values for TF-M secrets. This
allows the Trusted Firmware to work without adaptation during initial development
but it must be fully tailored before it is deployed.

Architecture support

The PSA Security Model is designed so that it can be implemented to run on all
variants of the Arm Cortex-M processor family. The file arch.cdefines Arm functions
for a specific Arm architectural revision.

Attestation

Attest_hal.c defines a URL for the verification and also the service lifecycle state
and attestation profile definition.

Boot seed

The file BootSeed.c provides a 32 byte random seed for the initial attestation
token. This ensures that each token is unique for each session.

Hardware interface

The HAL provides a set of hardware interface function in the spm_hal.c and tar
get cfg files. The spm_hal.c file provides functions to manage the following features:

Isolation management functions.
Secure IRQ interrupts.
Secure fault handlers.
Secure fault exception.
**Functions to get the entry point, stack address and VTOR setting for the
Nonsecure code.**
Device reset function.
Device ID

The device_id.c file contains a function to return the implementation ID. The implementation ID is a 256-bit number in the default file. This is defined as a hardcoded array.
This must be modified to read the device ID and, if necessary, take a SHA256 hash to
generate a unique ID of suitable size. This file also provides a hardware ID, and it is
suggested to use a European Article Number (EAN) code to guarantee a unique ID for
your device. Rather than hardwire this number, it would be best to modify the function
to place the EAN code in the Internal Trusted storage so that it can be provisioned.

NV counters

Provides a set of routines to manage the monotonic NV counters by default. These
are designed to use a standard FLASH memory. However, this file can be modified to
use dedicated counters if they are provided by the hardware.

Crypto_keys

Contains getter functions for a key derived from the hardware unique key and
also the symmetric or asymmetric initial attestation key and its key ID.

Initial attestation key material.

This file contains dummy values for the symmetrical and asymmetrical Initial Attestation Keys, which are stored in regions defined by the memory template.

TF-M RoT PK

Contains the hash values of the BL2 bootloader RoT public keys, which are used to validate the Secure and Nonsecure images during boot. We will look at these more closely in the final chapter.

Entropy source

By default, the TF-M is not configured with any entropy sources. So, while the security algorithms will work during development and testing, they are not using any random numbers. Before your device can be deployed as part of a real network, the microcontroller random number generator must be added to provide a real source of entropy.

Open tfm_mbedCrypto_config.h.

Comment out the *#define MBEDTLS_NO_DEFAULT_ENTROPY_SOURCES*.

This is the default setting which provides a NULL entropy source during development.

Uncomment *#define MBEDTLS_NO_PLATFORM_ENTROPY*.

mbedCrypto and mbedTLS can be used with both the windows and Linux operating systems. These feature-rich operating systems that provide a standard cryptographically strong random number generator. The entropy.c provides interface functions to use these platform entropy sources. We must enable this define to avoid trying to use these sources.

Uncomment *#define MBEDTLS_ENTROPY_HARDWARE_ALT*.

Now we can provide a custom entropy source that is available on our microcontroller. When this define is enabled an entropy source will be defined as follows:

```
mbedtls_entropy_add_source( ctx,
                            mbedtls_hardware_poll,
                            NULL,
                            MBEDTLS_ENTROPY_MIN_HARDWARE,
                            MBEDTLS_ENTROPY_SOURCE_STRONG );
```

Once enabled we must provide the function *mbedtls_hardware_poll()*, which is used to gather random data from the microcontroller TRNGas discussed in Chapter 4.

```
int mbedtls_hardware_poll( void *data,
                           unsigned char *output,
                           size_t len,
                           size_t *olen );
```

Exercise: Entropy

In its default installation, the Trusted Firmware has a platform layer that must be adapted to the microcontroller hardware. Within this layer are a set of entropy functions that must be configured to use a true source of randomness.

Locate exercise 12.4 in the pack installer and press the copy button

Make the secure project the active project

Open TFM::tfm_mbedcrypto_config.h

This file contains the build option for the Trusted Firmware mbedCrypto library. The defines used are effectively the same as we saw in the mbedTLS_config.h file.

Locate the MBEDTLS_TEST_NULL_ENTROPY define and comment it out.

This will disable the test entropy source.

Locate and uncomment the following defines

```
#define MBEDTLS_NO_PLATFORM_ENTROPY
#define MBEDTLS_ENTROPY_HARDWARE_ALT
```

This will enable the following function in entropy.c, which adds a custom entropy source called mbedtls_hardware_poll().

```
mbedtls_entropy_add_source( ctx, mbedtls_hardware_poll, NULL,
                            MBEDTLS_ENTROPY_MIN_HARDWARE,
                            MBEDTLS_ENTROPY_SOURCE_STRONG );
```

Open the RTE and enable the TRNG driver in device::SDK_Drivers:rng

Open system Code\SystemInit.c

This file contains the SystemInitHook() function, which is called by the startup code. We can extend this function to initialise the TRNG.

In SystemInit.c add the header #include "fsl_rng.h"

Add RNG_Init(RNG); to the end of the SystemInitHook() function

Now we can add the entropy gathering function we created in chapter four but renamed as mbedtls_hardware_poll().

Add the file LPC55S69-Entropy.c located in the project directory

Batch build both projects.

Now that the test entropy source has been removed, the Trusted Firmware is ready for use within a real application.

Secure partition startup

On entry to the TF-M startup code, the following actions will be performed to setup the secure partition before jumping to the start of the Nonsecure code.

Configure the secure main stack.

As the TF-M code may be started from the BL2 bootloader, it may not be on the device reset vector.

Seal the PSP stack.

Add the stack seal magic numbers as described in the next section.

Enable the fault handlers.

Set the fault priority to the highest and enable processor fault exceptions.

Route the reset to the SPM.

Configure the SYSRESETREQUEST bit to only be active in the secure NVIC.

Initialize the debug authentication.

Device specific. This is a void function and will need to be configured for your device.

Initialize the device partition isolation.

Configure the SAU, MPC, and PPC to create the trusted execution environment.

Initialize the platform.

Device specific. This is a void function and will need to be configured to support your device.

Configure coprocessors.

Enable the FPU if present and this will configure any coprocessors that are used by the device.

Validate the boot data.

This reads the bootloader measurements and checks that the shared data magic number provided by the bootloader is correct.

Configure the Nonsecure code.

Read and set the Nonsecure initial stack value, vector table offset register. Also read the Nonsecure reset handler so we are ready to jump to the Nonsecure code.

Configure all interrupts to target the NS state except for Secure peripherals.

This ensures that any interrupt not explicitly configured as a secure interrupt is routed to the nonsecure NVIC.

Enable the secure interrupts.

Enable the secure interrupts including the Security fault exception.

Load the SPM database.

Load the SPM services "database" structure g_spm_partition_db.

Set PSP Stack Limit.

Setup the PSP stack limit register.

Prioritize Secure IRQ.

Prioritize the Secure exceptions over the Nonsecure exceptions.

Declare the SPM state.

Set SPM state state Mark the SPM as ready for operation.

Start the secure services.

In the IPC model, it is necessary to initialize and start the secure service threads executing so that they are ready to accept connections.

Start The NSP code.

Leave the secure partition and jump to the Nonsecure image reset handler and start the application.

Stack sealing

As mentioned in the introduction to this chapter, the design of the TF-M firmware assumes that an attacker has control of the Nonsecure partition and can make rogue

TFM Secure Stack Image Limit

TFM Secure Stack Image Limit − sizeof(iovevc_args_t)

TFM Secure Stack Image Base

	Memory
	Partition iovec parameters
	Stack Seal
	Partition Stack

FIG. 12.18

Stack sealing. The main and process stacks are "sealed" to protect against underflow attacks.

No permission required.

calls into the SPE and manipulate the Nonsecure CPU registers. It would be possible to create a fake FUNC RETURN from the NSPE to the SPE which would cause the SPE to POP the stack potentially causing a stack underflow. In order to prevent this style of attack the TF-M places, a pair of stack sealing number at the top of the stack (Fig. 12.18).

These numbers are checked to ensure the integrity of the stack. If an underflow occurs and the sealing number is corrupted an exception will be generated. The value used for each stack seal number is 0xFEF5EDA5, which does not conflict with the FNC_RETURN signature or the TrustZone IRQ integrity signature and since it starts with 0xF cannot be used to return to a valid instruction address.

Conclusion

In this chapter, we have installed, configured and examined how the PSA Trusted Firmware works. Once the TF-M platform is fully operational, it provides a mandatory suite of security services to the application code in the nonsecure partition. While the reference platform can be used on any Cortex-M33 microcontroller, some additional effort is required to fully port the platform layer to a specific microcontroller. Ideally, over time, fully configured platform packs will be available that provides a ready to go system that just needs to be provisioned with the device secrets.

Trusted firmware secure services

13

Introduction

In this chapter, we will examine the TF-M security services and the API calls available to the Non-Secure application code, but first we will look at the TF-M Non-Secure client, which is used to pass the API calls across the isolation boundary.

Nonsecure client

The Non-Secure code contains a client and API definitions that are used to communicate with the Secure Partition Manager. The client supports both the Secure Function (SFN) call and the Inter-Process Calling (IPC) methods. Whichever calling method is used, an API function is first used to populate a structure with the service ID and the passed parameters before making a call across the isolation boundary.

Configuration

The Non-Secure code must be configured with the TF-M client by selecting the TFM::Core option in the RTE and selecting the calling type to match the configuration of the Secure partition code.

Next, we must add the support files for each of the mandatory services that will be used by the Non-Secure code (Fig. 13.1). If you are using the Attestation service, you will also need to add the QCBOR and T_COSE libraries. The T_COSE encryption type must be set to match the configuration of the attestation service in the Secure Partition.

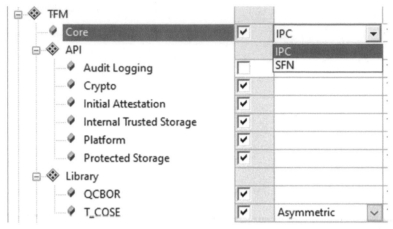

FIG. 13.1

Trusted Firmware Non-Secure client services. Add the Trusted Firmware Non-Secure client services in the RTE manager.

No permission required.

Once the files have been added to the RTE, you must include the Non-Secure interface header file in the application code.

```
#include "tfm_ns_interface.h"
```

TF-M client operation

We can access a service in the Secure partition by adding the service header file, for example, the cryptography API.

```
#include "psa/crypto.h"
```

Each of the services provide a client API function, which can be called directly from the application code.

```
psa_status_t psa_hash_setup(psa_hash_operation_t *operation,
                            psa_algorithm_t alg);
```

The operation structure is declared and initialized prior to calling the API function.

```
psa_hash_operation_t operation = PSA_HASH_OPERATION_INIT;
```

The NS API function will populate a structure with the Secure Function ID of the required service, and a handle used to manage the call:

```
struct tfm_crypto_pack_iovec iov = {
.sfn_id = TFM_CRYPTO_HASH_SETUP_SID,
.alg = alg,
.op_handle = operation->handle,
};
```

Then, place the calling parameters into input and output IO vector buffers, which are used to transfer data across the isolation boundary:

```
psa_invec in_vec[] = {
{.base = &iov, .len = sizeof(struct tfm_crypto_pack_iovec)},
};
psa_outvec out_vec[] = {
{.base = &(operation->handle), .len = sizeof(uint32_t)},
};
```

The API function then calls a dispatcher function which takes the Secure function name and ID as well as the IO vectors:

```
status = API_DISPATCH(tfm_crypto_hash_setup,
                              TFM_CRYPTO_HASH_SETUP);
```

The underlying dispatcher function is specific to the TF-M calling model selected:

```
define API_DISPATCH(sfn_name, sfn id)
tfm_ns_interface_dispatch((veneer_fn)tfm_##sfn_name##_veneer,
                              (uint32_t)in_vec,
                              ARRAY_SIZE(in_vec),
                              (uint32_t)out_vec,
                              ARRAY_SIZE(out_vec))
```

The tfm_ns_interface_dispatch() dispatcher function will use an RTOS mutex to lock the critical code.

```
os_wrapper_mutex_acquire(ns_lock_handle,
                              OS_WRAPPER_WAIT_FOREVER)
```

The API call structure is sent to the secure veneer function. The veneer function uses a supervisor call to enter the processor privileged mode prior to entering the secure partition. It will also add the partition ID and pass the API call structure to the Secure Partition Manager (SPM).

```
result = fn(arg0, arg1, arg2, arg3);
```

Once the message has been processed, the mutex is released.

```
os_wrapper_mutex_release(ns_lock_handle)
```

The IPC calling method used the same initial function to add the SID and prepare the IOVEC buffers. However, to send the API call, it then uses the connect\call\disconnect functions to communicate with the SPM and the endpoint security service.

Once the IO vectors have been populated, the NS Client will connect to the secure partition via the SPM.

```
psa_connect(FM_CRYPTO);
```

Once again the dispatcher function will be called:

```
status = API_DISPATCH(tfm_crypto_hash_setup,TFM_CRYPTO_HASH_SETUP);
```

However, this time it is aliased to support the IPC communication model and will generate a psa_call() to the secure partition.

```
#define API_DISPATCH(sfn_name, sfn_id)
psa_call(ipc_handle, PSA_IPC_CALL,
in_vec, ARRAY_SIZE(in_vec),
out_vec, ARRAY_SIZE(out_vec))
```

The call function will place the size of the IOVEC buffers in the ctrl_params structure and then call the original dispatcher function.

```
tfm_ns_interface_dispatch(
(veneer_fn)tfm_psa_call_veneer,
(uint32_t)handle,
(uint32_t)&ctrl_param,
(uint32_t)in_vec,
(uint32_t)out_vec);
```

When the transaction has finished, the connection to the secure partition is closed.

```
psa_close();
```

Security services

The Secure Partition Trusted Firmware provides the PSA mandatory security services cryptography, storage, auditing, attestation, and firmware update. Each service has an init function that is invoked on startup and does not need to be part of the application code.

Each security service provides a header file that defines an API and a return value. As part of our secure coding practice, any application code should always check the return value. The return value is of the type:

psa_status_t.

Ideally, you should get PSA_SUCCESS as a result. If the function fails, there are a wide range of error values that should be logged for future diagnostic use. The full range of error codes can be found in the header file.

psa/error.h.

After any operation with the secure services, you must also wipe any associated memory and variables in the Non-Secure code, including data stored on the stack or heap. Each security service provides an abort function which should be called if the results of a secure function are no longer required. You should also destroy any keys that are no longer in active use.

Secure storage service

The Trusted Firmware provides two storage volumes in the Secure Partition. These are Protected Storage (PS) and Internal Trusted Storage (ITS). Protected Storage is intended to provide storage for application "data at rest" and provides protection against software and hardware attack. The Internal Trusted Storage volume provides the highest level of security for device intimate data such as cryptographic keys, firmware measurements, and other device secrets.

Protected storage

The Protected Storage volume will generally be a region of the microcontroller FLASH though it could be an external volume such as serial FLASH memory. The PS storage volume can be located in either the Secure or Non-Secure partition through PSA storage functions are always located in the Secure Partition. The Protected Storage is different from the other services in that it is run as a service within the Application RoT rather than the PSA RoT. The protected storage is capable of providing confidentiality, integrity, and replay protection. However, depending on the threat model and user requirements, data may be stored without confidentiality or replay protection, while data integrity is always validated.

The protected storage volume is accessed through an API provided to the Non-Secure code by adding the header file "psa/protected_storage.h" to the application Non-Secure code. This provides the following storage API (Table 13.1):

Table 13.1 Protected storage API functions.

Function	Description
psa_ps_get	Retrieve data associated with a provided UID
psa_ps_set	Create a new or modify an existing key/value pair
psa_ps_get_info	Retrieve the metadata about the provided UID
psa_ps_remove	Remove the provided UID and its associated data from the storage
psa_ps_create	Reserves storage for the specified UID.
psa_ps_set_extended	Sets partial data into an asset based on the given identifier
psa_ps_get_support	Returns a bitmask with flags set for all the optional features supported by the implementation

When storing data, additional flags are used to control the security settings for a given data item. While confidentiality and anti-replay are optional, integrity is always applied.

In the case of public data, it is possible to disable encryption:

```
PSA_STORAGE_FLAG_NO_CONFIDENTIALITY
```

Similarly, we can also disable replay protection if required.

```
PSA_STORAGE_FLAG_NO_REPLAY_PROTECTION
```

We can also store an item as a constant so that one it has been written it cannot be updated. Such an immutable item can be created with the following flag.

```
PSA_STORAGE_FLAG_WRITE_ONCE
```

Data items are stored as key value pairs, which are referenced through a Unique Identifier (UID) using the type:

```
psa_storage_uid_tPS_Block = 0x01;
```

We can store a data item as follows:

```
psa_status_t res ;
size_t PS_BlockSize =20;
uint8_t PS_Blockdata[10] = "1234567890";
psa_storage_create_flags_t PS_CreateFlags = 0;
res = psa_ps_set( PS_Block, PS_BlockSize, PS_Blockdata,
PS_CreateFlags);
```

When data are stored, depending on the implementation, the modifying flags may be ignored. For example, you may request no confidentiality, but the storage service may be configured to always encrypt the data. We can check the actual storage state using the following API call:

```
struct psa_storage_info_t PS_block_info;
res = psa_ps_get_info(PS_Block, &PS_block_info);
```

which will return the capacity of the storage, the size of the data currently stored, and any flags that were set during creation.

If you need to create a storage item but only want to store part of the record, you must first create the item and then use the psa_ps_set_extended() function to add the data.

```
size_t PS_DataSize = 10;
size_t PS_Offset = 10;
If( psa_ps_get_support() == PSA_STORAGE_SUPPORT_SET_EXTENDED )
{
res = psa_ps_create(PS_Block, PS_BlockSize, PS_CreateFlags);
res = psa_ps_set_extended(PS_Block,PS_Offset, PS_DataSize,PS_
Blockdata );
}
```

Data items can be retrieved or partially retrieved in a similar fashion and if necessary deleted.

```
res =psa_ps_get(PS_Block, 0, PS_BlockSize, PS_Read_Blockdata,
&PS_Read_Size);
res = psa_ps_remove(PS_Block);
```

Exercise: Protected storage

This exercise uses the Protected Storage API to save and retrieve data to the protected storage volume.

Locate Exercise 13.1 in the pack installer and press the copy button.
Make the nonsecure project the active project.
Batch build both projects and start the debugger.
Open the RTE and the TFM::Secure Service branch.

The protected storage API is enabled as an encrypted volume.

In the secure project, open TFM::tfm_config.h

Protected Storage (PS)	
Flash Driver Number (Driver_FLASH#)	0
Create Flash Layout	☑
Validate Flash Metadata	☐
Rollback Protection	☐
Maximum Asset Size	2048
Maximum Number of Assets	8

FIG. 13.2

The secure code allows you to configure the protected storage volume and features.

Examine the configuration options for the protected storage volume (Fig. 13.2).

We can control the FLASH volume by selecting an appropriate CMSIS-FLASH driver. It is also possible to enable rollback protection and control the maximum item storage size and number of items that can be saved to the protected storage volume.

The "Create Flash layout" option will force the secure service to format the FLASH volume and erase all existing data.

Validate FLASH Metadata will force the secure service to check the item metadata during a read operation to ensure that it is not corrupted or subject to a malicious change.

If you change any of these options, you must also consider how any change to the size of the protected storage volume will impact the memory map defined in the original CMSIS Zone project.

Open app_main.c and step through the code.

The app-main thread uses each of the Protected Storage functions to save, retrieve and extend blocks of data into the secure FLASH volume.

Internal trusted storage

The Internal Trusted Storage is used to store a small number of high-value secrets and consequently always provides confidentiality, integrity, and replay protection. The Internal Trusted Storage is run as a service within the PSA Root of Trust, and the data will be stored in a small volume located in the internal secure FLASH memory. The API is defined by including the header file:

"psa/internal_trusted_storage.h"

and contains the following functions (Table 13.2):

Table 13.2 Internal trusted storage API functions.

Function	Description
psa_its_get	Reads a data entry
psa_its_set	Creates a data entry and saves the application data
psa_its_get_info	Returns data entry meta data (size and capacity) in the form of psa_storage_info_t
psa_its_get_remove	Deletes the data entry and frees the storage block

The Internal Trusted Storage functions operate with a similar but more limited API compared to the protected storage functions. When a data item is stored in the internal protected memory, the NO_CONFIDENTIALITY and PSA_STORAGE_FLAG_NO_REPLAY_PROTECTION have no effect, while the STORAGE_FLAG_WRITE_ONCE flag will always work.

We can now store secrets in the Internal Trusted Storage.

```
psa_status_t
psa_storage_create_flags_t ITS_CreateFlags = 0;
psa_storage_uid_t ITS_Block = 0x01;
size_t ITS_BlockSize =20;
uint8_t ITS_Blockdata[10] = "1234567890";
uint8_t ITS_Read_Blockdata[10];
size_t ITS_Read_Size = 0;

res = psa_its_set(ITS_Block,ITS_BlockSize,
                         ITS_Blockdata,
                         ITS_CreateFlags);

res =psa_its_get(ITS_Block,0,
                         10,
                         ITS_Read_Blockdata,
                         &ITS_Read_Size);

psa_its_remove(ITS_Block);
```

Exercise: Internal trusted storage

In this exercise, we will use the Internal Trusted Storage to store and retrieve a block of data.

Locate Exercise 13.2 in the pack installer and press the copy button.
Make the nonsecure project the active project.
Batch build both projects and start the debugger.
Open the RTE and the TFM::Secure Service branch.

The Internal Trusted Storage API is enabled and defaults to an encrypted volume with rollback protection.

In the secure project, open TFM::tfm_config.h

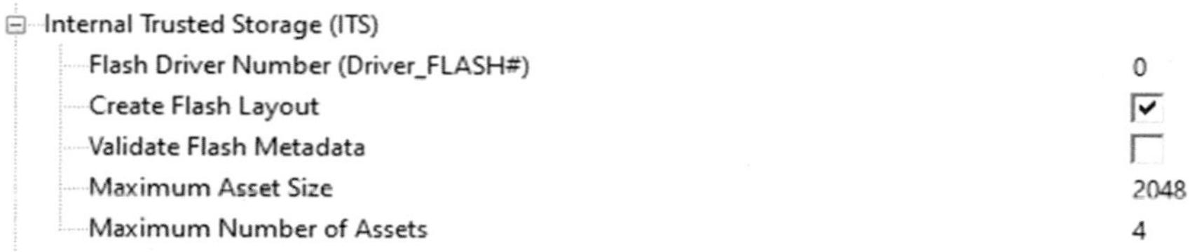

Internal Trusted Storage (ITS)	
Flash Driver Number (Driver_FLASH#)	0
Create Flash Layout	☑
Validate Flash Metadata	☐
Maximum Asset Size	2048
Maximum Number of Assets	4

FIG. 13.3

The secure code allows you to configure the ITS volume size and features.

Examine the configuration options for the Internal Trusted Storage volume (Fig. 13.3).

Like the protected storage, we can define the maximum storage size for each volume of data and the number of items that can be stored in the volume. We can also access the FLASH storage volume by selecting the configured CMSIS-FLASH driver.

In the nonsecure project, open app_main.c and examine the code.

The app-main thread uses each of the Internal Trusted Storage functions to save retrieve and extend blocks of data into the secure FLASH volume.

Run the code to store and retrieve data in the PSA internal Trusted storage.

Cryptography service

In the cryptography chapters, we saw how to use different algorithms by creating projects with a flat memory model that can be used with any Arm-based microcontroller. With the introduction of TrustZone, in order to create a secure application, we need to place the low-level cryptographic algorithms and their associated secrets in the secure partition. To solve this problem, a separate library called mbedCrypto has been created. The mbedCrypto library provides a set of abstraction layers for each group of algorithms. This allows us to place the sensitive functions in the Secure partition while the mbedTLS code responsible for the TLS protocol can remain in the Non-Secure partition (Fig. 13.4). It is likely that more functionality within mbedTLS will migrate to mbedCrypto over time.

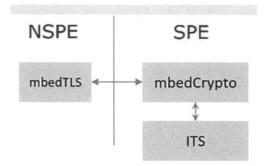

FIG. 13.4

mbedTls and mbedCrypto. mbedCrypto provides a secure cryptography service to mbedTLS.

No permission required.

The mbedCrypto library provides abstraction layers for the following groups of algorithms (Table 13.3):

Table 13.3 mbedCrypto abstraction layers.

Abstraction layer
Message DIGEST
Message authentication codes
Symmetric cipher
Key derivation
Random number
Key management
Asymmetric encryption
Hash and sign
Key agreement

Multipart operation

The symmetric cipher, MAC, and message digest abstraction layers may be used with a single block of data or are capable of working with large blocks of data or streaming data. A multipart operation consists of an initial setup function followed by a call to an update function. Once the data have been processed, the session can be terminated, and if appropriate, a final result can be calculated with a finish function.

To access the mbedCrypto functions, you must include the header *"psa/crypto.h"*.

Random

The mbedCrypto service provides a random function that are used to provide keying material and streams of random values (Table 13.4).

Table 13.4 mbedCrypto random function.

Function	Description
psa_generate_random	Return a buffer of random data

We can fill a local buffer with random data as follows.

```
uint8_t random[10] ;
status = psa_generate_random(random, sizeof(random));
```

Key management

In addition to the core cryptographic algorithms, mbedCrypto provides a rich API to create and manage encryption keys. By default, the Internal Trusted Storage is used to hold the encryption keys, but the API can be modified to target a secure key store provided by the underlying microcontroller. When using the key management API, the Non-Secure code and other security services reference the keys by identifiers, which are defined during the key generation process. When created, a key may be given a range of attributes and usage policies that allow it to be used by the Non-Secure code and/or other secure services. Each key is given a lifetime, which allows it to be persistent and be stored in the ITS until it is destroyed, or it may be a volatile key that has a lifetime limited to the current session. We can also control if a key is allowed to leave the Secure World by defining it as extractable or nonextractable. As an example, both a public and private key may be held in the Internal Trusted Storage. The private key would be labeled as nonextractable, while the public key would be defined as extractable. Once a key has been generated, an additional set of functions are used to manage its lifecycle, as shown in Table 13.5.

Table 13.5 mbedCrypto key management API.

Function	Description
psa_import_key	Import a key in binary format
psa_generate_key	Generate a key or key pair
psa_copy_key	Make a copy of a key
psa_purge_key	Remove nonessential copies of key material from memory
psa_destroy_key	Destroy a key

The capabilities of a key are stored in a structure *psa_key_attributes_t*. This structure contains a set of elements that define the following features (Table 13.6).

Table 13.6 mbedCrypto key attributes.

Attribute	Description
ID	The Key ID
Lifetime	Whether the key is persistent or volatile
Type	The key type and its algorithm
Keysize	The key size in bits
Usage flags	Allowed operations
Algorithm	The algorithms that may be used by the key
Location	If available, you can select additional storage volumes

When a key is created, we pass a unique integer value of type psa_key_id_t. This becomes the key ID that is used by the Non-Secure code to reference the key for all future operations. When a key is defined, we must also specify its usage policy as a set of flags (Table 13.7), which algorithms it can be used with and its bit size.

Table 13.7 mbedCrypto key usage flags.

Usage flag	Description
PSA_KEY_USAGE_EXPORT	Permission to export the key
PSA_KEY_USAGE_COPY	Permission to copy the key
PSA_KEY_USAGE_CACHE	Permission for the implementation to cache the key
PSA_KEY_USAGE_ENCRYPT	Permission to encrypt a message with the key
PSA_KEY_USAGE_DECRYPT	Permission to decrypt a message with the key
PSA_KEY_USAGE_SIGN_MESSAGE	Permission to sign a message with the key
PSA_KEY_USAGE_VERIFY_MESSAGE	Permission to verify a message signature with the key
PSA_KEY_USAGE_SIGN_HASH	Permission to sign a message hash with the key
PSA_KEY_USAGE_VERIFY_HASH	Permission to verify a message hash with the key
PSA_KEY_USAGE_DERIVE	Permission to derive other keys from this key

The Non-Secure code does not have access to the key and its attributes directly but can manage the key, and its attributes through a set of helper functions (Table 13.8). We again define the range of algorithms the key can be used for. Although this is already defined in key type, this second entry defines additional information necessary to use the algorithm, such as padding type.

Table 13.8 mbedCrypto attribute helper functions.

Function	Description
psa_set_key_id	Declare a key as persistent and set its key identifier
psa_get_key_id	Retrieve the key identifier from key attributes
psa_set_key_lifetime	Set the lifetime of a persistent key
psa_get_key_lifetime	Get the lifetime of a persistent key
psa_set_key_usage_flags	Declare usage flags for a key
psa_get_key_usage_flags	Retrieve the usage flags from key attributes
psa_set_key_algorithm	Declare the permitted algorithm policy for a key
psa_get_key_algorithm	Retrieve the algorithm policy from key attributes
psa_set_key_type	Declare the type of a key
psa_get_key_type	Retrieve the key type from key attributes
psa_set_key_bits	Declare the size of a key
psa_get_key_bits	Retrieve the key size from key attributes

The PSA crypto library also provides a set of high-level functions, which can be used to initialize, read, and reset the key attributes as a whole (Table 13.9). The reset function should be called after any operations on the key to wipe the Non-Secure attribute memory.

Table 13.9 mbedCrypto key attribute functions.

Function	Description
psa_key_attributes_init	Return an initial value for a key attribute object
psa_get_key_attributes	Retrieve the attributes of a key
psa_reset_key_attributes	Wipe the key attribute object to a freshly initialized state

Once a key has been created, it is stored in the Internal Trusted Storage. Within the Non-Secure code, it is then referenced by its ID. We can now use these functions to create a set of keys and store them in the ITS. First, declare and initialize the attributes object and the key ID:

```
psa_key_attributes_t attributes = PSA_KEY_ATTRIBUTES_INIT;
psa_key_id_ttest_key_id;
```

To manage our key, we can create a key ID value:

```
#define TEST_KEY_ID (psa_key_id_t) 1
```

This is stored in the attributes along with other the key parameters and policies.

```
psa_set_key_id(&attributes,TEST_KEY_ID)
psa_set_key_usage_flags(&attributes,PSA_KEY_USAGE_ENCRYPT
                        PSA_KEY_USAGE_DECRYPT );
```

```
psa_set_key_algorithm(&attributes, 0);
psa_set_key_type(&attributes, PSA_KEY_TYPE_AES);
psa_set_key_bits(&attributes, 128);
psa_set_key_lifetime(&attributes, PSA_KEY_LIFETIME_PERSISTENT);
```

Now we can store an existing key with psa_key_import() or generate a symmetrical key using a random process in the secure service.

```
status = psa_generate_key(&attributes, &test_key_id);
```

Once the key has been generated, the returned test_key_id will equal original define TEST_KEY_ID.

Once we have a set of keys, we can start to use the mbedCrypto algorithms.

Key derivation

For some algorithms, we will need to create ephemeral session keys. The mbedCrypto library provides a set of key derivation functions to manage these operations (Table 13.10).

Table 13.10 mbedCrypto key derivation functions.

Function	Description
psa_key_derivation_operation_init	Return an initial value for a key derivation operation object
psa_key_derivation_setup	Set up a key derivation operation
psa_key_derivation_get_capacity	Retrieve the current capacity of a key derivation operation
psa_key_derivation_set_capacity	Set the maximum number of bytes the derivation can return
psa_key_derivation_input_bytes	Provide an input for key derivation or key agreement
psa_key_derivation_input_key	Provide an input for key derivation in the form of a key
psa_key_derivation_key_agreement	Perform a key agreement using a shared secret as input
psa_key_derivation_output_bytes	Read some data from a key derivation operation
psa_key_derivation_output_key	Derive a key from an ongoing key derivation operation
psa_key_derivation_abort	Abort a key derivation operation
psa_raw_key_agreement	Perform a key agreement and return the raw shared secret

First create and initialize the key objects:

```
psa_key_attributes_t attributes = PSA_KEY_ATTRIBUTES_INIT;
psa_key_derivation_operation_t operation
=PSA_KEY_DERIVATION_OPERATION_INIT;
```

We must also create a salt to prevent lookup attacks:

```
const unsigned char salt[] = {0x1,0x2,0x3,0x4};
```

We can also select the underlying algorithm used for the derivation:

```
psa_algorithm_t alg = PSA_ALG_HKDF(PSA_ALG_SHA_256);
```

then define the characteristics of the required key:

```
size_t derived_bits = 128;
size_t capacity = PSA_BITS_TO_BYTES(derived_bits);
```

and then define the id's used to manage an existing and derived key:

```
psa_key_id_ttest_key_aes = 1;
psa_key_id_t derived key;
```

To derive the key, we can setup the key derivation algorithm and its bit size capacity:

```
status = psa_key_derivation_setup(&operation, alg);
status = psa_key_derivation_set_capacity(&operation, capacity);
```

Then, add the keying material:

```
status = psa_key_derivation_input_bytes(&operation,
            PSA_KEY_DERIVATION_INPUT_SALTsalt,
            sizeof(salt));

status = psa_key_derivation_input_key(&operation,
            PSA_KEY_DERIVATION_INPUT_SECRET,
            test_key aes);

status = psa_key_derivation_input_bytes(&operation,
            PSA_KEY_DERIVATION_INPUT_INFO,
            info,sizeof(info));
```

Then, define the key attributes:

```
psa_set_key_usage_flags(&attributes, PSA_KEY_USAGE_ENCRYPT);
psa_set_key_algorithm(&attributes, PSA_ALG_CTR);
psa_set_key_type(&attributes, PSA_KEY_TYPE_AES);
psa_set_key_bits(&attributes, 128);
```

Finally, derive the key:

```
status = psa_key_derivation_output_key(&attributes,&operation,
                                            &derived_key);
```

Symmetrical ciphers

The mbedCrypto service provides an abstraction layer for any symmetrical ciphers that have been enabled in the secure service (Table 13.11).

Table 13.11 mbedCrypto symmetrical cipher abstraction layer.

Function	Description
psa_cipher_encrypt	Encrypt a message using a symmetric cipher
psa_cipher_decrypt	Decrypt a message using a symmetric cipher
psa_cipher_operation_init	Return an initial value for a cipher operation object
psa_cipher_encrypt_setup	Set the key for a multipart symmetric encryption operation
psa_cipher_decrypt_setup	Set the key for a multipart symmetric decryption operation
psa_cipher_generate_iv	Generate an Initialization Vector (IV)
psa_cipher_set_iv	Set the Initialization Vector (IV)
psa_cipher_update	Encrypt or decrypt a message fragment in an active cipher operation
psa_cipher_finish	Finish encrypting or decrypting a message in a cipher operation
psa_cipher_abort	Abort a cipher operation

To use a symmetrical cipher, we can first setup the attributes objects and define the chaining method:

```
psa_status_t status;
psa_key_attributes_t attributes = PSA_KEY_ATTRIBUTES_INIT;
psa_algorithm_t alg = PSA_ALG_CBC_NO_PADDING;
uint8_t plaintext[block_size] = "Hello World";
uint8_t iv[block_size];
size_t iv_len;
uint8_t output[block_size];
size_t output_len;
psa_key_handle_t handle;
psa_cipher_operation_t operation = PSA_CIPHER_OPERATION_INIT;
```

Now we can open a test key and setup the cipher for multipart operation:

```
status = psa_cipher_encrypt_setup(&operation,test_key_aes, alg);
```

Before the first packet of plaintext, we must generate an IV:

```
status = psa_cipher_generate_iv(&operation,iv,
                                        sizeof(iv),
                                        &iv_len);
```

Then we can iterate through the data:

```
status = psa_cipher_update(&operation,plaintext,
                                    sizeof(plaintext),
                                    output,
                                    sizeof(output),
                                    &output_len);
```

Until we finish with the last packet:

```
status = psa_cipher_finish(&operation.output + output_len,
                                    sizeof(output) - output_len,
                                    &output_len);
```

Authenticated encryption with associated data

The AEAD algorithm is also provided as a set of API functions (Table 13.12).

Table 13.12 mbedCrypto AEAD abstraction layer.

Function	Description
psa_aead_encrypt	Process an authenticated encryption operation
psa_aead_decrypt	Process an authenticated decryption operation
psa_aead_operation_init	Return an initial value for an AEAD operation object
psa_aead_encrypt_setup	Set the key for a multipart authenticated encryption operation
psa_aead_decrypt_setup	Set the key for a multipart authenticated decryption operation
psa_aead_generate_nonce	Generate a random nonce for an authenticated encryption operation
psa_aead_set_nonce	Set the NONCE for an authenticated encryption or decryption operation
psa_aead_set_lengths	Declare the lengths of the message and additional data for AEAD
psa_aead_update_ad	Pass additional data to an active AEAD operation
psa_aead_update	Encrypt or decrypt a message fragment in an active AEAD operation
psa_aead_finish	Finish encrypting a message in an AEAD operation
psa_aead_verify	Finish authenticating and decrypting a message in an AEAD operation
psa_aead_abort	Abort an AEAD operation

We can use the AEAD algorithm to perform a simple encryption of a block of data. Here, we must provide the key ID, a NONCE, which must be unique for each session, the unencrypted associated data, and the input data, which will be encrypted:

```
status = psa_aead_encrypt(test_key_aead,PSA_ALG_CCM,
                                        nonce,
                                        sizeof(nonce),
                                        additional_data,
                                        sizeof(additional_data),
                                        input_data,
                                        sizeof(input_data),
                                        output_data,
                                        output_size,
                                        &output_length);
```

The same key and NONCE is used in the decryption function.

```
status = psa_aead_decrypt(test_key_aead,PSA_ALG_CCM,
                                        nonce,
                                        sizeof(nonce),
                                        additional_data,
                                        sizeof(additional_data),
                                        input_data,
                                        sizeof(input_data),
                                        output_data,
                                        output_size,
                                        &output_length);
```

We can also perform a multipart operation in a similar fashion to the symmetrical cipher above.

Message digest

The mbedCrypto library also provides an abstraction layer for the mbedTLS hashing algorithms (Table 13.13).

Table 13.13 mbedCrypto message digest abstraction layer.

Function	Description
psa_hash_compute	Calculate the hash (digest) of a message
psa_hash_compare	Calculate the hash (digest) of a message and compare it with a reference value
psa_hash_operation_init	Return an initial value for a hash operation object
psa_hash_setup	Set up a multipart hash operation
psa_hash_update	Add a message fragment to a multipart hash operation
psa_hash_finish	Finish the calculation of the hash of a message
psa_hash_verify	Finish the calculation of the hash of a message and compare it with an expected value
psa_hash_abort	Abort a hash operation
psa_hash_suspend	Halt the hash operation and extract the intermediate state of the hash computation
psa_hash_resume	Set up a multipart hash operation using the hash suspend state from a previously suspended hash operation
psa_hash_clone	Copy the state of an ongoing hash operation to a new operation object

We can perform a multipart hashing operation by first setting up the hash operation with the selected hash algorithm:

```
status = psa_hash_setup(&operation, alg);
```

Then we can apply packets of the data:

```
status = psa_hash_update(&operation, input, sizeof(input));
```

Until we reach the end of the data block when we can generate the final hash:

```
status = psa_hash_finish(&operation,actual_hash,
                                sizeof(actual_hash),
                                &actual_hash_len);
```

Or verify against an existing hash:

```
status = psa_hash_verify(&operation,expected_hash,
                                expected_hash_len);
```

Message authentication codes (MAC)

A set of MAC functions are also available. The base hashing algorithm can be selected at the start of the MAC operation (Table 13.14).

Table 13.14 mbedCrypto MAC abstraction layer.

Function	Description
psa_mac_compute	Calculate the Message Authentication Code (MAC) of a message
psa_mac_verify	Calculate the MAC of a message and compare it with a reference value
psa_mac_sign_setup	Set up a multipart MAC calculation operation
psa_mac_verify_setup	Set up a multipart MAC verification operation
psa_mac_update	Add a message fragment to a multipart MAC operation
psa_mac_sign_finish	Finish the calculation of the MAC of a message
psa_mac_verify_finish	Finish the MAC calculation and compare it with an expected value
psa_mac_abort	Abort a MAC operation

Like the hash algorithms, we can MAC a single packet of data or setup a multipart operation.

```
psa_mac_compute(test_key_mac,PSA_ALG_HMAC(PSA_ALG_SHA_256),
                        test_buffer,sizeof(test_buffer),
                        &mac,mac_size,&mac_len);

psa_mac_verify(test_key_mac,PSA_ALG_HMAC(PSA_ALG_SHA_256),
                        test_buffer,sizeof(test_buffer),
                        &mac,mac_len);
```

Asymmetric signing and encryption

The mbedCrypto library also supports a range of asymmetric algorithms for encryption\decryption and signing of data (Table 13.15). The abstraction layer supports both the RSA cryptosystem and the Diffie-Hellman key agreement algorithm. Signing can also be accomplished with RSA, DSA, or ECDSA.

Table 13.15 mbedCrypto Asymmetric Signing and Encryption abstraction layer.

Function	Description
psa_asymmetric_encrypt	Encrypt a short message with a public key
psa_asymmetric_decrypt	Decrypt a short message with a private key
psa_sign_message	Hash and sign a message with a private key
psa_verify_message	Verify the signature and hash of a message with a public key
psa_sign_hash	Sign an already-calculated hash with a private key
psa_verify_hash	Verify the signature of a hash or short message using a public key

Here we can sign a message using an already calculated hash. The key will define the algorithm though we must also specify a padding method:

```
status = psa_sign_hash (pk_handle,
                        PSA_ALG_RSA_PKCS1V15_SIGN_RAW,
                        hash,
                        sizeof(hash),
                        signature,
                        sizeof(signature),
                        &signature_length);
```

Key agreement

The Key Agreement API allows us to calculate a shared secret by combining our key with the public key from a peer (Table 13.16). We can also calculate the secret and derive a symmetric encryption key with a single API call.

Table 13.16 mbedCrypto key agreement abstraction layer.

Function	Description
psa_raw_key_agreement	Perform a key agreement and return the raw shared secret
psa_key_derivation_key_agreement	Perform a key agreement and use the shared secret as input to a key derivation

Once we exchange public keys with a peer, it is possible to calculate a shared secret.

```
psa_raw_key_agreement(PSA_ALG_ECDH,private_key,
                      &peer_key,
                      peer_key_length,
                      &output,
                      output_size,
                      &output_length);
```

Exercise: Cryptography service

The mbedCrypto Service is designed to run in the secure partition and provide essential cryptography algorithms to the nonsecure code. Mbed Crypto also provides a key storage and management API that allows secrets to be placed within the ITS where they can be referenced by the nonsecure code through ID's. Additionally, the keys may be bound to a specific service and function.

Locate Exercise 13.3 in the pack installer and press the copy button.
Make the nonsecure project the active project.
Batch build both projects and start the debugger.
Open the RTE and the TFM::Secure Service branch.

Here the nonsecure crypto service is enabled. This adds the client and the mbedCrypto.h header file.

In the secure project open TFM::tfm_config.h (Fig. 13.5).

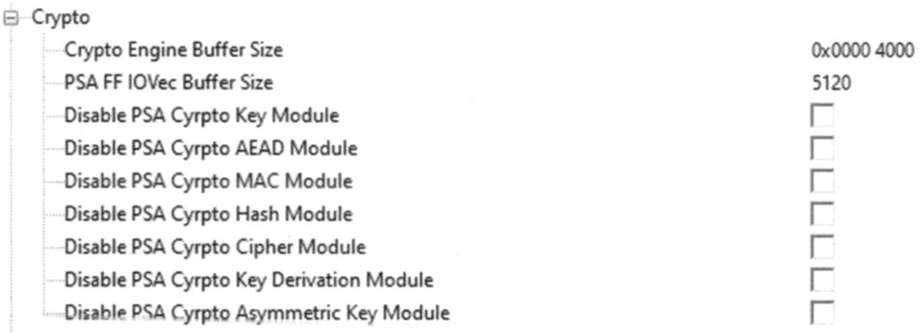

Crypto	
Crypto Engine Buffer Size	0x0000 4000
PSA FF IOVec Buffer Size	5120
Disable PSA Cyrpto Key Module	☐
Disable PSA Cyrpto AEAD Module	☐
Disable PSA Cyrpto MAC Module	☐
Disable PSA Cyrpto Hash Module	☐
Disable PSA Cyrpto Cipher Module	☐
Disable PSA Cyrpto Key Derivation Module	☐
Disable PSA Cyrpto Asymmetric Key Module	☐

FIG. 13.5

The secure code allows us to define the cryptography algorithms available to the nonsecure code.

This allows us to define how much memory is available to the cryptography service along with the size of the IO vectors used to pass data to and from the service. We can also disable unwanted algorithms.

Step through each of the following functions to exercise the cryptography algorithms provided by the mbedCrypto service. These are the same algorithms that we explored in Chapters 4–5.

```
mbedCrypto_symmetric_key_management();

mbedCrypto_asymmetric_key_management();
mbedCrypto_hash();
mbedCrypto_asymmetric_cipher();
mbedCrypto_symmetrical_cipher();
mbedCrypto_AEAD();
```

The mbedCrypto service acts as an Oracle where the nonsecure code can request a cryptography service without any knowledge of the encryption key.

Batch build both projects.
Start the debugger and step through the code to see the mbedCrypto API in action.

Attestation

An attestation service is used to create a token that is used to prove its identity and capabilities. The token can then be used to access resources on a server in place of a formal login. Existing web token schemes based on CBOR and JSON encoding are currently available to access HTTPS resources. However, these schemes do not fully meet the requirements of an IoT device. A new attestation token scheme called Entity Attestation Token (EAT) is used within the PSA Trusted firmware, which provides sufficient flexibility for IoT devices.

An Entity Attestation Token is a means for an IoT device to identify itself to a server and describe its characteristics as a set of security claims. A token is a blob of binary data, which is signed using the ECDSA algorithm to provide a guarantee of authentication. Typically a token will be encoded using CBOR and then encrypted and signed. While a token will generally carry fixed security claims, it may also be used to transfer a limited amount of process data. A good example of this would be "Number of units consumed" in a metering application.

Attestation token

A token will encode a number of security claims that are used to describe its origin and capabilities to the server. The Internet Assigned Numbers Authority maintains a registry of claims which may be used as templates for any given application. If a suitable token is not available, you can create your own security claims and token description. The format shown below is currently used (Table 13.17).

Table 13.17 Attestation token header claims.

Attestation fields	Description
Boot seed	A 32bit random value generated at startup
Challenge	A block of user supplied data
Implementation ID	The device PSA implementation ID
Instance ID	The device Instance ID
Profile ID	Profile definition, currently defaults to PSA_IOT_PROFILE_1
Security lifecycle	The device current lifecycle state
Measurement description	The Hash Algorithm used for the SW component measurements
SW components	A set of claims for each Software component

A claim is then added for each software component, typically this will be the Application Image, Trusted Firmware, and the PSA bootloader. Each claim is made up of the measurements shown in Table 13.18.

Table 13.18 Software component attestation claim.

SW component field	Description
Measurement value	Hash of the SW component
Signer ID	ID of the signing entity
SW component	Name of the SW component
SW COMPONENT version	The Version number in Major.Minor format

The token data will be encoded as a CBOR object and then will be encrypted and signed in a "CBOR Object Signing and Encryption" COSE format.

Attestation infrastructure

Alongside the token, a device will create an ECDSA key pair. The private key will be stored in the device itself, and the public key will be stored in a database that is part of an attestation server (Fig. 13.6).

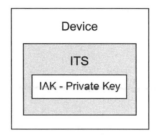

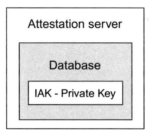

FIG. 13.6

Attestation key storage. The Initial Attestation private key is stored in the device while the public half is stored in a verification server.

No permission required.

The attestation server may be a public service or a private part of your system. When an IoT device wishes to communicate with a server, it first sends its token to the server. The server does not read the token but blindly passes the token to the attestation verification service for authentication using the instance ID to identify the matching public key. The attestation server will return a validation result to the server. If the token is found to be valid, the server can examine the claims made in the token and make a decision to grant the service request made by the IoT device (Fig. 13.7).

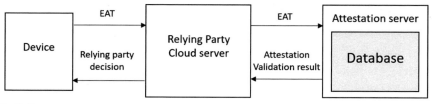

FIG. 13.7

Attestation infrastructure. An attestation token will pass through a cloud server to a verification service. The relying cloud service can then decide if it wants to onboard the device.

No permission required.

The header file "psa/initial_attestation.h" provides the Non-Secure code with an API to access the Attestation token and public key. The available functions are shown in Table 13.19.

Table 13.19 Non Secure attestation API.

Function	Description
psa_initial_attest_get_token	Retrieve the Initial Attestation Token
psa_initial_attest_get_token_size	Calculate the size of an Initial Attestation Token
tfm_Initial_attest_get_public_key	Get the attestation public key and associated elliptic curve

The Non-Secure code can create a token by providing a block of challenge data and then requesting the token.

```
#define TEST_TOKEN_SIZE (0x200)
#define TEST_CHALLENGE_OBJ_SIZE (32u)
static uint8_t token_buffer[TEST_TOKEN_SIZE];

static uint8_t challenge_buffer[TEST_CHALLENGE_OBJ_SIZE] =
{//32 bytes of user data};
uint32_t token_size;

attest_err = psa_initial_attest_get_token_size(TEST_CHALLENGE_OBJ_SIZE,
        &token_size);

attest_err = psa_initial_attest_get_token(challenge_buffer,
        TEST_CHALLENGE_OBJ_SIZE,
        token_buffer,
        &token_size);
```

Exercise: Attestation token

In this exercise, we will create and validate an Entity Attestation Token (EAT).

Locate Exercise 13.4 in the pack installer and press the copy button
Make the nonsecure project the active project
Batch build both projects and start the debugger
Open the RTE and the TFM::Secure Service branch

The Attestation API is enabled along with the crypto service

In the secure project, open TFM::tfm_config.c (Fig. 13.8).

```
⊟ Initial Attestation
    ├── Include optional Claims                                    ☐
    └── Include COSE Key-id                                        ☐
```

FIG. 13.8

The attestation options allow you to add custom 'claims' and a key ID for the verification server.

The asymmetric key ID is the SHA256 hash of the attestation public key. This is used by the attestation verification service to retrieve the correct public key from its database.

The "Include Optional Claims" selection will be removed from the final release.

In the nonsecure project open app_main().

The attestation API is used to first get the size of a token and then generate the token before storing it onto the SD card. To generate the token we provide a challenge in the form of a block of random data. The challenge is included within the token to prove it has been freshly created.

Run the code to generate the token and store it on the SD card.

We can now validate the token using a set of Python scripts provided by the TFM component pack.

Open the following directory in a DOS command window.

<PATH>\Keil_v5\ARM\PACK\ARM\TFM\<version>\tools\iat-verifier

Install the necessary Python modules with the following command.

pip3 install . (note there is a dot (.) at the end of this command)

Now validate the token using the following command.

python check_iat <path>/token.cbr

This will give a pass or fail on the Token format.

We can also check the signature with the following command.

check_iat -k <path>/key.pem <path>/token.cbr

Finally we can also decompile the token.

decompile_token -k <path>/key.pem <path>/token.cbr

Auditing

The PSA audit functions provides a way for the secure code to write audit log messages, which can be retrieved by the Non-Secure code.

Secure partition

The secure services and partition manager can write messages to the audit log using the API shown in Table 13.20.

Table 13.20 Secure audit functions.

Function	Description
psa_audit_add_record	Secure only Add a record to the audit log

Non-secure partition

The Non-Secure code can monitor and read the audit log (Table 13.21) using the header file "psa/initial_audit_api.h".

Table 13.21 Non-Secure audit functions.

Function	Description
psa_audit_retrieve_record	Retrieves a record at the specified index
psa_audit_get_info	Returns the total number and size of the records stored
psa_audit_get_record_info	Returns the size of the record at the specified index
psa_audit_delete_record	Deletes a record at the specified index

The Non-Secure code can read the audit log using this simple API.

```
psa_audit_get_info(numRecords,totalSize);
for(n=0;n<numRecords;n++){
psa_audit_get_record_info(n,&curRecSize);
psa_audit_retrieve_record(n,sizeof(auditBuf),NULL,0,&curRecSize);
printf("%s", auditBuf);
psa_audit_delete_record(n);
}
```

Exercise: Audit

The audit log is generated secure partition and accessed by the nonsecure code. The nonsecure audit client provides a minimal API to manage the audit records.

Locate Exercise 13.5 in the pack installer and press the copy button.
Make the nonsecure project the active project.
Batch build both projects and start the debugger.
Open the RTE and the TFM::Secure Service branch.
Check that the audit logging client is enabled.

In the secure project the Audit logging is enabled in the RTE and currently has no further configuration options.

The client API provides functions to get the total number of audit records their total stored size and the size of a particular record.

```
psa_audit_get_info(&num_records, &stored_size);
psa_audit_get_record_info(0, &recordSize);
```

We can then read and delete a specific record.

```
psa_audit_retrieve_record(0,          //record index
                LOCAL_BUFFER_SIZE, //buffer size
                0,                  //challenge token currently NULL
                0,                  //challenge token size
                &auditBuffer[0],   //record buffer
                &recordSize);      //record buffer size
```

Build the project and start the debugger.
Step through the code in app_main() to see the audit API in action.

Lifecycle

Finally the Non-Secure code can request the current lifecycle state using the API call shown in Table 13.22 and provided by the header "psa/lifecycle.h".

The lifecycle state is returned in bits [15:8] while bits [7:0] are reserved for future implementation defined states.

Table 13.22 Lifecycle API.

Function	Description
psa_rot_lifecycle_state	Returns the current lifecycle state of the PSA RoT

Provisioning

Once the TF-M software has been installed onto the Secure partition, it must be provisioned with all the necessary device secrets so that it fully enters into its operational lifecycle. This can be achieved during manufacture by installing a provisioning program into the NSPE. The provisioning program is used to download the necessary secrets into the SPE and the TF-M ITS storage. Table 13.23 shows the range of the TF-M device intimate data.

Table 13.23 Trusted Firmware provisioning requirements.

Secret	Type	Storage
Hardware unique key	Symmetric key	ITS or device keystore
Initial attestation key	Asymmetric private key or symmetric key	ITS or device keystore
Instance ID	Hash of initial attestation key	ITS or device keystore
Implementation ID	32Byte Platform ID	Image
Hardware ID	EAN	Image
TLS CA cert	X.509	PS or Image
TLS device cert	X.509	PS or Image
TLS device private key	Asymmetric private key	ITS or device keystore
RoT key	Asymmetric public key	ITS or device keystore
Device secure boot	X.509 public key	Device specific
Device debug	X.509 public key	Device Specific

Conclusion

In this chapter, we have seen how to communicate between the Application in the NSPE and the TF-M platform in the SPE. We have also seen the range of available services within the secure partitions and how to provision the TF-M for its operational lifetime. In the next chapter, we will look at adding the Second Stage Bootloader (BL2), which will allow us to perform essential updates over the lifetime of the device.

The PSA Secure Bootloader

Introduction

As we saw in Chapter 9, the PSA security model defines a two-stage "multisigner" boot process that bases the device security on a validated "chain of trust." The first two links in this chain are the microcontroller Secure Boot, BL1 and the PSA Secure Bootloader, BL2. The second-stage bootloader BL2 is a standard part of the TF-M firmware and is derived from an open-source project called MCUBoot. During the development process, it is normal to design the application code without the BL2 bootloader fitted. This allows us to add code to the main application and download it using the debugger without having to continually recreate signed images. Once we are happy with the main application, it is possible to add the BL2 stage. This will mean making changes to the overall memory map with the CMSIS-Zone utility. As we will see, this is a straight forward process that makes use of the underlying memory layout template discussed in Chapter 12.

Updatable bootloader

When the BL2 bootloader is enabled, it will be added to the start of the Trusted Firmware image to execute on entry to the secure world code after the BL1 code has completed. The BL2 bootloader then becomes the initial Root of Trust. During normal operation, the BL2 bootloader will validate the secure and nonsecure images before passing control to the entry point of the Secure World Trusted Firmware image. If any new firmware images are available, the BL2 bootloader will inspect the new firmware and, if appropriate, will update the current active image. The firmware update process can also be managed by a firmware update service, which is part of the Trusted Firmware. The firmware update service provides an API to the nonsecure code and is designed to work in cooperation with the BL2 bootloader.

The device memory must be divided into a slot pair called the primary and secondary slot for each managed image. Each image is designed to execute in place from its primary slot. The secondary slot is used as a download and staging area for a candidate update image. Downloading a new image into the secondary slot is done by the application where the firmware update client provides the low-level FLASH management functions. When a candidate image is placed in the secondary slot, a device reset or a firmware update install function in the application code can trigger the bootloader to inspect the new image. If appropriate it will update the primary slot and restart the processor.

The bootloader is designed to manage images that have been built to "execute in place" from absolute addresses rather than position-independent code. The BL2 bootloader provides a number of strategies for updating the primary image. Depending on which strategy is selected, an additional swap slot may be required, as shown in Fig. 14.1.

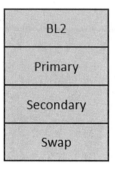

FIG. 14.1

Single image bootloader memory map. Bootloader memory map to support a single update image.

No permission required.

If the BL2 bootloader is configured to use a single primary and secondary slot, the secure and nonsecure images must occupy a contiguous memory space so that they can be concatenated together and updated as a single monolithic entity. This means that we cannot update either partition independently, which is far from ideal in a practical system.

Fortunately, the BL2 bootloader can also manage multiple images with additional primary and secondary slots. This allows us to provide separate primary and secondary slots for both the secure and nonsecure images and update them independently. When BL2 is configured to support multiple images, the bootloader can also check version dependencies to ensure that both images are mutually compatible before any update is performed. This gives us a lot more flexibility in both the memory layout and image update management (Fig. 14.2).

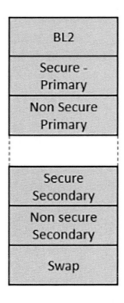

FIG. 14.2

Dual image bootloader memory map. The bootloader can also support multiple images with individual primary and secondary slots.

No permission required.

Upgrade strategies

BL2 provides four update strategies, one of which must be selected at design time.

Update strategies.

Update strategy	Description
Overwrite	Copy image in the secondary slot into the primary slot
Swap	Preserve the current primary image using the swap slot
Xip	Execute directly from the primary or secondary slot
RAM	Copy image to RAM and execute

Overwrite

The simplest form of update is to validate the secondary slot's image and then copy it directly into the primary slot by overwriting the existing image. This update strategy precludes any form of rollback and should only be used where the device does not have enough FLASH memory to provide the swap region.

Swap

BL2 provides a swap strategy that preserves the current primary image by copying it to the swap region during an update process. When stored in the swap slot, any image that is marked as encrypted in the metadata will automatically be re-encrypted during the copy process. This ensures that the code is never exposed to an attacker outside of the primary slot. Once the current image has been stored in the swap slot, the new update will be copied into the primary slot and if necessary, decrypted. When the update is first placed in the primary slot, it can be marked as a test swap. After reset, the new image will start execution, and if this is successful, the application will mark itself as OK. If this does not happen when the device is next rebooted, the BL2 bootloader will automatically perform a rollback to the original saved image and delete the failed update image.

Execute in place

It is also possible to select a "no-swap" update method. Here, each stored image (primary and secondary) is compiled to execute from their respective slots. When the bootloader starts, it will inspect the version number of each image and then start execution of the image with the highest version number. This means that the update client must be capable of downloading a new image into the slot, which is currently holding the oldest version. It would be tempting to build the code as position independent execution rather than absolute addresses. However, you may find that some library code is built to execute from absolute addresses. The upshot of this is that you would have to ensure that a new image is built to execute from the available slot.

RAM

In the case where the microcontroller is designed to execute code from RAM rather than FLASH, it is possible for the BL2 bootloader to copy the contents of the secondary slot into the execution RAM. This is suitable for custom SoC or asymmetrical devices, which may have a mixture of processor types such as Cortex-A and Cortex-M.

Firmware update service

The Trusted Firmware provides a firmware update service FWU, which provides an API to the nonsecure application software. This allows the application to manage updates in cooperation with the BL2 bootloader. The firmware update service provides functions to manage, store, and update a candidate image in a secondary slot staging area. However, the application will be responsible for providing the mechanism to download the update image either by a communications channel or other local interface. This process will vary between different cloud provides, but the firmware update service provides a standard low-level foundation that can be used by any vendor.

The firmware update client manages the update process through the stages shown in Fig. 14.3.

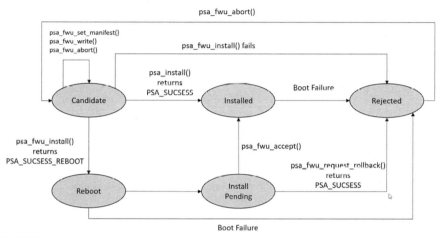

FIG. 14.3

Firmware update process. The firmware client manages the update process through a series of states.

No permission required.

The update image must be stored using the psa_fwu_write() function. This supports downloading and storing the image as multipart blocks so that it can work with constrained devices. Once the full image has been downloaded to the staging area, we can start the update process with psa_fwu_install(). In the case of executable images, this will return with PSA_SUCSESS_REBOOT, and we can restart the device with psa_fwu_request_reboot(). When the device restarts, it will enter the BL2 bootloader, which will validate the candidate image and perform the necessary update. If this is successful, the device will boot the new image, which, if we are using the swap strategy, must use psa_fwu_accept() to mark itself valid. If the device fails to boot or mark itself valid the update will be rejected and rolled back to the original. If the update is not an executable image but some form of custom ancillary data, the psa_fwu_install() function will update it directly and return PSA_SUCSESS.

The nonsecure API functions are shown in Table 14.1.

Table 14.1 Firmware update API.

Function	Description
psa_fwu_set_manifest()	Stores a manifest object and associates it with a particular image ID
psa_fwu_query()	Returns information for an image of a particular image ID
psa_fwu_write()	Writes an image to its staging area
psa_fwu_install()	Starts the installation of an image
psa_fwu_abort()	Aborts an ongoing installation and erases the staging area of the image
psa_fwu_request_reboot	Requests the platform to reboot
psa_fwu_request_rollback	Requests the platform to roll back the rmware belonging to the caller and any other image that is dependent on that firmware. This is only used when the caller detects a fatal error after an update
psa_fwu_accept()	Indicates to the bootloader that the upgrade was successful
psa_fwu_get_image_id_iterator	Gets an iterator for use with psa_fwu_get_image_id
psa_fwu_get_image_id_next	Advances an initialized iterator object
psa_fwu_get_image_id_valid	Determines whether an iterator object is valid or not
psa_fwu_get_image_id	Returns the image ID

While the update client is designed to work with the BL2 bootloader and its metadata the API provides a psa_fwu_set_manifest() function that allows other metadata formats to be stored alongside the associated image, this is intended to support other third-party bootloaders.

The update candidate image is stored in the staging slot using the psa_fwu_write() function. Once the image is ready, we can call the install function. This has several return values depending on the image type.

```
install_multiple_images(void *image,
                        size_t image_size,
                        psa_image_id_tid))
{
        psa_status_t rc;
        psa_image_id_t needed_image;
        psa_image_version_t needed_version;
//------------------
/* the code here downloads the update image in chunks /
/* and stores the image with psa_fwu_write(); */
//------------------
        rc = psa_fwu_install(id,
                             &needed_image,
                             &needed_version);
```

If the image has a version dependency, we can recursively call the install_multiple_images() function to download the required image. When all the images have been downloaded, it will return with PSA_SUCCESS_REBOOT. After a reboot, BL2 will update all of the new images. The dependency information is stored in the image metadata when it is signed by the BL2 bootloader scripts. The needed_image and needed_version parameters return the dependency information.

```
if (rc == PSA_SUCCESS_DEPENDENCY_NEEDED) {
    int new_image_size = 0;
    void *new_image = retrieve_image_from_wherever(&needed_image,
    &needed_version, &new_image_size);
//Make a recursive call to download and store the next required
//image

install_multiple images(new_image, new_image_size, &needed_image);

}
```

Once the final image is present, the install function will request a reboot and the BL2 bootloader will update all the available images.

```
if (rc == PSA_SUCCESS_REBOOT) {
    psa_fwu_request_reboot();
}
```

Where the install function is able to fully manage the update without a reboot, a PSA_SUCSESS will be returned.

```
else if (rc == PSA_SUCCESS) {
/* other success */ }
else {
/* handle failures /*
 }
```

Image encapsulation

Before a new image can be downloaded into the secondary slot, it must be extended with supporting BL2 metadata. The BL2 metadata is added using a python script called imgtool that postprocesses the update image binary or hex file to provide an encapsulated update image again in either binary or hex format. The imgtool script can be integrated into the build process to automatically (and painlessly) provide a ready to go update image.

The imgtool script adds a header and image metadata, which contains the necessary upgrade configuration information for the bootloader. An additional image trailer region located at the end of the image slot acts as a workspace used to record the progress of an image update. This allows the bootloader to resume an update in the event of a power loss or other unexpected interruption. Finally, a signature is calculated so that the image and metadata can be checked for integrity and authenticity. In addition to image signing, the update image may be stored in an encrypted format while it is held in its secondary or swap slots (see Fig. 14.4). The image header metadata and image trailer are stored in both the primary and secondary slots, so the start of the image will be offset from the start of the slot by the header and any additional padding. The total header size is controlled by a switch in imgtool.

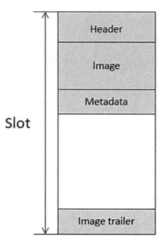

FIG. 14.4

Image with BL2 metadata. The image is encapsulated with a header, metadata, and an image trailer.

No permission required.

The image header is used to provide some basic information about the execution image, such as its size, load address, and version information. This is stored in a structure as shown below and is appended to the start of the image.

```
struct image_header {
uint32_t ih_magic;
u;int32_t load_addr
uint16_t ih_hdr_size;/* Size of image header (bytes). */
uint16_t ih_protect_tlv_size;/* Size of protected TLV area (bytes). */
uint32_t ih_img_size;/* Does not include header. */
uint32_t ih_flags;/* IMAGE_F_[...]. */
struct image_version ih_ver;uint32_t _pad1;
};
```

Further image metadata is stored at the end of the image as a set of records in a custom "Type Length Value," TLV, encoding format. This allows the imgtool to add a collection of configuration settings where each element is preceded by its TLV tag. This allows the BL2 bootloader to parse the configuration metadata stored in the protected TLV area (Fig. 14.5) in a similar fashion to a JSON record but without the overhead of storing everything as ASCII values.

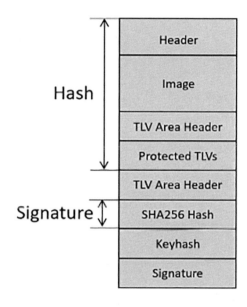

FIG. 14.5

The image with header and BL2 metadata. The image configuration data are stored as TLV tags and are signed to guarantee integrity and authentication.

No permission required.

The metadata includes two hash values. The first hash is used to protect the integrity of the image by taking an SHA-256 hash from the start of the header to the end of the protected TLV records. This hash is stored within the metadata, and it is also used as the basis of a signature that is placed at the end of the metadata. The second message digest is a hash of the public key of the key pair used to generate the signature. We will look at BL2 key management later in this chapter.

The image trailer is located at the end of the image slot and acts as a workspace that records the update progress, swap status, and image status (Fig. 14.6).

The swap status region provides a set of three records for each flash sector in the current slot. These records are used to monitor the progress of an image update through the erase, program, and validate cycle. The minimum size for each swap

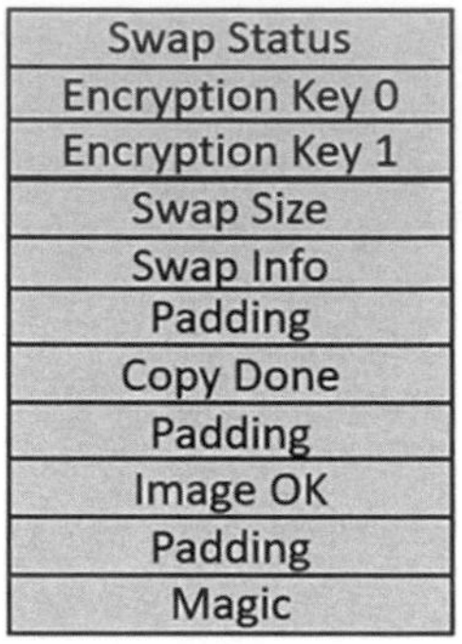

Swap Status
Encryption Key 0
Encryption Key 1
Swap Size
Swap Info
Padding
Copy Done
Padding
Image OK
Padding
Magic

FIG. 14.6

The image trailer structure. The image trailer is located at the end of the slot and provides a workspace for the BL2 bootloader.

No permission required.

record is a single byte. In practice, each record will be the minimum write size of the microcontroller FLASH memory. If the update image has been encrypted by the imgtool, the symmetrical cipher keys for both images will be wrapped by a further asymmetrical key pair and stored in the image trailer. We will look at this later in the chapter. The image trailer also contains three fields Swap info, copy done and Image_Ok. The BL2 bootloader uses these fields in both the primary and secondary slots to decide if it should start the primary image executing, perform an update or a firmware rollback. In the case of multiple images, we can define version dependencies between each image.

Image signing

The image signing process is managed by a python script called imgtool.py. The script can be used to generate the signing keys and then sign and, if required, encrypt the candidate image. The image files can be processed in either a hex or binary format. In the following examples, for simplicity, we will download the update files as HEX files using the debugger.

Security counter

The imgtool adds the security counter value as a tag in the TLV protected area in addition to the firmware image version number. The BL2 bootloader stores the current value of the security counter in a monotonic counter and will not install any update with a lower value security counter. The security counter is used to prevent a rollback to an earlier version, but it does not need to be incremented with each new image. Updates with a security counter value equal to the value stored in the microcontroller will be installed. This is intended to give some flexibility to downgrade to a version with the same security counter value.

Bootloader signing keys

The BL2 bootloader uses an asymmetrical key pair to prove the integrity and authenticity of the images that are located in both the primary and secondary slots. The private key is used to sign the image, while the public key must be available to the bootloader firmware. The BL2 bootloader has two methods of storing the public key. The first method is to store the key in the BL2 image and place a hash of the key in the metadata of the update image. The bootloader will then check that the stored key matches the hash in the image before it proceeds with the image validation. The second approach is to reverse the process: a hash of the public key is stored within the bootloader, and the full public key is stored in the image metadata. Either way, we are not concerned with the secrecy of the public key, just that it is validated by the B1 secure boot to establish a Root of Trust. In the following examples, we will look at using both methods.

Exercise: BL2 first project

In this project, we are going to build and download images in a project configured with the BL2 bootloader. In this project, we will also go through the mechanics of building and signing the application and update images to match the project memory map. We will then check the operation of the BL2 bootloader by going through a cycle of updating the secure and nonsecure application images.

First, install Python 3 from the link below and add it to the windows path. The link below is to the current version, and this may be superseded, so please install the latest version.

https://www.python.org/download/releases/3.0/.

Now install the Image Tool supporting packages using the Python package installer (Table 14.2), which can be invoked using the command line "python pip install <pakagename>."

Table 14.2 Required Python packages.

Package	Note
Cryptography	Minimum version 2.6
CBOR	Minimum version 1.0.0
intelHex	Minimum 2.3.0
Click	Minimum 8.0.0

We will also use a binary to hex converter called srec_cat.exe. This is a useful utility that can be used to concatenate and convert binary files to a hex format along with many other operations. The download page is given below:

https://sourceforge.net/projects/srecord/files/srecord-win32/.

A manual page is given below:

http://srecord.sourceforge.net/man/man1/srec_cat.html.

Open the pack installer and select project 14.1 and press the Copy button.

The project is a multiproject workspace and contains a total of four subprojects. The project includes the imgtool utility in the scripts directory. This is to ensure that it matches the instructions in this example. Once you are familiar with its operation, you check for later versions, which should be used with a real project.

The first three projects are the active executables: the BL2 bootloader plus projects for the secure and nonsecure images. The final project is a programmer project, which is used to load updated images into the secure and nonsecure secondary slots (Fig. 14.7).

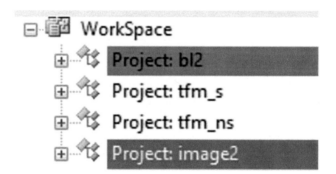

FIG. 14.7

Project workspace. The project workspace has four images, BL2, the secure and nonsecure partitions, and an update image.

No permission required.

Select the tfm_s project and open its project options.
Select the user tab (Fig. 14.8).

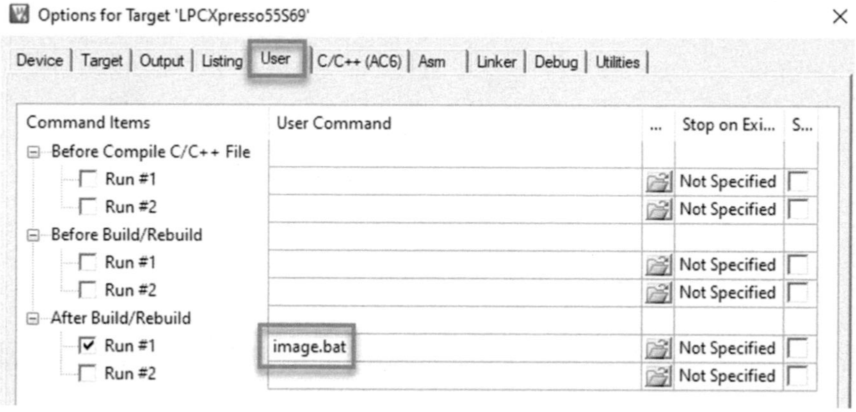

FIG. 14.8

Image postprocessing. At the end of a build process, the user tab can invoke a custom batch file for postprocessing.

No permission required.

The build process has been extended to run the image batch file at the end of a build process in the "options for target\User" menu.

The image batch file contains the following commands (Table 14.3).

Table 14.3 imgtool options.

Command	Description
imgtool sign	Invoke imgtool to perform a signing operation
-k root-rsa-3072_1.pem	Use the RSA public/private keypair
--public-key-format full	Embed the public key in the image metadata. Alternatively, you can store the key in the MCU hardware and embed its hash
--align 1 --pad --pad-header	Header padding
--boot-record NSPE	Generate boot measurements
-H 0x400	Header size
-S 0x18000	Slot size
-s auto	Security counter
-v 1.0.0	Version
-d "(1,0.0.0+0)"	Dependencies
--overwrite-only	Update strategy
Objects\tfm_ns.hex Objects\tfm_ns_signed.hex	Input and output Hex files

The Python script processes the project HEX file to calculate its signature and add the BL2 metadata. The -H option sets the size of the metadata header to 1 KB to match the settings in the linker file. Since the metadata will be copied into the primary slot along with the image, this means that the vector table is offset by 0x400 from the start of the primary slot.

Build the projects using the batch build option.

This will generate HEX files which contain the program image plus the BL2 metadata.

For the code to work correctly with the bootloader, we must download the HEX files rather than the unprocessed linker.axf file that is normally used by the debugger.

This can be done by adding a script file to the FLASH programming utilities dialog to customize the standard download process (Fig. 14.9).

FIG. 14.9

Download script. A custom script can be added to download the HEX files in place of the standard AXF linker file.

No permission required.

Select the bootloader project.
Open the options for Target menu and select the Utilities tab.

In the utilities tab, the flash.ini file contains a script command that is used to load the processed HEX file. We will again use the INCREMENTAL keyword to load the symbol set for each application so we can debug seamlessly between all the active images.

```
LOAD ".\Objects\tfm_ns.hex" INCREMENTAL
LOAD ".\Objects\tfm_s.hex" INCREMENTAL
LOAD ".\Objects\bootloader.hex" INCREMENTAL
```

The update project has a similar script that is used to preprocess and download the update images into the secondary slots.

Select Download/Erase to completely erase the FLASH.
Select the bootloader project.
Start the debugger.

This will run the script and download the three project files.

Open a terminal window and set the serial parameters to 115200 8/n/1.
Run the code.

The bootloader will output informational messages.

As the secondary slots are empty, the bootloader will validate the primary images and then pass execution to the secure code.

Exit the debugger.
Select the update project.
Select download/FLASH.

This will download updated versions of the secure and nonsecure projects to the secondary slots. These projects are identical except that the startup message has been modified to show the image has been upgraded.

The preprocessing file has been changed to update the version number and optionally you can increase the security counter value.

```
imgtool sign -k root-rsa-3072.pem --public-key-format full --align
1 --pad --pad-header --boot-record SPF -H 0x400 -S 0x28000 -s
auto -v 1.2.1 -d "(0,0.0.0+0)" --overwrite-onlyObjects\tfm_s.hex
Objects\tfm_s_signed.bin
```

Now the serc_cat utility is used to offset the start address to place the update images in the secondary slots.

```
srec_cat Objects\tfm_s_signed.bin -Binary -offset 0x60000 -o
Objects/tfm_s_signed_update.hex -Intel
```

Select the bootloader project and restart the debugger.
Run the code.

The BL2 bootloader will now detect the updated versions in the secondary slots and perform an overwrite upgrade to the primary slots. Once it has finished, it will again pass control to the entry point of the secure code, and the application will run as before but with updated firmware that displays the modified startup messages.

BL2 configuration

When the BL2 bootloader is added to the Trusted Firmware, it is located in the Secure Partition. Therefore, we need to adjust the project memory map to accommodate the bootloader image and divide the FLASH memory primary and secondary slots for the secure and nonsecure images.

Go back to project 14.1.

Alongside the Microvision projects there is a separate directory containing a CMSIS-Zone project.

Start the CMSIS-Zone utility.
Import the project from the zone directory.
Open the main zone file (Fig. 14.10).

Name	Permis...	Size	Start	End	bl2	tfm	Info
∨ ▦ Memory							
∨ ⦿ FLASH	rx	646656 B	0x00000000	0x0009DDFF	☑	☐	Flash
⦿ IMAGE_1_NS	rx,n	64 KB	0x00030000	0x0003FFFF	☑	☑	Non-secure Image Primary slot
⦿ IMAGE_2_NS	rx,n	64 KB	0x00060000	0x0006FFFF	☑	☐	Non-secure Image Secondary slot
∨ ⦿ FLASH_S	rx,c	646656 B	0x10000000	0x1009DDFF	☑	☐	Flash (Secure)
⦿ IMAGE_BL2	rx,s	64 KB	0x10000000	0x1000FFFF	☑	☐	Bootloader Image
⦿ IMAGE_1_S	rx,c	128 KB	0x10010000	0x1002FFFF	☑	☑	Secure Image Primary slot
⦿ IMAGE_2_S	rx,c	128 KB	0x10040000	0x1005FFFF	☑	☐	Secure Image Secondary slot
⦿ SCRATCH	rx,c	128 KB	0x10070000	0x1008FFFF	☑	☐	Scratch area for Bootloader
⦿ SST	rx,s	16 KB	0x10090000	0x10093FFF	☐	☑	Secure Storage area
⦿ ITS	rx,s	8 KB	0x10094000	0x10095FFF	☐	☑	Internal Trusted Storage Area
⦿ NV_COUNTERS	rx,s	512 B	0x10096000	0x100961FF	☐	☑	Non-volatile Counters
⦿ FLASH_FFR	rx	8 KB	0x0009DE00	0x0009FDFF	☐	☑	Flash FFR
⦿ FLASH_FFR_S	rx,c	8 KB	0x1009DE00	0x1009FDFF	☐	☑	Flash FFR (Secure)
⦿ ROM	rx	128 KB	0x03000000	0x0301FFFF	☐	☑	Boot ROM
⦿ ROM_S	rx,s	128 KB	0x13000000	0x1301FFFF	☐	☑	Boot ROM (Secure)
⦿ SRAMX	rwx	32 KB	0x04000000	0x04007FFF	☐	☑	SRAMX
⦿ SRAMX_S	rwx,c	32 KB	0x14000000	0x14007FFF	☐	☑	SRAMX (Secure)
⦿ SRAM	rw	272 KB	0x20000000	0x20043FFF	☐	☑	SRAM Banks 0-4
⦿ SRAM_S	rw,s	272 KB	0x30000000	0x30043FFF	☐	☑	SRAM Banks 0-4 (Secure)
⦿ USB_SRAM	rw	16 KB	0x40100000	0x40103FFF	☐	☑	USB SRAM
⦿ USB_SRAM_S	rw,s	16 KB	0x50100000	0x50103FFF	☐	☑	USB SRAM (Secure)

FIG. 14.10

CMSIS-Zone project. The bootloader memory map is added to the Zone project.

No permission required.

This segments the memory into regions for the bootloader, the application primary and secondary slots, the swap region, and the shared memory region.

Open the nonsecure zone map.

The secure and nonsecure FLASH regions are further subdivided to allocate FLASH memory for the bootloader metadata. Here, the BL2 header is allocated 1 KB, making the start address of the nonsecure code 0x30400. The start address of the secure application is offset in a similar fashion (Fig. 14.11).

Name	Permis...	Size	Physical	cm33_core0	Info
▧ LPC55S69					Cortex-M33, 320kB on-chip SRAM, 6
∨ ▦ Memory					
⦿ HEADER_NS	rx,n	1 KB	0x00030000	0x00030000	Non-secure Image Header for Bootlo
⦿ CODE_NS	rx,n	62 KB	0x00030400	0x00030400	Non-secure Application CODE sectio
⦿ TRAILER_NS	rx,n	1 KB	0x0003FC00	0x0003FC00	Non-secure Image Trailer for Bootloa
⦿ FLASH_FFR	rx	8 KB	0x0009DE00	0x0009DE00	Flash FFR
⦿ ROM	rx	128 KB	0x03000000	0x03000000	Boot ROM
⦿ SRAMX	rwx	32 KB	0x04000000	0x04000000	SRAMX
> ⦿ DATA_NS	rw,n	144 KB	0x20020000	0x20020000	Non-secure Application DATA sectio
⦿ USB_SRAM	rw	16 KB	0x40100000	0x40100000	USB SRAM

FIG. 14.11

Nonsecure memory map. Layout of the nonsecure partition when the bootloader is added.

No permission required.

Open the bootloader zone memory map.

This places the bootloader code at the start of the secure FLASH region so that it will start execution immediately after the ROM secure boot code. A region called DATA_BOOT is also created at the start of the secure memory to act as the shared memory between the bootloader and the secure partition code. This occupies the first 1 KB of the secure RAM. This area is also allocated to the secure main stack space, so information shared between the bootloader and the secure code will be available as the secure code starts (Fig. 14.12).

∨ 🖿 Memory					
⬦ FLASH	rx	646656 B	0x00000000	0x00000000	Flash
⬦ FLASH_S	rx,c	646656 B	0x00000000	0x10000000	Flash (Secure)
∨ ⬦ IMAGE_BL2	rx,s	64 KB	0x00000000	0x10000000	Bootloader Image
⬦ CODE_BL2	rx,s	64 KB	0x00000000	0x10000000	Bootloader CODE section
⬦ IMAGE_1_S	rx,c	128 KB	0x00010000	0x10010000	Secure Image Primary slot
⬦ IMAGE_1_NS	rx,n	64 KB	0x00030000	0x00030000	Non-secure Image Primary slot
⬦ IMAGE_2_S	rx,c	128 KB	0x00040000	0x10040000	Secure Image Secondary slot
⬦ IMAGE_2_NS	rx,n	64 KB	0x00060000	0x00060000	Non-secure Image Secondary slot
⬦ SCRATCH	rx,s	128 KB	0x00070000	0x10070000	Scratch area for Bootloader
⬦ NV_COUNTERS	rx,s	512 B	0x00096000	0x10096000	Non-volatile Counters
∨ ⬦ SRAM_S	rw,s	272 KB	0x20000000	0x30000000	SRAM Banks 0-4 (Secure)
⬦ DATA_BOOT	rw,s	1 KB	0x20000000	0x30000000	Boot shared DATA section
⬦ DATA_BL2	rw,s	117 KB	0x20000400	0x30000400	Bootloader DATA section
⬦ HEAP_BL2	rw,s	4 KB	0x2001D800	0x3001D800	Bootloader HEAP section
⬦ STACK_BL2	rw,s	6 KB	0x2001F800	0x3001F800	Bootloader STACK section

FIG. 14.12

Project memory layout. The full project layout with bootloader, secure and nonsecure images, and staging area.

No permission required.

The zone definitions are used to produce the linker memory maps and the memory description files that incorporate the BL2 memory layout.

Select the bootloader project.
Open the RTE Select the TF-M::Bootloader option (Fig. 14.13).

FIG. 14.13

Adding the BL2 code to project. The BL2 code can be added to a project using the RTE Manager.

No permission required.

When the bootloader is added, we need a range of subcomponents. These include the platform support files that are used to access the microcontroller hardware. The mbedCrypto security service is also added.

Press the Resolve button to add the necessary platform files and mbedCrypto (Fig. 14.14).

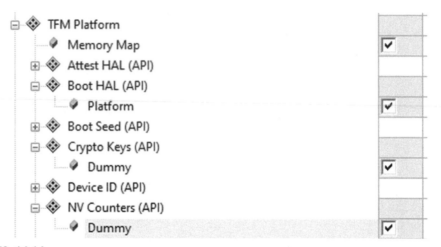

FIG. 14.14

Additional components used by the bootloader. The bootloader requires access to a range of TF-M components.

No permission required.

The BL2 bootloader is added to the workspace as a new project. When selected within the RTE, it is added as a full executable with its own main() function, and the user code provides a system_init() function to configure the device clocks. The Arm fork of the MCU Boot project is designed to access the hardware through standard CMSIS drivers, so in addition, we need to add drivers for the FLASH memory and a USART. Depending on the support provided by the Silicon Vendor, these may exist as part of the CMSIS device family pack. If they are not available, templates are provided so that you can develop your own (Fig. 14.15).

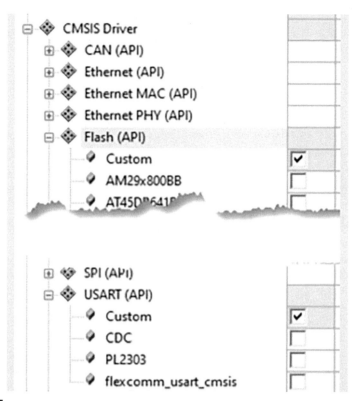

FIG. 14.15

CMSIS drivers. The bootloader requires a CMSIS FLASH driver and also a USART driver during development.

The CMSIS USART driver provides a channel for the bootloader diagnostics and can be disabled for production code in the bootloader configuration file.

Open bl2_config.h

This is a templated file that contains the configuration options for the bootloader. Here, we can select the update strategy and signature type and the number of supported images. The current project is configured for separate secure and nonsecure images. Currently, the RAM and No_Swap update strategies only support a single image. If you need to use either of these options, the secure and nonsecure partitions must be arranged as one contiguous memory block so they can be managed as one image. The final option, "Hardware Key," allows us to define how the public key is managed within the BL2 bootloader (Fig. 14.16).

```
☐ MCUBoot Configuration
    Upgrade Strategy                    Overwrite Only
    Signature Type                      RSA-3072
    Number of Images                    2
    Hardware Key                        ☑
    Logging Level                       Info
```

FIG. 14.16

Bootloader configuration wizard. bl2_config.h provides a configuration wizard for the update strategy and key selection.

No permission required.

Updating the bootloader keys

The BL2 bootloader uses an RSA or EC-DSA key pair to validate the active and stored images. The default version of the BL2 bootloader uses a set of demo keys that must be replaced with production keys before the code is used in a real-world system. The BL2 bootloader supports the use of multiple key pairs, so it is possible for each image to be signed by a dedicated key. The private keys are used to sign the images before they are downloaded by the update client. The public keys must be stored in the device so that they can be used to validate the images when the bootloader starts. The BL2 bootloader provides two methods of storing the keys. The simplest method is to embed the keys in the bootloader image when it is compiled. When the image is signed by the private key, a hash of the public key is stored in the metadata. The BL2 image will be validated by the secure boot, and the BL2 public keys will be checked against the hashes in the image metadata. The disadvantage of this method is that the keys are fixed within the resident BL2 image and cannot be changed without updating the whole bootloader.

Exercise: Bootloader keys

In this example, we will generate a new set of image keys for the BL2 bootloader and embed them within the BL2 image.

Go to the pack installer and copy Example 14.2

We can generate a new set of keys using the imgtool script as follows:
```
imgtool.py keygen -k <key file>.pem -t rsa-3027
```
and then extract the public key using
```
imgtool.py getpub -k <key_file>.pem
```

Open the ns project directory
Open a command window
Run the genkey batch file

The genkey batchfile will create and store the new private keys into the secure and nonsecure projects. It will also print the public keys to the console window.

This creates a "C" array which can be embedded in the bootloader.

```
/* Autogenerated by imgtool.py, do not edit. */
const unsigned char rsa_pub_key[] = {
    0x30, 0x82, 0x01, 0x8a, 0x02, 0x82, 0x01, 0x81,
    0x00, 0xb6, 0x0c, 0x3a, 0x37, 0x2c, 0x4d, 0xd5,

    ..............................

    0xe6, 0x60, 0x7e, 0x33, 0x7f, 0xb1, 0x83, 0xf8,
    0x1b, 0x02, 0x03, 0x01, 0x00, 0x01,
};
const unsigned int rsa_pub_key_len = 398;
```

Set BL2 as the active project.
Open the file TFM/keys.c
Update the contents of the public key arrays by copying the newly generated public keys into the arrays.
If necessary adjust the size of rsa_pub_key_len.
Open the file bl2_config.h
Make sure the hardware key option is unchecked (Fig. 14.17).

Option	Value
⊟ MCUBoot Configuration	
Upgrade Strategy	Overwrite Only
Signature Type	RSA-3072
Number of Images	2
Hardware Key	☐
Logging Level	Info

FIG. 14.17

Placing the verification keys in the bootloader image. Uncheck use hardware key to place the verification keys in the bootloader image.

No permission required.

This will force the bootloader to use the keys embedded in the BL2 image.

Rebuild the bootloader.
Rebuild the secure and nonsecure images.

This will recreate the secure and nonsecure images and regenerate their signed images using the new private keys.

The public key is embedded in the bootloader. In order to verify it, we must place its hash in the signed image metadata. This is done using the imgtool -K option.

```
python ../scripts/imgtool.py sign -l ../tfm_s/layout.txt -k root-
rsa-3072.pem -K hash --align 1 -v 1.2.3+4 -s 42 -H 0x400 Objects/
tfm_s.bin Objects/tfm_s_signed.bin
```

Start the debugger.
The code will now boot using the new image keys.

Bootloading by hardware key

The second method allows us to store the hashes of the public keys in the Internal Trusted Storage. In this version, when the image is created, the public key is stored in the image metadata and can be measured against the stored hash. Each hash is used to validate the matching public key, which is then used to validate the matching image. The advantage of this method is that the hashes may be provisioned separately from the BL2 image. This allows us to use test keys during development and then switch to production keys without having to update the BL2 image. However, for this example, the public key hashes are included as part of the image and are located in tfm_rotpk.c.

Go back to the previous example.
Set the bootloader as the active example.

Before we regenerate the images, we must change the imgtool options to embed the full public key into the metadata. This time the -K option is used to embed the full private key into the bl2 metadata.

```
python ../scripts/imgtool.py sign -l ../tfm_s/layout.txt -k root-
rsa-3072.pem -K full --align 1 -v 1.2.3+4 -s 42 -H 0x400 Objects/
tfm_s.bin Objects/tfm_s_signed.bin
```

Open the image.bat file in both the secure and nonsecure projects and change the -K option from hash to full.
In the bl2_config.h configuration image check the hardware key option.
Build the bootloader project.
This will re-run each of the image batchfile to regenerate the secure and nonsecure signed images.
Start the debugger.

The project will now boot using the independently provisioned hardware keys and hashes.

Image encryption

If the secondary slots are located in external flash memory or are otherwise vulnerable, it is possible to encrypt the update. This will generate a symmetrical encryption key, which will be wrapped by the public half of a second RSA key pair using the following addition to the imgtool command line.

```
-E enc-rsa2048-pub.pem
```

The executable image will now be encrypted, and the wrapped encryption key will be stored in the image trailer. In the current version of BL2, the private half of the encryption wrapping key is stored in the array enc_priv_key[], which is in the keys.c file and can be enabled by ticking the encryption option in the bl2_config.h configuration wizard.

Open build.bat and Add the encryption option -E enc-rsa2048-pub.pem to encrypt the update images.
Enable the encryption option in the bl2_config.h file.
Rebuild the BL2 bootloader and the project images.
Start the debugger to download the images.

Use the memory window to inspect the secure update slot and compare this to the existing image in the primary slot.

The images are the same so while the primary slot contains unencrypted code the secondary will contain "meaningless" encrypted data.

Run the code to check the images update and execute OK.

Measured boot

In addition to the primary, secondary, and swap slots, the memory layout defines a RAM region, which is shared between the BL2 bootloader and the secure, trusted firmware.

The measured boot option is added to the imgtool a TLV record will be added to the metadata. This stores a boot record for the image, which is a set of key-value items, as shown below.

```
key_value_list = [
  SW_COMPONENT_TYPE, sw_type,
  SW_COMPONENT_VERSION, sw_version,
  SIGNER_ID, sw_signer_id,
  MEASUREMENT_DESCRIPTION, sw_measurement_type,
  MEASUREMENT_VALUE, sw_measurement_value];
```

This data is encoded as a CBOR map object, and on successful validation, the bootloader will copy the record to the shared region of memory. This information is then used to construct the claims required for an attestation token, as discussed in Chapter 13.

Conclusion

The PSA Secure Bootloader and Firmware Update Client complete the suite of software components required to meet the goals of the security model. We now have a complete platform that will turn a low-cost microcontroller into a secure IoT device that can connect to a wide range of commercial cloud servers. Now our IoT device will become part of complex systems, which integrate sensors, data, and applications to impact many areas of everyday life. Perhaps most importantly, IoT devices will act as smart sensors to gather the vast amounts of data required to train Deep Learning Networks. At the same research projects have devised Neural Networks small enough to run on today's microcontrollers. Alongside this new ARM IP in the form of a microneural processing unit, microNPU, provides a huge performance uplift with low power consumption. Allowing us to create applications that were previously impossible with small microcontrollers. Welcome to the AIoT.

Bibliography

In the bibliography below, I have listed the most useful resources used to help write this book. Many of these are available online, and I have included a pdf copy with the tutorial examples to save you typing in the long URLs.

Chapter 1 Introduction

Book

Click here to kill everybody—Bruce Schneier—ISBN9780393608892

Paper

Lone actor terrorism and SIMAD

    http://www.millennium-project.org/special-studies/
    special-studies-simad-and-lone-wolf/

Cyberattack on critical infrastructure

    jsis.washington.edu/news/
    cyberattack-critical-infrastructure-russia-ukrainian-power-grid-attacks/

Arm cyber security manifesto 2018/2019

    https://www.arm.com/resources/manifesto/iot-security

Web resource

General security blog

    https://www.schneier.com/

IoT security association

    https://www.iotsecurityfoundation.org/

Chapter 2 Platform security architecture

Book

Embedded systems security—David Kleidermacher, Mike Kleidermacher—ISBN: 9780123868879

Specification

PSA Certified™ level 1 questionnaire

    https://www.psacertified.org/development-resources/certification-resources/

Web resource

    https://www.trustedfirmware.org/projects/tf-m/
    https://www.psacertified.org/

Chapter 3 Development tools and device platform

Book

Definitive guide to the arm Cortex-M23 and Cortex-M33—Joseph Yiu—ISBN: 9780128207369

Designers guide to Cortex-M processors family—Trevor Martin—ISBN: 9780081006344

Specification
ARM®v8-M architecture reference manual—ddi0553
https://developer.arm.com/documentation/ddi0553/latest
Web resource
MDK getting started
www2.keil.com/mdk5/install/
Hardware
Xpresso LPC55S69 development board
https://www.nxp.com/design/development-boards/lpcxpresso-boards/
lpcxpresso55s69-development-board:LPC55S69-EVK
Click wifi ESP module
https://www.mikroe.com/wifi-esp-click
Software
Keil MDK
https://www2.keil.com/mdk5
Tera term
https://osdn.net/projects/ttssh2/releases/

Chapter 4 Cryptography—The basics
Book
Understanding cryptography—Christof Parr, Jan Pelzl—ISBN: 9783642041013
Paper
Verified correctness and security of mbedTLS HMAC-DRBG—Katherine Q. Ye, et al.
https://arxiv.org/abs/1708.08542#:~:text=We%20have%20formalized%20
the%20functional,a%20hybrid%20game%2Dbased%20proof
A statistical test suite for random and pseudorandom—NIST
Number Generators for Cryptographic Applications
https://tsapps.nist.gov/publication/get_pdf.cfm?pub_id=906762
Web resource
Understanding cryptography online lectures
https://www.youtube.com/channel/UC1usFRN4LCMcfIV7UjHNuQg
Trusted firmware security center
https://developer.trustedfirmware.org/w/mbed-tls/security-center/
Software
Hash Calc Software
https://www.slavasoft.com/hashcalc/
Statistical test suite improved source code
https://github.com/arcetri/sts

Chapter 5 Cryptography—Secure communications
Book
Implementing SSL/TLS—Joshua Davis—ISBN: 9781118038772
Software
XCA X.509 certificate creation and management
https://hohnstaedt.de/xca/

Chapter 6 IoT networking and data formats
Book
MQTT essentials—Gaston C. Hillar—ISBN: 9781787285149
Introduction to JavaScript object notation—Lindsay Bassett—ISBN: 9781491929483
Paper
AN 312 IoT connectors for MDK-Middleware
    https://www.keil.com/appnotes/files/apnt_312.pdf
Specification
MQTT Version 3.1.1
    http://docs.oasis-open.org/
The JavaScript object notation (JSON) data interchange format—RFC: 8259
    https://datatracker.ietf.org/doc/html/rfc8259
Concise binary object representation (CBOR)—RFC: 7049
    https://datatracker.ietf.org/doc/html/rfc7049
Enumeration of cbor tags
    https://www.iana.org/assignments/cbor-tags/cbor-tags.xhtml
Software
Mosquitto MQTT Broker
    https://mosquitto.org/download/
MQTT.fx PC client
    http://mqttfx.jensd.de/index.php/download

Chapter 7 Using an IoT Cloud service
Paper
AWS IoT developers guide
    docs.aws.amazon.com/iot/latest/developerguide/iot-dg.pdf
Specification
Web resource
    https://aws.amazon.com/iot/
AWS free tier account
    aws.amazon.com/free
Free tier terms and conditions
    https://aws.amazon.com/frcc/?all-frcc-ticr.sort-by=itcm.additionalFields.
    SortRank&all-free-tier.sort-order=asc

Chapter 8 Software attacks and threat modelling
Book
Secure coding in C and C++—Robert C. Seacord—ISBN: 9780132981972
Threat modelling: Designing for security—Adam Shostack—ISBN: 9781118809990
Threat modelling—Izar Tarandach, Matthew J. Coles, ISBN: 9781492056508
Paper
Return-oriented programming on a Cortex-M processor—Nathanael R. Weidler et al.
    https://ieeexplore.ieee.org/document/8029521
ADTool: Security analysis with attack-defense trees—Barbara Kordy et al.
    https://link.springer.com/chapter/10.1007/978-3-642-40196-1_15

Web resource
OWSAP Internet of things project
https://wiki.owasp.org/index.php/
OWASP_Internet_of_Things_Project#tab=IoT_Top_10
Common attack pattern enumeration and classification
https://capec.mitre.org/data/index.html
EoP threat modelling card game
https://www.microsoft.com/en-gb/download/details.aspx?id=20303
Security cards
https://securitycards.cs.washington.edu/
Threat modelling tool
https://docs.microsoft.com/en-us/azure/security/develop/threat-modeling-tool
OWASP threat dragon
http://docs.threatdragon.org/#downloads
Threat dragon tutorial
http://docs.threatdragon.org/#threat-model-diagrams
Attack/defense trees AD tool
https://satoss.uni.lu/members/piotr/adtool

Chapter 9 Building a defence with the PSA security model
Specification
Platform security architecture security model—DEN 0079
https://developer.arm.com/-/media/Files/pdf/PlatformSecurityArchitecture/
Architect/DEN0079_PSA_SM_ALPHA-03_RC01.
pdf?revision=2c567adf-c6e3-432b-90f7-b0f5358c43ec

Chapter 10 Device partitioning with the TrustZone security peripheral
Paper
AN291 using TrustZone on Armv8-M
https://www.keil.com/appnotes/docs/apnt_291.asp
Arm® TrustZone Technology for the Armv8-M Architecture ARMv8-M Memory
Protection Unit
https://developer.arm.com/documentation/100690/latest/
Software
Trust zone utility
https://arm-software.github.io/CMSIS_5/Zone/html/zTInstall.html

Chapter 11 The NXP LPC55S69 A Reference IoT Microcontroller
Book
LPC55S69 user manual
AN12283 LPC55S69 Secure Boot
AN12324 LPC55Sxx usage of the PUF and Hash Crypt to AES coding
AN12278 LPC55S69 Security Solutions for IoT
https://www.nxp.com/products/processors-and-microcontrollers/
arm-microcontrollers/general-purpose-mcus/lpc5500-cortex-m33/
high-efficiency-arm-cortex-m33-based-microcontroller-family:LPC55S6x

Web resource
NXP LPC55S59 secure provisioning tool
> https://www.nxp.com/design/software/development-software/mcuxpresso-
> software-and-tools-/mcuxpresso-secure-provisioning-tool:MCUXPRESSO-
> SECURE-PROVISIONING
> https://www.psacertified.org/certified-products/

Chapter 12 Trusted firmware
Paper
Armv8-M Secure Stack Sealing—Uma Maheswari Ramalingam, Thomas Grocutt,
Peter Smith
> https://developer.arm.com/support/arm-security-updates/armv8-m-stack-sealing
Specification
Trusted System Base Architecture—DEN0083
> https://developer.arm.com/ /media/Arm%20Developer%20
> Community/PDF/PSA/DEN0083_PSA_TBSA-M_1.0-bet2.
> pdf?revision=5f9de99f-a7b5-4851-b041-f698521bf6bf
Firmware framework—DEN0063
> https://developer.arm.com/-/media/Files/pdf/PlatformSecurityArchitecture/
> Architect/DEN0063-PSA_Firmware_Framework-1.0.0-2.
> pdf?revision=2d1429fa-4b5b-461a-a60e-4ef3d8f7f4b4&la=en&hash=BE8C59
> DBC98212591E1F935C2312D497011CD8C7
Firmware framework extensions—aes0039
> https://developer.arm.com/documentation/aes0039/latest
Web resource
> https://www.trustedfirmware.org/projects/tf-m/
> https://git.trustedfirmware.org/TF-M/trusted-firmware-m.git/

Chapter 13 Security services
Specification
Cryptography service—IHI0086
> https://developer.arm.com/documentation/ihi0086/latest/
Storage service—IHI0087
> https://developer.arm.com/-/media/Files/pdf/PlatformSecurityArchitecture/
> Implement/IHI0087-PSA_Storage_API-1.0.0.pdf?revision=810a2412-bca0-
> 46e1-a801-f48729a32e47
Attestation service—IHI0085
> https://developer.arm.com/-/media/Files/pdf/PlatformSecurityArchitecture/
> Implement/IHI0085-PSA_Attestation_API-1.0.2.pdf?revision=eef78753-c77e-
> 4b24-bcf0-65596213b4c1
Attestation token specification
> https://tools.ietf.org/id/draft-tschofenig-rats-psa-token-00.html

Chapter 14 PSA secure bootloader
Specification
Platform security boot guide—DEN0072

https://developer.arm.com/documentation/den0072/0101/

Firmware update service—IHI 0093

https://developer.arm.com/documentation/ihi0093/latest/

mcuboot project home page

www.mcuboot.com

Software

Python 3

https://www.python.org/download/releases/3.0/

SRECORD utilities download

https://sourceforge.net/projects/srecord/files/srecord-win32/

Srec_cat manual

http://srecord.sourceforge.net/man/man1/srec_cat.html

Index

Note: Page numbers followed by *f* indicate figures and *t* indicate tables.

Printed in the United States
by Baker & Taylor Publisher Services